NATIONALITY AND STATELESSNESS IN THE INTERNATIONAL LAW OF REFUGEE STATUS

International refugee law anticipates state conduct in relation to nationality, statelessness and protection. Refugee status under the Convention relating to the Status of Refugees 1951 and regional and domestic instruments referring to it can be fully understood only against the background of international laws regarding nationality, statelessness, and the consequences of national status or the lack of it. In this significant addition to the literature a leading practitioner in these fields examines, in the light of international law, key issues regarding refugee status including identification of 'the country of his nationality', concepts of 'effective nationality', and the inclusion within 'persecution' of a range of acts or omissions focused on nationality.

Nationality and Statelessness in the International Law of Refugee Status

Eric Fripp

MA (St Andrews) LLM MA LLM (London)
of Gray's Inn, Barrister

With a Foreword by
The Rt Hon Sir Konrad Schiemann

Former Lord Justice of Appeal, former Judge of the
Court of Justice of the EU

•HART•
PUBLISHING
OXFORD AND PORTLAND, OREGON
2016

Hart Publishing
An imprint of Bloomsbury Publishing Plc

Hart Publishing Ltd
Kemp House
Chawley Park
Cumnor Hill
Oxford OX2 9PH
UK

Bloomsbury Publishing Plc
50 Bedford Square
London
WC1B 3DP
UK

www.hartpub.co.uk
www.bloomsbury.com

Published in North America (US and Canada) by
Hart Publishing
c/o International Specialized Book Services
920 NE 58th Avenue, Suite 300
Portland, OR 97213-3786
USA

www.isbs.com

First published 2016

Reprinted 2017

British Library Cataloguing-in-Publication Data
A catalogue record for this book is available from the British Library.

ISBN: HB: 978-1-78225-921-3
ePDF: 978-1-78225-923-7
ePub: 978-1-78225-922-0

Library of Congress Cataloging-in-Publication Data

Names: Fripp, Eric, author.

Title: Nationality and statelessness in the international law of refugee status / Eric Fripp, MA (St Andrews) LLM MA LLM (London) of Gray's Inn, Barrister ; with a foreword by the Rt Hon Sir Konrad Schiemann former Lord Justice of Appeal, former Judge of the Court of Justice of the EU.

Description: Oxford ; Portland, OR : Hart Publishing, 2016. | Includes bibliographical references and index.

Identifiers: LCCN 2016019867 (print) | LCCN 2016020007 (ebook) | ISBN 9781782259213 (hardback : alk. paper) | ISBN 9781782259220 (Epub)

Subjects: LCSH: Refugees—Legal status, laws, etc. | Citizenship. | Stateless persons—Legal status, laws, etc. | Statelessness.

Classification: LCC K3230.R45 F75 2016 (print) | LCC K3230.R45 (ebook) | DDC 341.4/86—dc23

LC record available at https://lccn.loc.gov/2016019867

Typeset by Compuscript Ltd, Shannon

Foreword

I do not recollect being taught anything about refugee law in the course of the acquisition of two law degrees at Cambridge around 1960. I knew refugees, but nothing about the law relating to them. Indeed there was not all that much. One thought of it as a problem of the past. Alas, events have proved us wrong. There is little that is more immediately relevant.

This is a work of careful and formidable scholarship which fulfils the expectations raised by the author's Preface. It seeks to clarify the underlying relationship between international refugee law and other areas of international law. Mr Fripp has read very widely—not only the relevant treaties and academic writings, but also the case law of international, common law and other jurisdictions. The citations are set out at sufficient length to enable one to understand the gist of what has been said and to see whether one should examine the cited source in greater detail. The work is very clearly organised and presented so that one can rapidly arrive at the centre of whatever one happens to be investigating at the time. Yet a prolonged perusal of the work shows one that the subdivisions into which it is organised form part of a well thought through whole. While the author's prime contribution is in organising and presenting this wide material he does not shrink from the occasional personal query or thought prompted by the cited material.

I have no doubt that this book was worth the enormous amount of effort and thought which has clearly been put into its production. It is an important and useful contribution in a field which daily becomes of more and more importance. Law is always liable to disorganised fragmentation as people specialise in this or that branch. As a judge I was permanently conscious of the danger of solving the immediate problem in front of me at the risk of creating problems for the future. This book should help judges to avoid at least some of the many pitfalls and should be of interest to lawyers and legislators in the field all round the world.

Konrad Schiemann
February 2016

Table of Contents

Preface

Immediately after the Second World War changes took place which significantly advanced the position of the natural person in relation to international law. Hersch Lauterpacht asserted that the individual 'has acquired a status and a stature which have transformed him from an object of international compassion into a subject of international right'.[1] Georges Scelle, the eminent French teacher of international law and jurist, stated that 'this doctrinal battle has been won ... the immense majority of authors recognise individuals as subjects of international law'.[2]

However, the role of the State in the international community and in international law remained central, and this is directly reflected in the international law created since the Second World War for the identification and protection of refugees. The builders of new international law structures viewed States as the bedrock of any new protective regime, a perspective contrasting sharply with Hannah Arendt's scepticism as to the ability or willingness of States to safeguard human rights:

> [C]ontrary to Arendt's lack of confidence in the ability of nation-states to guarantee the rights of stateless persons, postwar liberal internationalism optimistically viewed citizenship, safeguarded in time of crisis by international organization, as the natural guardian of human rights. As such, the stateless condition was repairable through reinstatement into a community of rights, the sovereign nation-state kept in check by international guarantees.[3]

The reliance upon the State by those designing new protections for the individual within international law is understandable given the long-standing centrality of the State to international law. From this follows the importance of nationality in international law. As Jennings and Watts stated, in *Oppenheim's International Law*:

> To the extent to which individuals are not directly subjects of international law, nationality is the link between them and international law. It is through the medium of their nationality that individuals can normally enjoy benefits from international law. This has consequences over the whole area of international law. Such individuals as do not possess any nationality enjoy, in general, only limited protection, since if they are aggrieved by a state there is no national state which is competent to take up their case. As far as

[1] H Lauterpacht, *International Law and Human Rights* (Praeger, 1950) 4.
[2] G Scelle, *Manuel de droit international public* (Domat-Montchrestien, 1948) 511.
[3] GD Cohen, *In War's Wake: Europe's Displaced Persons in the Postwar Order* (OUP, 2012).

> international law is concerned, there is, apart from obligations (now quite extensive) expressly laid down by treaty—and in particular the general obligation, enshrined in the Charter of the United Nations, to respect human rights and fundamental freedoms—no restriction upon a state maltreating such stateless individuals. On the other hand, if individuals who possess nationality are wronged abroad, it is, as a rule, their home state exclusively which has a right to ask for redress … It is for this reason that nationality is very important for international law.[4]

Nationality was therefore central to the thinking of those responsible for devising and operating international refugee protection. In April 1948 Paul Weis, then Legal Adviser in the International Refugee Organisation (IRO), writing as the Universal Declaration of Human Rights was being drafted, observed that 'It is through his connection with a particular state by the ties of nationality that the individual finds his place in international law'. Because of this, linkage to a State by nationality and by citizenship, the measure of membership in a State under domestic law, represented 'one of the most effective means to safeguard and assure the human rights of the individual'.[5]

The emphasis upon nationality in the then nascent system for refugee protection under international law operated by the IRO was challenged thereafter only briefly and ineffectively. In February 1949 eminent intellectuals including Albert Einstein, Aldous Huxley, François Mauriac, John Dos Passos, Bertrand Russell, and George Bernard Shaw wrote to United Nations Secretary-General Trygvie Lie. Their letter suggested that refugees should be freed from the obligation to seek a nationality in order to guarantee their rights through membership in a nation, because 'sheer force of events [has given them] the feeling of belonging to a community larger than one nation. Indeed, History made them citizens of the world, and they should be treated as such'. According to the signatories the situation of post-war refugees offered unprecedented opportunity '[to] let the ideal of world-citizenship subsist not exclusively in theories and programs, but also in courageous experimenting and in a genuine respect for the human person.' The IRO responded in robust terms:

> Here are people to whom you say: be proud of your statelessness, remain this way and become the first world citizens! … But stateless persons know all too well what they desire: to stop being stateless. Not out of sentimentality, but to obtain asylum, passport, a work permit, or access to a hospital.[6]

Against this background it was natural that the Convention relating to the Status of Refugees 1951 (CSR51) would in its construction reflect the continuing importance in international affairs of the State and hence of nationality. The

[4] R Jennings and A Watts (eds), *Oppenheim's International Law*, vol 1 ('Peace') (9th edn, OUP, 1992) Pt 1, 849, §376.

[5] P Weis to E Stone, 28 April 1948, IRO Records 43AJ-202.

[6] IRO Records 43AJ-232.

most important part of the provision for inclusion within the CSR51 regime as a refugee is article 1A(2) CSR51. The first paragraph of this definition as now most commonly applied includes a person who 'owing to well-founded fear of being persecuted for reasons of race, religion, nationality, membership of a particular social group or political opinion, is outside the country of his nationality and is unable or, owing to such fear, is unwilling to avail himself of the protection of that country; or who, not having a nationality and being outside the country of his former habitual residence …, is unable or, owing to such fear, is unwilling to return to it'.

This work focuses on interpretation of the provisions at article 1 CSR51 establishing the rubric for qualification as a refugee under that instrument. It seeks in particular to identify and to give adequate consideration to the multiple respects in which the content of article 1 CSR51 reflects understandings of nationality and statelessness in the broader body of international law. Such norms inform article 1 CSR51 in significant respects, and may be critical to the question of whether any given individual is inside or outside its protective ambit. The task of interpretation is not straightforward, in part because it follows from the status of CSR51 as a 'living instrument', requiring interpretation in the light of current international conditions, that it is necessary to assess not the historic state of development of international law as regards nationality and statelessness, but its present situation, in order to interpret article 1 CSR51. Over the lifetime of CSR51 there have been extensive developments in international norms concerning nationality and statelessness. Most dramatically, important changes over time have included the increasing acknowledgment of a customary law principle of non-discrimination, the development of international laws concerning statelessness by the Convention relating to the Status of Stateless Persons 1954 and the Convention on the Reduction of Statelessness 1961, and the influence of a growing body of international human rights norms affecting, or potentially affecting, actions or omissions by States in relation to the creation or destruction of nationality. In other areas there has been development of principles, and of international instruments, in areas that previously were almost untouched by international law, such as for instance nationality in situations of state succession.

This work therefore applies to the interpretation of relevant parts of CSR51 an international law of nationality and statelessness which, though in part reflecting the long-standing concept of international law as the body of legally binding rules regulating the relations of States (within which nationality has an obvious part), has also been shaped by the principle of non-discrimination and the international law of human rights. No recent attempt has been made to draw together the current international law of nationality and statelessness and to analyse systematically the effect thereof upon the scope of CSR51.

I owe a particular debt to earlier writers on the international law of nationality and statelessness. By some distance the greatest debt is owed to Paul Weis, whose *Nationality and Statelessness in International Law*, published in its first edition 60 years ago, was described by Louise Holborn as 'the first thorough treatise on the existence and nature of rules of public international law relating to nationality and statelessness'.[7] Born in Vienna, Weis suffered internment in Dachau before escaping in April 1939 to the United Kingdom, where he later naturalised. He served as Legal Adviser in the IRO between 1947 and 1951, and then between 1951 and 1967 was successively Legal Adviser then Director of the Legal Department in the Office of the United Nations High Commissioner for Refugees (UNHCR). After retirement from the UNHCR he was United Kingdom Expert on the Council of Europe Committee on Refugees and Asylum, ultimately chairing that Committee. A second edition of *Nationality and Statelessness in International Law* was released in 1979. As a leading expert both in refugee law and in the international law of nationality and statelessness, who was present at the creation of modern refugee law, he represents an important human link between these fields. The title of the current work acknowledges that in many respects what I have sought to do is to continue to the present date, and to apply particularly to the interpretation of article 1 CSR51, relevant parts of Weis's treatise, read in the light of the work of other commentators, judicial and other decisions, and developments in the law.

Before the publication of Weis' book in 1956, there had been two significant works addressing the issue of recognition under international law, a mechanism of international law not restricted or even mainly applied to nationality, but brought to bear upon it by international law practice and latterly by article 1 of the Convention on Certain Questions Relating to the Conflict of Nationality Laws 1930. The first of these, by Hersch Lauterpacht (*Recognition in International Law*, 1947) was shortly followed by another, by Ti-Chiang Chen (*The International Law of Recognition, with Special Reference to Practice in Great Britain and the United States*, 1951). Richard Plender in his *International Migration Law* (1972, second edition, 1988) then provided important reflections on aspects of international nationality law. Since Weis' second edition in 1979 and Plender's in 1988 there has been no single work of similar stature in English addressing a broad span of the international law of nationality and statelessness.

In recent decades, the interpretation of certain elements of article 1 CSR51 has undergone particular development. As regards the key concept of 'persecution', important early commentators such as Vernant[8] and Grahl-Madsen[9] could anticipate the possibility of international human rights law coming to provide a more developed framework for interpretation, but this could only begin to become a developed reality after a body of binding human rights norms had first come into force and then gained wide acceptance. The International Convention on the Elimination of All Forms of Racial Discrimination entered into force in 1969, as

[7] L Holborn, Review of *Nationality and Statelessness in International Law* by Paul Weis and *The Refugee and the World Community* by John George Stoessinger (1957) 51(2) *American Political Science Review* 528, 528.

[8] J Vernant, *The Refugee in the Post-War World* (George Allen & Unwin, 1953) 7–8.

[9] A Grahl-Madsen, *The Status of Refugees in International Law*, vol I (AW Sijthoff, 1966); vol II (AW Sijthoff, 1972) 201, §84.

did the International Covenant on Civil and Political Rights and the International Covenant on Economic and Social Rights in 1976. Only as an international framework of human rights standards was created could a systematic analysis of the protective ambit of CSR51 be adequately developed. That process has ultimately been greatly advanced by the work of Guy Goodwin-Gill[10] and James Hathaway,[11] authors of important works on international refugee law now in further editions.[12] Where the subject matter of this work overlaps with theirs, I have sought to complement these more expansive accounts by a particular focus upon nationality law and statelessness.

International refugee law, which did not exist before the First World War and had a relatively limited content before the Second World War, is now a substantial field in its own right with CSR51 at its core. This development deserves to be welcomed. However a potential risk inherent in the attainment of specialism and weight by international refugee law is to the identification of its place within the wider fabric of international law, not isolated from this but rather influenced by the law in other areas themselves subject to change and development.

This work therefore surveys the scope of critical provisions of CSR51 invoking nationality, in the light of an up to date assessment of the body of international law relating to nationality and statelessness. But it might be asked, if this is a topic which has been neglected, might that neglect not be deserved? Is there good reason to explore the international law of nationality and statelessness as these bear on interpretation of what might be called the international law of refugee status, that is, the law as to who is and who is not within the ambit of CSR51 or kindred instruments?

Ultimately the answers to those questions can only be ascertained by following the enquiry set out later in this book. But four general points might be made at this point.

First, the factual and legal situations which CSR51 was designed to address were themselves frequently focused upon discriminatory manipulation of nationality, including most notoriously the imposition of statelessness by denationalisation. The paradigm refugee situations in the interwar period were the wholesale denationalisation measures entered into most infamously by the Union of Soviet Socialist Republics, Fascist Italy and Nazi Germany, with the consequence that millions of men and women were either deprived of nationality and left stateless, or reduced to a nationality denoting connection to the State on the international level, but divorced from the protections attached to social membership denoted as citizenship. To ignore this prehistory to CSR51 is to risk fundamental error as to the concern of States to address any recurrence of similar acts which underlay the creation of CSR51.

[10] G Goodwin-Gill, *The Refugee in International Law* (Clarendon Press, 1983) 38–46.

[11] J Hathaway, *The Law of Refugee Status* (Butterworths Canada, 1991) 105.

[12] G Goodwin-Gill and J McAdam, *The Refugee in International Law* (3rd edn, OUP, 2007); J Hathaway and M Foster, *The Law of Refugee Status* (2nd edn, CUP, 2014).

Second, concern regarding state manipulation of nationality, including the imposition of statelessness on the basis of discrimination, is regrettably not obsolete or irrelevant today. If anything, discriminatory conduct by States in relation to nationality or citizenship appears to have acquired a greater relevance to refugee law in recent years in contexts including the position of persons of Eritrean national background in Ethiopia, persons of Haitian national origin born in the Dominican Republic, Bidoon in Kuwait and elsewhere, and Rohingya in Myanmar. In States including Canada, the United States, and important European countries, concerns with security, terrorism, and assimilation of migrants, underlie a growth of interest in the use or threat of denationalisation. To other States control over nationality is important as a potential route to escape human rights or other obligations, including continued presence by persons in their own countries. As James Goldston, Executive Director of the Open Society Justice Initiative, stated in 2006:

> Across broad swaths of the globe, the treatment of noncitizens—so-called foreigners and aliens, migrants, refugees, asylum seekers, stateless persons, and others who, by virtue of their exclusion from the political community, enjoy some formal legal protection but little influence—is worsening precisely as states are increasingly bestowing, denying, or retracting citizenship as a political weapon. In countries with high rates of immigration, problems of access are common; in postcolonial countries, deprivation is often the main concern. Racial and ethnic discrimination commonly worsen the problems faced by noncitizens, many of whom are members of minority groups.[13]

Third, there is a risk of fragmentation amongst different international law regimes, with consequential deterioration of understanding of international law generally and of particular regimes. As early as 1953, C Wilfred Jenks noted the absence of a general legislative body of the international community as a result of which international law remained a highly decentralised system. He envisaged the potential need for international lawyers to address the risk of isolation of regimes from general international law:

> In the absence of a world legislature with a general mandate, law-making treaties are tending to develop in a number of historical, functional and regional groups which are separate from each other and whose mutual relationships are in some respects analogous to those of separate systems of municipal law.[14]

The scope for differentiation and consequential fragmentation has been greatly increased by the volume of international law which has come into existence since the Second World War. The isolation of certain regimes from others and from the wider body of international law, referred to as 'fragmentation', was addressed in 2006 by the Study Group of the International Law Commission chaired by

[13] J Goldston, 'Holes in the Rights Framework: Racial Discrimination, Citizenship, and the Rights of Noncitizens' (2006) 20(3) *Ethics & International Affairs* 321, 322.

[14] CW Jenks, 'The Conflict of Law-Making Treaties' in *British Yearbook of International Law* 1953 (OUP, 1954) 401, 403.

Martii Koskenniemi,[15] which identified the existence of a system of international law involving potentially interacting norms at different levels, which might relate to each other through interpretation or might conflict.[16] The treatment of international refugee laws within the broader fabric of international law, including international norms relating to nationality and statelessness, is in this context clearly desirable.

Fourth, the interpretation and application of CSR51 is a matter of the greatest possible importance to those affected and they, and those charged with understanding and applying refugee law, deserve assistance of the highest possible standard, consistent with the importance of the regime. The full understanding of the scope of the regime and its consistent application possesses enormous importance for those concerned with the application of the regime or the adjudication of disputes, as well as those laying claim to status under it.

The structure of the work is as follows. In Part I, which contains important matters of background, chapter one considers definitions, in particular those of the key terms 'nationality' and 'statelessness', and the content of international law relating to those areas relevant to interpretation of key provisions in article 1 CSR51. Chapter two provides a brief account of the prehistory and history of the formation of international refugee law, identifies key provisions in the centrepiece of that law, CSR51, and points to relevant provisions in other, generally regional, regimes. Chapter three contains a short account of the principled basis for interpretation of CSR51. In Part II, which contains the chapters focusing upon interpretation of particular provisions, chapter four considers the interpretation of 'nationality' as one of the reasons enumerated at article 1A(2) as necessary for a well-founded fear of persecution to qualify the possessor as a refugee. Chapter five treats the interpretation of the term 'nationality' in the context of identification of the State or States of reference in relation to other requirements of the refugee definition at article 1A(2) CSR51. Thereafter chapter six considers the relevance of acts or omissions concerning nationality or kindred matters to the critical term 'persecution' in the same article. Two shorter chapters address invocations of nationality or related terms in the context respectively of cessation under article 1C CSR51 (chapter seven) and of exclusion under article 1E CSR51 (chapter eight).

Whilst it is hoped that the whole exercise will be considered valuable, it is suggested that a number of significant conclusions emerge:

— First, 'country of nationality' in article 1A(2) CSR51 means country of actual current nationality. Whilst a line primarily of Canadian authority has developed which treats the phrase as including a country whose nationality a claimant does not actually possess at the time of assessment, and

[15] International Law Commission, Report on the Work of the Fifty-eighth session (2006) Ch 12, 'Conclusions of the Work of the Study Group on the Fragmentation of International Law: Difficulties arising from the Diversification and Expansion of International Law' (UN Doc A/61/10).

[16] Ibid, §252.

this whilst remaining a minority view has attracted intermittent reference in other jurisdictions, the underlying conclusion in these authorities is not consistent with CSR51, whatever the position as a matter of domestic authority.

— Second, in identifying the 'country of nationality' in article 1A(2) CSR51, principles concerning recognition (and non-recognition) of nationality may be significant, where action by a State of origin changing nationality status is inconsistent with important norms of international law. This is perhaps particularly relevant in situations of deprivation of nationality (denationalisation) by reason of discrimination.
— Third, a particular approach is needed to situations in which plural nationality is present. Whilst these cases are distinct by reason of the existence of a link of nationality, the existence of a non-persecutory country of nationality does not elide the potential existence of 'valid reason based on well-founded fear' cited in the second paragraph of article 1A(2) CSR51, and the refugee definition may therefore still be engaged notwithstanding that at least one non-persecuting country of nationality may be identified. Whilst the jurisprudence and commentary does not identify a consistent approach to such cases, there are functional parallels both to 'protection elsewhere' (protection outside the country of origin or of claim) situations and to the so-called 'internal protection alternative' concept (protection within a country of nationality in an area free from relevant risk), and this greatly assists the development of a cohesive understanding as to how article 1A(2) CSR51 applies in such situations. An approach supported by interpretation of article 1A(2) CSR51, and designated as 'national protection alternative', is developed in chapter five.
— Fourth, arbitrary deprivation of nationality linked to statelessness and exclusion and brought about by relevant discrimination is likely in many cases to represent a substantial breach of international law, and to constitute persecution for purposes of article 1A(2) CSR51.

The law continues to change and develop, but I have sought to provide an account of it valid, to the best of my ability, to today, 1 February 2016.

Eric Fripp
Shillingstone, Dorset
and
Lamb Building, Elm Court, Temple, London
1 February 2016

Acknowledgements

There are many people to whom I wish to express thanks as this work emerges from gestation. The idea of writing it came from the effort of ordering past thoughts and experience, and the discovery of new and interesting issues, in researching a paper for delivery at the first Global Statelessness Forum, sponsored by the United Nations High Commissioner for Refugees and the Statelessness Programme of Tilburg University and held in The Hague in September 2014. Laura van Waas managed the Statelessness Programme (now the Institute on Statelessness and Inclusion) and David Baluarte and Hélène Lambert delivered interesting papers within the session.

I have benefited greatly from the willingness of leading scholars and practitioners in the refugee law field, including in particular Guy Goodwin-Gill and James Hathaway, to discuss issues and to provide detailed and constructive reflections in answer to my queries. Malte Jaguttis kindly answered questions concerning aspects of German approaches to international law and Reinhard Marx assisted with others concerning refugee law in Germany. Simon Cox, Chris Desira and Ellis Wilford have read all or important parts of the volume and provided helpful comments. In Chambers at Lamb Building, David Sellwood and Christel Querton have assisted with research as has my (now former) pupil Rachel Kerr. Various issues have been discussed with Richard Drabble QC. In relation to Ethiopia and Eritrea, which after 1998 provided the locus for my growing exposure to the interaction of denationalisation and refugee law, the expertise and commitment of experts on those countries—and in particular John Campbell, Lionel Cliffe and Günter Schröder—has been invaluable.

My Clerks at Lamb Building, particularly Gary Goodger, Senior Clerk, and Phil Silverman, Clerking Team Leader for immigration, asylum and nationality, have been supportive throughout.

Over the years I have had the benefit of great encouragement and support from my parents Robert Fripp and Carol Burtin Fripp and my brother Will Fripp. The support of my wife Satwant Gill has, as in so many other things, been indispensable to the completion of this project.

Finally I am grateful to Hart Publishing. Sinead Moloney saw promise in the project and has backed it consistently and her staff have vindicated her, and my, confidence throughout.

Any mistake in the text is my own.

1 February 2016

List of Acronyms and Abbreviations

ACHPR81	African Charter on Human and Peoples' Rights 1981
ACHRWC90	African Charter on the Rights and Welfare of the Child 1990
ACERWC	African Committee of Experts on the Rights and Welfare of the Child
ACHR69	American Convention on Human Rights 1969
ACHR04	Arab Charter on Human Rights 2004
CJEU	Court of Justice of the European Union
CPED06	Convention for the Protection of All Persons from Enforced Disappearance 2006
CEDAW79	Convention on the Elimination of All Forms of Discrimination against Women 1979
CRS61	Convention on the Reduction of Statelessness
CRPD06	Convention on the Rights of Persons with Disabilities 2006
CRC89	Convention on the Rights of the Child 1989
CAT84	Convention against Torture and other Cruel, Inhuman or Degrading Treatment or Punishment 1984
CRS61	Convention on the Reduction of Statelessness 1961
CSR51	Convention relating to the Status of Refugees 1951
CSSP54	Convention relating to the Status of Stateless Persons 1954
CASSS06	Council of Europe Convention on the Avoidance of Statelessness in Relation to State Succession 2006
ECOWAS	Economic Community of West African States
ECN97	European Convention on Nationality 1997
ECHR50	European Convention on Human Rights and Fundamental Freedoms 1950
IACHR	Inter-American Court of Human Rights
ICERD66	International Convention on the Elimination of All Forms of Racial Discrimination 1966
ICSPCA48	International Convention on the Suppression and Punishment of the Crime of Apartheid 1948
ICCPR66	International Covenant on Civil and Political Rights 1966

ICESCR66	International Covenant on Economic, Social, and Cultural Rights 1966
ICJ	International Court of Justice
ILC	International Law Commission
IHRL	International Human Rights Law
IRO	International Refugee Organisation
MCI	Minister of Citizenship and Immigration (Canada)
MEI	Minister of Employment and Immigration (Canada)
MIEA	Minister for Immigration & Ethnic Affairs (Australia)
MIMIA	Minister for Immigration & Multicultural & Indigenous Affairs (Australia)
RSAA	Refugee Status Appeals Authority (New Zealand)
SSHD	Secretary of State for the Home Department (United Kingdom)
VCLT69	Vienna Convention on the Law of Treaties 1969
UDHR48	Universal Declaration of Human Rights 1948
UNHCR	United Nations High Commissioner for Refugees
UNHRC	United Nations Human Rights Committee

Table of Cases

International

Court of Justice of the European Union

European Court of Human Rights and European Comission of Human Rights

International Court of Justice

Permanent Court of International Justice

Other International Decisions

Domestic

Australia

Canada

Egypt

France

Germany

India

Ireland

New Zealand

Poland

Switzerland

United Kingdom

United States

Table of Treaties and Other International Materials

European Union

Regulations

Directives

International

Table of Domestic Legislation

Part I

Background

1

Nationality, Citizenship, Statelessness

Nationality is the expression of affiliation to a State for purposes of international law. The classical position that nationality falls to the reserved domain of the State in principle remains in force, and nationality can be created only by municipal law. However, state exclusivity is balanced by the increasing development of international standards relevant to state conduct affecting nationality, and breach of international conventions, international custom and principles of law generally recognised with regard to nationality, will be relevant to whether the bestowal or removal of status by a State will be recognised on the international plane.

Contents

A. Nationality Defined

A1. General Definition

1.1 The *Oxford English Dictionary* sets out several meanings of 'nationality', including 'national quality or character', 'Nationalism; attachment to one's country or nation; national feeling' and 'The fact of belonging to a particular nation; spec. a legal relationship between a state and an individual involving reciprocal rights and duties'. The root concept 'nation' is defined as:

> An extensive aggregate of persons, so closely associated with each other by common descent, language, or history, as to form a distinct race or people, usually organised as a separate political state and occupying a definite territory.
>
> In early examples the racial idea is usually stronger than the political; in recent use the notion of political unity and independence is more prominent.[1]

1.2 The dictionary entry states the existence of two potential concepts, related to but independent of the other, either of which may underlie the idea of a 'nation' in a particular case. One of these is a term exclusively of law, the other one of society and politics. This is wholly consistent with the observation of Paul Weis, who, writing in 1956 at the start of his very important study of *Nationality and Statelessness*

[1] J Simpson and E Weiner (eds), *The Oxford English Dictionary* (2nd edn, Clarendon, 1989) vol X 231, 234, 235.

in International Law (a second edition was published in 1979),[2] emphasised the existence of two senses in which the term 'nationality' might be employed:

> The term 'nationality' in the sense in which it is used in this book is a politico-legal term denoting membership of a State. It must be distinguished from nationality as a historico-biological term denoting membership of a nation. In the latter sense it means the subjective corporate sentiment of unity of members of a specific group forming a 'race' or 'nation' which may, though not necessarily, be possessed of a territory and which, by seeking political unity on that territory, may lead to the formation of a State.[3]
>
> Nationality in that sense, which is essentially a conception of a non-legal nature belonging to the field of sociology and ethnography, is not the subject of this work. The use of the same term for two different notions, belonging to two different branches of science is, however, not merely accidental. It can be explained by historic-genetic reasons and is not entirely irrelevant when treating nationality as a legal concept, as will be shown later.[4]

Weis noted the origin of the root term 'nation' as the Latin word '*natio*', but this provides only a starting point in definition of the modern term 'nation' and its extension 'national'—the Latin term possessed a range of potential meanings including 'people, tribe, kin, genus, class, flock' as well as legal membership.[5] Equivalent terms exist in many other languages, including for example French (*nationalité*), German (*Nationalität*), Italian (*nazionalità*) and Spanish (*nacionalidad*).[6] 1.3

Whilst the Latin word clearly illustrates antecedent usage, the meaning focused upon both by Weis, and in this work, is nationality as that term is generally employed in the context of international and national laws, that is, as 'a politico-legal term denoting membership of a State'. This meaning reflects appropriation of the earlier, broader usage of the term in order to give a name to the legal connection of membership or affiliation as between an individual and the State, as opposed to the relationship between a subject and a monarch. This core legal meaning of 'nationality' as denoting legal connection between individual and State is surprisingly recent. It seems to have its first roots in the development, after the French Revolution in 1789, of legal language referring to nationhood as emanating from the popular will rather than from shared fealty to a monarch.[7] According to Zernatto and Mistretta, '"Nationalité" as a term denoting State membership was confirmed officially by the 1835 Sixth Edition of the *Dictionnaire de l'Académie Française*'.[8] 1.4

---

[2] P Weis, *Nationality and Statelessness in International Law* (2nd edn, Brill, 1979).

[3] P Weis, *Nationality and Statelessness in International Law* (Stevens, 1956).

[4] Weis (n 2 above) 3.

[5] R Plender, *International Migration Law* (2nd edn, Martinus Nijhoff, 1988) 10–12; Weis (n 2 above) 4.

[6] Weis (n 2 above) 4.

[7] A Boll, *Multiple Nationality and International Law* (Martinus Nijhoff, 2006) 65; Plender, *International Migration Law* (n 5 above) 10–12.

[8] G Zernatto and A Mistretta, 'Nation: The History of a Word' (1944) 6(3) *The Review of Politics* 351; M Koessler, '"Subject", "Citizen", "National", and "Permanent Allegiance"' (1946–47) 56 *Yale Law Journal* 58, 61.

1.5 In international law, 'nationality' means not simply membership of a State, but 'attachment to that State for purposes of international law,' the attachment necessarily being of a form indicative of affiliation or membership. Harvard Law School research done in the 1920s, and later cited with approval by Plender, defined nationality in this context as 'the status of a natural person who is attached to the State by the tie of allegiance'.[9] In *Messih v Minister of the Interior* (1950) 28 ILR 291, the Egyptian Conseil d'État concluded that nationality 'is the juridical and political link which unites an individual with a State' and that 'its rules form part of public law'. *Oppenheim's International Law* further asserts that 'Nationality is the principle link between individuals and international law',[10] whilst Dörr, in the *Max Planck Encyclopedia of Public International Law*, states that 'the legal bond of nationality becomes the essential element of the individual's legal status under international law'.[11]

1.6 It has been held that the legal relationship of nationality must reflect a particular connection between a national and the State of his nationality. In the *Nottebohm* case (*Liechtenstein v Guatemala*) [1955] ICJ Reports 4 (at 20), the majority finding in the International Court of Justice was:

> According to the practice of States, to arbitral and judicial decisions and to the opinions of writers, nationality is a legal bond having as its basis a social fact of attachment, a genuine connection of existence, interests and sentiments, together with the existence of reciprocal rights and duties. It may be said to constitute the juridical expression of the fact that the individual upon whom it is conferred, either directly by the law or as the result of an act of the authorities, is in fact more closely connected with the population of the State conferring nationality than with that of any other State. Conferred by a State, it only entitles that State to exercise protection vis-à-vis another State, if it constitutes a translation into juridical terms of the individual's connection with the State which has made him its national.

As will be seen later, this decision potentially impacts upon international law as regards the recognition and opposability of a nationality asserted on the basis of a State's laws. But it is important to recognise both that the 'social fact of attachment' or 'genuine connection' held inherent in nationality by the Court may be minimal whilst still effective for the purpose of sustaining status as a national, and also that the 'social fact' and 'genuine connection' cannot *create* the legal status of nationality.

1.7 Nationality, existing at the level of international law, follows from membership of the State defined by its municipal law, which in the modern era is most often

---

[9] Plender, *International Migration Law* (n 5 above) 39.

[10] R Jennings and A Watts (eds), *Oppenheim's International Law*, vol 1 ('Peace') (9th edn, OUP, 1992) Pt 2, 857, §379.

[11] O Dörr, 'Nationality' in *Max Planck Encyclopedia of Public International Law* (online edn, OUP, 2015).

referred to as citizenship. The congruence between the two concepts—nationality and citizenship—is so close that the terminology denoting state membership under domestic law ('citizenship' in most States today—in the United Kingdom formerly 'subject' and now 'British citizen' status, '*Staatsangehörigkeit*' in Germany) is frequently if imprecisely also used to refer to the usual extension of that status on to the international plane as 'nationality'.[12] By contrast the term 'alien' denotes a person who is not a national of a particular State, whether a national of another State or without any nationality. In comparative domestic practice there has over time been a substantial movement towards the preferential use of 'citizen' rather than 'subject', as language indicative of feudal rather than constitutional relationships has fallen into disfavour. However, the precise word or phrase employed in municipal law, whether citizen, or subject, or something else, is irrelevant on the plane of international law.

At the level of legal theory the national of a State has been characterised as an extension of the sovereignty of the State itself, following the eighteenth-century Swiss philosopher, diplomat and legal theorist Emmerich de Vattel. In 1758 Vattel wrote that 'Whoever uses a citizen ill, indirectly offends the state, which is bound to protect this citizen; and the sovereign of the latter should avenge his wrongs'.[13] The Vattelian concept of the citizen as an extension of the State, also known as the 'Vattelian fiction' provides the theoretical justification for the interest in protection of a national by the State of nationality, even where the national is on the territory of another State which therefore possesses territorial supremacy. By doing so the Vattelian fiction provides the theoretical foundation for interrelationship of sovereignties as between that of the territorial State and that of the state of an alien's nationality, and hence represents a factor offsetting in some part what had been advanced in classical international law as the absolute supremacy of the territorial State. The protection of its national by a State against a State possessing territorial supremacy is known as 'international protection' or 'diplomatic protection'. Amerasinghe, a leading authority on diplomatic protection, has said that: **1.8**

> even though this protection is based on what has come to be called a fiction, it is a valuable source of protection which has not outlived its usefulness ... It might be said that, though a person—natural or juridical—suffers the primary injury, it is through, and because of, a legal relationship between States that his interests have come to be and are protected.[14]

---

[12] The term '*ressortissant*' is frequently used in the French text of treaties where the term 'national' is employed in the English text. Weis concluded, in the light of the decision of the French Cour de cassation in *Prince Elie de Bourbon-Parma v Auroux es qualité ministère public* (1923) *Clunet* 904–30, that the French term had a somewhat wider meaning than 'national', also including other protected persons ('protégés') and perhaps resident aliens under temporary protection.

[13] E de Vattel, *The Law of Nations, Or, Principles of the Law of Nature, Applied to the Conduct and Affairs of Nations and Sovereigns, with Three Early Essays on the Origin and Nature of Natural Law and on Luxury* (translated 1797, trans anonymous, B Kapossy and R Whatmore (eds)) (Liberty Fund, 2008) Bk II, 298, §71.

[14] C Amerasinghe, *Diplomatic Protection* (OUP, 2008) 6.

1.9 The relationship between sovereignty embodied in the person of a national and that rooted in territorial supremacy arises on the plane of international law. In *Barcelona Traction (Belgium v Spain (Second Phase)* [1970] ICJ Reports 3, the International Court of Justice at [33] described the legal relationship created by entrance to the territory of a state by an alien as including obligations on the part of the receiving State:

> When a State admits into its territory foreign investments or foreign nationals, whether natural or juristic persons, it is bound to extend to them the protection of the law and assumes obligations concerning the treatment to be afforded them.

1.10 The representation of the interests of a State embodied in its national as against another State is part of the law of international protection, also known as diplomatic protection. Diplomatic protection is not exercisable against a State of nationality and is distinct from the separate system of protection of individuals represented by international human rights laws. Despite the initiation of a global human rights regime diplomatic protection has not disappeared, and remains important within international law. The exercise of diplomatic protection by a State classically depends upon nationality, although surrogate exercise for resident refugees and stateless persons represents a potential broadening in recent years. Reflecting the classical position Plender observed that:

> in the absence of treaty terms or other special provisions to the contrary, a State may not make specific representation to another State concerning the individual who is not a national of the complainant State. The principle remains basic to the international diplomatic and legal system, even though it has been somewhat attenuated as a result of the development of rules of international law governing human rights.[15]

1.11 Weis closed his groundbreaking study in 1956 with a striking set of observations subsequently repeated in the second edition of his work. For Weis the international law of nationality was not static, and questions concerning that law required reference to the important functions of nationality in international society. He believed that the further development of the law of nationality was bound to be linked with the continued development of the individual's position in international law, most visibly by the creation and continuation of international human rights laws:

> One last word about the relationship between nationality and the rights of individuals. Questions of nationality cannot be dissociated from the functions of nationality. These functions may differ in international law and in municipal law, but they are closely interlinked. From the aspect of municipal law nationality confers rights and interposes obligations on the individual. With the enactment of the Charter of the United Nations human rights and fundamental freedoms are no longer solely a matter of domestic concern. If nationality is not a purely formal concept, the efforts for the development of

---

[15] Plender, *International Migration Law* (n 5 above) 42. On diplomatic protection see Amerasinghe (n 14 above) and R Ziegler, 'Protecting Recognized Geneva Convention Refugees Outside their States of Asylum' (2013) 25(2) *International Journal of Refugee Law* 235.

international law relating to nationality can hardly be separated from the efforts for the integration of human rights in international law and for their guarantee by the safeguards of international law. The further development of international law in the field of nationality is thereby closely, if not inseparably, linked with the entire development of the position of the individual in international law.[16]

A2. Relationship Between National and International Law

i. General Features

Nationality is a concept which expresses a status or link operating on the level of international law but which rests on the underlying creation of a particular status by municipal law. Nationality and citizenship are created and maintained by the domestic law of the State—most frequently, given the importance of these areas to citizens, its constitutional law.[17] As a concept of law, nationality is not created by mere practice, unless in the system of laws observed in the State in question such practice is held to have legal status. An arbitrary or mistaken disavowal by the State of nationality status in general does not undermine the continuity of that status, if the status is in fact established by the law of the same State and the disavowal itself is not given constitutive (or deconstitutive) force under the domestic legal order. In the 1955 *Nottebohm* decision, the view of the majority of judges in the International Court of Justice (ICJ) emphasised the international character of nationality as being compatible with variation in domestic laws regarding citizenship: 1.12

> The character thus recognized on the international level as pertaining to nationality is in no way inconsistent with the fact that international law leaves it to each State to lay down the rules governing the grant of its own nationality. The reason for this is that the diversity of demographic conditions has thus far made it impossible for any general agreement to be reached on the rules relating to nationality, although the latter by its very nature affects international relations. It has been considered that the best way of making such rules accord with the varying demographic conditions in different countries is to leave the fixing of such rules to the competence of each State. On the other hand, a State cannot claim that the rules it has thus laid down are entitled to recognition by another State unless it has acted in conformity with this general aim of making the legal bond of nationality accord with the individual's genuine connection with the State which assumes the defence of its citizens by means of protection as against other States.[18]

In recent decades the development of international human rights law (IHRL) and of regional and domestic human rights laws has created, at least in theory, 1.13

[16] Weis (n 3 above) 259–60 repeated in Weis (n 2 above) 256.

[17] Weis (n 2 above) 29. The United Kingdom, without a law of citizenship given explicit constitutional status, is unusual in this respect.

[18] *Nottebohm* (*Liechtenstein v Guatemala*) [1955] ICJ Rep 4, 26.

protections for the individual not depending upon nationality and in the main applicable without regard to it. This represents a dramatic change from the position before the Second World War, when in the absence of establishing international standards States were seen as able to act against their own nationals, within their territories, with near complete impunity. As a result, a foreign national resident in a State, to whom diplomatic protection by a State of nationality might be extended, and who could flee and expect to enter his or her own State of nationality, might well have been in a better position than a national of the home State itself, who could look to no external protector.[19] However, the link of nationality between individual and State is still very important to the individual, providing his or her primary operative link with the international system. This is emphasised by one of the primary general texts, *Oppenheim's International Law*:

> It is through the medium of their nationality that individuals can normally enjoy benefits from international law. This has consequences over the whole area of international law. Such individuals as do not possess any nationality enjoy, in general, only limited protection, since if they are aggrieved by a state there is no national state which is competent to take up their case. As far as international law is concerned, there is, apart from obligations (now quite extensive) expressly laid down by treaty—and in particular the general obligation, enshrined in the Charter of the United Nations, to respect human rights and fundamental freedoms—no restriction upon a state maltreating such stateless individuals. On the other hand, if individuals who possess nationality are wronged abroad, it is, as a rule, their home state exclusively which has a right to ask for redress … It is for this reason that nationality is very important for international law.[20]

ii. Nationality and Citizenship

1.14 The distinction between nationality and citizenship has been described already at paragraph 1.7 above. Nationality and citizenship may be indivisible under a particular system of nationality law, but this is not inevitably the case. In theory at least it appears that a State can create nationality without granting effective citizenship, or may call into being a form of citizenship which does not extend to nationality on the international plane. *Oppenheim's International Law* states that 'In principle, and subject to any particular international obligations which might apply, it is not for international law but for the internal law of each state to determine who is, and who is not, to be considered its national'.[21] Weis describes the

[19] An example of this is afforded by the historian Timothy Snyder's relating that for a period between the Nazi consolidation of power in Germany in spring 1933, and until Polish policy and/or practice changed some years later, Jews of Polish nationality resident in Germany by reason of their nationality enjoyed some degree of protection from the oppression delivered upon Jews of German nationality: T Snyder, *Black Earth: The Holocaust as History and Warning* (Penguin Random House, 2015) 35.

[20] Jennings and Watts (n 10 above) 849, §376.

[21] Ibid, 852.

State's exclusivity in the sphere of nationality as an aspect of its very character as a State: 'The right of a State to determine who are, and who are not, its nationals is an essential element of its sovereignty'.[22] This freedom of States gives considerable latitude as regards the conditions for obtaining or holding either nationality or citizenship. Schwarzenberger has observed that 'For purposes of his own municipal law, a territorial sovereign may deny to groups of inhabitants ... all or most rights of citizenship, yet still consider himself entitled to protect them in relation to other subjects of international law'.[23]

iii. The Interaction of State Exclusivity and International Law

1.15 Although it had long been thought that States possessed something approaching unlimited freedom of action in relation to nationality, the past century has brought an increasing recognition that a nationality status which is valid under domestic law may not be effective on the international plane. *Oppenheim's International Law* states that:

> Thus, although nationality is essentially an institution of the internal laws of states, and the international application of the notion of nationality law in any particular case must be based on the nationality law of the state in question, the determination by each state of the grant of its own nationality is not necessarily to be accepted internationally without question.[24]

1.16 The reasons why 'the determination by each state of the grant of its own nationality is not necessarily to be accepted internationally without question' lie in the existence of distinct standards established in international law. Weis identifies national sovereignty and international law as interacting in relation to nationality:

> This conception of nationality as a matter falling primarily into the domestic legislative sphere of the State is just as consistent with the existence of rules of international law in the field of nationality as the conception of sovereignty is consistent with international law itself. Nationality cannot be a matter falling within the competence of municipal law to the exclusion of international law.[25]

1.17 An illustrative parallel is that offered in *Brownlie's Principles of Public International Law*, namely the delimitation of territorial boundaries:

> National law prescribes the extent of the territory of a state, but this prescription does not preclude an international forum from deciding questions of title in its own way, using criteria of international law. A sovereignty in principle unlimited by the existence

---

22 Weis (n 2 above) 65.

23 G Schwarzenberger, *A Manual of International Law* (5th edn, Stevens, 1967) 141–42.

24 Jennings and Watts (n 10 above) 853, §378, citing *Nottebohm* (*Liechtenstein v Guatemala*) [1955] ICJ Rep 4, 20, 26.

25 Weis (n 2 above) 65.

of other states is ridiculous. For instance, as regards the delimitation of the territorial sea, the [International Court of Justice] in *Anglo-Norwegian Fisheries* allowed that in regard to rugged coasts the coastal state is in the best position to appraise the local conditions dictating the selection of baselines, but the Court did not support complete autonomy. The conferral of nationality as a status is in this respect akin to a process of delimitation.[26]

1.18 The same work cautions against 'relying on abstract statements purporting to establish the boundaries of the reserved domain' and adds the observation that the degree of exclusivity reserved to the State may depend upon the particular context: 'Nationality is not confined either to the reserved domain or the realm of state relations: in principle it has two aspects, either of which may be dominant depending on the facts and type of dispute'.[27] In this context *Oppenheim's International Law* states that:

> although nationality is essentially an institution of the internal laws of states, and the international application of the notion of nationality in any particular case must be based on the nationality law of the state in question, the determination by each state of the grant of its own nationality is not necessarily to be accepted internationally without question.[28]

1.19 The relevance of international legal standards in the context of nationality is now confirmed authoritatively both by leading commentators and by treaty and customary international law. Plender concluded in 1988 that 'international relations have so developed, in the course of the present century, that very many aspects of the law of nationality are now removed from the reserved domain of domestic jurisdiction',[29] and *Brownlie's Principles of Public International Law* states, at 2012, that 'There are compelling objections of principle to the doctrine of the complete freedom of states in the present context'.[30] Even where the reserved domain applies, a State may bind itself by obligations to other States. An early example of contemporary political relevance, and interesting as predating the identification or development of the broader body of standards now understood as relevant, is provided by article 61 of the Treaty of Trianon 1920, formally concluding the First World War between the Allied Powers and the Kingdom of Hungary. It provides that:

> Every person possessing rights of citizenship *(pertinenza)* in territory which formed part of the territories of the former Austro-Hungarian Monarchy shall obtain *ipso facto* to the exclusion of Hungarian nationality the nationality of the State exercising sovereignty over such territory.

An amendment by Hungary to the Hungarian Nationality Act which came into force in 2011 allowing any Hungarian-speaking descendant of a Hungarian

---

26 J Crawford (ed), *Brownlie's Principles of Public International Law* (8th edn, OUP, 2012) 510.
27 Ibid.
28 Jennings and Watts (n 10 above) 853, §378.
29 Plender, *International Migration Law* (n 5 above) 144.
30 Crawford (ed), *Brownlie's Principles of Public International Law* (n 26 above) 509.

national or person of probable Hungarian origin to apply for Hungarian nationality, is considered by neighbouring States on the territory of the former Austria-Hungary to breach the express restriction in the Treaty of Trianon upon re-extension of Hungarian citizenship beyond the territorial boundaries of the current State.[31]

The 1923 Advisory Opinion of the Permanent Court of International Justice concerning *Nationality Decrees Issued in Tunis and Morocco on 8 November 1921* [1923] PCIJ Series B No 4 represents an important watershed in understanding of the relationship between domestic competence and international law in the sphere of nationality. The dispute followed legislation by the metropolitan French government and the government of Tunis, then a French protectorate, that every person born in Tunis to a parent also born there would be a Tunisian and a French citizen. The United Kingdom protested the automatic application of the decrees to British subjects in that territory, and declined to recognise the decrees as effective as regards any person entitled to British nationality who might be born in Tunis. The Court had to decide whether or not, as France maintained, the dispute between France and the United Kingdom concerned matters 'solely within the domestic jurisdiction' of France. The Court concluded that 'in principle' nationality represented a reserved domain, but added an important qualification: **1.20**

> 40. The question whether a certain matter is or is not solely within the jurisdiction of a State is an essentially relative question; it depends upon the development of international relations. Thus, in the present state of international law, questions of nationality are, in the opinion of the Court, in principle within this reserved domain.
>
> 41. For the purpose of the present opinion, it is enough to observe that it may well happen that, in a matter which, like that of nationality, is not, in principle, regulated by international law, the right of a State to use its discretion is nevertheless restricted by obligations which it may have undertaken towards other States. In such a case, jurisdiction which, in principle, belongs solely to the State, is limited by rules of international law.

In 1930 an International Conference for the Codification of International Law was held in The Hague under the auspices of the League of Nations. Nationality, including the question of the relationship between domestic and international law in relation to nationality, was a primary area selected for examination at the Conference. The Preparatory Committee prepared a Schedule of Points seeking information from States. Point 1 ('Right of each State to regulate the Acquisition and Loss of its Nationality') was set out as follows: **1.21**

> It appears necessary to take as the point of departure the proposition that questions of nationality are in principle matters within the sovereign authority of each State and that in principle a State must recognise the right of every other State to enact such legislation

[31] European Union Democracy Observatory, 'UPDATE: Changes in the Hungarian Citizenship Law and adopted on 26 May 2010', July 2010, available at: eudo-citizenship.eu/docs/CountryReports/recentChanges/Hungary.pdf; A Peters, 'Les changements collectifs de nationalité' in *Droit international et nationalité* (Pedone, 2012) 169.

as the latter considers proper with regard to the acquisition and loss of its nationality. The consequence should be that any question as to the acquisition or loss of a particular nationality by any person is to be decided by application of the law of the State of which the person is claimed to possess, or not possess, the nationality.

Are there, however, limits to the application of these two principles? Is there no limit to the right of the State to legislate in this matter? Is a State bound in every case to recognise the effects of the law of the other State?[32]

The preparation for the Conference, the Conference itself, and ensuing agreements represented important developments in the identification of principles recognised by States.

1.22 From the outset of preparation for the Conference, the very exercise of systematically seeking and recording the views of States, then unprecedented, was of great importance, helping to identify areas of consensus. The replies of States show a range of views. A number of representative examples have been quoted below to illustrate common themes in opinions both of the majority and of significant minorities. It can be seen that some States in Latin America particularly stressed adherence to an exclusive or near-exclusive protection of state authority—perhaps understandably given the frequent use of international law at that time by more powerful States to justify external intervention in the affairs of smaller States. An example is Chile, whose recognition of other countries' nationality laws was said to be expressly subordinated to the protection of Chile's own:

The Chilean Government regards it as a fundamental and unalterable principle that the question of the acquisition and loss of its nationality falls solely within the domestic jurisdiction of each State. It accordingly recognises, and holds that it is compelled to recognise, the effects of the law of other States concerning nationality but only in so far as this recognition does not involve the surrender or infringement of its own provisions regarding the acquisition and loss of Chilean nationality.[33]

This might be called the absolutist position, whereby for a State its own laws ultimately stand regardless of conflict with the laws of any other State. It is however strongly focused upon the issue of conflict between domestic laws of different States, not identifying any distinct body of international standards as relevant.

1.23 Egypt adopted a more nuanced position, acknowledging that express restriction by treaty might limit exclusivity, but seeking to exclude 'so-called principles' of the type frequently used by European powers, and protesting the proliferation of capitulations, or concessionary zones of operation for nationals of external States shielded from control of the host State:

The fact that in Egypt many foreign countries enjoy the benefit of capitulations causes much inconvenience to the Egyptian Government in the exercise of its sovereign rights

---

32 S Rosenne, *League of Nations Conference for the Codification of International Law*, vol I (Oceana, 1975) 13.

33 Ibid, 14.

in questions of nationality. Egypt therefore would welcome an unequivocal declaration to the effect that States are entitled to settle without appeal all questions of nationality within their own territories, the only restrictions being those contained in express provisions of treaties, to the exclusion of all so-called principles derived from an existing state of affairs or vague usage.[34]

The German response referred to limitations upon national powers, but in terms limited to conflict of laws rather than to any separate body of principle at the level of international law: 1.24

> The general principle that all questions relating to the acquisition or loss of a specific nationality shall be governed by the laws of the State whose nationality is claimed or contested should be admitted. The application of this principle, however, should not go beyond the limits at which the legislation of one State encroaches on the sovereignty of another. For example, a State has no power ... to confer its nationality on all the inhabitants of another State or on all foreigners entering its territory. Further, if the State confers its nationality on the subjects of other States without their request, when the persons in question are not attached to it by any particular bond, as, for instance, origin, domicile, or birth, the States concerned will not be bound to recognise such naturalisation.[35]

Other replies went beyond identifying limitations limited to conflict between different domestic laws, to assert the existence of at least some discrete standards at the international level. The Danish Government responded that: 1.25

> The above principle, namely, the sovereignty of the State and the duty of recognising the sovereignty of other States in this connection cannot be pushed to extremes, but should be subject to certain restrictions. It can be recognised in its entirety only in relation to the grounds for the acquisition and loss of nationality generally recognised by the community of States.[36]

In contrast Australia accepted the possibility of restrictions upon States in 'exceptional' cases, but insisted that acceptance of the general doctrine of the freedom of States remained good only whilst no State sought to move away, under cover of that exclusivity, from principles normally followed in the past: 1.26

> [The fact that] in general, questions relating to its nationality fall solely within the domestic jurisdiction of the State ... does not, however, exclude the possibility that, in exceptional cases, the right of the State to legislate on the subject may be restricted by the duties which it owes to other States, and that legislation which it may pass in breach of such duties may not involve a corresponding obligation on the part of those other States to recognise such legislation. This question is not likely to be of practical importance so long as legislation as to nationality does not depart from the general principles normally followed by States in the past.[37]

34 Ibid, 15.
35 Ibid, 13.
36 Ibid, 14–15.
37 Ibid, 13.

1.27 The United Kingdom reply gave understandable prominence to the recent decision of the Permanent Court of International Justice (PCIJ) in its favour against France in the *Nationality Decrees* case:

> His Majesty's Government ... accept the general principle that it is for the State to determine the rules relative to the acquisition and loss of its nationality. In general, therefore, questions relating to the enjoyment or non-enjoyment of its nationality fall solely within the domestic jurisdiction of the State.
>
> The mere fact, however, that nationality falls in general within the domestic jurisdiction of a State does not exclude the possibility that the right of the State to use its discretion in legislating with regard to nationality may be restricted by duties which it owes to other States [reference to the *Nationality Decrees* case]. Legislation which is inconsistent with such duties is not legislation which there is any obligation upon a State whose rights are ignored to recognise. It follows that the right of a State to legislate with regard to the acquisition and loss of its nationality and the duty of another State to recognise the effects of such legislation are not necessarily coincident.[38]

Amongst other States responding on the point, South Africa stated that 'there is no obligation on the other States to recognise legislation which is not consistent with such duties, or which is prejudicial to their own rights as States', and Bulgaria cited both exclusion of exceptions and the relevance of widely expressed duties amongst States: 'questions connected with the acquisition and loss of nationality come within the sovereign jurisdiction of each State, there being no exceptions to this rule. The right of every State to legislate in this matter is limited only by the necessities of common courtesy and justice'.[39]

1.28 Finally, the United States identified over-extensive naturalisation provisions as a particular problem, and strongly asserted the existence of international legal standards applicable to nationality:

> [T]he Government of the United States has always recognised ... that the acquisition or loss of the nationality of a particular State are matters which pertain primarily to domestic policy and are therefore to be determined by the domestic law of that State, it does not admit that a State is subject to no limitations in conferring its nationality on individuals. It has proceeded upon the theory, which is believed to be sound, that there are certain grounds generally recognised by civilized States upon which a State may properly clothe individuals with its nationality at or after birth, but that no State is free to extend the application of its laws of nationality in such a way as to reach out and claim the allegiance of whomsoever it pleases. The scope of municipal laws governing nationality must be regarded as limited by consideration of the rights and obligations of individuals and of other States.[40]

1.29 In the replies both jointly and severally, three features are notable. The first is the priority given to domestic law as the exclusive source of nationality, in line with

---

[38] Ibid, 17.
[39] Ibid, 13-14.
[40] Ibid, 16.

the recognised principle that it is for the State to determine the rules relative to the acquisition and loss of its nationality. The second is that notwithstanding agreement as to the existence of a general principle, a balance of opinion pointed to the existence of potential areas of exception, even if the scope of any such exception was evidently difficult to define with precision. The principle of domestic freedom in relation to matters of nationality might itself be circumscribed in scope, limited to 'grounds for the acquisition and loss of nationality generally recognised by the community of states' (Denmark). Such freedom even if not restricted in this way was admitted to be limited by the need to resolve cases of conflict between different domestic legal regimes (Germany, South Africa). But it might also be limited by broad and difficult to define factors such as 'the necessities of common courtesy and justice' (Bulgaria) or 'the general principles normally followed by States in the past' (Australia). The right of the State might be limited by duties owed to other States (United Kingdom), or by duties owed to other States as well as 'the rights and obligations of individuals' (United States). Even States which were more sovereigntist in their replies, and desirous of excluding unquantified obligations which might be invoked by more powerful States, accepted that treaty obligations might affect the extent of a State's freedoms (Egypt). As Brownlie subsequently noted:

> In view of the element of contradiction, and the rules noted above, the statements in the replies of governments to the effect that 'in principle' the question of nationality falls within the exclusive competence of States lose much of their effect: at least they can no longer be regarded as presenting an absolute bar as a matter of principle. What is significant is that the majority of replies accepted the position that the right to determine nationality was not unlimited.[41]

The third notable feature is that both the enquiry and every response touching on this referred to external standards as undermining not the initial validity of action under domestic law, but the obligation of any other State to give recognition to a situation resulting from such action.

The primary instrument concluded at the Conference was the Convention on Certain Questions Relating to the Conflict of Nationality Laws 1930. Whilst overall this represented particular rather than general international law—that is, it became binding only as between parties to the treaty—it is likely that some of its provisions reflected customary international law, including articles 1 and 2, the primary provisions in the Convention dealing with the basis of nationality law and relationship of domestic and international law: **1.30**

> Article 1
>
> It is for each State to determine under its own law who are its nationals. This law shall be recognised by other States in so far as it is consistent with international conventions,

---

[41] I Brownlie, 'The Relations of Nationality in Public International Law' in *British Yearbook of International Law* 1963 (OUP, 1965) 298.

> international custom, and the principles of law generally recognised with regard to nationality.
>
> Article 2
>
> Any question as to whether a person possesses the nationality of a particular State shall be determined in accordance with the law of the State.

Article 1 distinguishes between the determination of nationality under domestic law, which is reserved to States, and recognition of the result by other States, which depends expressly upon compliance with 'international conventions, international custom, and the principles of law generally recognised with regard to nationality'. So the nationality of State A is determined by the domestic law of State A, but if State A has acted otherwise than consistently 'with international conventions, international custom, and the principles of law generally recognised with regard to nationality' other States are not obliged to recognise the resulting status. Article 2 states that any nationality question shall be determined on the basis of the domestic law of the State in question. This emphasises that neither another State nor any other institution may create nationality of State A: an example would be the case in which an individual has lost nationality of State A under the law of that country by reason of marriage to a national of State B, then divorces and upon divorce loses the nationality of State B. State B's law cannot validly provide that an individual who is granted nationality of State B by naturalisation on the basis of marriage to a national of State B, shall in the event of divorce lose the nationality of State B and resume any original nationality which was lost upon naturalisation. Here only State A may restore its nationality: State B cannot validly purport to do so.

1.31 It appears likely that articles 1 and 2 in the 1930 Convention represent a statement of already existing customary international law, as opposed to particular international law binding only upon the parties. The Convention itself left open the question as to whether any part of its content was seen as reflecting customary international law: article 18 provides expressly that 'The inclusion of the above-mentioned principles and rules in the Convention shall in no way be deemed to prejudice the question whether they do or do not already form part of international law'. Article 1 was cited by the ICJ in the *Nottebohm* case (*Liechtenstein v Guatemala*) [1955] ICJ Reports 4, at 23, with no suggestion that this was restricted to particular international law, and leading texts cite it likewise as expressing international law of wide application.[42] Brownlie considered that 'With its limitations, article 1 remains a useful authority for the view that international law sets limits to the power of a State to confer nationality'.[43] Certainly the 1930 Conference has lasting significance in the field of nationality. Weis concluded in 1979 that the Conference 'must certainly be seen as a landmark in any investigation into the problem of nationality in international law', and that 'Taken as a whole

---

[42] For instance Jennings and Watts (n 10 above) 852–53, §378.

[43] Brownlie (n 41 above) 299.

and read with a critical eye, the preparatory documents and transactions of the Conference contain important information as to existing international law in the field of nationality'.[44] Hersch Lauterpacht considered the 1930 Convention to be a highly significant instrument, in part because it prompted a substantial movement amongst States towards amendment of their nationality laws in line with its principles.[45] More recently the language of article 1 has been echoed in the European Convention on Nationality 1997 (ECN97), which provides by its article 3 that 'Each State shall determine under its own law who are its nationals', balancing this by the statement that 'This law shall be accepted by other States in so far as it is consistent with applicable international conventions, customary international law and the principles of law generally recognised with regard to nationality'. The influence of the 1930 Convention belies what has been in fact a relatively small degree of participation by States: even today there are only 20 States Parties.[46]

In a 'Report on the Elimination or Reduction of Statelessness' prepared in 1953 for the International Law Commission (ILC) by Special Rapporteur Córdova, he concluded, giving particular regard to deprivation of nationality by reason of its significance as a cause of statelessness, that international law provided standards which in principle were applicable both to the creation and to the removal of nationality: **1.32**

> 14. It follows that international law sets forth the limits of the power of a State to confer its nationality. The power necessarily implies the right to deprive an individual of that nationality; consequently international law may also restrict the authority of the State to deprive a person of its own nationality. There are cases in which international law considers that a certain national legislation is not legal because it comes into conflict with the broader interests of the international community.
>
> 15. In the present state of international law, it is not, therefore, unwarranted to affirm that the right of individual States to legislate in matters of nationality is dependent upon and subordinate to the rules of international law on the subject, and that, therefore, these questions of nationality are not, as has been argued, entirely reserved for the exclusive jurisdiction of the individual States themselves.[47]

At that time—as at the time of the 1930 Conference—it could be said that insofar as the existence of a body of international law standards relevant to nationality was accepted, the content was not extensive. The decades since the 1930 Convention and the 1953 Report have seen a substantial growth in the body of laws bearing on the conduct of States as regards nationality. In particular, the development of IHRL and the international law relating to statelessness since the Second World

[44] Weis (n 2 above) 26 and 28.

[45] *Yearbook of the International Law Commission*, vol 1 (1952) 125.

[46] Noted at treaties.un.org/pages/LONViewDetails.aspx?src=LON&id=512&chapter=30&lang=en.

[47] ILC, 'Report on the Elimination or Reduction of Statelessness' (1953) UN Doc A/CN.4/64; ILC, *Yearbook of the International Law Commission*, vol II (1963) 167 [14]–[15].

War, and the principle of non-discrimination in international law, have greatly increased the volume and density of *materiel* within the categories identified at article 1 of the 1930 Convention as 'international conventions, international custom, and the principles of law generally recognised with regard to nationality'.

1.33 It is striking that this body of standards has in general not been created by treaty-making activity directly focusing upon the international law concerning nationality. Relatively few treaties have directly targeted questions of nationality and recognition since the 1930 Convention, though there have been two treaty instruments, the Convention relating to the Status of Stateless Persons 1954 (CSSP54) and the Convention on the Reduction of Statelessness 1961 (CRS61), concerning statelessness. The Council of Europe by ECN97 marked a renewal of interest in the topic following the break-up of the Union of Soviet Socialist Republics and Socialist Federal Republic of Yugoslavia. In 1999 the ILC, in its 'Draft Articles on Nationality of Natural Persons in relation to the Succession of States', included a preambular paragraph '[e]mphasizing that nationality is essentially governed by internal law within the limits set by international law', a theme justified in the ensuing Report which states that 'the competence of States in this field may be exercised only within the limits set by international law'.[48] In 2006 the 'Draft Articles on Diplomatic Protection of the International Law Commission' defined the 'state of nationality of a natural person' at article 4 as 'a State whose nationality that person has acquired, in accordance with the law of that State, by birth, descent, naturalization, succession of States, or in any other manner, not inconsistent with international law'.[49] What has occurred in the place of more substantial treaty-making activity is that the growth of IHRL coupled with recognition of a customary law principle of non-discrimination has, in conjunction with the treaty-making which has occurred, led to the identification of norms affecting state conduct in respect of nationality.

1.34 The present situation is not one which could have been predicted at the time of the 1930 Conference. Then, many foresaw the development of more detailed international rules concerning nationality. Szymon Rundstein was one of the foremost international lawyers in Europe in the 1930s, one of three members of the Sub-Committee on Nationality of the League of Nations Committee of Experts, charged with identifying questions of law relating to nationality ripe for codification at the 1930 Conference, and then the Polish delegate to the Conference itself. He agreed with his German contemporary Gerhard Liebholz that 'the deliberately arbitrary use of State authority without regard to the legislation of other States constitutes a violation of general principles of international law as an intentional abuse of rights. It would not have to be recognised by other States, being an act

[48] ILC, *Yearbook of the International Law Commission*, vol II(2) (1999) 23–24.

[49] ILC, 'Draft Articles on Diplomatic Protection' (2006)Official Records of the General Assembly (GAOR) Sixty-first Session, Supp 10 (UN Doc A/61/10).

ultra vires'.[50] Looking outwards he envisaged successive stages of development by which nationality could become fully regulated by international law. These, as paraphrased later by Weis, were as follows:

> i. initially, rules for the solution of conflicts [between different municipal legal systems] if they occur;
> ii. over time, the devising of rules to prevent conflicts of municipal nationality laws;
> iii. ultimately, the creation of a uniform international code regarding nationality.[51]

Rundstein believed the 1930 Conference had moved forward the first two objectives of enabling the resolution or avoidance of actual or potential conflicts—but he also acknowledged that generally recognised principles of nationality continued to be lacking, save for the principle of active or effective nationality employed by international tribunals in the particular context of diplomatic protection.[52] Looking today at the stage of development Rundstein identified, it can be seen that there has been little movement towards the creation of a uniform international law of nationality constraining the shape of national laws. But on the other hand, there has been a development which Rundstein could not have foreseen and was not able to see initiated, namely the creation after 1945 of a growing body of IHRL and identification of an international law principle of non-discrimination.[53] Despite the absence of any uniform international law of nationality there have since 1945 been substantial further restrictions placed upon the liberty of States in the area of nationality, most critically in the development of international human rights but also in other respects, such as the recognition and development of general anti-discrimination norms and creation of measures for the reduction of statelessness. 1.35

iv. Domestic Law is Not a Defence to Breach of International Law

It is a long-established principle of international law that a State cannot avert responsibility for an international law wrong by reliance upon its own constitutional or other law, or some lacuna in this, as enabling or justifying its action. The principle was established in the *Alabama Claims* arbitration,[54] in which the United States sought, and recovered, substantial damages from the United Kingdom for permitting the Confederate States to fit out vessels as commerce raiders in British 1.36

---

50 S Rundstein, 'Die allgemeinen Rechtsgrundsätze des Völkerrechts und die Fragen der Staatsangehörigkeit' (1932) XVI Band *Zeitschrift für Völkerrecht* 14–71, cited at Weis (n 2 above) 87.

51 Weis (n 2 above) 87.

52 Ibid and see para 1.104 below.

53 Rundstein, by then one of the foremost international lawyers of his day, was killed in 1942 at Treblinka concentration camp.

54 Reports of International Arbitral Awards, *Alabama Claims of the United States of America against Great Britain*, Award rendered on 14 September 1872 by the tribunal of arbitration established by Article I of the Treaty of Washington of 8 May 1871, Vol XXIX, 125–34.

shipyards during the American Civil War, the absence of domestic law prohibition upon such activity in the United Kingdom being found irrelevant. More recently articles 27 and 46 of the Vienna Convention on the Law of Treaties 1969 have codified this as regards treaties, the first of these stating that 'A party may not invoke the provisions of its international law as justification for its failure to perform a treaty', and the latter providing a limited exception if consent to be bound on the international plane was given in breach of domestic law authority, in a way which would be objectively evident to any State conducting itself in the matter in accordance with normal practice and in good faith, and if 'a rule of its internal law of fundamental importance' is concerned. The ILC in its Articles on the Responsibility of States for Internationally Wrongful Acts 2001 provides explicitly that 'The characterization of an act of a State as internationally wrongful is governed by international law. Such characterization is not affected by the characterization of the same act as lawful by internal law'.

A3. Nationality Requires Existence of a State

1.37 The concept of nationality in international law interacts with a separate international law concept, that of the State:

> [T]he first obvious fact is that the concept of nationality is consubstantial with the concept of the State. The existence of a nationality presupposes the existence of a sovereign State. On this point, international law and legal theory are unanimous.[55]

In May 2010 an Expert Meeting at Prato organised by the United Nations High Commissioner for Refugees (UNHCR) examined questions relating to the definition of statelessness, that is, the absence of a nationality. In relation to the question of whether there is a State to which a relevant link of nationality might extend, the Summary Conclusions state that:

> When applying the definition it will often be prudent to look first at the question of 'State' as further analysis of the individual's relationship with the entity under consideration is moot if that entity does not qualify as a 'State'. In situations where a State does not exist under international law, the persons are *ipso facto* considered to be stateless unless they possess another nationality.[56]

The observation is obviously as apt in the context of ascertaining nationality as it is in the related context of ascertaining its absence.

[55] African Commission on Human and Peoples' Rights, *The Right to Nationality in Africa* (Study undertaken by the Special Rapporteur on the Rights of Refugees, Asylum Seekers, Migrants and Internally Displaced Persons in Africa (Maya Sahli Fadel)) (Banjul, ACHPR, 2015) 13.

[56] UN High Commissioner for Refugees (UNHCR), *Expert Meeting: The Concept of Stateless Persons under International Law: Summary Conclusions* (May 2010) 2.

At the level of social science a frequently cited definition of the State is that of Weber, from a pamphlet in 1919: 1.38

> Yet what is a 'political' association, considered from a sociological point of view? What is a 'state'? This too cannot be defined sociologically in terms of the content of its activities. There is hardly a task which has not been undertaken by some political association at some time or other, is no task of which it could be said that it is always, far less *exclusively*, the preserve of those associations which are defined as political (in today's language: states) or which were historical predecessors of the modern state. In the last analysis the modern state can only be defined sociologically in terms of a specific *means* (*Mittel*) which is peculiar to the state, as it is to all other political associations, namely physical violence (*Gewaltsamkeit*). 'Every state is founded on force (*Gewalt*)' as Trotsky once said at Brest-Litovsk. That is indeed correct. If there existed only social formations in which violence was unknown as a means, *then* the concept of the 'state' would have disappeared; *then* that condition would have arisen which one would define, in this particular sense of the word, as 'anarchy'. Violence is, of course, not the normal or sole means used by the state. There is no question of that. But it is the means specific to the state. At the present moment the relation between the state and violence is a particularly intimate one. In the past the most diverse kinds of association—beginning with the clan—have regarded physical violence as a quite normal instrument. Nowadays, by contrast, we have to say that a state is that human community which (successfully) lays claim to the *monopoly of legitimate physical violence* within a certain territory, this 'territory' being another of the defining characteristics of the state. For the specific feature of the present is that the right to use physical violence is attributed to any and all associations or individuals only to the extent that the state for its part permits this to happen. The state is held to be the sole source of the 'right' to use violence.[57]

In international law, the standards providing the basis of any determination as to whether a particular entity is a State are not fully settled. In particular there has been a long-standing dispute between those who believe that recognition of a State by other States is declaratory, and those who believe recognition to be constitutive (whose views are sometimes referred to as 'positivism').[58] Crawford summarises the direction of movement by the observation that:

> If the effect of positivist doctrine in international law was to place the emphasis in matters of statehood on the question of recognition, the effect of modern doctrine and practice has been to return the attention to issues of statehood and status independent of recognition. Nevertheless there has long been no generally accepted and satisfactory legal definition of [the criteria for achievement of] statehood.[59]

Crawford has illustrated the problem by reference to observations of two of the most prominent international lawyers of the early to mid-twentieth century, Brierly 1.39

---

[57] M Weber, 'The Profession and Vocation of Politics' in P Lassman and R Speirs (eds), *Political Writings* (trans R Speirs, first publication 1919, this publication CUP, 1994) 310–11.

[58] See Crawford, 'Introduction' to H Lauterpacht, *Recognition in International Law* (CUP, 1947, reprinted with new 'Introduction' by Crawford, 2013).

[59] J Crawford, *The Creation of States in International Law* (2nd edn, OUP, 2006) 37.

and Scelle, in the course of work by the ILC concerning a proposed Declaration on the Rights and Duties of States:

> Brierly ... argued that 'the definition [of "State"] would be difficult to establish and highly controversial', though he added that 'the word was commonly used in documents and speech, and its meaning had been understood without definition'. Scelle was more emphatic: he 'had been active in international law for more than fifty years and still did not know what a State was and he felt sure that he would not find out before he died. He was convinced that the Commission could not tell him'.[60]

1.40 Notwithstanding continued dispute as to whether recognition is partly or wholly constitutive of statehood, there is a degree of consensus as to the existence of a number of conditions which are held to be essential qualifications for statehood. The core account is at article 1 of the Montevideo Convention on the Rights and Duties of States 1933, by which it is declared that '[t]he state as a person of international law should possess the following qualifications: (a) a permanent population; (b) a defined territory; (c) government; and (d) capacity to enter into relations with the other states'. *Brownlie's Principles of International Law* notes this 'brief enumeration' as 'often cited', but 'no more than a basis for further investigation', observing that 'Not all the conditions are necessary, and in any case further criteria must be employed to produce a working definition'.[61]

1.41 The basic criteria in the Montevideo Convention have been fleshed out concisely by *Oppenheim's International Law*:

> A state proper is in existence when a people is settled in a territory under its own sovereign government. There are therefore four conditions which must obtain for the existence of a state.
>
> There must, first, be a *people*. A people is an aggregate of individuals who live together as a community though they may belong to different races or creeds or cultures, or be of a different colour.
>
> There must, second, be a *territory* in which the people is settled, although there is 'no rule that the land frontiers of a State must be fully delimited and defined; they may indeed be disputed. But it matters not whether the country is small, or large; it may consist, as in the case of city states, of one town only'.
>
> There must, third, be a *government*—that is, one or more persons who act for the people and govern according to the law of the land. A state calls for a community organised as a political unit (*polis*) as distinguished from, say, a tribe. But once a state is established, temporary interruption of the effectiveness of the government, as in a civil war, or as a result of belligerent occupation, is not inconsistent with the continued existence of the state.
>
> There must, fourth and last, be a *sovereign* government. Sovereignty is supreme authority, which on the international plane means not legal authority over all other states but rather legal authority which is not in law dependent on any other earthly authority. Sovereignty

[60] Ibid, 38.
[61] Ibid, 128.

> in the strict and narrowest sense of the term implies, therefore, independence all round, within and without the borders of the country.
>
> Of these four elements needed before a community may be regarded as a state, some may at times exist only to a diminished extent, or may even be temporarily absent, without the community necessarily ceasing to be a state. Thus the existence of a civil war may affect the continued effective existence of a government, or relations with other states may affect the degree to which sovereignty is retained, while the state nevertheless continues to exist. In some extreme cases it may do so in only a much attenuated form.[62]

The requirement for a people and for a fixed territory does not imply a minimum standard—the Vatican City is recognised as a State with a population of fewer than 1000 people, and Tuvalu with fewer than 10,000. Nauru, Palau, San Marino, Monaco, Liechtenstein, and St Kitts and Nevis, all had recorded populations well below 50,000 in 2005. As to territory, the Vatican City's territorial extent was only 0.4 square kilometres and that of Monaco 1.5. The reflection in *Oppenheim's International Law* that 'A state calls for a community organised as a political unit (*polis*) as distinguished from, say, a tribe' may unconsciously carry forward aspects of earlier subjectivities in international law which tended to treat as void less familiar forms of social organisation, and there is probably no reason why, given satisfaction of other requirements, a State may not be contiguous with the people and territory of a tribe. As to sovereignty, appreciations of the question have to be carefully nuanced. Voluntarism appears to be a requirement. For instance, the Republic of China (Taiwan) would appear potentially capable of satisfying the essential criteria, but its government has not asserted independence of the People's Republic of China so the best position is that it has not established full sovereignty—albeit possibly having the capacity to do so.

On the approach held by many modern commentators, recognition is not in itself constitutive of statehood but may in general be taken as indicative of the view of recognising States that the entity is a State, through meeting the Montevideo Convention standards. **1.42**

A4. Modes of Acquisition and/or Loss of Nationality

i. Acquisition

Nationality may be acquired in any one of a number of ways. Weis distinguished between 'original' and 'derivative' acquisition. Within the first category he stated that: **1.43**

> The two principles on which acquisition of nationality (original acquisition) is based are *jus soli* and *jus sanguinis*—acquisition of nationality by birth in the territory of the

[62] Jennings and Watts (n 10 above) 120–22, §34.

> State, and acquisition of nationality by descent whereby, as a rule, an illegitimate child acquires at birth the nationality of his mother, a legitimate child that of his parents or, if the parents are of different nationalities, that of the father.[63]

For most States one or both of these will provide the backbone of their domestic nationality law. In 1929 whilst the 1930 Convention was in contemplation, researchers at Harvard found that 17 States had nationality laws based exclusively upon *ius sanguinis*, another 25 States had nationality laws based primarily upon *ius sanguinis*, two States had nationality laws based equally upon *ius soli* and *ius sanguinis*, and 26 States had nationality laws based principally upon *ius soli* with influence of *ius sanguinis*.[64] A few years later, in 1935, another commentator found that 48 States had nationality laws based upon *ius sanguinis*, 29 States had nationality laws based upon *ius soli* and two States had nationality laws based equally upon *ius soli* and *ius sanguinis*. *Ius soli* was, and remains, the dominant principle in the Americas.[65] The Harvard Law Research project published in 1929 proposed that every State be required to select either *ius soli* or *ius sanguinis* and to base its law upon one of these models.[66] Later, at the 1930 Conference, France and Uruguay asserted that these two models were of necessity mutually exclusive and that this exclusivity itself represented a general principle of customary international law.[67] 'Derivative' acquisition for Weis included naturalisation 'in the wider sense of the term' including 'acquisition by marriage, legitimation, option, acquisition of domicile, entry into State service', and grant of naturalisation in the narrow sense of grant on application.[68]

1.44 Although the dominance of *ius soli* and *ius sanguinis* prompted van Panhuys to judge that these methods of acquisition in particular are 'sanctioned by customary international law', the validity of elevating statistical dominance to legal principle in this context has been doubted by others including Weis and Brownlie.[69] Examples of States not employing either exist—for instance nationality of the Vatican City depends not by birth or by descent but upon appointment to a specified employment coupled with residence, and this has not been suggested as undermining the status of the Vatican City as a State. Weis observed that in the practice of States *ius soli* and *ius sanguinis* themselves tended to interact to produce composites:

> The very fact … that the nationality law of a majority of States combines both principles makes their exclusive character a matter of degree. In the absence of historical

---

[63] Weis (n 2 above) 95.

[64] Harvard Law Research (1935) 29 *American Journal of International Law* 2nd sup, 29.

[65] DV Sandifer, 'A Comparative Study Relating to Nationality by Birth and Loss of Nationality' (1935) 29 *American Journal of International Law* 248, 256.

[66] Harvard Law Research (n 64 above) 29.

[67] Weis (n 2 above) 96.

[68] Ibid.

[69] HF van Panhuys, *The Role of Nationality in International Law* (Sijthoff, 1959) 160–61; Weis (n 2 above) 96; Brownlie (n 41 above) 303.

examples it is a matter of conjecture whether a nationality law based equally on *ius soli* and *ius sanguinis* would be regarded as inconsistent with international law or the general principles.[70]

In *Lay Kon Tji v MIMA* [1998] FCA 1380, (1998) 158 ALR 681, Finkelstein J judged that van Panhuys in attributing particular status under international law to *ius soli* and *ius sanguinis* 'may be going too far'. He implicitly placed greater weight on the quoted view of Weis, to the effect that: **1.45**

> *Jus soli* and *jus sanguinis* are undoubtedly the predominant modes of acquisition of nationality by municipal law. Whether there is a generally recognised principle of law to that effect is a moot question. It is not a rule of international law. Concordance of municipal law does not yet create customary international law; a universal consensus of opinion of States is equally necessary.[71]

In a survey giving attention to both views, prior to but not cited in the *Lay Kon Tji* decision, Brownlie characterised the view of Weis as a cautious one, suggesting that whilst accepting a positive authority for *ius soli* and *ius sanguinis* in international law would give rise to 'a proposition obviously much too dogmatic', Weis 'is thought to underestimate the evidence of the opinion of States'.[72] In the light of the various views the question as to whether any principle arises from the factual prevalence of *ius soli* and *ius sanguinis*, and the extent of such a principle, cannot be regarded as fully settled. **1.46**

In *Lay Kon Tji*, Finkelstein J rejected as over-extensive the proposition that acquisition of nationality invariably had a voluntary character, noting that this was plainly not correct as regards 'original nationality' acquired at birth: **1.47**

> The derivative acquisition of nationality is that acquired by naturalisation. Naturalisation includes not only the acquisition of nationality on application to the conferring state but its acquisition by circumstances such as marriage, subjugation after conquest, acquisition of domicile, legitimation and the like: see Weis at 98. In other words, derivative nationality is nationality that is conferred in consequence of an application or that is acquired by operation of law but it does not include the acquisition of nationality at birth. Thus derivative nationality could include both the voluntary and the involuntary acquisition of nationality.

Weis further observed that there was no general duty applicable to States which required the amelioration or avoidance of involuntary statelessness:

> To the extent that there are no rules of international law imposing a duty on States to confer their nationality, and few, if any, rules denying or restricting the right of States to withdraw their nationality, one may say that statelessness is not inconsistent with international law.[73]

---

[70] Weis (n 2 above) 96.

[71] Finkelstein J referred to Weis' 1956 (first) edition (n 3 above 96), but the text appears in identical terms in the second edition (ibid, 98).

[72] Brownlie (n 41 above) 312.

[73] Weis (n 2 above) 162. The absence of a general duty does not mean that there are no duties at all—see for instance the Convention on the Reduction of Statelessness 1961, articles 1–10.

His concluding that there was no broad duty of this type did not prevent him from also concluding in 1979 that international law non-discrimination standards gave rise to a narrower international law prohibition on discriminatory denationalisation (see para 1.69 below).

1.48 The broader question as to whether there is a general right to acquire nationality by derivative means, whether initially without a nationality or otherwise, has consistently been answered in the negative. Plender, considering article 15 of the Universal Declaration of Human Rights 1948 (UDHR48), concluded that there was no inherent human right to naturalisation:

> Article 15, however, resembles Article 14. Just as the right under Article 14 to 'seek and enjoy asylum' is not equated with the right to receive it, so the right to a nationality, pronounced in Article 15, is not the same as the right to demand that any particular State grant nationality to an individual. The famous rule in the *Nottebohm* case, which requires a real and substantial connection between an individual and the State espousing his claim as one of its nationals, is a principle in respect of the *opposability* of nationality. It cannot be asserted, at least in the present state of international law, that an individual is entitled to be granted the nationality of a State with which he has real and substantial connections, even if he would otherwise be stateless.[74]

1.49 Mathew has expressed a similar conclusion as regards acquisition of nationality, though citing human rights-based constraints on exclusive state competence:

> Still, State freedom in matters of nationality is now limited by the prohibition on arbitrary—particularly discriminatory—withdrawal of nationality and discriminatory denial of the benefits attaching to a nationality.[75]

1.50 These views concerning the absence of any general 'right to acquire nationality' or 'right to naturalise' have been cited in a number of decisions, for instance that of the New Zealand Refugee Status Appeals Authority in *Refugee Appeal No 72635/01* [2002] NZRSAA 344 regarding refugee claims by Kuwaiti Bidoon. A subsequent decision in *Refugee Appeal No 74467* [2004] NZRSAA 283 came to a very different decision on the facts, but did not reject the earlier elaboration of applicable principles.

1.51 The dominance of *ius soli* and *ius sanguinis* has been criticised by a number of commentators. In the absence of safeguards their conjunction may produce statelessness, as where someone born on the territory of State A to parents who are nationals of States B and C does not acquire nationality (citizenship) by *ius soli* because the parents are aliens on the territory, and does not acquire it alternatively by *ius sanguinis* because of a restraint on transmission where birth is outside the territory. More fundamentally, a prominent academic and former senior Dutch

---

[74] R Plender, 'The Right to a Nationality as Reflected in International Human Rights Law and the Sovereignty of States in Nationality Matters' (1995) 49 *Austrian Journal of Public International Law* 43, 43–44.

[75] P Mathew, 'Lest we Forget: Australia's Policy on East Timorese Asylum-Seekers' (1999) 11(1) *International Journal of Refugee Law* 7, 22.

politician, Ernst Hirsch Ballin, has suggested that the domination of *ius soli* and *ius sanguinis* is not logically acceptable, resulting in a situation in which individuals are recognised as nationals without regard to the actual connection they have to a country and creating, in the absence of sufficient provision for naturalisation, a class of persons connected to the territory but excluded from nationality: he endorses the argument of Shachar, looking at the huge numbers of undocumented aliens in the United States, for a new *ius nexus* principle based upon 'the degree of rootedness, the presence of a genuine bond' which would operate as a basis for citizenship alongside *ius soli* and *ius sanguinis*.[76]

Taking together original and derivative means of acquisition, a description of the primary modes of acquisition of nationality, as listed in *Oppenheim's International Law*, can be enlarged as follows: **1.52**

> *Birth*—most people acquire at least one nationality at birth, and this in most cases occurs because of a domestic law entitlement based upon parentage or descent (*ius sanguinis*) or by reason of birth on the national territory or some legal extension of it, such as a ship or aircraft registered in a State (*ius soli*). Most States adopt one or both of these basic principles, with many in practice operating a composite of the two.
>
> *Naturalisation*—States may provide for their nationality to be given to someone who is a non-national, whether that person is an alien or a stateless person. Domestic laws may provide that this occurs automatically, as by marriage to a national, legitimation or adoption as a child, completion of military service, or other means. Alternatively they may provide for nationality by grant of this after application, requiring satisfaction of standards such as good character, presence on or other connection with the territory, and so on. Some states will make naturalisation conditional on release from, or renunciation of, a prior nationality (see below).
>
> *Redintegration*—The word means 'restoration of the whole of something from a part of it'–this means in the present context that laws may provide for resumption of nationality by persons who had lost this, for example by taking a second nationality which is then itself lost.
>
> *Annexation and Cession*—Where a territory is ceded by one State to another which annexes it the inhabitants of that territory are considered by customary international law to acquire the nationality of the annexing State and to lose that of the ceding one, subject to realisation by municipal laws.[77]

Redintegration has a compound character rather than being an entirely separate concept. It is a reaffirmation of original acquisition, which shares with derivative acquisition the feature of not being acquired (at the time of redintegration) at birth.

---

[76] E Hirsch Ballin, *Citizens' Rights and the Right to be a Citizen* (Brill/Nijhoff, 2014) 83; A Shachar, *The Birthright Lottery, Citizenship and Global Inequality* (Harvard University Press, 2009) 111–13; A Shachar, 'Earned Citizenship: Property Lessons for Immigration Reform' (2011) 23 *Yale Journal of Law & the Humanities* 110.

[77] Jennings and Watts (n 10 above) 869–77, §§383–91.

ii. Loss

1.53 The primary means of loss of nationality enumerated in *Oppenheim's International Law* are those described below:

> *Release*—An individual may be released from the nationality of that State by a decision taken on behalf of the State following request by the individual.
>
> *Renunciation* – An individual may be permitted to renounce nationality as of right, without having to obtain a decision of the State allowing this. Some states (consistently with article 7 CRS61) will make renunciation dependent upon that individual not becoming stateless in consequence.
>
> *Deprivation*—A State may provide for deprivation of its nationality, for instance where this was acquired by fraud or misrepresentation, or on other grounds including undertaking military service in another State, voting in another State, treason against the State of nationality, prolonged residence abroad, evasion of military service, or the taking of the nationality of another State.
>
> *Expiration*—Some States provide that nationality expires after a certain period abroad, for example the United States provided by section 352 of its Nationality Law 1952 that naturalised citizens lose US nationality by continuous residence of 3 years or more in the territory of birth or original nationality, a provision the US Supreme Court in *Schneider v Rusk* 377 US 163 (1964), quashed as unconstitutional by reason of discrimination against naturalised citizens.
>
> *Substitution*—Some States provide that an individual will lose nationality automatically by acquisition of the nationality of another State.

1.54 Expiration and substitution might be treated as subcategories of deprivation rather than as separate concepts. The UN Secretary-General has in effect followed this course, treating 'arbitrary deprivation of nationality' as covering arbitrariness in the context of 'all non-voluntary means by which nationality may be lost including those which occur automatically by operation of the law and those requiring decision by administrative authorities'.[78]

iii. Denationalisation

1.55 Denationalisation is a term which, in relation to nationality, may be employed in a narrow sense to denote deprivation of nationality in a specific context, for example, as a penalty by a court following criminal conviction. But it is more widely used in relation to the removal of a person's nationality, whether by administrative

---

[78] UN Human Rights Council (UNHRC), *Human rights and arbitrary deprivation of nationality: report of the Secretary-General*, 14 December 2009 (UN Doc A/HRC/13/34) para 23, available at: www.refworld.org/docid/4b83a9cb2.html.

or judicial decision or by operation of law. Weis defined denationalisation in this wider sense as 'deprivation of nationality by decision of administrative authorities, or even by operation of law, on certain grounds, such as entry into foreign military service'.[79] The term is used in this work to denote any deprivation of nationality by the State, whether by administrative or judicial decision or action or by operation of law. Although in a different context the term might reasonably extend to voluntary renunciation, this is not the sense in which it is employed in the present work. The line between denationalisation in the instant sense and renunciation may require some reflection: for example, a State which pressurises individuals into so-called 'voluntary' renunciation—for instance by offering remission of lengthy imprisonment or hard labour—could realistically be described as engaged in denationalisation.

A significant aspect of denationalisation is that from it there generally follows removal of the attributes or expectations ordinarily following from possession of nationality by a natural person. In particular, as Plender has observed: **1.56**

> A State's obligation to admit its own nationals to its territory could easily be circumvented if it were always open to the State to withdraw its nationality from those whom it wished to exclude ... It is unlikely that the Soviet, German, Italian, and Turkish authorities would have pursued their policies of denaturalization had they not been persuaded that the decrees would be effective to relieve those States of their obligations in respect of the individuals or groups concerned.[80]

Before at least the final decades of the nineteenth century neither derivative acquisition nor denationalisation was frequent. In 1956 Weis noted that deprivation of nationality had not been a widespread feature of international life before the twentieth century:

> Deprivation of nationality by a unilateral act of the State was known in the municipal legislation of the nineteenth century almost exclusively as a penal measure consequential upon conviction for certain crimes. Since then, statutory legislation providing for deprivation of nationality has developed on similar lines in many countries. A number of grounds for denationalisation have been created which are common to many systems, although one cannot speak of uniform legislation ... Within different States the law varies to the extent of providing for automatic loss of nationality on certain grounds (for instance, entry into foreign military service) and for deprivation by an individual act of State only on other grounds (such as disloyal conduct).[81]

International law first encountered denationalisation as a substantial issue in the aftermath of the First World War. Large-scale resort to denationalisation by multiple States in that period created serious difficulties both for millions of individuals and for other States. The First World War, the collapse of major powers, the political sensitivities of the revolutionary regime in Russia, and the creation **1.57**

---

[79] Weis (n 2 above) 120.
[80] Plender, *International Migration Law* (n 5 above) 144.
[81] Weis (n 2 above) 118.

of new States based on ethnic or language divisions, left very large numbers of persons alienated from their places of previous habitual residence or nationality, deprived of access to protection by a State as nationals. By 1926 almost 10 million persons were estimated to be without national protection in Europe.[82] This phenomenon explains the development of a focus upon denationalisation beginning from the 1920s. At that time international law disclosed a near-total absence of restraints upon denationalisation by States. As Weis noted of the earlier situation:

> Denationalisation gave rise to hardly any discussion as to the consistency of this measure with international law as long as it was applied on a limited scale, mainly as a penal measure in connection with criminal convictions. The question of the admissibility of denationalisation arose only when States began, for political reasons, to deprive great numbers of their nationals of their nationality, and particularly when Soviet Russia resorted to mass denationalisation.[83]

1.58 The Soviet action included a decree of the All Russia Central Executive Committee and Council of People's Commissars of 15 December 1921 withdrawing Russian citizenship from, *inter alia*, all persons remaining outside Russia for more than five years without receiving new documents from the Union of Soviet Socialist Republics (USSR), those who had left after 7 November 1917 without authorisation of the authorities of the USSR, and any person who had served voluntarily in armies fighting the Soviets or had 'in any way' participated in counter-revolutionary organisations.[84] Writing in 1926, Sir John Fischer Williams, a former Assistant Legal Adviser to the Home Office, observed that 'No denationalization on any such scale as this has hitherto been known to history'.[85] Much later Plender noted that:

> During the present [twentieth] century the practice of withdrawing nationality from dissident individuals or groups has become increasingly widespread. In the 1920s, between one and two million people were deprived of their Soviet citizenship by the Bolsheviks. The German Reich followed a similar policy in respect of Jews in the 1930s. Measures of a comparable character (although on a smaller scale) were adopted during the same decade by the Italian and Turkish authorities.[86]

1.59 In most cases denationalisation was accompanied by expulsion or exclusion from the national territory, whether immediately or later. It generally represented either punishment for assumed or actual political difference from the new regime or a means to the removal of particular individuals or groups. Denial of access to the territory, and deprivation of the possibility of diplomatic protection, often provided the apparent motivation for denationalisation.

---

[82] A Zolberg, A Suhrke and A Aguayo, *Escape from Violence: Conflict and the Refugee Crisis in the Developing World* (OUP, 1989) 18.

[83] Weis (n 2 above) 120.

[84] British Parliamentary Paper, *Nationality and the Naturalization Laws of certain Foreign Countries*, Misc No 2, 1927 (Cmd 2852).

[85] J Fischer Williams, 'Denationalization' (1927) 8 *British Yearbook of International Law* 45, 46.

[86] Plender, *International Migration Law* (n 5 above) 144.

Whilst the interwar refugee regimes described in chapter two, section A1, alleviated the difficulties of many denationalised persons, the international law of the time imposed little restraint upon the States responsible for large scale denationalisation, and given a paucity of deterrence, the problem increased over the period. Beginning in the 1930s, Nazi and Fascist regimes developed their own regimes of denationalisation. Most notoriously, Nazi Germany took steps against its own citizens first by the Law on the Revocation of Naturalisations and the Deprivation of the German Citizenship of 14 July 1933, which rescinded nationality grants to a large number of persons, many of them Jews or political opponents of the Nazis,[87] and then by the Reich Citizenship Law of 15 September 1935, which deprived German Jews and others of Reich citizenship to which civil rights were attached, whilst leaving them still subject to the duties attached to nationality. The denationalisation laws, and removal of citizenship rights from persons who retained nationality, were not confined to Jews, but they were a primary target. Sir John Hope Simpson noted in a 1939 survey that: **1.60**

> The denationalisation laws of the Third Reich were not confined to Jews, but were mainly directed against them. The Nuremberg Laws of 1935 had left the Jews as German subjects but not German citizens. A further step towards the outlawry of Jews was in contemplation, for the State Secretary Stückart announced in June 1938 … that in future children born to Jews would be stateless, not merely disfranchised German subjects, as their parents already are under the Nuremberg Laws. In October 1938 identity cards in lieu of the passports held by Jews were issued; they bear the imprint 'J' to indicate that the bearer is a Jew.[88]

A secondary phenomenon was the effective denial of documentation of citizenship, or of the right to return, to frustrate the exercise of rights attaching to citizenship or the usual international law prerogative of a State of sojourn, of expulsion to a State of nationality: the historian Timothy Snyder, referring to Jews possessing Polish citizenship resident in Germany and Austria, and faced with expulsion from those countries, noted that before the Second World War Poland as their country of nationality sought by intransigent administration to obstruct the exercise of their right of return from Germany or Austria to its territory, and Germany's right to expel them as aliens: **1.61**

> [A]fter the *Anschluss*, the Polish government demanded that all of its citizens living abroad register with embassies—and in October, right before the deadline, instructed its ambassador in Berlin not to stamp the passports of Jews. The Germans could see where this was headed, and responded by deporting about 17,000 Polish Jews to Poland in late October. Very often these were people whose entire lives had been spent in Germany.[89]

---

[87] Weis (n 2 above) 119.

[88] J Hope Simpson, *The Refugee Problem, Report of a Survey* (OUP, 1939) 135. Marrus states that the idea of marking identity documents with the infamous 'J' was suggested to the German authorities not by any German but by the head of the Swiss border police, Heinrich Rothmund, to aid Switzerland in identifying and excluding Jews seeking refuge at its border: MR Marrus, *The Unwanted: European Refugees from the First World War Through the Cold War* (2nd edn, Temple UP, 2002) 157.

[89] T Snyder, 'In the Cage, Trying to Get Out' (24 October 2013) 60(16) *New York Review of Books*, available at: www.nybooks.com/articles/archives/2013/oct/24/herschel-grynszpan-cage-trying-get-out/.

1.62 By the outbreak of war in 1939, the attempt to extend protection under international law to new refugees, whether expressly deprived of nationality or citizenship or otherwise, had ground virtually to a halt. After the outbreak of the Second World War Nazi Germany by the 11th Decree under the 1935 Law, issued on 25 November 1941, provided that a Jew of German nationality who had his usual place of abode abroad at the date of its coming into effect lost German nationality forthwith: this affected not only those who had fled Germany, but also those already transported to camps outside its territory.[90]

1.63 Snyder has pointed to the removal of those facing persecution from the protection of nationality or citizenship, and the selective destruction of States to destroy protection of nationals or citizens, as a major part of the Nazi campaign of genocide: 'Citizenship is the name of a reciprocal relationship between an individual and a sheltering polity. When there was no state, no one was a citizen, and human life could be treated carelessly'.[91] The manipulation of citizenship and nationality therefore played a central role in the Nazi persecutions in Europe, and the contemporary absence of international law restraint upon this was emblematic of failure by the international community.

1.64 Even after the defeat of Germany in 1945 large-scale denationalisation occurred, in the transfer (expulsion) of German and other minorities from other States to German territory after the defeat of Germany, under the Potsdam Protocol agreed by the main allies. Hofmann lists some significant cases and relevant legal instruments:

> Mass denaturalization of ethnic minorities occurred on a large scale immediately after World War II, notably in Czechoslovakia (Presidential Decree of 2 August 1945) affecting nationals of German and Hungarian origin; in Poland (Law on the Exclusion of Hostile Elements from Polish Society of 6 May 1945 [Journal of Laws No 17 item 96], as amended by the Decree of 2 February 1946 and Decree of 13 September 1946, as amended by the Law of 18 November 1948) affecting nationals of German origin; and in Yugoslavia (Citizenship Act of the Federal People's Republic of Yugoslavia of 1 July 1946 as amended by the Law of 1 December 1948) also affecting nationals of German origin.[92]

Additionally Poles were excluded from Ukraine, Belarus and Lithuania.[93] Whilst some resident populations had acted as a fifth column prior to and during the

---

[90] The original law had not removed German nationality from Jews, but rather had created the status of 'citizen of the Reich', defined at article 2(1) thereof as 'that subject only who is of German or kindred blood and who, through his conduct, shows that he is both desirous and fit to serve the German people and Reich faithfully'. Article 2(3) provided that 'Only the citizen of the Reich enjoys full political rights in accordance with the provision of the laws'.

[91] T Snyder, *Black Earth: The Holocaust as History and Warning* (Tim Duggan Books, 2015) 220.

[92] R Hofmann, 'Denaturalization and Forced Exile' in *Max Planck Encyclopedia of Public International Law* (online edn, OUP, 2015) 2013 [6].

[93] J-M Henckaerts, *Mass Expulsion in Modern International Law and Practice* (Martinus Nijhoff, 1995) 9.

years of Nazi ascendency, denationalisation and exclusion from the territory affected many who had not, and even some who had actively resisted the Nazis.[94] Henckaerts judged the post-war expulsions 'a tragic anomaly', contrasting condemnation in the Nuremberg Trials of Axis wartime deportations.[95] Although there is controversy as to the consistency of those actions with international law even as then understood, it seems virtually certain that such actions would, if repeated today in the face of current IHRL, be viewed as contrary to international law: 'Where population transfers used to be accepted as a means to settle ethnic conflict, today, forced population transfers are considered violations of international law'.[96]

The persecutions of the interwar and Second World War period illustrated a serious flaw in international practice regarding nationhood and human rights, whereby the latter was guaranteed only through membership in a national State. As highlighted by Arendt in *The Origins of Totalitarianism*, first published in 1951: **1.65**

> The proclamation of human rights was also meant to be a much-needed protection in the new era where individuals were no longer secure in the estates to which they were born or sure of their equality before God as Christians. In other words, in the new secularized and emancipated society, men were no longer sure of these social and human rights which until then had been outside the political order and guaranteed not by government and constitution, but by social, spiritual, and religious forces.[97]

Arendt saw the reliance upon human rights language in the period preceding the Nazi persecutions as delusive, given the ultimate reliance upon States for the protection of rights and the evasion of responsibility by States made possible through regimes of denationalisation and exclusion not subject to any effective constraint by international society: **1.66**

> The Rights of Man, supposedly inalienable, proved to be unenforceable—even in countries whose constitutions were based on them—whenever people appeared who were no longer citizens of any sovereign state.
>
> By itself the loss of government protection is no more unprecedented than the loss of a home. Civilised countries did offer the right of asylum to those who, for political reasons, had been persecuted by their governments, and this practice, though never officially incorporated into any constitution, has functioned well enough throughout the nineteenth and even in our century. The trouble arose when it appeared that the new categories of persecuted were far too numerous to be handled by an unofficial practice

[94] G Macdonogh, *After the Reich: From the Liberation of Vienna to the Berlin Airlift* (John Murray, 2007) 158–61.

[95] Ibid.

[96] E Rosard, 'The Right to Return under International Law Following Mass Dislocation: The Bosnia Precedent' (1998) 19 *Michigan Journal of International Law* 1091, 1120. See also C Meindersma, 'Population Exchanges: International Law and State Practice—Part 1' (1997) 9(3) *International Journal of Refugee Law* 335; and C Meindersma, 'Population Exchanges: International Law and State Practice—Part 2' (1997) 9(4) *International Journal of Refugee Law* 613.

[97] H Arendt, *The Origins of Totalitarianism* (2nd edn, Houghton Mifflin Harcourt, 1973) 291.

> destined for exceptional cases. Moreover, the majority could hardly qualify for the right of asylum, which implicitly presupposed political or religious convictions which were not outlawed in the country of refuge. The new refugees were persecuted not because of what they had done or thought, but because of what they unchangeably were—born into the wrong kind of race or the wrong kind of class or drafted by the wrong kind of government.[98]

Her oft-quoted characterisation of nationality as 'the right to have rights' follows from her analysis of imposed statelessness as a paradigmatic form of exclusion from rights regimes within human community, so that:

> The calamity of the rightless is not that they are deprived of life, liberty, and the pursuit of happiness, or of equality before the law and freedom of opinion—formulas which were designed to solve problems within particular communities—but that they no longer belong to any community whatsoever. Their plight is not that they are not equal before the law, but that no law exists for them.[99]

1.67 As the events of the Second World War period receded into the past, a survey of States quoted by Weis in 1956 indicated that in 1953 some did not admit any possibility of denationalisation in their law. States which did provide for it cited as primary current or recent grounds: (i) entry into foreign military or State service or acceptance of foreign distinctions; (ii) departure or extended sojourn abroad; (iii) conviction for specified offences; (iv) political attitude or activities including disloyalty or disaffection, acts prejudicial to the State or its interests, collaboration with the enemy; and (v) 'racial and national' grounds.[100] Many States which did have domestic law provision for denationalisation afforded broader grounds for potential denationalisation as regards those who had become citizens by naturalisation, rather than by original means.

1.68 Setting aside the 'anomaly' of the post-war action against ethnic Germans and others, denationalisation as exemplified by Nazi and Fascist laws appears to have been a central part of the complex of evils the international community sought to address by establishing and broadening international law of human rights and creating the international refugee law regime of which the Convention relating to the Status of Refugees 1951 (CSR51) has become the core instrument. Instances of denationalisation have continued to occur, though the phenomenon is sometimes described by States in terms which avoid admission that denationalisation is intended. Plender refers to the effective denationalisation and/or expulsion from Uganda of persons of South Asian background in the early 1970s:

> The Ugandan authorities under … Idi Amin Dada did not purport to withdraw Ugandan citizenship from the Asian community in 1972 but declared a policy of scrutinising the claim to Ugandan citizenship of each Asian resident and of imprisoning those residents whose claims to citizenship were found to be false. The effect on the departure of the

---

[98] Ibid, 293–94.
[99] Ibid, 295–96.
[100] Weis (n 2 above) 117–27.

> Asian community was much the same as it would have been in the event of a candid act of denaturalization.[101]

Since the period of the Nazi persecutions there has been a substantial development **1.69**
and evolution of international legal standards regarding non-discrimination, human rights and statelessness affecting, *inter alia*, authoritative views regarding the freedom of States to denationalise their citizens. This is well illustrated by the evolution in the view of Weis, a leading early commentator on CSR51 and the international law of nationality. In 1956, in the first edition of *Nationality and Statelessness in International Law*, he noted that:

> While the practice of States and judicial decisions seem to recognise the right of each State to determine freely the conditions for the loss of its nationality, municipal measures which lead to deprivation of nationality are looked at askance by most writers on international law, and publicists have frequently endeavoured to prove the existence of rules of international law restricting this right.[102]

Weis concluded with evident reluctance that 'the views of those who have tried to establish as a mandatory rule of existing law what must certainly be regarded as a sound and desirable rule for the future, find no justification in the present state of international law'.[103] However in the second edition of the same work, published in 1979, Weis noted the considerable intervening developments in international law—notably CRS61 and the International Covenant on Civil and Political Rights 1966 (ICCPR66), and endorsed the proposition that prohibition of discriminatory denationalisation might be regarded as a rule of international law:

> Considering that the principle of non-discrimination may now be regarded as a rule of international law or as a general principle of law, prohibition of discriminatory denationalisation may be regarded as a rule of present-day international law. This certainly applies to discrimination on the ground of race which may be considered as contravening a peremptory norm of international law but also, in the present writer's view, to discrimination on the other grounds mentioned in the Charter of the United Nations, ie sex and religion.[104]

He considered this a 'possible exception' from the general liberty of a State, save where bound by treaty, to mandate the loss of its nationality.[105]

In 1988 Plender concluded that developments in IHRL, especially article 12(4) **1.70**
ICCPR66, the *travaux préparatoires* of which '[make] clear that this provision is so framed as to exclude the permissibility of an act of denaturalization directed against an ethnic group or dissident individual or minority, with the object of depriving such persons of the right to return to their country of origin' had had a

---

[101] Plender, *International Migration Law* (n 5 above) 144.
[102] Weis (n 3 above) 126–27.
[103] Ibid, 128.
[104] Weis (n 2 above) 125.
[105] Ibid, 126.

'profound effect' on the development of international law,[106] so that 'The evidence suggests that in current international law a State cannot always release itself of its obligation to admit certain of its own nationals to its territory by promulgating a decree which deprives such persons of their nationality.[107]

1.71 A significant more recent example, both because of the numbers affected and because significant refugee status issues had thereafter to be addressed in many other countries, is that of Ethiopia. Eritrea had seceded from Ethiopia in 1993 without a full working through by either State of the effect in the field of nationality. After the outbreak of war between them in 1998, Ethiopia and Eritrea each interned and expelled many persons perceived as nationals of the other, applying loose criteria of membership which, certainly in the case of Ethiopia, resulted in effective denationalisation. Human Rights Watch in a subsequent report stated that:

> Ethiopian authorities launched a vast campaign to round up and expel people of Eritrean origin from Ethiopia in June 1998. Most had been born in Ethiopia when Eritrea was still held to be a part of that country—and had no other recognized citizenship other than Ethiopian. Most adults had spent all or most of their working lives in Ethiopia, outside of Eritrea. Ethiopian authorities in June 1998 announced the planned expulsion of residents who posed a security risk to the state, to include members of Eritrean political and community organizations, and former or current members of the Eritrean liberation front.
>
> The Ethiopian authorities moved almost immediately to carry out arrests and to expel Eritreans and those of Eritrean origin in a manner that became increasingly indiscriminate over time. No meaningful steps were made to determine 'risk' on a case-by-case basis—or to distinguish between those who had formally assumed Eritrean nationality and Ethiopian nationals distinguished only by their Eritrean origin.[108]

1.72 In the aftermath of those events, the Eritrea–Ethiopia Claims Commission in its Partial Award of 17 December 2004 was to hold that certain individuals had effectively been dual nationals and that where Ethiopia had 'devised and implemented a system applying reasonable criteria to identify individual dual nationals thought to pose threats to its wartime security', deprivation was not shown to be arbitrary, but that by contrast, where persons were permitted to remain but treated arbitrarily as aliens, then:

> [c]onsidering that rights to such benefits as land ownership and business licenses, as well as passports and other travel documents were at stake, the Commission finds that this wide-scale deprivation of Ethiopian nationality of persons remaining in Ethiopia was under the circumstances arbitrary and contrary to international law.[109]

---

106 Plender, *International Migration Law* (n 5 above) 147.

107 Ibid, 149.

108 Africa Division, Human Rights Watch, *The Horn Of Africa War: Mass Expulsions and the Nationality Issue (June 1998–April 2002)* (2003), available at: www.hrw.org/report/2003/01/29/horn-africa-war/mass-expulsions-and-nationality-issue.

109 *Eritrea Ethiopia Claims Commission, Partial Award: Civilians Claims—Eritrea's Claims 15, 16, 23 & 27–32*, Permanent Court of Arbitration, The Hague, 17 December 2004, available at: www.pca-cpa.org/ER%20Partial%20Award%20Dec%20048515.pdf?fil_id=148, esp §72, §75.

More recently denationalisation, including denationalisation resulting in statelessness, has continued to occur, although on a smaller scale. A number of States have made use of denationalisation on political, ethnic or religious grounds, whilst others, particularly in the West, cite security concerns in the wake of 11 September 2001 and subsequent events as justification for the expansion or increased use of relevant powers, and/or increased use of others. In 2014 the Islamic Human Rights Commission pointed to current laws and practices both in Gulf Arab and in Western countries as cause for concern: **1.73**

> This report aims to reflect on the legal phenomenon of denationalisation as a political weapon against targeted groups of people who are excluded from the entire state system, on the grounds of their political, cultural or religious affiliation. The creation of stateless people by nation states is becoming a widespread phenomenon with global dimensions.
>
> More specifically, in Bahrain, the UAE, Kuwait and Qatar, the power of the executive to revoke citizenship has been used as part of strategies for managing popular uprisings, while in some Western countries, including the UK, the executive has ramped up a controversial programme to revoke citizenship on national security grounds.[110]

iv. State Succession

'State succession occurs when there is a definitive replacement of one state by another in respect of sovereignty over a given territory, that is, a replacement in conformity with international law'.[111] Succession is deemed to occur only when there is a *permanent* displacement of sovereign power over a territory from one entity to another: mere changes in control not displacing sovereignty, such as belligerent occupation, do not bring about succession. The law of state succession is not wholly self-contained. A leading text notes a common fault of writers as being the tendency 'to consider particular issues in isolation from the matrix of rules governing the subject-matter' emphasising instead 'The need to consider problems precipitated by a change of sovereignty in relation to the particular body of legal principles'.[112] In the present context, this implies the need to consider issues of state succession together with the body of international law concerned with nationality (including statelessness) and with other significant norms including non-discrimination and international human rights. **1.74**

State succession has been a significant generator of statelessness over time. As a matter of international law theory, the new sovereign on the territory inherits no link to citizens of its predecessor. Hence Weis wrote that 'In the case of universal **1.75**

---

[110] C Aiena, *Stripping of Nationality as a Weapon of Political Suppression: The Cases of Bahrain, United Kingdom, United Arab Emirates And Kuwait* (IHRC, 2014) 4.

[111] Crawford (ed), *Brownlie's Principles of Public International Law* (n 26 above) 422.

[112] Ibid, 438.

succession [complete annexation or incorporation into a new State], the predecessor State is extinguished and its nationality ceases to exist. All persons who were nationals of the predecessor State cease to be such'.[113] In 1968 Mohammed Bedjaoui, as Special Rapporteur for Succession of States in Respect of Rights and Duties Resulting from Sources Other Than Treaties, reported to the ILC that:

> In all cases of succession, traditional or modern, there is in theory no succession or continuity in respect of nationality. The successor State does not let the inhabitants of the territory retain their former nationality. This is a manifestation of its sovereignty.[114]

The term 'succession of States' therefore refers to the fact of replacement of one State by another, but without any implication that citizens or residents of the territory of an earlier entity will inherit rights or obligations upon the formation of a new State.[115]

1.76 In the early 1990s the attention of the international community was refocused on questions of nationality in relation to state succession by urgent problems consequential to the collapse of the USSR. In 1995 a new Special Rapporteur, Václav Mikulka, reported on the significance of the issue:

> 30. The change of nationality resulting from State succession is a matter of great importance because it occurs on a collective basis and has numerous serious consequences for the persons involved. Nationality is a precondition for the exercise of a number of political and civil rights. But this matter also has important implications with respect to the exercise of the sovereign powers of the States concerned, ie, the successor and predecessor State.
>
> 31. But as this matter belongs primarily to the sphere of internal law, no serious attempt has ever been made to set up a universal instrument providing for a uniform solution to the problem. Nor has the Commission been anxious to deal with the problem of nationality in relation to that of State succession, which it discussed for nearly 20 years. Nationality has once again become an issue of special interest for the international community against the backdrop of the emergence of new States ... The manner in which problems relating to nationality in the context of State succession are being resolved has become a matter of concern to the international community.[116]

1.77 The problems emerging from new situations of state succession have been considered in various fora apart from the United Nations, notably at the regional level. In 2006 the Council of Europe Convention on the Avoidance of Statelessness in relation to State Succession (examined in chapter six, section C5.iv) came into being. In 1999 the ILC published 'Draft Articles on Nationality of Natural Persons

---

[113] Weis (n 2 above) 136.

[114] ILC, 'First Report on Succession of States in Respect of Rights and Duties Resulting from Sources Other Than Treaties', M Bedjaoui, Special Rapporteur (1968) (UN Doc A/CN.4/204) 11 [133].

[115] *Official Records of the United Nations Conference on Succession of States in respect of Treaties*, vol III (UN Doc A/CONF.80/4) 6 (Vienna, 4 April–6 May 1977).

[116] ILC, 'First report on State succession and its impact on the nationality of natural and legal persons submitted by the Special Rapporteur, Mr Mikulka' (UN Doc A/CN.4/467) (17 April 1995).

in Relation to the Succession of States', with a detailed commentary. The foundational principle for the draft instrument is expressed at article 1:

> Article 1: Right to a nationality
>
> Every individual who, on the date of the succession of States, had the nationality of the predecessor State, irrespective of the mode of acquisition of that nationality, has the right to the nationality of at least one of the States concerned, in accordance with the present draft articles.

The application of the principle to different circumstances is explored in later articles. In 2011 the United Nations General Assembly invited States to take into account the Draft Articles and to consider the creation of regional instruments, emphasising the value of the Draft Articles as guidance to States dealing with succession issues.[117]

From the matters above it can be seen that the establishment of binding standards specifically regarding nationality in situations of state succession is a recent and still developing phenomenon. But an extremely important principle is that state succession does not represent a sphere separate from established international law norms of non-discrimination, already-extant binding human rights standards, and standards aimed at the reduction or elimination of statelessness.[118] **1.78**

A5. Nationality and 'the Operation of its Laws' by the State

As indicated separately in the context of statelessness (see section C below), article 1(1) CSSP54 provides that 'For the purpose of this Convention, the term "stateless person" means a person who is not considered as a national by any State under the operation of its law'. The UNHCR *Handbook on Protection of Stateless Persons* identifies 'its law' in this context as requiring analysis of the legal system of the relevant State as a whole: **1.79**

> 22. The reference to 'law' in Article 1(1) should be read broadly to encompass not just legislation, but also ministerial decrees, regulations, orders, judicial case law (in countries with a tradition of precedent) and, where appropriate, customary practice.[119]

---

[117] Resolution 66/92 adopted by the General Assembly on 9 December 2011 (Nationality of natural persons in relation to the succession of States) (UN Doc A/RES/66/92) (13 Jan 2012).

[118] See, eg, J Blackman, 'State Successions and Statelessness: The Emerging Right to an Effective Nationality Under International Law' (1998) 19 *Michigan Journal of International Law* 1141; A Zimmermann, 'State Succession and the Nationality of Natural Persons: Facts and Possible Codification' in P Eisemann and M Koskenniemi(eds), *Succession: Codification Tested against the Facts* (Hague Academy of International Law/Martinus Nijhoff, 2000); and I Ziemele, 'State Succession and Issues of Nationality and Statelessness' in A Edwards and L van Waas, *Nationality and Statelessness Under International Law* (CUP, 2014). For examination of the recent case of Sudan/South Sudan see M Sanderson, 'Statelessness and Mass Expulsion in Sudan: A Reassessment of the International Law', 12 *Northwestern Journal of International Human Rights* 74 (2014).

[119] UNHCR, *Handbook on Protection of Stateless Persons* (30 June 2014) [22], available at: www.refworld.org/docid/53b676aa4.html.

1.80 That *Handbook* identifies reference to 'the operation of' those laws by state authorities as encompassing something wider than the simple understanding and application of its laws by the State, implicitly extending to 'implementation in practice' which may extend to the State not respecting its own system of laws, even to the extent of 'ignor[ing] its substance':

> 23. Establishing whether an individual is not considered as a national under the operation of its law requires a careful analysis of how a State applies its nationality laws in an individual's case in practice and any review/appeal decisions that may have had an impact on the individual's status. This is a mixed question of fact and law.
>
> 24. Applying this approach of examining an individual's position in practice may lead to a different conclusion than one derived from a purely formalistic analysis of the application of nationality laws of a country to an individual's case. A State may not in practice follow the letter of the law, even going so far as to ignore its substance. The reference to 'law' in the definition of statelessness in Article 1(1) therefore covers situations where the written law is substantially modified when it comes to its own implementation in practice.

1.81 In *Pham v SSHD* [2015] UKSC 19, [2015] 3 All ER 1015 the United Kingdom Supreme Court considered the interpretation of the phase 'under the operation of its law' in the article 1(1) CSSP54 definition, which had been transposed into a domestic law protection against deprivation of British nationality creating statelessness. The case concerned a naturalised British citizen of Vietnamese origin deprived of British nationality, whose possession of its nationality was unacknowledged by the Socialist Republic of Vietnam. The Court did not find it necessary on the facts of the case to consider whether to endorse or reject the approach set out by the UNHCR. Lord Carnwath, outlining the factual situation, stated that:

> 36. Nor is there any evidence that the government issued a ministerial decree, or adopted any other form of practice or position which could be treated as equivalent to 'law', even in the broadest sense used by the UNHCR. Rather the implication is that it has simply declined, no doubt for policy reasons, to make any formal decision on the appellant's status, whether under the operation of its own nationality law or at all.

In conclusion Lord Carnwath accepted that some reference to practice was necessary, but that a line might fall to be drawn at some point:

> 38. I would accept that the question arising under article 1(1) of the 1954 Convention in this case is not necessarily to be decided solely by reference to the text of the nationality legislation of the state in question, and that reference may also be made to the practice of the government, even if not subject to effective challenge in the courts. However, there is in my view no evidence of a decision made or practice adopted by the Vietnamese government, which treated the appellant as a non-national 'by operation of its law', even adopting the broadest view of those words as interpreted by the UNHCR.

At [66] Lord Mance concluded, referring to Lord Carnwath's earlier recitation of relevant parts of the UNHCR guidance, that 'it is, as Lord Carnwath indicates (para 29), unnecessary on this appeal to express any concluded view on whether or how far practice may supersede law in relation to the concept of statelessness under article 1(1)', not referring to Lord Carnwath's acceptance of the potential significance to be given to 'the practice of the government, even if not subject to effective challenge in the courts'. Lord Sumption (at [101]) differed expressly from Lord Carnwath: 'I am not convinced that practice can stand for law in article 1(1) of the 1954 Convention, nor that any relevant practice was proved in this case'. The outcome on this point is blurred by Lord Neuberger, Lady Hale and Lord Wilson, who did not give separate judgments, agreeing expressly with Lords Carnwath, Mance and Sumption.

What can be taken from article 1(1) CSSP54, however, is that this gives a definition of statelessness which might ultimately be held to extend beyond the strict law of the country of nationality, to what may be an 'operation of' its laws by the State modifying or withholding the benefit of the law. Nationality, by contrast, has not classically been interpreted in this way, and the Convention on Certain Questions Relating to the Conflict of Nationality Laws 1930 defines nationality as status 'under its law' (article 1) and requires questions as to nationality to be dealt with 'in accordance with the law of the State'. 1.82

A6. Incidents of Nationality

i. Entry/Remaining in the Country of Nationality

Plender states that: 1.83

> The principle that every State must admit its own nationals to its territory is accepted so widely that its existence as a rule of law is virtually beyond dispute. The principle is often implied by those who assert that each State has the right to deny admission to aliens. Among the more specialised writers, those who defend the existence of the principle include François, Weis, Goodwin-Gill, and Van Panhuys. The latter states that the duty to admit nationals is considered so important a consequence of nationality that it is almost equated with it. The Court of Justice of the European Community, in [*Van Duyn v Home Office (Workers)* [1974] EUECJ R-41/74, [1974] ECR 1337, 1351], held it 'a principle of international law ... that a State is precluded from refusing its own nationals the right of entry or residence'.
>
> Nevertheless, the precise meaning of the principle is disputed and in some respects obscure. The first problem is that of identifying the quality of the obligation; for it remains to be determined whether the duty of admission is merely the corollary of a second State's right to expel aliens, or the product of an internationally protected right to return to one's own country. The second difficulty is [whether] a State is under any duty to permit nationals from outlying territories or dependencies to enter the metropolitan territory. The third problem [is] the denaturalization of an individual or minority,

followed by expulsion. In such cases, the question arises whether a foreign State has any duty to recognize the efficacy of the denaturalization.[120]

1.84 The right of expulsion and duty of admission noted by Plender have been expressly linked by most commentators. In 1959 van Panhuys, having surveyed the corpus of earlier international law learning, observed that:

> A State's duty to admit its own nationals corresponds to the right of expulsion of the foreign State.
>
> ...
>
> The duty to admit nationals is considered so important a consequence of nationality that it is almost equated with it ... This duty corresponds to the right of expulsion of the State of residence ... Both rules are consequences of customary international law and are closely connected with the essence of nationality, that is, as long as the foreign national did not acquire the nationality of the State of residence, it is presumed that he belongs to the politico-legal community of his own State and consequently, the responsibility for him lies, according to international law, at the door of his State.[121]

1.85 Van Panhuys stated that the position was varied in the case of a dual national. A country of nationality was not bound to grant admission to its national if faced with expulsion by another country of nationality: 'A State whose national also possesses other nationalities is not in duty bound to admit him unless the pertinent request comes from a non-national State'.[122]

1.86 *Oppenheim's International Law* also notes the nationality of an individual as important both in relation to diplomatic protection, and in the obligation of the State of nationality to accept the return of a national:

> The function of nationality becomes apparent with regard to individuals abroad ... especially on account of one particular right and one particular duty of every state towards all other states. The right is that of protection over its nationals abroad which every state holds, and occasionally vigorously exercise, as against other states ... The duty is that of receiving on its territory such of its nationals as are not allowed to remain on the territory of other states. Since no state is obliged by international law to allow foreigners to remain within its boundaries, it may, for many reasons, happen that certain individuals are expelled from all foreign countries. The state of nationality of expelled persons is bound to receive them on its territory.[123]

1.87 The editors of that work concluded that the duty of admission was engaged by a second State wishing to expel an alien to a country of nationality and was not an individual right under customary international law: 'According to international law the duty of admission only exists towards foreign States and not towards the

---

[120] Plender, *International Migration Law* (n 5 above) 133.
[121] van Panhuys (n 69 above) 56.
[122] Ibid.
[123] Jennings and Watts (n 10 above) 857–58, §379.

national, though the custom, not to deny admission to nationals, is sometimes reflected in municipal law'.[124]

1.88 In 1972 the principle was tested as regards the United Kingdom by President Idi Amin's expulsion from Uganda of many persons of Asian origin. A large number were, under the laws then in force, British subjects and therefore of British nationality. In the House of Lords the Lord Chancellor, Lord Hailsham LC, on the day following the Ugandan announcement that expulsion would be enforced, stated that:

> the Attorney General, acting in his capacity as the professional legal adviser to the Government ... advised us that in international law a State is under a duty as between other States to accept in its territories those of its nationals who have nowhere else to go. If a citizen of the United Kingdom is expelled, as I think illegally from Uganda, and is not accepted for settlement elsewhere, we could be required by any State where he then was to accept him. I think that is good law; I also think it is part of the international facts of life.[125]

That statement adds the significant caveat that a national must have 'nowhere else to go' prior to the State of nationality being obliged to allow entry to its territory.

1.89 Since the Second World War IHRL has set in place a range of positive rights including an effective right of entry and residence for nationals. Article 13(2) UDHR48 provides that 'Everyone has the right to leave any country, including his own, and to return to his [her] country'. Article 12(4) ICCPR66 further provides that 'No one shall be arbitrarily deprived of the right to enter his [her] own country'.[126] These are further examined in chapter six, section C2.ii.

1.90 Other human rights instruments also prohibit expulsion in particular situations. For instance articles 5(d)(i)–(ii) in the Convention on the Elimination of All Forms of Racial Discrimination 1966 (ICERD66) require States Parties to prohibit and eliminate discrimination as to race, colour, or national or ethnic origin in enjoyment of the rights to freedom of movement and residence, and 'the right to leave any country, including one's own, and to return to one's country'. The standards of IHRL applicable in this context are considered in greater detail elsewhere. The content of relevant norms is particularly important in the context of the present work for a number of reasons. First, IHRL is widely acknowledged as possessing an important role in relation to the interpretation of the qualifying conditions for refugee status under article 1A(2) CSR51, in particular as regards

---

124 Ibid.

125 HL Deb 14 September 1972, vol 335, col 497.

126 In *Van Duyn v Home Office (Workers)* [1974] EUECJ R-41/74, [1974] ECR 1337, [22] the European Court of Justice cited the right of individual entry and residence by nationals as a principle of international law. The Court did not distinguish between customary law and international human rights law as authority for this proposition, but the principle it expressed is better supported by the latter.

the meaning of 'persecution' in the first paragraph of that article (as examined in chapter six hereto). Second, human rights standards are generally acknowledged as exerciseable by individuals as beneficiaries, something not so far established in relation to the duty to admit under customary international law. Third, recent decades have seen the development of a substantial *corpus* of decisions and 'soft law' lending substance to core rights.

ii. Diplomatic Protection

1.91 Nationality makes possible 'international protection', also known as 'diplomatic protection', by reason of the right of a person's State of nationality to grant protection to him or her in relation to other States. In doing this, the State in principle does not act to assist its national, but in its own interest, relying upon the so-called 'Vattelian fiction' described at paragraph 1.8 above. As Commissioner Neilson stated in 1931 in the United States–Mexico Special Claims Commission, in a dissenting decision on the *Naomi Russell* case (*United States v Mexico*) (1931) 4 RIAA 805, 'Nationality is the justification in international law for the intervention of one government to protect persons and property in another country'. An effective short description is provided by Dugard in the *Max Planck Encyclopedia of Public International Law*:

> Under international law, a State is responsible for injury to an alien caused by that State's wrongful act or omission ... Diplomatic protection is the procedure employed by the State of nationality of the injured person to secure protection of that person, and to obtain reparation for the internationally wrongful act inflicted. Such protection extends to both natural and legal persons. As diplomatic protection is part of the law of State responsibility, the International Law Commission (ILC) has defined diplomatic protection, for the purpose of its Draft Articles, as consisting of the invocation by a State 'of the responsibility of another State for an injury caused by an internationally wrongful act of that State to a natural or legal person that is a national of the former State with a view to the implementation of such responsibility' (Art 1 ILC Draft Articles on Diplomatic Protection (2006) ['Draft Articles']). This definition was noted with approval by the International Court of Justice (ICJ) in the *Ahmadou Sadio Diallo Case (Republic of Guinea v Democratic Republic of the Congo)* [[2007] ICJ Rep 20] para 39.

The ILC's Draft Articles on Diplomatic Protection delineate the group of persons to whom diplomatic protection may be provided. Article 3(1) in the Draft Articles confirms the normal principle that 'The State entitled to exercise diplomatic protection is the State of nationality', where by article 4 'a State of nationality means a State whose nationality that person has acquired, in accordance with the law of that State, by birth, descent, naturalization, succession of States, or in any other manner, not inconsistent with international law'. The ILC Articles also posit an express confirmation of the principle's extension, reflecting ideals of surrogate protection, so that a State may exercise diplomatic protection in respect of stateless persons and refugees who are lawfully and habitually present within its territory, save in respect of an injury caused by an internationally wrongful act of the State of nationality of the refugee.[127]

Diplomatic protection in international law is the exclusive prerogative of the State of nationality (or other State in line with accepted principles, such as, under the ILC Draft Articles, the stateless person or refugee who is lawfully and habitually resident in a state's territory). Any obligation of the State to the individual arises under national, often constitutional law, so that, for example, the 1870 Constitution of the German Empire provided by article 3, paragraph 6, that 'Against foreign States all Germans equally have the right to demand the protection of the Reich'. In the *Slaughterhouse cases* 83 US 36, 79 (1873), Miller J in the US Supreme Court stated that: 1.92

> Another privilege of a citizen of the United States is to demand the care and protection of the Federal government over his life, liberty, and property when on the high seas or within the jurisdiction of a foreign government. Of this there can be no doubt, nor that the right depends upon his character as a citizen of the United States.

iii. Internal Protection

Though this has been gradually but dramatically altered in recent years, classical international law regarded as a matter of exclusive competence the treatment by a State of its own nationals on its territory. This has now been changed by the growth of IHRL, in tandem with the establishment under the Convention relating to the Status of Refugees 1951 (CSR51) that international protection arises by reason of failure of internal protection from persecution. However, legal theory in many countries has posited the existence of some form of protection owed to nationals on its territory. Weis distinguishes diplomatic protection from 'the *internal, legal* protection which every national may claim from his State of nationality under its municipal law ie, the right of the individual to receive protection of his person, rights and interests from the State', citing as an example the concept of *Rechtsschutz* (legal protection) by which protection of nationals internally is the subject of state duty and individual right.[128] Internal protection in the sense relevant here is primarily a concept of legal theory to be given expression, or otherwise, in domestic law. 1.93

A7. Dual or Plural Nationality

Dual or plural nationality is increasingly frequent, for reasons which include the elimination of discriminatory laws which formerly removed the nationality of 1.94

[127] ILC, 'Draft Articles on Diplomatic Protection' (2006) (n 49 above).
[128] Weis (n 2 above) 32–33 citing G Jellinek, *System Der Subjectiven Öffentlichen Rechte* (Mohr, 1892) 349–51.

women upon marriage to a foreign national (and consequentially prevented transmission of that nationality to children of a mixed marriage) and more recently the gradual change of attitude to plural nationality by States identified elsewhere, leading to reduced legal provision for automatic expatriation or loss of nationality. Plural nationality can arise at birth from the interaction of different domestic systems regarding nationality: for instance where a nationality law based on *ius soli* ascribes nationality of a State of birth on the basis of birth on the territory, whilst the domestic law of a parent's State of nationality, based on *ius sanguinis* ascribes nationality through descent, or alternatively where parents are of different nationalities and both States of nationality ascribe nationality to the new child on the basis of *ius sanguinis*. In addition, dual nationality may come into being subsequent to birth, through an individual naturalising in one country and thereafter holding the new nationality whilst maintaining the original one. 'Dual nationality' denotes specifically the holding of two nationalities, and the phrase may also describe one of those nationalities ('the nationality of X is her dual nationality'), whereas 'plural nationality' may be used to encompass any situation in which at least two nationalities are possessed, or describe one of them.

1.95 Dual nationality was, as Spiro has said,

> not a pressing issue in a world of low mobility … To the extent the vast majority of individuals were born, lived, and died in the same realm, early modern Europe did not supply the conditions to create any substantial incidence of dual nationality.[129]

This however changed with the development of relatively large-scale migration and the formation of new national States, initially the United States of America and subsequently others, keen to defend their sovereignty as embodied in the persons of their subjects or citizens:

> Dual nationality emerged as a serious threat to inter-State order, with States pressing competing claims on individuals or attempting to protect nationals from the claims of another State of nationality. In the 19th and early 20th centuries, dual nationality arose most prominently as a result of the naturalization by the United States of America ('US') of individuals from States refusing to recognize the possibility of expatriation. Under the feudal doctrine of perpetual allegiance ('once a subject, always a subject'), as of the beginning of the 19th century most European States refused to accept the naturalization of subjects before another sovereign and continued to claim them as their own … States did not want 'to release a national from his allegiance and thereby lose a potential soldier'.[130]

1.96 Reflecting this negative view of States, the Preamble to the Convention on Certain Questions Relating to the Conflict of Nationality Laws 1930 recorded the States Parties as 'Being convinced that it is in the general interest of the international community to secure that all its members should recognise that every person

---

[129] P Spiro, 'Multiple Nationality' in *Max Planck Encyclopedia of Public International Law* (online edn, OUP, 2015) 5.

[130] Ibid.

should have a nationality and should have one nationality only'. Article 3 of the same agreement provides that:

> Article 3
>
> Subject to the provisions of the present Convention, a person having two or more nationalities may be regarded as its national by each of the States whose nationality he possesses.

Further, article 5 of the 1930 Convention provided that: **1.97**

> Article 5
>
> Within a third State, a person having more than one nationality shall be treated as if he had only one. Without prejudice to the application of its law in matters of personal status and of any conventions in force, a third State shall, of the nationalities which any such person possesses, recognise exclusively in its territory either the nationality of the country in which he is habitually and principally resident, or the nationality of the country with which in the circumstances he appears to be in fact most closely connected.

This does not appear to express customary international law, and so is only binding as between signatory States. Piotrowicz has observed that even if article 5 of the 1930 Convention theoretically applied to the identification of nationality under CSR51 (which, on the assumption that the provision was not expressive of customary international law, was not the case), it was expressly phrased as without prejudice to 'any conventions in force', so that any duty created by article 5 would have to be subordinate to the express terms in the second paragraph of article 1A(2) CSR51 (see chapter five, section B7).[131]

In the post-Second World War era, and particularly in recent decades, there have been substantial changes to state attitudes and consequent practice. Hailbronner suggests that a significant motivation has been recognition of the interests of immigrants in connection with their country of origin, whilst marking integration by taking the nationality of the State of residence, noting that the effectiveness of such policies is not universally accepted.[132] Spiro concludes that both State and individual interests are seen as having come into more substantial alignment with dual nationality: **1.98**

> 15. These trends toward greater acceptance of dual nationality coincide with changed State interests. Dual nationals are unlikely to provoke bilateral disputes in an age of human rights. States are constrained from mistreating individuals as such and not simply by virtue of alternate national ties. States may also have an interest in maintaining ties with large (and usually relatively prosperous) diaspora populations for economic reasons, which explains the move on the part of many immigrant-sending States not only

---

[131] R Piotrowicz, '*Lay Kon Tji and Minister for Immigration & Ethnic Affairs*: The Function and Meaning of Effective Nationality in the Assessment of Applications for Asylum' (1999) 11(3) *International Journal of Refugee Law* 544, 551.

[132] K Hailbronner, 'Nationality' in TA Aleinikoff and V Chetail (eds), *Migration and International Legal Norms* (TMC Asser Press, 2003) 80.

to tolerate but to embrace dual citizenship among those who would in the past have been expatriated upon naturalization in a state of new residence.

> 16. Multiple nationality can now also be conceived as serving individual interests. As States have abandoned conscription or made it contingent on residence (also the case with taxation), … the burdens of citizenship have grown lighter. Dual nationality has become a status that an individual might seek to maintain. Emigrant populations have otherwise been faced not only with the choice of sentimental loyalties but also with the prospect of losing certain rights in their homelands upon the forfeiture of their original nationality. Nationality has been central to individual identity. Insofar as an individual might want to identify with more than one nation, dual citizenship can be framed as a matter of individual autonomy, in other words, as a matter of rights.[133]

1.99 The fact of an individual holding plural nationality may be obscured where that nationality is not utilised. Piotrowicz made this point in a comment addressing the question of Portuguese nationality as held by East Timorese at the relevant time. Because of the particular context he refers particularly to *ius sanguinis* as a source of poorly realised or obscure nationality:

> Citizenship law often works in this way. Because many countries allow their nationality to be passed on purely by birth to a parent of that nationality (*jus sanguinis*), it means that nationality of such countries can be passed on for generations, and hence possessed by individuals who have no idea of their status. The nationality laws of Poland and Germany, for instance, operate in this way. Individuals may be unaware of their Polish or German nationality, but they possess it, whether they like it or not. Should they wish to activate it, for instance by applying for a passport or taking up residence, they do so on the foundation of that existing status: they do not *acquire* nationality. Portugal's law operates in the same way: East Timorese who seek the rights of Portuguese citizenship are not acquiring a new status: they are formalising an existing entitlement which has been with them since the moment of birth.[134]

1.100 Many persons likely believe themselves not to be plural nationals, because their primary allegiance is to the nationality of a State whose nationality laws prohibit dual or plural nationality. But the laws of one State cannot abrogate the nationality of another. In the East Timorese asylum claims adjudicated in Australia before Indonesia withdrew from East Timor and the territory became independent, one argument raised against consideration of Portuguese nationality as relevant was that the applicants were Indonesian citizens under the law of that State, and it did not permit plural nationality. That argument was rejected as incompatible with the principles of international law relating to nationality:

> It was rightly dismissed as incorrectly seeking to reach a conclusion about Portuguese law based on Indonesian law. To have sustained such an argument would have contradicted not only the [articles 1 and 2 of the 1930] Convention on the Conflict of Nationality Laws, but also general international law pertaining to State jurisdiction. Portuguese

---

133 Spiro (n 129 above) 15–16.

134 Piotrowicz, '*Lay Kon Tji and Minister for Immigration & Ethnic Affairs*' (n 131 above) 555.

> citizenship law was a matter for the Portuguese and, to some extent, international law. Indonesia's law was irrelevant.[135]

International law would, subject to human rights-based safeguards and international standards concerning statelessness, permit Indonesia to withdraw or withhold its nationality from persons possessing another nationality. It does not permit Indonesia to abrogate the equivalent laws of Portugal.

Indeed, a country may, for political or other reasons, be reluctant to publicise or clarify the effect of its nationality laws, or to enable meaningful access to the benefit of these, even where entitlement is clear: a classic example is the situation described by the Inter-American Court of Human Rights in *Yean and Bosico v Dominican Republic* [2005] Inter-American Court of Human Rights (Series C) No 130 (8 September 2005), a case arising because of endemic denial in the Dominican Republic of birth registration to children of Haitian origin, motivated by desire to prevent proof of entitlement to citizenship based on *ius soli*. **1.101**

A8. Minimum Content

There is no convincing authority as to whether nationality exists for purposes of international law only when this status possesses a minimum content in municipal law. If this were so then if the State excluded the potential exercise of international protection, or access to the territory, it would be said that the status given to the individual by the State did not reach minimum requirements for nationality on the international plane. The more common view is that insofar as nationality is created and maintained by municipal rather than international law, there can be no uniform international standard for the attributes attached to it. As Weis wrote in 1956 (and reiterated in 1979): **1.102**

> There is, therefore, not *one* definition of nationality as a conception of municipal law, but as many definitions as there are States, unless one wishes to choose a general definition such as "nationality denotes a specific relationship between individual and State conferring mutual rights and duties as distinct from the relationship of the alien to the State of sojourn".[136]

In principle it would be possible for the international community to conclude agreements defining nationality for international law purposes as extant only where particular attributes are guaranteed to holders of the status by municipal law so that recognition depends upon minimum content. But there is no evidence that doing so is a priority for States. Against this background it is understandable

---

[135] R Piotrowicz, 'Refugee Status and Multiple Nationality in the Indonesian Archipelago: Is there a Timor Gap?' (1996) 8(3) *International Journal of Refugee Law* 319, 342.

[136] Weis (n 2 above) 29.

that in 2010 discussion of precisely this point at an Expert Meeting sponsored by the UNHCR was indecisive:

> For the purposes of the 1954 Convention, 'national' is to be understood by reference to whether the State in question regards holders of a particular status as persons over whom it has jurisdiction on the basis of a link of nationality. Several participants were of the view that in practice it is difficult to differentiate between the possession of a nationality and its effects, including, at a minimum, the right to enter and reside in the State of nationality and to return to it from abroad, as well as the right of the State to exercise diplomatic protection. Otherwise, according to this view, nationality is emptied of any content.[137]

1.103 A striking feature of the discussion is the absence of any authority for the proposition that a status will not be a nationality at all if minimum conditions are not satisfied, though such a nationality would be diminished in content and ineffective in regard to the generally expected effects of nationality as between national and State. The Reich Citizenship Law of 15 September 1935, reflecting the malign discrimination of the Nazi regime as regards a significant part of the population, provides a potential example, which the international community appears to have viewed not as removing nationality, but as discriminating in relation to citizen status and indicating a denial of national protection. It has to be noted also, that a nationality, without one or more expected effects, might be brought into existence by reason of some motivation other than malignity or discrimination—for instance some form of status seen as carrying nationality but having an intermediate character in municipal law.

A9. 'Effective Nationality'

1.104 The phrase 'effective nationality' arises in several contexts in different areas of international law. It bears a number of different meanings in law, several of which are contested, and its language is extremely wide, which may tend to obscure rather than enhance the clarity of any underlying concept. First, 'effective nationality' represents a method of distinguishing one or more nationalities from others on the basis of greater 'effectiveness' in respect of some specified incident of nationality—so that the actual meaning can be determined only after identification of the matter justifying characterisation as 'effective'. The most frequent use of the term 'effective nationality' in international law is in relation to diplomatic protection. Within that field it identifies a principle of disputed legitimacy and scope requiring identification of a primary or dominant nationality in a plural national (in relation not only to natural persons but also legal ones). In the *Canevaro* case (*Italy v Peru*) (1912) Scott 2 Hague Court Reports 284–96 the Permanent Court of Arbitration considered claims against Peru by Italy seeking to exercise diplomatic

[137] UNHCR, *Expert Meeting* (n 56 above) 2–3.

protection in respect of a dual Italian–Peruvian national. The Court found on the basis of extensive conduct by the claimant in respects indicative of exercise of Peruvian citizenship, including standing as a candidate for the Peruvian Senate and acting as Consul General in Peru for the Netherlands, that 'whatever [his] status as a national may be in Italy, the Government of Peru has a right to consider him a Peruvian citizen and to deny his status as an Italian claimant'. In the *Nottebohm* case (*Liechtenstein v Guatemala*) [1955] ICJ Reports 4, the principle was controversially extended to bar protection of its national by Liechtenstein against Guatemala, which had been a long-standing country of habitual residence at the time of the acts prompting the action, but had never been the claimant's country of nationality. Equivalent principles have been identified in cases of dual or plural nationality not including the respondent State. Article 5 of the 1930 Convention had provided that:

> Within a third State, a person having more than one nationality shall be treated as if he had only one. Without prejudice to the application of its law in matters of personal status and of any conventions in force, a third State shall, of the nationalities which any such person possesses, recognise exclusively in its territory either the nationality of the country in which he is habitually and principally resident, or the nationality of the country with which in the circumstances he appears to be in fact most closely connected.

The principle is applied relatively recently in numbers of decisions by the Iran–United States Claims Tribunal. An illustration is the *Asghar* case (1990) 24 Iran–US CTR 242–43. In the same Tribunal the rule has also been subject in practice to a compromise interpretation as requiring only satisfaction of a minimum level of linkage beyond nationality with the State of protection: *Dallal Case* (1983) 3 Iran–US CTR 10.[138] In 2006 the ILC's Draft Articles attempted to codify practice by articles 6 ('Multiple nationality and claim against a third State') and 7 ('Multiple nationality and claim against a State of nationality').[139] Similar principles are applied in other contexts, for instance within European Union law as regards jurisdiction, recognition and enforcement of decisions in matrimonial and child law matters: see for instance *Hadadi (Area of Freedom, Security & Justice)* [2009] EUECJ C-168/08.

Second, 'effective nationality' might be used as a term asserting that a legal status of nationality is 'effective', in that it carries either all incidents thought to attach to possession of nationality, or a particular characteristic providing the focus for the term's use. 'Effective nationality' in this sense might equally be expressed as nationality plus a specific additional requirement of endorsement thereof as meeting a particular expectation regarding its content or the consequence of possessing it. This usage occurs regularly in jurisprudence and commentary regarding refugee status, where question arises as to whether a nationality (generally a **1.105**

[138] See also D Bederman, 'Nationality of Individual Claimants before the Iran–United States Claims Tribunal' (1993) 42 *International & Comparative Law Quarterly* 119.

[139] ILC, 'Draft Articles on Diplomatic Protection' (2006) (n 49 above).

second or further nationality) is relevant for consideration in relation to refugee status: for example, *Jong Kim Koe v MIMA* [1997] FCA 306, [1997] ALR 695; *Lay Kon Tji v MIMA* [1998] FCA 1380, (1998) 158 ALR 681; *Katkova v Canada (MCI)* (1997) 130 FTR 192; *R v SSHD ex p Milisavljevic* [2001] EWHC Admin 203, [2001] Imm AR 580, [2001] All ER(D) 165 (March); and *Dolma v Canada (MCI)* [2015] FC 703. The cases and commentary however show a high level of doubt and disagreement as to the content of 'effective nationality'– for instance see the cogent criticism of the Australian decision in *Lay Kon Tji* by Piotrowicz.[140] The issue is addressed in detail in chapter five, section B7, where it is suggested that resort to the term 'effective nationality' has caused confusion and uncertainty, and that interpretation of article 1A(2) CSR51 shows that a better approach may be set out.

1.106 Third, a status might be said to constitute 'effective nationality' if it is not a nationality in the legal sense, as defined previously in this chapter, but is thought to display some characteristic or characteristics which mean that though actual nationality is not present, something parallel to nationality, defined by the specific aspect or consequence chosen by the user of the term, is present: 'effective nationality' in this sense might equally be expressed as '*de facto* nationality', a formulation which at least has the relative advantage over 'effective nationality' of identifying as a definitive characteristic the absence of 'nationality' in legal terms. A kindred usage potentially denotes closeness to legal nationality—someone is so close to possession of a legal nationality that he or she is 'effectively' a national even if 'not yet' holding that status. This sense is quite close to concepts described by reference to the Canadian cases of *Bouianova v Canada (MEI)* (1993) 67 FTR 74 and *Canada (MCI) v Williams* [2005] FCA 126, [2005] 3 FCR 429, 253 DLR (4th) 449, though the phrase is not used in either case. In this sense 'effective nationality' is simply a descriptor, not carrying any established legal meaning or significance, though capable of confusion with the preceding sense of the term.

1.107 Overall, it may be felt that the phrase 'effective nationality' is potentially useful as a descriptive phrase where the intended meaning is fully clarified, but use without further express specification of assumptions risks obscuring rather than illuminating the concept referred to. Against this background it is understandable that the United Kingdom Upper Tribunal in *KK and others (Nationality: North Korea) Korea CG* [2011] UKUT 92 preferred to set aside the term and to focus upon whether (in that case) South Korean nationality provided a relevant level of 'protection'– albeit certain difficulties not dissimilar to those described above also arise in relation to the latter term—as explored in detail in chapter five, sections B2, B4 and B7. Although the language of 'effective nationality' has been a feature of a number of significant refugee law cases, it is considered that absence of clarity including the potential for multiple relevant meanings favours avoiding the continued use of the term in relation to the international law of refugee status—see in particular chapter 5 section B7.

---

[140] Piotrowicz, '*Lay Kon Tji and Minister for Immigration & Ethnic Affairs*' (n 131 above).

A10. Recognition and Non-Recognition

i. Non-Recognition in General

1.108 As already seen, article 1 of the 1930 Convention Relating to the Conflict of Nationality Laws distinguished between the domestic law of a State as the origin of nationality, and the obligation to recognise this on the international plane. The validity of actions or omissions of the State fall to be scrutinised on the plane of international law by external international law standards, and a situation which flies in the face of such standards risks non-recognition. *Oppenheim's International Law* states, as regards 'the principle of non-recognition', that:

> Recognition will not, of course, be granted to a state or government which does not meet the requirements for recognition. Even where those requirements are satisfied, states may nevertheless not grant recognition; for example, when the non-recognising state regards the grant of recognition as entirely a matter of policy, or where to grant it would be inconsistent with particular international obligations binding upon the non-recognising state.
>
> Recognition may also be withheld where a new situation originates in an act which is contrary to general international law. The principle of *ex iniuria ius non oritur* is well established in international law, and according to it acts which are contrary to international law cannot become a source of legal rights for a wrongdoer. Furthermore, where a situation is found to be illegal, states for whom that finding is binding have an obligation to bring that illegal situation to an end. There is, however, no settled view how far as a matter of international law the unlawful act is to be regarded as null and void, or as voidable, or as merely giving rise to a claim by an injured state for redress.
>
> To grant recognition to an illegal act or situation will tend to perpetuate it and to be of benefit to the state which has acted illegally.
>
> ...
>
> The development ... to an international legal obligation to withhold recognition of illegal conduct has been hesitant and incomplete. States do not in practice acknowledge any general obligation under international law permanently to withhold recognition of illegal acts or their consequences.[141]

1.109 National courts are in general reluctant to enquire into the actions of foreign States: for instance in *MacKay v McAlexander, Acting District Director INS*, ILR 28, 268 F 2d 35 (9th Cir 1959) the US Court of Appeals supported a decision declining to question the validity under the law of that country of a Canadian naturalisation decree relating to the father of the appellant, who sought to resist deportation from the United States on the basis that his father's Canadian naturalisation was invalid so had not brought about the loss of his US citizenship. In England and Wales the attitude of the courts to questions of foreign nationality law has varied

[141] Jennings and Watts (n 10 above) 183, §54.

between treatment of the domestic law of a foreign State as decisive in all events, on the one hand, and on the other a more provisional approach, including willingness to treat as ineffective in England and Wales ordinances viewed as oppressive or arbitrary. In *Stoeck v Public Trustee* [1921] 2 Ch 67, Russell J (at 82) followed the former course, concluding that:

> Whether a person is a national of a country must be determined by the municipal law of that country. Upon this I think all text writers are agreed. It would be strange were it otherwise. How could the municipal law of England determine that a person is a national of Germany? ... In truth there is not and cannot be such an individual as a German national according to English law.

This does not prevent foreign courts from making decisions of fact regarding foreign nationality laws and their bearing upon the position of individuals. Such decisions are required for many purposes including the adjudication of entitlement to refugee status. As McLaughlin J put it in *Fedorovski, Re Judicial Review* [2007] NIQB 119 [2008] NI 193:

> 16. The ultimate decision about grant or refusal of citizenship to any person is entirely within the remit of the administrative and judicial authorities of the Republic of Ukraine. For me to make any determination of citizenship would be an unauthorised trespass upon the jurisdiction of its courts and the sovereignty of the Republic of Ukraine and I repeat I make no attempt at such a determination. The function of this court is to inform itself of the relevant citizenship laws and to consider the factual circumstances surrounding the personal, social and family history of the applicant for asylum ... On the basis of the facts available to me, and reading the law of the Ukraine as explained to me by the document from the Ministry of Foreign Affairs and the evidence of Ms Khanna, an expert whose evidence is unchallenged and which I accept, I am satisfied that the decision of the immigration authorities of the United Kingdom to remove the applicant from the United Kingdom to the Ukraine is entirely rational and legal. I am satisfied there are strong reasons to believe the applicant would be admitted to the state of Ukraine as a Ukrainian national under the Ukrainian law of citizenship.

1.110 The principles applicable to recognition or non-recognition of nationality follow, with variations reflecting the difference in context, principles also applicable to recognition of States,[142] governments, or belligerency. In *Recognition in International Law*, one of the most significant systematic examinations of recognition in international law, Lauterpacht argued that recognition or non-recognition had a strong legal character and was critical to the existence and functioning of the international law regime:

> International law acknowledges as a source of rights and obligations such facts and situations as are not the result of acts which it prohibits and stigmatises as unlawful. Thus, for example, secession from an existing State, although constituting a breach of the law of

[142] A distinction in this context is that according to one school of thought recognition of States has constitutive power, ie, an entity becomes a State by recognition: see Crawford, 'Introduction' to Lauterpacht, *Recognition in International Law* (n 58 above) xx–liv.

the State concerned, is not contrary to international law ... Although rebellion is treason in the eyes of municipal law, it results—when followed by the establishment of an effective government wielding power over the entirety of national territory with a reasonable prospect of permanence and with the consent or acquiescence of the people—in a duty of other States to recognise the [new government] ... For the same reason ..., once a rebellion has assumed dimensions of widespread hostilities in the form of a civil war as understood by international law, there arises the duty to admit the consequences of the situation ... and to recognise a state of belligerency.

These forms of recognition [of statehood, government, and belligerency] have been most conspicuous in international practice. But the same principle applies to any other situation created in a manner not inconsistent with international law.

...

It follows from the same principle [acknowledgement as a source of rights and obligations only of such facts and situations as are not the result of acts which international law prohibits and stigmatises as unlawful] that facts, however undisputed, which are the result of conduct violative of international law cannot claim the same right to be incorporated automatically as part of the law of nations. They do not impose upon other States the duty of recognition. They may, if they so wish and if, in exceptional circumstances, they deem it compatible with the maintenance of the authority of international law, recognize them as creating internationally valid rights as against themselves. If they do so, it is a concession they are under no duty to grant. On the other hand, they may announce their intention to treat in the future such unlawful acts as devoid of any validity in international law. They may go further and obligate themselves in a mutually binding instrument not to validate as part of international law the consequences of an unlawful act. Such a duty of non-recognition may follow indirectly from obligations of a different character previously undertaken. This distinction between acts consistent with and those contrary to international law enables us to understand the principle of non-recognition in terms of the general doctrine of recognition conceived as an act of application of international law.[143]

According to Lauterpacht, recognition and non-recognition possess a central importance in the international system as a significant part of its reaction to the consequences of acts which violate established standards of international law: **1.111**

In a properly constituted political society the function—which is perhaps the most important function of any legal system—of ascertaining the presence of conditions of legal capacity and existence is performed by impartial organs delegated by the law for that purpose. In international society that task is as a rule fulfilled by individual States acting on their own responsibility and endowed with wide discretion in the appreciation of the relevant facts. That discretion is unfettered only in the meaning that, at present, the State which takes a decision on the issue of recognition is not accountable for acts to any superior jurisdiction. In essence, it is a discretion determined by international law. In granting or refusing recognition the State administers international law; it does not perform a legally indifferent act of national policy. In the imperfectly developed

[143] Lauterpacht, *Recognition in International Law* (n 58 above) 409–10, §119.

international society States are often called upon to act in the fulfilment of a legal duty or in the assertion of their legal interest without being directly and immediately responsible to a higher authority. This does not mean that in these matters States are not bound by law at all. They enjoy freedom of decision in ascertaining the facts and assessing their significance. They are not free to assert the liberty to disregard the facts or to act in defiance of them.[144]

1.112 Ti-Chiang Chen, a Chinese contemporary of Lauterpacht, also emphasised the systemic importance for international law of recognition and non-recognition:

> In every legal community the law, however weak, does not succumb to acts of violence without resistance, and the doctrine of non-recognition serves the purpose of preserving the legal *status quo ante* before the submission of the dictates of circumstances. One can reject the doctrine only if the non-recognition is unduly prolonged and eventually unsuccessful.[145]

1.113 Lauterpacht linked recognition and non-recognition to the dictum *ex injuria ius non oritur*:

> The principle *ex injuria jus non oritur* is one of the fundamental maxims of jurisprudence. An illegality cannot, as a rule, become a source of legal right to the wrongdoer. This does not mean that it cannot produce any legal results at all. For it gives rise to a legal liability of the lawbreaker; it may become, in the interests of intercourse and general security, a source of rights for third persons acting in good faith ... But to admit that, apart from well-defined exceptions, an unlawful act, or its immediate consequences, may become *suo vigore* a source of legal right for the wrongdoer is to introduce into the legal system a contradiction which cannot be solved except by a denial of its legal character. International law does not and cannot form an exception to that imperative alternative.[146]

1.114 It was acknowledged by Lauterpacht that the application of this maxim might be affected by another potentially opposing dictum, *ex factis jus oritur* (law arises from facts):

> Law, once established, tells us what, under pain of compulsion, is the right conduct; it is not a generalisation of actual behaviour; its validity is not affected by wrongful acts. On the other hand, while law, so long as it is valid, is unaffected by a violation of its rules, its continuous breach, when allowed to remain triumphant, ultimately affects the validity of the law. As the sociological basis of the legal system as a whole is ultimately determined by the social realities of consent and power, so also the validity of its individual rules cannot in the long run be divorced from that foundation. Law conceived as an enforceable rule of conduct is to a large extent determined by what we judge to be socially feasible and practicable. Continued acquiescence in or toleration of illegality is a powerful element in the formation of such judgment.

---

[144] Ibid, 33–34, §14.

[145] T-C Chen, *The International Law of Recognition, with Special Reference to Practice in Great Britain and the United States* (Stevens, 1951) 415.

[146] Lauterpacht, *Recognition in International Law* (n 58 above) 420–21, §124.

However, although accumulation of illegal conduct, when tolerated or left unpunished by the society, may have the consequence of changing the law and of sanctioning rights originating in illegality, no such result can be attributed to single acts of lawlessness, however successful. International law, being a weak law, is fully exposed to the impact of the phenomenon to which jurists have referred as the 'law-creating influence of facts'. But unless law is to become a convenient code for malefactors, it must steer a middle course between the law-creating influence of facts and the principle, which is the essence of law, that its validity is impervious to individual acts of lawlessness. Law is a body of rules operating under the aegis of a system of force actually operative in society. This does not mean that all breaches of the law, if successful, become part of the legal order. A balance must be achieved somewhere. It cannot be found in the immediate validation of the illegal act; it must be sought in considerations of a general nature which would justify the legislator in incorporating the result of the illegality as part of the law. In the absence of such incorporation, a provisional balance may be found, in the international sphere, in *de facto* recognition combining the necessities of international intercourse with the maintenance of an essential legal principle.[147]

In 1955 the ICJ decided the *Nottebohm* case (*Liechtenstein v Guatemala*) [1955] ICJ Reports 4, which, whilst primarily concerned with opposability in the bilateral context, and considered in more detail in that context below, may have some continuing relevance also in the context of recognition. Even if the extent of that relevance is limited, the decision may still be seen as an important watershed in the identification of nationality created by the State of nationality as not binding in all circumstances upon other States. **1.115**

In 1958, looking at the 1930 Convention and subsequent developments relevant to nationality in international law, Parry endorsed non-recognition based upon the 'admitted exceptions to the duty to recognise foreign nationality laws' of inconsistency with 'international conventions or international custom and the generally recognised principles of international law with regard to nationality', though he also concluded that the 1930 Convention did not create a coherent positive duty to recognise foreign nationality laws.[148] In 1959 Mann acknowledged this, but suggested that 'the question remains whether Article 1 does not also contain a negative duty, which may be full of meaning'.[149] **1.116**

In relation to recognition on the level of international law in the modern era, the ICJ has indicated the need for distinction between the welfare of persons affected by illegal measures and an overall requirement of non-recognition directed at the State in question. In the *Namibia* Advisory Opinion, the Court said of non-recognition of South Africa's occupation and administration of Namibia that: **1.117**

125. In general, the non-recognition of South Africa's administration of the Territory should not result in depriving the people of Namibia of any advantages derived from

[147] Ibid, 426–27, §127.

[148] C Parry, 'The Duty to Recognise Foreign Nationality Laws' in (1958) *Zeitschrift für Öffentliches Recht (Festgabe für Alexander N Makarov)* 337, 360–68.

[149] F Mann, 'Review of Festgabe Makarov' in (1958) *British Yearbook of International Law* (OUP, 1959) 425, 427.

international co-operation. In particular, while official acts performed by the Government of South Africa on behalf of or concerning Namibia after the termination of the Mandate are illegal and invalid, this invalidity cannot be extended to those acts, such as, for instance, the registration of births, deaths and marriages, the effects of which can be ignored only to the detriment of the inhabitants of the Territory.[150]

1.118 There have also been important decisions of the highest courts both in the United Kingdom and in Australia concerning recognition of nationality. The decision of the House of Lords in *Oppenheimer v Cattermole* [1976] AC 249, directly applicable to denationalisation, is outlined in the next section, which relates specifically to recognition of denationalisation. Questions of recognition were examined in a different context by the High Court of Australia (Mason CJ, Brennan, Deane, Dawson, Toohey, Gaudron and McHugh JJ) in *Sykes v Cleary* [1992] HCA 60, (1992) 176 CLR 77. The case concerned eligibility for public office in Australia, where statute barred nationals of other States (including plural citizens) therefrom. Brennan J delivered the judgment of the Court:

> 7. However, recognition by our municipal law of the effect of foreign law on status and allegiance is subject to a further qualification. In times of war, common law courts have refused to recognize changes in the status either of British subjects ((55). See *R v Lynch* (1903) 1 KB 444) or of enemy aliens ((56) *R v The Home Secretary; Ex parte L* (1945) KB 7; *Lowenthal v Attorney-General* (1948) 1 All ER 295) under the law of the foreign hostile power. In these cases, non-recognition has been justified on the ground of public policy ((57) *Oppenheimer v Cattermole* (1976) AC, at p 275). But there is no reason why the doctrine of public policy should be confined to that situation. If recognition of status, rights or privileges under foreign law would extend the operation of s 44(i) of the Constitution to cases which it was not intended to cover, that section should be construed as requiring recognition of foreign law only in those situations where recognition fulfils the purpose of s 44(1). To take an extreme example, if a foreign power were mischievously to confer its nationality on members of the Parliament so as to disqualify them all, it would be absurd to recognize the foreign law conferring foreign nationality. Section 44(i) is concerned to ensure that foreign powers command no allegiance from or obedience by candidates, senators and members of the House of Representatives; it is not concerned with the operation of foreign law that is incapable in fact of creating any sense of duty, or of enforcing any duty, of allegiance or obedience to a foreign power. It accords both with public policy and with the proper construction of s 44(i) to deny recognition to foreign law in these situations ... However, there are few situations in which a foreign law, conferring foreign nationality or the rights and privileges of a foreign national, is incapable in fact of creating a sense of duty, or is incapable of enforcing a duty, of allegiance or obedience to a foreign power. One such situation does occur when the foreign law, purporting to affect nationality of persons who have had no connection or only a very slender connection with the foreign power, exceeds the jurisdiction recognized by

[150] *Legal Consequences for States of the Continued Presence of South Africa in Namibia (South West Africa) notwithstanding Security Council Resolution 276* (1970) (Advisory Opinion) [1971] ICJ Rep 16, 56 [125].

international law. That is the situation described by Lord Cross ((58) supra, fn (53)) in which international law does not recognize the jurisdiction of the foreign power.

More recently the ILC's Articles on Responsibility of States for Internationally Wrongful Acts 2001 by article 41 assert a positive duty of non-recognition upon States in certain circumstances: 1.119

Article 41: Particular consequences of a serious breach of an obligation under this chapter

1. States shall cooperate to bring to an end through lawful means any serious breach within the meaning of article 40.
2. No State shall recognize as lawful a situation created by a serious breach within the meaning of article 40 ['a serious breach by a State of an obligation arising under a peremptory norm of general international law [where a] breach of such an obligation is serious if it involves a gross or systematic failure by the responsible State to fulfil the obligation'], nor render aid or assistance in maintaining that situation.
3. This article is without prejudice to the other consequences referred to in this Part and to such further consequences that a breach to which this chapter applies may entail under international law.

The positive duty at article 41(2) would potentially attach to nationality changes brought about by aggression or breaching prohibitions against slavery and the slave trade, genocide, and racial discrimination and apartheid.[151] But more broadly it can be said that today, international human rights standards, the international law relating to non-discrimination, and the international law relating to statelessness, all represent sources of norms which may affect recognition.

ii. Denationalisation in Particular

Issues of recognition versus non-recognition in relation to nationality have been most to the fore in relation to denationalisation. Over time courts in different States have had to consider whether to recognise the consequences of denationalisation, with the large-scale expatriation measures of the USSR and of Nazi Germany in the 1920s and 1930s providing a particular early test over a significant period of time and across different jurisdictions. 1.120

In some instances important questions have been examined at the level of national law: for instance the Nazi decree of 25 November 1941 was in 1968 found by Germany's own Federal Constitutional Court in *BVerfG 23, 98—2 BvR 557/62 of 14 February 1968* (*'Ausbürgerung I'*) to have 'violated fundamental principles', to 1.121

[151] ILC, 'Draft Articles on Responsibility of States for Internationally Wrongful Acts, with Commentaries' (UN Doc A/56/10), available at: legal.un.org/ilc/texts/instruments/english/commentaries/9_6_2001.pdf), commentary on articles 40 and 42.

have been 'irreconcilable with justice' and therefore null and void from the outset ('*ex tunc*').[152]

1.122 In 1927 Sir John Fischer Williams deplored in strong terms the effect of the earlier mass denationalisation by the USSR, but there was no body of law to point to which constrained human rights abuses by States against their own citizens, or against stateless persons. Beyond the delict by the USSR against other States which were left unable to expel aliens from their own territory to that of the USSR, Williams could point to little more than the irreconcilability of denationalisation and expulsion with international order and humanitarian care:

> It is no longer possible simply to send undesirables abroad. Slops may be thrown out of the windows of a settler's hut on a prairie; in a town such a practice is inadmissible. English law has long abandoned the practice of transportation—partly no doubt from the fact that no temperate colony is now sufficiently under home control to allow of a practice ... Formerly states welcomed migrants without discrimination; they now for the most part discourage them.[153]

1.123 Searching for a legal standard capable of affording remedy for the situation he perceived, Williams had to look to the breach of territorial sovereignty of other States threatened by the Soviet action:

> What then is the conclusion of the whole matter? There will be general agreement that a state cannot, whether by banishment or by putting an end to the status of nationality, compel any other state to receive one of its own nationals whom it wishes to expel from its own territory. There will also be general agreement that a state is bound to receive back across its frontiers any individual who possesses its nationality or who is one of its '*ressortissants*'. If so, it follows that while positive international law does not forbid a state unilaterally to sever the relationship of nationality so far as the individual is concerned, even if the person affected possesses or acquires no other nationality, still a state cannot sever the tie of nationality in such a way as to release itself from the international duty, owed to other states, of receiving back a person denationalized who has acquired no other nationality, should he be expelled as an alien by the state where he happens to be.[154]

1.124 A full survey of the cases of the interwar period is impossible here. In relation to the Soviet denationalisations, the Swiss Federal Court held in *Tcherniak v Tcherniak* (1929) 56 *Clunet* 208 that the Soviet instruments had no effect in Switzerland, but the decision was overturned in *Lempert v Bonfol* (1929) 7 *Annual Digest* 290, in which the issue was whether the child of a Swiss mother and a father denationalised by the Soviet Union became a Swiss national as the child of a stateless person—something which only came about if the denationalisation were treated as effective. The Polish Supreme Court came to a like decision in 1927 in *Rajdberg v Lewi* 4 AD (1927–28) 314, No 219, the issue being whether the plaintiff,

---

[152] See also *BVerfG 54, 53—2 BvR 842/77* of 15 April 1980 ('*Ausbürgerung II*').

[153] Fischer Williams (n 85 above) 57.

[154] Ibid, 61.

a denationalised Russian, should be treated as a stateless person entitled as such to League of Nations protection.

In 1933 Lauterpacht, writing about law within the international community, characterised actions of the Soviet Union and Italy, which resulted in many cases in statelessness, as instances of abuse of rights by those States: **1.125**

> There is no clear rule of international law at present which limits the freedom of action of States in this respect, but it is submitted that the indiscriminate exercise by a State of the right of denationalizing its subjects, when coupled with the refusal to receive them when deported from a foreign country, constitutes an abuse of rights which could hardly be countenanced by an international tribunal.[155]

As to the Nazi instruments, the US Court of Appeals in *Schwartzkopf v Uhl*, 137 F 2d 898 (2nd Cir 1943) treated the Nazi denationalisation provision as effective, so that an individual stripped of German nationality was held entitled to *habeas corpus* as a stateless person, something which would have been denied him had he been found to be a German (and therefore enemy) national. In England and Wales it was held by a Divisional Court in *R v Home Secretary ex p L* [1945] 1 KB 7 that an individual affected by the Nazi denationalisation was not entitled to *habeas corpus* because as a matter of policy, recognition of loss of nationality by enemy aliens was not given during wartime, a decision subject almost immediately to powerful criticism.[156] In 1946 in Switzerland, the Swiss Federal Tribunal in *Levita-Mühlstein v Département Fédéral de Justice et Police* 70 Arrêts du Tribunal Fédéral Suisse (1946) 407 declined to recognise the Nazi decree as effective within Swiss territory, supporting this by reference to Swiss public policy rather than international law. The effect however was the loss of Swiss nationality by the Swiss-born wife of an individual stripped of nationality under the Nazi laws, who was found by the Tribunal to be German with the effect that his spouse lost Swiss nationality upon her marriage. **1.126**

A common feature of many cases including, for example, *Schwartzkopf v Uhl*, in which the Nazi decree was treated as effective, *Levita-Mühlstein*, in which it was not, and *ex p L*, in which the question was not reached because of the intervening domestic judicial policy of non-recognition during wartime, was that it was in the interest of the individual in each case to have the decree treated as effective—in the first and third cases because this meant access to *habeas corpus*, and in the second because this would have meant that the wife of the affected individual retained her Swiss nationality rather than losing it through marriage to a denationalised German. The decisions are not permanent authority for the necessity of recognising denationalisation regardless of circumstances, and this is particularly so given **1.127**

---

155 H Lauterpacht, *The Function of Law in the International Community* (OUP, 1933) 308–09.

156 See, *inter alia*, F Mann, '*R v Home Secretary ex p L* (Case Comment)' (1945) 61 *Law Quarterly Review* 126; H Lauterpacht, 'The Nationality of Denationalised Persons' (1948) *Jewish Yearbook of International Law* 164, republished in E Lauterpacht (ed), *International Law; Being the Collected Papers of Hersch Lauterpacht*, vol 3 (CUP, 1977) ch 1, 397–98.

that at the time neither IHRL in a developed form nor CSR51 nor CRS61 existed. In 1948 Lauterpacht, in a comment upon *ex p L* pointed to:

> overwhelming considerations of fairness and equity [which] demand that, in so far as the law allows, the victims of persecution should not be exposed to the hardships and losses attaching to a nationality of which they were deprived by a valid decree of the State responsible for the persecution.[157]

He noted that:

> Public policy, of which public morality is a not inconsiderable element, would seem to demand that the State should not identify itself with a measure of injustice inherent in the attempt to make the victims of the persecution pay for the policy and misdeeds of their persecutors.[158]

Another critic was Mann:

> In these circumstances [the application was made not by an enemy alien who had 'thrown off' his disability for the purpose of improving his status, but by a Jew who, by virtue of a Nazi decree of 1941 expatriating all German Jews resident outside Germany, had been deprived of his German nationality] the decision is remarkable for other reasons. Firstly, while employing language which went further than the decision required, Viscount Caldecote [the Lord Chief Justice] seemed to doubt whether a change from enemy nationality to statelessness during war-time could be 'permitted' or recognized for any purposes. It is submitted that the well-known relativity of public policy excludes a hard-and-fast answer. Where the change of status comes into conflict with the exigencies of war it will not be recognized, but this cannot alter the fact that persons in the position of the applicants are stateless and, in many connexions, will have to be recognized as such.[159]

Those cases, in which avoidance of further harm to those affected by denationalisation measures favoured recognition of statelessness, are distinct in significant respects from, for example, the situation of a denationalised individual seeking refugee status by reason of denationalisation and consequences thereof.

1.128 Since article 1 of the 1930 Convention identified recognition as depending upon consistency 'with international conventions, international custom, and the principles of law generally recognised with regard to nationality', what has changed very greatly is the surrounding international law framework. As early as 1963, before ICCPR66, the International Covenant on Economic, Social and Cultural Rights 1966 (ICESCR66) and ICERD66 came into being, Brownlie observed that in relation to nationality of another State arising as a consequence of acts inconsistent with international law, such as aggression or over-extensive nationality law, a State 'may refuse to give effect to change of nationality because it regards the origin of

[157] Lauterpacht, *International Law; Being the Collected Papers of Hersch Lauterpacht* (n 156 above) 398.

[158] Ibid, 400.

[159] Mann, '*R v Home Secretary ex p L*' (n 156 above) 126–27.

the change ... to be contrary to international law'.[160] In relation to denationalisation in particular, he commented that:

> principle and existing practice give some support to and, at the least, do not contradict certain positions. If the deprivation is part and parcel of a breach of an international duty then the act of deprivation will be illegal. If the deprivation is not a part of a delictual act but merely involves denationalization of groups of citizens domiciled within the frontiers of a State, who lack any other links, then there is no delict—as there would be, for example, if they were forced to try to gain admission illegally in neighbouring States—but the deprivation is not entitled to recognition by others because it disregards the doctrine of effective link and represents an attempt to avoid the responsibilities of territorial sovereignty and statehood ... It is perhaps not surprising that existing practice and jurisprudence do not support a general rule of illegality.[161]

1.129 Later the courts in England and Wales had again to consider the consequences of measures adopted by the Nazi regime in Germany between 1933 and 1945 depriving individuals of nationality on political, racial, or religious grounds, without the intervention of judicial policy of non-recognition during wartime. The question raised by the case was whether a naturalised British subject of German–Jewish origin, who had left Germany in 1939 as a result of Nazi persecution, was exempt from taxation in England on a pension which he received from the Federal Republic of Germany from 1953 by reason of his many years of work before 1939 in a Bavarian orphanage. His claim to exemption from taxation in England on that income depended upon whether he had remained a German national so had dual nationality after naturalisation in the United Kingdom. The Court of Appeal in *Oppenheimer v Cattermole (Inspector of Taxes)* [1973] Ch 264 followed the approach taken in earlier cases, of declining to look beyond German law which on its analysis had rescinded nationality.[162]

1.130 This was criticised severely by experts. In 1973 Mann identified the Nazi instrument of 1941 as one which 'may be held to be incapable of recognition or application on the ground that it is contrary to public international law, or alternatively, to public policy'.[163] He pointed to the previous work of Lauterpacht on recognition and to his maxim of *ex iniuria ius non oritur* as providing guidance in a selective application of recognition and non-recognition based upon deterrence of state misconduct balanced by avoidance of harm to the individual.[164] In 1974, prior to consideration of the case in the House of Lords, Merrills broadly supported Mann:

> Of course, nationality is a matter on which States are extremely sensitive, but it is difficult to see why an English court in deference to this sensitivity should seem to condone legislation which is contrary both to declared British policy on race relations and to world wide condemnation of racial discrimination. There are today few matters on

---

[160] Brownlie (n 41 above) 326–27.
[161] Ibid, 339–40.
[162] Ibid, 273.
[163] F Mann, 'The Present Validity of Nazi Nationality Laws' (1973) 89 *Law Quarterly Review* 194.
[164] Ibid, 202–07.

> which States are generally agreed, but the wrongfulness of racial discrimination is one and there would seem to be every reason for an English court to refuse such legislation its imprimatur.
>
> In general the aim of protecting the interests of individuals seems likely to be best served by refusing to recognise arbitrary denationalisations.[165]

The views of Merrills and Mann differ as to whether avoidance of harm in individual circumstances justified recognition (Mann) or whether non-recognition was obligatory, the deterrence of mischief by States having an absolute priority (Merrills). The position of Mann implicitly gained support through later developments such as the *Namibia* Advisory Opinion of the ICJ (see para 1.117 above), and is believed to be on current evidence the better one of the two.

1.131 On appeal, the House of Lords considered the case in *Oppenheimer v Cattermole* [1976] AC 249. Lord Cross of Chelsea (at 276H–278G), delivering the most widely supported speech, held that a racially discriminatory and confiscatory law of the type represented by Nazi measures represented an infringement of human rights so serious that the courts ought to refuse to recognise it:

> It may be said, perhaps, that though international law sets limits to the jurisdiction of sovereign states so far as concerns the granting of nationality it sets no limits whatever to their power to withdraw it. I am not prepared to accept that this is so. I think, for example, that Martin Wolff, Private International Law, 2nd ed, p 129, may well be right in saying that, if a state withdraws its citizenship from some class of its citizens living within its borders to which it has taken a dislike and of whom it would be glad to be rid, other states are not obliged to regard such people as 'stateless'. ... [In the case at bar] the 1941 decree did not deprive all 'emigres' of their status as German nationals. It only deprived Jewish emigres of their citizenship. Further, as the later paragraphs of the decree show, this discriminatory withdrawal of their rights of citizenship was used as a peg upon which to hang a discriminatory confiscation of their property. A judge should, of course, be very slow to refuse to give effect to the legislation of a foreign state in any sphere in which, according to accepted principles of international law, the foreign state has jurisdiction. He may well have an inadequate understanding of the circumstances in which the legislation was passed and his refusal to recognise it may be embarrassing to the branch of the executive which is concerned to maintain friendly relations between this country and the foreign country in question. But I think ... that it is part of the public policy of this country that our courts should give effect to clearly established rules of international law ... what we are concerned with here is legislation which takes away without compensation from a section of the citizen body singled out on racial grounds all their property on which the state passing the legislation can lay its hands and, in addition, deprives them of their citizenship. To my mind a law of this sort constitutes so grave an infringement of human rights that the courts of this country ought to refuse to recognise it as a law at all.

165 JG Merrills, 'One Nationality or Two? The Strange Case of *Oppenheimer v Cattermole*' (1974) 23 *International & Comparative Law Quarterly* 143, 152, 156.

The ultimate decision owed much to reaction by the members of the panel to commentary by Mann, *inter alia*, pointing to the intervening decision of the German Federal Constitutional Court in 1968 which had found the 1941 decree void.[166] Lord Cross noted that the case before the House of Lords was relatively unusual in that the appellant argued that he remained a German national rather than the contrary: 1.132

> There are no doubt practical objections to [refusing to recognise the Decree as law], for in many, if not most, cases the persons affected by the 1941 decree would not have wished to remain German nationals. Dr Mann in his article[167] ... quotes several cases in which courts in different countries, while characterising the 1941 decree as 'atrocious' or 'barbarous', have yet given effect to it for this reason.[168]

Lord Cross *en passant* indicated some reservation as to whether, as Mann had suggested 'in the final analysis the overriding consideration is believed to be that a lawyer must not ever enforce a statute which constitutes a wrong' and that ultimately recognition fell to be considered on the basis of the maxim *ex injuria jus non oritur*: 'But it surely cannot be right for the question whether the decree should be recognised or not to depend on the circumstances of the particular case'.[169] 1.133

Space does not permit an exhaustive account of every instance of non-recognition in recent decades. An important example followed the purported foundation of independent 'homeland' or 'Bantustan' entities in furtherance of the apartheid policy of the Government of South Africa. Four such entities were created: Transkei, Bophuthatswana, Venda and Ciskei. Millions of black South Africans were effectively deprived of their South African nationality and dealt the nationality of a new entity with which they might have little connection. In its Resolution 2775(XXIV)(E) of 29 November 1971 the United Nations General Assembly condemned the policy as aimed at the division and disempowerment of black South Africans in pursuit of apartheid, and by Resolution 3411 (XXX)(D) of 28 November 1971 it reaffirmed that the establishment of Bantustan entities was a measure designed to destroy the territorial integrity of South Africa in breach of the principles of the Charter of the United Nations and called upon 'all Governments and organisations not to deal with any institutions or authorities of the Bantustans or to accord any form of recognition to them'. Responding on behalf of the United Nations Security Council to the so-called independence of Venda, the President of the Council employed strikingly forceful language: 1.134

> The Security Council condemns the proclamation of the so-called 'independence' of Venda and declares it totally invalid. This action by the South African regime, following

---

[166] Mann, 'The Present Validity of Nazi Nationality Laws' (n 162 above). See also F Mann '*Oppenheimer v Cattermole* Revisited' (1981) 97 *Law Quarterly Review* 194, 220–22; JG Merrills, '*Oppenheimer v Cattermole*—The Curtain Falls' (1975) 24 *International & Comparative Law Quarterly* 617.

[167] Mann, 'The Present Validity of Nazi Nationality Laws' (n 163 above).

[168] *Oppenheimer v Cattermole* [1976] AC 249, 276H–278G.

[169] Ibid, 278.

> similar proclamations of Transkei and Bophuthatswana, denounced by the international community, is designed to divide and dispossess the African people and establish client states under its domination in order to perpetuate apartheid. It further aggravates the situation in the region and hinders international efforts for just and lasting solutions … The Security Council calls upon all Governments to deny any form of recognition to the so-called 'independent' bantustans; to refrain from any dealings with them; to reject travel documents issued by them; and urges Member Governments to take effective measures to prohibit all individuals, corporations and other institutions under their jurisdiction from having any dealings with the so-called 'independent' bantustans.[170]

None of the 'bantustan' entities was ever recognised as a State by the international community. Each was formally reabsorbed into South Africa as part of the subsequent transition from *apartheid*. Crawford identifies the reason for non-recognition as connected with the underlying breach of international law in the 'fundamental denial of equality on the grounds of race or ethnic origin'.[171]

1.135 The evolution of international legal standards within IHRL and as regards statelessness, and the effect of these upon the freedom of States to denationalise their citizens, is illustrated by the change in the view of Weis, the leading early commentator on CSR51 and the international law of nationality. In 1956, in the first edition of *Nationality and Statelessness in International Law*, he noted that 'publicists have frequently endeavoured to prove the existence of rules of international law restricting the right of each State to determine freely the conditions for the loss of its nationality'[172] and concluded that 'the views of those who have tried to establish as a mandatory rule of existing law what must certainly be regarded as a sound and desirable rule for the future, find no justification in the present state of international law'.[173]

1.136 In the second edition of the same work, published in 1979, Weis noted the considerable developments in international law—notably ICCPR66 and CRS61, and then expressed a changed view:

> Considering that the principle of non-discrimination may now be regarded as a rule of international law or as a general principle of law, prohibition of discriminatory denationalisation may be regarded as a rule of present-day international law. This certainly applies to discrimination on the ground of race which may be considered as contravening a peremptory norm of international law but also, in the present writer's view, to discrimination on the other grounds mentioned in the Charter of the United Nations, ie sex and religion.[174]

1.137 Weis considered this a 'possible exception' from the general liberty of a State, save where bound specifically by treaty, to mandate the loss of its nationality.[175]

---

170 UN Doc S/13549, 21 September 1979, quoted by J Dugard, *Recognition and the United Nations* (Grotius Books, 1987) 101,

171 Crawford, *The Creation of States in International Law* (n 59 above) 344–45.

172 Weis (n 3 above) 126–27.

173 Ibid, 128.

174 Weis (n 2 above) 125.

175 Ibid, 126.

In 1988 Plender noted that developments in IHRL, especially the coming into force of ICCPR66 had had a 'profound effect' on the development of international law,[176] so that: 1.138

> The evidence suggests that in current international law a State cannot always release itself of its obligation to admit certain of its own nationals to its territory by promulgating a decree which deprives such persons of their nationality. A decree which discriminates on racial grounds, or is in any other sense 'arbitrary', need not be recognized by other States as effective to derive of their nationality those to whom it purports to apply.[177]

iii. Other Instances of Non-Recognition

Denationalisation is likely the paradigm case in which non-recognition principles may require consideration in the context of refugee status determination. However, at least three other situations may be identified in which consideration may have to be given to the issue of recognition: 1.139

i. A change of nationality resulting from a serious breach of human rights or another serious breach of international law, such as an act of genocide.
ii. An over-extensive nationality law contrary to the sovereignty of other States, as in the *Tunis Decrees* case and as identified in *Oppenheimer v Cattermole* at 277, referring to *Schwarzkopf v Uhl*: 'If a foreign country purported to confer the benefit of its protection on and to exact a duty of allegiance from persons who had no connection or only a very slender connection with it our courts would be entitled to pay no regard to such legislation on the ground that the country in question was acting beyond the bounds of any jurisdiction in matters of nationality which international law would recognise. In this respect I think that our law is the same as that of the United States as stated by the Circuit Court of Appeals, Second Circuit, in *United States ex rel Schwarzkopf v Uhl* ((54) (1943), 137 F 2d 898)'. Schwarzenberger instanced the principle by observing that 'If a territorial sovereign claims as his national an individual who, prima facie, appears more closely connected with another subject of international law, difficulties arise. For instance, a State which has made the cult of the moon goddess its State religion may grant its nationality to the adherents of this faith wherever they happen to dwell. Yet, while, under the municipal law of that State, any devotee of this creed is entitled to the privileges of citizenship, other [States] need not recognise this nationality'.[178]
iii. The case in which the person on whom nationality is conferred by naturalisation has no connection, or only a slender connection with the State whose nationality is created: *Oppenheimer v Cattermole (Inspector of Taxes)* [1976]

---

[176] Plender, *International Migration Law* (n 5 above) 147.
[177] Ibid, 149.
[178] Schwarzenberger (n 23 above) 141–42.

AC 249 at 277; *Sykes v Cleary*, above, at 112. In that circumstance the requirement for a 'genuine link' in *Nottebohm* terms might be held to militate against recognition on the plane of international law as well as domestic policy—although the application of this principle to broad issues of recognition on the international plane even on the widest possible interpretation is likely to include solely the most extreme cases—as noted below the primary relevance of *Nottebohm* appears to be in the different context of opposability, rather than in recognition.

1.140 As a matter of completeness it may be noted that non-recognition may also arise as a result of domestic policy. A non-exhaustive list of observed cases suggests the following as potentially within national practice:

i. A State may decline to recognise the loss of a nationality of an enemy State during wartime on the grounds of public policy, *R v The Home Secretary; Ex parte L* (1945) KB 7, 10; *Lowenthal v Attorney-General* (1948) 1 All ER 295, 299.
ii. It has been said that according to customary international law when territory is transferred to a new sovereign by conquest or cession the people of the territory become nationals of the new government only by their consent: *United States; ex rel Schwarzkopf v Uhl*, 137 F 2d 898 (1943).
iii. Also in wartime, a State may choose not to recognise renunciation of its own nationality or the naturalisation of its own national by an enemy State.

A11. Opposability

1.141 A question related to that of recognition or non-recognition is that of opposability of nationality. This generally arises in the context of claims between States, where one State seeks to bring a claim against another for harm to a national of the State bringing the claim. Amerasinghe describes the 'general rule' as being:

> that a person, whether natural or juridical, must have the nationality of the State claiming injury at the time at which the injury is inflicted, in order that there may be an actual violation of the substantive rules of international law relating to injuries to aliens.[179]

The concept of opposability of nationality in this context means, essentially, 'capable of reliance excluding dispute by another': so that 'opposable' means that the State taking an action (in the present context, by granting or withdrawing nationality) cannot enforce the validity of grant or withdrawal against another State. The term, adopting the French usage '*opposable à*', translates somewhat awkwardly into English.

1.142 The best known decision on opposability of nationality is that of the International Court of Justice in the *Nottebohm* case.[180] Mr Nottebohm was until 1939 a German national who had since 1905 resided in Guatemala where he with his two brothers

[179] Amerasinghe (n 14 above) 91.
[180] *Nottebohm (Liechtenstein v Guatemala)* [1955] ICJ Rep 4, 20.

had substantial business interests which he directed from 1937. In 1939, anticipating the risk that, in the event of Guatemala and Germany coming to be at war, he could face treatment as an enemy alien in Guatemala, he travelled to Liechtenstein in October and obtained its nationality after a stay of 11 days, paying substantial sums to obtain waiver of the usual three-year residency requirement. As a result of his naturalisation in Liechtenstein his German nationality was automatically withdrawn. He then returned to Guatemala and to the management of his business interests. Shortly after that country declared war on Germany—late in 1943—he was interned by the Guatemalan authorities and then transferred to a United States military base. Three days later Mr Nottebohm was transferred from Guatemala to the United States and he was then interned in the United States until the end of 1945. Whilst he was interned substantial personal and business assets in Guatemala were allegedly seized without confiscation through domestic proceedings alleging treasonous conduct by Mr Nottebohm against Guatemala, which he could not answer adequately by reason of his internment in the United States. In a subsequent dissenting judgment referring to this history Judge Read noted that 'In such circumstances I am bound to proceed on the assumption that Liechtenstein might be entitled to a finding of denial of justice, if the case should be considered on the merits'.[181]

After his release Mr Nottebohm travelled to and sought the diplomatic protection of Liechtenstein against Guatemala. Guatemala challenged Liechtenstein's ability to rely upon its naturalisation of Nottebohm in a claim brought against a country with which he had had a much stronger association. Mr Nottebohm was not able to rely upon connections he had developed through having taken up residence in Liechtenstein after release from internment, because of the so-called 'rule of continuous nationality', based upon the aim of deterrence of selective search for a State ready to exercise protection after the events to which a claim attaches: **1.143**

> [B]y the long-established rule of continuous nationality, no claimant is entitled to diplomatic protection of the State whose assistance is invoked unless such claimant was a national of that State at the time when the claim arose and continuously thereafter until the claim is presented.[182]

The same commentator cites UK policy in 1985: '[Her Majesty's Government] will not take up the claim unless the claimant is a United Kingdom national and was so at the date of the injury'.[183]

It was not contested that Mr Nottebohm at the date of the acts he complained of was a national of Liechtenstein under the laws of that State, or that Liechtenstein **1.144**

[181] Ibid, 34–35.

[182] Amerasinghe (n 14 above) 99, citing correspondence from the US Assistant Secretary of State for Congressional Relations to the Chairman of the House of Representatives Committee on Foreign Affairs, reprinted at (1982) 77 *American Journal of International Law* 836. For Amerasinghe's wider account of the continuous residence 'rule' see Amerasinghe (n 14 above) 96–106.

[183] Amerasinghe, ibid 98, citing C Warbrick, 'Protection of Nationals Abroad: Current Legal Problems' (1988) 37 *International & Comparative Law Quarterly* 1006.

had been entitled to grant nationality to him. But the Court did not regard this as creating a situation in which Guatemala was at the international level bound by the Liechtenstein naturalisation:

> It is for Liechtenstein, as it is for every sovereign State, to settle by its own legislation the rules relating to the acquisition of its nationality, and to confer that nationality by naturalization granted by its own organs in accordance with that legislation. It is not necessary to determine whether international law imposes any limitations on its freedom of decision in this domain ... Nationality serves above all to determine that the person upon whom it is conferred enjoys the rights and is bound by the obligations which the law of the State in question grants to or imposes on its nationals. This is implied in the wider concept that nationality is within the domestic jurisdiction of the State.
>
> But the issue which the Court must decide is not one which pertains to the legal system of Liechtenstein. It does not depend on the law or on the decision of Liechtenstein whether that State is entitled to exercise its protection, in the case under consideration. To exercise protection, to apply to the Court, is to place one-self on the plane of international law. It is international law which determines whether a State is entitled to exercise protection and to seise the Court.
>
> The naturalization of Nottebohm was an act performed by Liechtenstein in the exercise of its domestic jurisdiction. The question to be decided is whether that act has the international effect here under consideration.
>
> International practice provides many examples of acts performed by States in the exercise of their domestic jurisdiction which do not necessarily or automatically have international effect, which are not necessarily and automatically binding on other States or which are binding on them only subject to certain conditions: this is the case, for instance, of a judgment given by the competent court of a State which it is sought to invoke in another State.[184]

1.145 The majority found that Liechtenstein had no right to extend its protection to Nottebohm, because in order to be capable of being invoked against another State, nationality had to correspond with specific factual criteria not met in the instant case prior to the acts complained of:

> The character thus recognized on the international level as pertaining to nationality is in no way inconsistent with the fact that international law leaves it to each State to lay down the rules governing the grant of its own nationality. The reason for this is that the diversity of demographic conditions has thus far made it impossible for any general agreement to be reached on the rules relating to nationality, although the latter by its very nature affects international relations. It has been considered that the best way of making such rules accord with the varying demographic conditions in different countries is to leave the fixing of such rules to the competence of each State. On the other hand, a State cannot claim that the rules it has thus laid down are entitled to recognition by another State unless it has acted in conformity with this general aim of making the legal

184 *Nottebohm* case (*Liechtenstein v Guatemala*) [1955] ICJ Rep 4, 20–21.

> bond of nationality accord with the individual's genuine connection with the State which assumes the defence of its citizens by means of protection as against other States.
>
> ...
>
> According to the practice of States, to arbitral and judicial decisions and to the opinions of writers, nationality is a legal bond having as its basis a social fact of attachment, a genuine connection of existence, interests and sentiments, together with the existence of reciprocal rights and duties. It may be said to constitute the juridical expression of the fact that the individual upon whom it is conferred, either directly by the law or as the result of an act of the authorities, is in fact more closely connected with the population of the State conferring nationality than with that of any other State. Conferred by a State, it only entitles that State to exercise protection vis-à-vis another State, if it constitutes a translation into juridical terms of the individual's connection with the State which has made him its national.[185]

The Court's approach may have taken some aspects of the theory of 'effective nationality', normally used to distinguish amongst two or more countries of nationality, and referred to at paragraph 1.104 above, as a starting point for its approach, though it was not suggested that Mr Nottebohm had been a dual national—he had never taken Guatemalan citizenship and his German nationality fell away upon his naturalising in Liechtenstein. It found that the facts revealed 'on the one hand, the absence of any bond of attachment between Mr Nottebohm and Liechtenstein and, on the other hand, the existence of a long-standing and close connection between him and Guatemala, a link which his naturalization in no way weakened'. It concluded that there had at the relevant time been no sufficient bond of attachment, whereas there was 'a long-standing and close connection between him and Guatemala'. The naturalisation 'was lacking in the genuineness requisite to an act of such importance, if it is to be entitled to be respected by a State in the position of Guatemala. It was granted without regard to the concept of nationality adopted in international relations'. To the Court it was also important that the motive for naturalisation it ascribed to Nottebohm was to avoid the effect of the law of belligerency, 'to enable him to substitute for his status as a national of a belligerent State that of a national of a neutral State'. These appear to be matters the ICJ considered as vitiating the necessary claim by Liechtenstein that at the time of the acts complained of in 1943–45, Nottebohm was a national who could look to the protection of that country as against Guatemala. Given the circumstances there had not at that time been a 'social fact of attachment, a genuine connection of existence, interests, and sentiments' sufficient that Guatemala was required to acknowledge protection by Liechtenstein. Accordingly the ICJ concluded that 'Guatemala is under no obligation to recognize a nationality granted in such circumstances' and that 'Liechtenstein consequently is not entitled to extend its protection to Nottebohm vis-à-vis Guatemala and its claim must, for this reason, be held to be inadmissible'.[186] **1.146**

[185] Ibid, 20.
[186] Ibid, 26.

1.147 The decision remains controversial, and there is doubt as to the exact nature and extent of the principle or principles established by it. There was powerful dissent in Opinions by Judges Klaestad and Read and by Judge ad hoc Guggenheim.[187] The core principle of the majority appears to be that in bilateral proceedings the existence of a relevant bond is a precondition for attribution of nationality notwithstanding that its domestic law identifies that individual as a national.[188] This is the interpretation, *inter alia*, of Amerasinghe:

> [T]he principle [in the *Nottebohm* case] is at least limited to situations where, firstly, the person concerned has no genuine or effective connection with the claimant State and, secondly, where his connection with the respondent State is clearly genuine and more effective even though he may not have the nationality of that State. Not only is the second requirement a necessary feature of the rule but it is clear that relevance of a genuine link becomes one based on a comparison between the person's relationship with the respondent State and the claimant State.[189]

1.148 Subsequent international decisions have tended to ascribe a narrow reading to the *Nottebohm* judgement. In the 1958 decision of the Italian–United States Conciliation Commission in the *Flegenheimer claim* (1958) 25 ILR 91, the Commission argued that the ICJ had itself restricted the scope of its decision by affirming its relative nature. It further held that the requirement of an effective link was established for the sole purpose of resolving cases involving dual nationals, stating that

> when a person is vested with only one nationality, which is attributed to him or her either *iure sanguinis* or *iure soli*, or by a valid naturalization entailing the positive loss of the former nationality, the theory of effective nationality cannot be applied without the risk of causing confusion. It lacks a sufficiently positive basis to be applied to a nationality which finds support in a State law.[190]

1.149 The ILC in its 2006 'Draft Articles on Diplomatic Protection' at article 4 adopted a restrictive view:

> Article 4
>
> State of nationality of a natural person
>
> For the purposes of the diplomatic protection of a natural person, a State of nationality means a State whose nationality that person has acquired, in accordance with the law of that State, by birth, descent, naturalization, succession of States, or in any other manner, not inconsistent with international law.[191]

---

[187] Ibid 28, 34 and 50 respectively.

[188] See Crawford (ed), *Brownlie's Principles of Public International Law* (n 26 above) 513–18.

[189] Amerasinghe (n 14 above) 116.

[190] Italian–United States Conciliation Commission, *Flegenheimer claim* (1958) 25 ILR 91, 150.

[191] ILC, 'Draft Articles on Diplomatic Protection with Commentaries' (2006) in Report of the International Law Commission, Fifty-eighth Session (1 May–9 June and 3 July–11 August 2006) (UN Doc A/61/10) 17.

The Commentaries of the ILC are clear in their support for a restrictive understanding: 1.150

> (5) Draft article 4 does not require a State to prove an effective or genuine link between itself and its national, along the lines suggested in the *Nottebohm* case, as an additional factor for the exercise of diplomatic protection, even where the national possesses only one nationality. Despite divergent views as to the interpretation of the case, the Commission took the view that there were certain factors that served to limit *Nottebohm* to the facts of the case in question, particularly the fact that the ties between Mr Nottebohm and Liechtenstein (the Applicant State) were 'extremely tenuous' compared with the close ties between Mr Nottebohm and Guatemala (the Respondent State) for a period of over 34 years, which led the International Court of Justice to repeatedly assert that Liechtenstein was 'not entitled to extend its protection to Nottebohm vis-à-vis Guatemala'. This suggests that the Court did not intend to expound a general rule applicable to all States but only a relative rule according to which a State in Liechtenstein's position was required to show a genuine link between itself and Mr Nottebohm in order to permit it to claim on his behalf against Guatemala with whom he had extremely close ties.[192]

More recently the ICJ has returned to the issue of diplomatic protection and nationality in the *Ahmadou Sadio Diallo (Republic of Guinea v Democratic Republic of the Congo) Case* [2010] ICJ Reports 639. Mr Diallo was a businessman of Guinean nationality which he acquired at birth. He settled in the DRC from 1964 establishing a substantial business. He was arrested in the DRC in 1988–89 and held by state authorities, though no proceedings were pursued, and then in 1995–96 was arrested once more, detained and expelled. Guinea asserted its entitlement to exercise diplomatic protection of its national. The DRC did not challenge its ability to do so, which might be seen as a realistic acknowledgement that the *Nottebohm* principle would not extend to a situation in which the nationality of the protecting state was acquired by original rather than derivative means. 1.151

Although early writers, in particular during the interwar period, frequently use the language almost interchangeably, opposability may be seen either as parallel to wider principles of recognition across some part of its sphere of operation or as a special form of recognition within the law of diplomatic protection. Opposability is however not necessarily co-extensive with recognition, nor is the inverse proposition supportable. 1.152

A12. Nationality Documentation

Weis notes two forms of document as internationally accepted proofs of nationality: national passports and consular certificates.[193] Additionally, and 1.153

---

[192] Ibid, 32–33.
[193] Weis (n 2 above) 222.

notwithstanding that these are not formal proofs of nationality, some reference to birth certificates and kindred documents is justified. These forms of documentation are addressed in turn below.

i. National Passports and Travel Documents

1.154 The use of the term 'passport' has changed considerably over time. Sibley states that it was first used in an English statute in 1548 to denote a written permission for absence from duty given by a person in military authority to a soldier.[194] In the next century it was used for 'sea briefs' for shipping, and a treaty between the United Kingdom and Denmark in 1670 stated that 'letters of passport' might be required of travellers on land.[195] Thereafter, the term appears to have denoted, *inter alia*, documents issued by a State to resident aliens, a function described more recently in the course of submissions by the Attorney General to the House of Lords in 1945:

> [W]hen protection depended on the strong arm of the feudal lord, aliens were granted by the Crown an executive protection against our laws, the passport enabling them to pass freely in this country, protected from the ordinary operation of laws. which were highly restrictive and penal as regards foreigners. It was a document permitting them to travel within the state's own boundaries.[196]

1.155 It appears to have been only in the nineteenth century that the primary current usage of the term, as a national passport, or document issued by a State to its own nationals for purposes of travel abroad, came into common usage.[197] In *R v Brailsford* [1905] 2 KB 730 Lord Alverstone CJ provided a definition, subsequently quoted with approval by Lord Jowitt, delivering the majority decision in *Joyce v Director of Public Prosecutions* [1946] AC 347 at 369:

> The terms of a passport are familiar. It is thus described by Lord Alverstone CJ, in *R v Brailsford* (1): 'It is a document issued in the name of the sovereign on the responsibility of a minister of the Crown to a named individual, intended to be presented to the governments of foreign nations and to be used for that individual's protection as a British subject in foreign countries'.[198]

Lord Jowitt LC added (at 369), that a passport:

> by its terms … requests and requires in the name of His Majesty all those whom it may concern to allow to allow the bearer to pass freely without let or hindrance and to afford

[194] N Sibley, 'The Passport System' (1906) *Journal of the Society of Comparative Legislation* 26, 32.

[195] Ibid, 30; K Diplock, 'Passports and Protection in International Law' (1946) *Transactions of the Grotius Society* 42, 45.

[196] Record of submission by Hartley Shawcross AG in *Joyce v Director of Public Prosecutions* [1946] AC 347, 358, citing E Churchill, 'The Crown and the Alien' (1920) *36 Law Quarterly Review* 402.

[197] Weis (n 2 above) 223.

[198] *Joyce v Director of Public Prosecutions* [1946] AC 347, 369.

him every assistance and protection of which he may stand in need. It is, I think, true that the possession of a passport by a British subject does not increase the sovereign's duty of protection, though it will make his path easier. For him it serves as a voucher and means of identification.

Possession of a passport is not in every circumstance decisive as to nationality. As Plender noted: **1.156**

> State practice in the issuance of passports is so varied, however, that it is impossible to establish a connection in international law between the issuance of a passport and the acquisition or tenure of nationality. The problem is not merely that many States issue travel documents of various kinds to travellers of foreign nationality but that some States issue passports, in the strict sense of the term, to aliens of defined classes.[199]

Although a passport is not necessarily proof of nationality, it may and frequently will serve this purpose. In 1986 Grahl-Madsen indicated the breadth of conventions relating to passports, criticising broad statements as to the characteristics of a passport as rigid and contrary to actual international practice: **1.157**

> According to one traditional view, a passport is "a document of identity issued by a state, ordinarily to its own nationals, which requests foreign governments to grant the bearer safe and free passage and all lawful aid and protection while within their jurisdiction, and implicitly guarantees that they will be readmitted to the issuing country." This description offers little guidance in practical terms. A passport need not necessarily be issued by a state; it is not always trustworthy as an identity document or proof of citizenship; and it does not always contain an explicit request to foreign governments. It does, however, implicitly guarantee the readmittance of the bearer to the territory of the issuing (state) authority. A passport *could* be all the things suggested in the above description, but it *need* not be any of them.[200]

It is important to recognise that even a passport designed to evidence nationality is not more than that—the document is declaratory of a status or relationship (nationality) not constitutive of it. Whilst theoretically a State could shape a nationality law so that possession of a defined document was constitutive ('he or she is unconditionally a citizen if in present possession of a valid citizenship document') no example of this is known. **1.158**

A passport which does evidence nationality will generally be a primary means of demonstrating the possession of that nationality, though other documents may be relevant depending upon the circumstances. Paragraph 320(3) of the United Kingdom Immigration Rules (HC 395) for instance provides that the 'Grounds on which entry clearance or leave to enter the United Kingdom is to be refused' include 'failure by the person seeking entry to the United Kingdom to produce to the Immigration Officer a valid national passport or other document satisfactorily **1.159**

---

199 Plender, *International Migration Law* (n 5 above) 150.

200 A Grahl-Madsen, 'Protection of Refugees by their Country of Origin' (1986) 11 *Yale Journal of International Law* 362, 367. The internal quotation is from D Turack, *The Passport in International Law* (Heath, 1972) 15 in turn citing a 1953 statement of the Canadian Department of External Affairs.

establishing his identity and nationality', which reflects the modern importance of national passports without closing out the possibility of other fully equivalent documents, or of 'non-national' passports.

1.160 States may still issue passports or documents with equivalent functions to non-nationals, and the category of persons to whom such non-national passports may be issued is not coterminous with the group of those to whom diplomatic protection may be extended: a State may issue a passport even where international law would not allow it to extend diplomatic protection.[201]

ii. *Travel Documents*

1.161 Certain international agreements provide for the issuance by a State Party, and thereafter for mutual recognition of, documents for use in travel, meeting the function of national passports for those with access thereto. This practice notably grew after the First World War with 'Nansen passports' issued to denationalised Russian and other refugees as then defined, the 'London Travel Document' issued to refugees under the Agreement on the Adoption of a Travel Document for Refugees 1946 and, much more significantly as regards current practice, travel documents under article 28 CSR51 and its equivalent in CSSP54 respectively.[202] Each travel document under CSR51 or CSSP54 states on its face that 'This document is issued solely with a view to providing the holder with a travel document which can serve *in lieu* of a national passport. It is without prejudice to and in no way affects the holder's nationality'. Weis has said that 'The main features of the travel documents issued to non-nationals under international agreements are that they have to be recognised by the other Contracting States and that, as a rule, they entitle the holder to return to the issuing country'.[203]

iii. *Consular Certificates*

1.162 Weis employed this term compendiously to delineate certificates of registration issued by consular officers:

> [D]ocuments certifying that the holder has been entered in the register of nationals resident within the area for which the consulate is competent, and which is kept by the

---

[201] Plender, *International Migration Law* (n 5 above) 150.

[202] In *Tcherniak v Tcherniak*, decided by the Cour de Justice de Genève on 29 November 1927 (reproduced at Official Collection of Decisions, 54, II, 225; Annual Digest 1927–28, No de *Procès* 39), it was held for instance that 'the possession of a Nansen certificate was not proof of loss of Soviet nationality; the Nansen certificates were, according to international agreements, delivered to persons who did not enjoy the protection of the USSR; loss of protection did not, however, allow to conclude therefrom with certainty loss of nationality'. Cited Weis (n 2 above) 222, fn 9.

[203] Weis (n 2 above) 222.

> consular officer concerned ... The register is, therefore, primary evidence, the certificate secondary evidence, of the fact of registration as a national.[204]

Such registration is not in general required by international law, and any system of registration will be established by domestic law. It may have any of a number of purposes according to the priorities and laws of the State of nationality: monitoring or enabling contact with those nationals who have taken up residence in a foreign State or States, or some of them, enabling participation in domestic elections or other voting processes, or responding or enabling response to circumstances in the State of sojourn. Only some systems of registration will provide strong evidence of nationality. Registration may be mandatory or optional, depending upon the law of the State. For example, the US State Department now operates a website and database within its 'Smart Traveler Enrolment Program' allowing American citizens to register overseas residence or travel information, to enable it to assist and communicate with citizens in any particular territory or generally in the event of emergency.[205] Although registration in general takes place for municipal purposes, it may have important consequences, such as displacing a presumption of expatriation or enabling the passage of nationality to children born to a national residing outside his or her country of nationality. **1.163**

Evidential requirements for registration will be a matter of national law: they may include production of a valid passport, satisfaction of evidential requirements equivalent to those applicable to passports, or other criteria. The rigour of evidential requirements is likely to reflect the purpose of registration, and to reflect in whether registration is accepted as proof of nationality without more. **1.164**

iv. Birth Certificates or Other Documents

It will be obvious that evidence of birth is not direct evidence of nationality. But as Weis noted: **1.165**

> Another method of proving nationality has been the production of evidence of facts the existence of which confers nationality according to municipal law, *ie*, birth in the territory in *ius soli* countries, descent from parents possessing the nationality concerned in *ius sanguinis* countries, or of a combination of facts required as a condition for the possession of nationality under municipal law. In some cases, evidence of certain facts given by witnesses or an affidavit has been admitted in the absence of other evidence or as corroborative evidence.[206]

Because of this, deprivation of particular documentation, aimed at or with the effect of denying evidence which would prove entitlement to citizenship and **1.166**

---

[204] Ibid, 229.
[205] At: step.state.gov/step/.
[206] Weis (n 2 above) 216.

hence nationality, is a serious matter potentially impinging upon the fundamental rights of those affected. In *Yean and Bosico* [2005] Inter-AM Ct HR (series C) No 130 (8 September 2005) the Inter-American Court of Human Rights found that the State's failure to ensure birth certification for children of Haitian migrants breached several rights under the Inter-American Convention, including article 20 (right to nationality), article 24 (equality before the law), article 19 (protection of minor children) and article 1(1) (non-discrimination):

> 3. In its application, the Commission alleged that the State, through its Registry Office authorities, had refused to issue birth certificates for the Yean and Bosico children, even though they were born within the State's territory and that the Constitution of the Dominican Republic (hereinafter 'the Constitution') establishes the principle of *ius soli* to determine those who have a right to Dominican citizenship. The Commission indicated that the State obliged the alleged victims to endure a situation of continued illegality and social vulnerability, violations that are even more serious in the case of children, since the Dominican Republic denied the Yean and Bosico children their right to Dominican nationality and let them remain stateless persons until September 25, 2001.

A13. Proof of Nationality

1.167 In principle, proof of nationality falls to be dealt with within national law and practice. The claimant must establish his or her nationality as part of the claim, subject to the shared responsibility noted in the UNHCR *Handbook*[207] and appropriate evidential and procedural rules. The United Kingdom Immigration and Asylum Tribunal has held that nationality, where contested, must be established by the claimant as part of the proof of a claim: *K v SSHD (Afghanistan)* [2002] UKIAT 04412. This is unexceptionable, save that the ability of a claimant to do so must be understood in context. The essential framework will be a fair recognition of the potential complexity of nationality issues and of the relative roles and capabilities of both applicant and State of application. This requires the application, in a manner which is sensitive to the particular situation, of the principle identified in the *Handbook* as a 'shared duty':

> 196. It is a general legal principle that the burden of proof lies on the person submitting a claim. Often, however, an applicant may not be able to support his statements by documentary or other proof, and cases in which an applicant can provide evidence of all his statements will be the exception rather than the rule. In most cases a person fleeing from persecution will have arrived with the barest necessities and very frequently even without personal documents. Thus, while the burden of proof in principle rests on the applicant, the duty to ascertain and evaluate all the relevant facts is shared between the applicant

[207] UNHCR, *Handbook and Guidelines on Procedures and Criteria for Determining Refugee Status under the 1951 Convention and the 1967 Protocol relating to the Status of Refugees*, Reissued, Geneva, December 2011, §§74–76 [205].

and the examiner. Indeed, in some cases, it may be for the examiner to use all the means at his disposal to produce the necessary evidence in support of the application.

In many cases agents of a State which has a politicised or uncertain system of nationality law cannot be expected to be reliable or disinterested assistants (whether this is the country of origin or a country of possible dual nationality), and expectation of approach to state authorities may well be unreasonable where risk could result to some person through this—whether a claimant or family members or connections in the country of origin. Actions or statements of state authorities may have to be put in context with other evidenced facts: as for instance by a panel (SIJs PR Lane and S Ward) of the Upper Tribunal (Immigration and Asylum Chamber) in the United Kingdom in *ST (Ethnic Eritrean—nationality—return) Ethiopia CG* [2011] UKUT 252 (IAC), where a claimant who stated that she had been denationalised by Ethiopia had been accompanied to the Embassy by a lawyer to evidence her position: **1.168**

> 100. The interchange between the appellant and Mr Hart [the lawyer accompanying the appellant] and the Ethiopian Embassy in December 2010 fits well with the expert evidence, both as to the procedures and attitudes of the London Embassy and elsewhere. In particular, it chimes with the evidence of Mr Schröder, that the authorities 'had no interest whatsoever in getting back the 10,000 to 15,000 Eritreans who had fled Ethiopia for third countries'... The evidence of Mr Hart and the appellant is also compatible with the interviews held by Dr Campbell with Messrs Tesfaye and Haileselassie Suba.
>
> ...
>
> 113. Given the evidence we have already encountered about the arbitrary behaviour of the Ethiopian authorities, together with the evidence concerning the behaviour of embassy staff, and in the light of the background evidence, which discloses a generally problematic approach to the rule of law in Ethiopia, I find that there is considerable force in Mr Schröder's evidence regarding the way in which Article 22 of the 1999 Proclamation is applied in practice.

In some States asylum seekers are not expected to approach a country of origin prior to status determination, though in non-state persecution cases for example, this might be relaxed. Grahl-Madsen recognised the difficulties as early as 1966: **1.169**

> [I]n the case of refugees it is hardly feasible to apply to the authorities of the country where they fear persecution in order to have their national status authentically determined. The authorities of the country of refuge must therefore reach their decision by other means. In this connexion, laws and regulations in force in the refugee's country of origin, known decisions of the authorities of that country, the curriculum vitae of the applicant, and available documents, especially national passports, aliens passports, and other travel documents, may be of particular importance.[208]

One of the most reliable means of assessing foreign nationality laws will be advice of lawyers from that jurisdiction expert in its nationality law. But specialists in the field may be few or difficult to identify impartially, and lawyers in States where **1.170**

---

[208] A Grahl-Madsen, *The Status of Refugees in International Law*, vol I (AW Sijthoff, 1966) 155, §70.

nationality laws are politicised and the rule of law is imperfect may well themselves be unwilling or unable to provide advice to a foreign authority or regarding a person or situation of which the State in question has a strong view enforced by threat of official or unofficial sanction.[209] Even expert evidence provided in good faith and without negligence may conflict. In *Al-Jedda v SSHD* [2008] UKSIAC 66/2008 (23 May 2008), the United Kingdom Special Immigration Appeals Commission faced a division between experts. The primary question was whether the subject's Iraqi nationality had survived naturalisation in the United Kingdom in 2000 or had lapsed but been automatically restored by Iraqi legislation enacted after the fall of Saddam Hussain in 2003. If he remained an Iraqi national then the Secretary of State was not restrained by law from denationalising him. The Commission found that evidence of experts instructed on both sides failed to provide an adequate basis for decision, forcing it to seek its own interpretation of the original Iraqi legal materials adapting an approach to interpretation combining that evidence with domestic (United Kingdom) technique:

> 6. The result of these shortcomings in the expert evidence is that we cannot decide the critical questions of Iraqi law by reference only to the expert evidence which we have received. [Counsel] submits that, in those circumstances, we should reach our own conclusions about the meaning and effect of Iraqi law, applying English canons of construction to it. The task is made more difficult by the fact that the texts which we have to consider are in translation from the Arabic: and, as Mr Edge explained, Arabic words are often capable of bearing more than one meaning. The approach which we have adopted is to attempt, with the aid of Mr Edge and Judge Al Saedi, to discern the meaning and effect of Iraqi laws by applying a familiar domestic technique: to analyse the words used against the historical and statutory background in such a way as to give effect to the apparent intention of the legislators; and, in so doing, to attempt to resolve anomalies and absurdities in a way that does least violence to the language and apparent purpose of the laws.

The validity of that approach is undermined by the reference to adoption of potentially alien techniques of interpretation to decide a question concerning the laws of Iraq. Such a course (unless Iraqi law itself incorporates an interpretive technique similar to those of the United Kingdom jurisdictions) is contrary to the specific provisions of the Convention Relating to the Conflict of Nationality Laws 1930.

i. Presumption of Nationality from Passport

1.171 The UNHCR *Handbook on Procedures and Criteria for Determining Refugee Status* provides that:

> 93. Nationality may be proved by the possession of a national passport. Possession of such a passport creates a *prima facie* presumption that the holder is a national of the

[209] States of relevance in this regard include, in the relatively recent experience of the author, Bahrain, Myanmar and Saudi Arabia.

country of issue, unless the passport itself states otherwise. A person holding a passport showing him to be a national of the issuing country, but who claims that he does not possess that country's nationality, must substantiate his claim, for example, by showing that the passport is a so-called 'passport of convenience' (an apparently regular national passport that is sometimes issued by a national authority to non-nationals). However, a mere assertion by the holder that the passport was issued to him as a matter of convenience for travel purposes only is not sufficient to rebut the presumption of nationality. In certain cases, it might be possible to obtain information from the authority that issued the passport. If such information cannot be obtained, or cannot be obtained within reasonable time, the examiner will have to decide on the credibility of the applicant's assertion in weighing all other elements of his story.

The UNHCR *Handbook on Protection of Stateless Persons* sets out an equivalent but not identical advice: 1.172

95. Authentic, unexpired passports raise a presumption that the passport holder is a national of the country issuing the passport. However, this presumption may be rebutted where there is evidence showing that an individual is not actually considered to be a national of a State, for example where the document is a passport of convenience or the passport has been issued in error by an authority that is not competent to determine nationality issues. In such cases the passport is not a manifestation of a State's position that the individual is one of its nationals. No presumption is raised by passports that are counterfeit or otherwise fraudulently issued.[210]

The Immigration and Refugee Board of Canada in the 2010 version of its Interpretation of the Convention Refugee Definition states that: 1.173

2.1.2. Establishing Nationality

Each state determines under its own laws who are its nationals. Determining nationality is a question of fact. Nationality can be established by examining the relevant laws (constitution, citizenship legislation) and their interpretation (most authoritatively, by officials of the relevant government), and the state practice of the country in question. Possession of a national passport as well as birth in a country can create a rebuttable presumption that the claimant is a national of that country. However, the claimant can adduce evidence that the passport is one of convenience or that he or she is not otherwise entitled to that country's nationality. Recourse to paragraph 89 of the UNHCR *Handbook* is necessary only when a person's nationality cannot be clearly established.[211]

The guidance in the *Handbook on Procedures and Criteria for Determining Refugee Status* was relied upon by Shore J in the Canadian Federal Court in *Yah Abedalaziz v Canada (MCI)* [2011] FC 1066: 1.174

[42] Paragraph 93 of the *Handbook on Procedures and Criteria for Determining Refugee Status*, Geneva, September 1979, recognizes the existence of a *prima facie* presumption that a passport holder is a national of the country of issue. The mere assertion by the

[210] UNHCR, *Handbook on Protection of Stateless Persons* (n 119 above).

[211] Immigration and Refugee Board of Canada, *Interpretation of the Convention Refugee Definition in the Case Law, 31 December 2010, 4.3*, available at: www.irb-cisr.gc.ca/Eng/BoaCom/references/LegJur/Pages/RefDef.aspx.

passport holder that it was issued as a matter of convenience for travel purposes only is not sufficient to rebut the presumption of nationality (*Mathews v Canada (MCI)*, 2003 FC 1387, 127 ACWS (3d) 528 at paragraph 11; *Adar v Canada (MCI)* (1997), 1997 CanLII 16800 (FC), 132 FTR 35, 71 ACWS (3d) 1151).

[43] The RPD noted that the applicant had already held a Jordanian passport with a national identity number and had clearly claimed to be a Jordanian citizen. Therefore, the RPD drew a negative inference with respect to the credibility of the applicant, who claimed to be a Jordanian citizen and then went back on this statement:

...

[45] Based on the evidence submitted to the RPD, it was reasonable for the RPD to find that the applicant, a Palestinian who was born in Jordan, whose parents are Jordanian citizens, and who is a Jordanian passport holder, had not rebutted the presumption that the holder of a passport is a citizen of the issuing country.

1.175 The current United States Citizenship and Immigration Services (USCIS) Asylum Officer Basic Training Course provides, under the heading 'identifying nationality', the following guidance:

i. Passports

i. Presumption of nationality

Possession of a passport creates a presumption that the holder is a national of that country, unless the passport states otherwise.

ii. Overcoming the presumption of nationality

(i) There may be reliable information that a travel document or passport does not establish citizenship. The asylum officer must consider the circumstances under which the applicant obtained the passport and available information on whether a country issues passports to non-nationals.
(ii) Some countries have issued passports to non- nationals for the sole purpose of allowing these individuals to leave the country issuing the passport.
(iii) Some applicants have obtained passports through misrepresentation or payment of bribes.
(iv) An unsupported assertion by the holder that a passport was issued only for travel purposes is generally insufficient to rebut the presumption of nationality. However, an assertion that a passport is a travel document only, combined with information indicating that the issuing country issues passports to non-nationals for travel purposes, and a consistent and detailed explanation of the circumstances could rebut the presumption of nationality established by the passport.

When determining whether the presumption of citizenship created by the presentation of a passport is overcome, the officer must weigh all of the available evidence, including the applicant's testimony.[212]

---

[212] USCIS Asylum Officer Basic Training Course, *Asylum Eligibility Part I: Definitions; Past Persecution* 8–9, available at: www.uscis.gov/sites/default/files/USCIS/Humanitarian/Refugees%20%26%20Asylum/Asylum/AOBTC%20Lesson%20Plans/.

In *Palavra v INS*, 287 F 3d 690, 694 (8th Cir 2002), the Eighth Circuit of the US Court of Appeals by a majority found that the administrative authorities responsible for decision-making had materially erred in law, in failing to give adequate or any consideration to affidavit evidence that valid passports produced by the claimants in fact did not confirm possession of nationality. Circuit Judge Richard S Arnold set out the judgment of the majority: 1.176

> 8. No doubt the use of Croatian passports is evidence in support of the position taken by the BIA. All sides agree, however, that the passports are not conclusive. Their apparent effect—that their holders are citizens of Croatia—can be rebutted by other evidence. The BIA's opinion states that the Palavras 'have presented absolutely no evidence that the passports are not valid or in some way indicate anything less than full nationality and citizenship of Croatia'.
>
> 9. We can accept that the Croatian passports are 'valid', and that there is no reason to suppose that they are not. There is considerable evidence in this record, however, 'indicat[ing] [some]thing less than full nationality and citizenship of Croatia' ... According to the affidavit, which we have no reason to disbelieve at this point, all four of the Palavras were born in and lived in that part of Yugoslavia that is now Bosnia-Herzegovina. The family had lived there at least four generations. None of them had ever lived in Croatia, although they are ethnic Croatians. They wanted to come to the United States to get treatment for an eye condition for their son ... They were not able to obtain passports from the government of Bosnia-Herzegovina because of 'the strained situation between the ethnic Croats, which we were and are, and the Bosnian government and the majority ethnic group living in and controlling the Bosnian government' ... with the intervention of a government official, in a few days, 'Croatian passports were issued to us'... They owe no loyalty or allegiance to the country of Croatia, and have no connection to it either by residence or oath.
>
> 10. The affidavit explains that Croatian passports were issued to the Palavras as a humanitarian accommodation by the government of a country with which they had ethnic identification. We are at a loss to explain the statement of the BIA that this evidence in no way indicates anything less than full nationality and citizenship of Croatia. It seems to us that that is precisely what it indicates.

The decision provides a valuable example of the importance which should be attached in this context to avoiding fixed views, attention to context in examination of nationality law and practice in other countries, and achieving good understanding of the surrounding facts. Presumptions may be helpful but excessive or rote reliance upon these or other fixed rules is likely to be detrimental.

ii. Assessment of Evidence

In *Kim v Canada (MCI)* 2010 FC 720, Hughes J in the Canadian Federal Court, observed, in relation to the extent to which a refugee claimant can 'control' the award of citizenship in another country, that: 1.177

> [8] Such an issue eventually requires an examination of the laws, jurisprudence, practice and politics of that country. In a perfect world such an examination would be conducted

on the basis of one or more opinions of legal professionals entitled to practice in the relevant country and skilled in that area. These opinions are received as factual matters but involve questions of law.

[9] In a less than perfect world, where a refugee claimant usually has limited funds and resources and limited time to prepare a case, reference is made to other sources in deciding what may be the situation in the other country. In the present case, the Applicants were only advised a few days before the hearing that an issue would be made as to whether they could acquire South Korean citizenship.

1.178 Where questions of any complexity arise as to whether an individual possesses nationality a broad variety of evidence may be useful. This is a sphere in which, in the context of the 'shared burden' identified by the *Handbook*,[213] the differential capacities of the applicant and of the State considering the applicant's claim are highly relevant. The State may have information from its own consular officials or legal department, as well as from the State referred to in the claim, and frequently also has a greater capacity to identify and absorb evidence of third parties such as United Nations agencies or non-governmental organisations. As to the range of material which may be useful on issues of nationality, the UNHCR *Handbook on Protection of Stateless Persons* provides a relatively detailed guidance which, whilst particularly addressed to statelessness and requiring some adaption in the refugee context, is still useful:

(1) Types of evidence

83. Statelessness determination requires a mixed assessment of fact and law. Such cases cannot be settled through analysis of nationality laws alone as the definition of a stateless person requires an evaluation of the application of these laws in practice, including the extent to which judicial decisions are respected by government officials. The kinds of evidence that may be relevant can be divided into two categories: evidence relating to the individual's personal circumstances and evidence concerning the laws and other circumstances in the country in question.

84. Evidence concerning personal history helps identify which States and nationality procedures need to be considered in determining an applicant's nationality status. In any given case, the following non-exhaustive list of types of evidence may be pertinent:

— testimony of the applicant (eg written application, interview);
— response(s) from a foreign authority to an enquiry regarding nationality status of an individual;
— identity documents (eg birth certificate, extract from civil register, national identity card, voter registration document);
— travel documents (including expired ones);
— documents regarding applications to acquire nationality or obtain proof of nationality;
— certificate of naturalization;

[213] Para 196.

- certificate of renunciation of nationality;
- previous responses by States to enquiries on the nationality of the applicant;
- marriage certificate;
- military service record/discharge certificate;
- school certificates;
- medical certificates/records (eg attestations issued from hospital on birth, vaccination booklets);
- identity and travel documents of parents, spouse and children;
- immigration documents, such as residence permits of country(ies) of habitual residence;
- other documents pertaining to countries of residence (for example, employment documents, property deeds, tenancy agreements, school records, baptismal certificates); and
- record of sworn oral testimony of neighbours and community members.[214]

As indicated earlier (see section A5 above) the extent to which practice is relevant remains controversial.

In *Urgen v Holder* (2 October 2014) the Second Circuit of the United States Court of Appeals (Winter, Parker, Hall CJJ) held, on an application for review, that the Board of Immigration Appeals had erroneously insisted that an applicant establish his nationality through documentary evidence: **1.179**

> The government concedes that the BIA did not reach the issue of Urgen's credibility but argues that there was no need to consider his testimony because he failed to meet the threshold of establishing his 'Tibetan nationality'. Because Tibet is today part of the People's Republic of China, we understand the government and BIA's reference to 'Tibetan nationality' to mean 'Chinese nationality'. *See Dhoumo v BIA*, 416 F 3d 172, 175 (2d Cir 2005) (per curiam). Regardless, the practical consequence of the government's position is to impose a requirement that an asylum applicant establish his or her nationality through documentary evidence alone. While we have recognized that an applicant's 'nationality, or lack of nationality, is a threshold question in determining his eligibility for asylum', *id* at 174, there is no requirement that this showing be made through non-testimonial evidence. Such a requirement directly contradicts the statute and controlling precedent, and it 'ignore[s] the proposition that an applicant can meet his burden of proof based on credible testimony alone', *Zaman v Mukasey*, 514 F 3d 233, 238 n 4 (2d Cir 2008) (per curiam). *See* 8 USC § 1158(b)(1)(B)(ii) (providing that '[t]he testimony of the applicant may be sufficient to sustain the applicant's burden without corroboration'); *accord* 8 CFR § 1208.13(a). By failing to review the IJ's credibility determination, or otherwise consider Urgen's testimony, the BIA denied him the 'potential benefit' of establishing his asylum eligibility through credible testimony alone. *See Diallo v INS*, 232 F 3d 279, 287 (2d Cir 2000).

The principles to be applied to questions of nationality are mirrored in some other decisions in which nationality is not in question, but the effects thereof are considered to be critical. In *Lay Kon Tji v MIMA* [1998] FCA 1380, (1998) 158 ALR 681, **1.180**

214 UNHCR, *Handbook on Protection of Stateless Persons* (n 119 above).

Finkelstein J addressed evidence in the case going to whether Portugal, established as a country of nationality, would admit or otherwise deploy 'protection' of an East Timorese applicant for refugee status in Australia:

> This communique confirms what the Ambassador had previously advised the Department, namely that East Timoreans are not automatically regarded as Portuguese nationals. It indicates the view of Portugal that for an East Timorese to become a national he or she must make an application to become a national and that application may not be granted. If it does nothing else, this communique also demonstrates the potential danger confronting an Australian court or tribunal when determining the existence of an 'effective nationality' in the absence of a clear indication from the state concerned that the claimed nationality is recognised to exist. This is not to say that Australian courts and tribunals can avoid their obligation to determine such issues when they come up for consideration. But it serves to emphasise that questions such as are here under consideration must be approached with a good deal of caution because of the potentially serious consequences that may flow from a wrong decision.

iii. Expectation of Application to Authorities of State in Certain Circumstances

1.181 In the Scottish case of *R v SSHD ex p Bradshaw* [1994] Imm AR 359, Lord MacLean, sitting in the Outer House of the Court of Session, considered the petition of a former citizen of the USSR who was living in the United Kingdom when her State of nationality collapsed and the Russian Federation and the Ukraine were established. She obtained indefinite leave to remain by a deceit, asserting that she continued to cohabit with her Scottish husband when they had in fact separated. After this emerged in the context of divorce proceedings, action was taken by the Home Office to curtail her continuing stay. Having failed to challenge the finding by the Secretary of State of dishonesty, which supported the further conclusion that she was an illegal entrant to the United Kingdom, she also asserted that she was stateless. She had not made any application to either of the successor States and through her counsel stated that she did not wish to. At 366–67 Lord MacLean observed that:

> Since questions of foreign law are in issue I am not prepared to reach an opinion without either hearing oral evidence or receiving affidavits from those authoritatively qualified to advise me on the nationality laws of the Russian federation and the Ukraine. Besides, it seems to me that before a person can be said to be stateless in terms of the definition in [CSSP54], he or she would have had to apply to those states which might consider her to be and might accept her as a national. It would be surprising if the Ukraine did not accept her as a national, if she were to apply to them. After all, she enters the Ukraine freely, it appears. Indeed, I was left with the suspicion ... that the petitioner did not wish to obtain the nationality of either state lest that diminished her chances of remaining within the United Kingdom.

1.182 *Bradshaw* was not a refugee case. In *Bouianova v Canada (MEI)* (1993) 67 FTR 74 Rothstein J prior to rejecting the argument of the applicant that she should not be treated as a national of the Russian Federation, following the collapse of the USSR, attached considerable weight to the apparent election not to make enquiries with the Russian authorities. On the facts there was no question of fear of persecution as from the Russian Federation:

> I do not think the necessity of making an application, which in these circumstances is nothing more than a mere formality, means that a person does not have a country of nationality just because they chose not to make such an application.

In a subsequent refugee case in England, *Tecle v SSHD* [2002] EWCA Civ 1358, the Court of Appeal concluded that on the facts a subordinate tribunal had been entitled to treat as relevant to credibility the failure of the applicant, who had been born in Eritrea and whose claim was based upon acts of the Ethiopian authorities, to ascertain her standing vis-a-vis Eritrea by direct approach to the authorities. Although an asylum case, it was one in which the applicant's fear of persecution was not directed against Eritrea: **1.183**

> 23. In my judgment, given the material from the British Embassy which was before the adjudicator and the Tribunal in this case, the Tribunal was entitled, having regard to that and having regard to the CIPU report, to take an adverse view of the fact that the appellant, on whom the burden of proof lay, had not contacted the Eritrean Embassy in London and made an application, supported by the appropriate witnesses, for citizenship.

Later, in a materially similar case, the United Kingdom Immigration Appeal Tribunal in *YL (Nationality, Statelessness, Eritrea, Ethiopia) Eritrea CG* [2003] UKIAT 00016 observed that the observations of Lord MacLean could not be read directly across to such cases: **1.184**

> 46. We would accept that in asylum cases the *Bradshaw* principle has to be qualified to take account of whether there are valid reasons for a claimant not approaching his or her embassy or consulate—or the authorities of the country direct—about an application for citizenship or residence. In some cases such an approach could place the claimant or the claimant's family at risk, because for example it would alert the authorities to the fact that the claimant has escaped pursuit by fleeing the country. However, by no means can there be a blanket assumption that for all claimants such approaches would create or increase risk. It is a matter to be examined on the evidence in any particular case. The 1979 UNHCR Handbook does not require a different position to be taken: paragraph 93 clearly contemplates a case-by-case approach.

In *Canada (MCI) v Williams* [2005] FCA 126, [2005] 3 FCR 429, 253 DLR (4th) 449, the Canadian Federal Court of Appeal (Décary, Létourneau and Nadon JJA) held that an individual was expected to seek recourse to a state of nationality or potential nationality. The judgment of Décary JA, concurred in by other members of the panel, endorsed observations in the earlier *Bouianova* decision: **1.185**

> [22] This 'control' test also reflects the notion which is transparent in the definition of a refugee that the 'unwillingness' of an applicant to take steps required from him to gain state protection is fatal to his refugee claim unless that unwillingness results from the very fear of persecution itself.

Hathaway and Foster have identified the potential for serious error, were a decision like *Tecle* or *Williams* erroneously understood as creating or pointing to a principle that a perceived failure to take relevant steps in itself justifies rejection of a protection claim: in this context the impact of conduct is best understood as a matter which may go to the ability of an applicant to make good her case evidentially.[215] At least in *Tecle* and *MA (Ethiopia)* this appears to have been the position: in *Tecle* 'the Tribunal was entitled … to take an adverse view of the fact that the appellant, on whom the burden of proof lay, had not contacted the Eritrean Embassy in London' and this is echoed in *MA (Ethiopia)*. In each case the observation affirms the justification, in context, for the drawing of a negative inference.

1.186 The *Bradshaw* decision, or the underlying principle as understood subsequently, was applied later by McLaughlin J in *Fedorovski, Re Judicial Review* [2007] NIQB 119 [2008] NI 193. The Court of Appeal of England and Wales applied the same principle, citing *Bradshaw*, in *MA (Ethiopia) v SSHD* [2009] EWCA Civ 289, [2010] INLR 1. This was an asylum case, in which the appellant claimed to have been denationalised and excluded from Ethiopia. In one of the two substantial judgments Elias LJ, with whom Mummery and Stanley Burnton LJJ concurred on the point, observed that:

> 50. In my judgment, where the essential issue before the AIT is whether someone will or will not be returned, the Tribunal should in the normal case require the applicant to act *bona fide* and take all reasonably practicable steps to seek to obtain the requisite documents to enable her to return. There may be cases where it would be unreasonable to require this, such as if disclosure of identity might put the applicant at risk, or perhaps third parties, such as relatives of the applicant who may be at risk in the home state if it is known that the applicant has claimed asylum. That is not this case, however. There is no reason why the appellant should not herself visit the embassy to seek to obtain the relevant papers. Indeed, as I have said, she did so but wrongly told the staff there that she was Eritrean.

Stanley Burnton LJ commented:

> 83. The Tribunal was entitled, having regard to that and having regard to the CIPU report, to take an adverse view of the fact that the appellant, on whom the burden of proof lay, had not contacted the Eritrean Embassy in London and made an application.

1.187 The judgment notably accepts that there will be circumstances in which it is not reasonable to expect an approach to be made, as where the applicant or others might be put at risk by this. The unfortunate complication to this is that it may be difficult to show that the making of an enquiry would involve negative

[215] J Hathaway and M Foster, *The Law of Refugee Status* (2nd edn, CUP, 2014) 62.

consequences, because the overall credibility of the applicant needed to establish this is held by circular reasoning to depend upon the fact of the enquiry. Also, the finding as to whether the claimant has good reason for failing to approach the relevant diplomatic authorities may not be made before the decisive hearing, so that the claimant cannot measure whether to make an approach after a rejection of the claim to good reason for refraining. There is also the problem that an individual's actions in approaching the agents of his or her putative State may be viewed as provocative, and perhaps as an attempt to establish a claim to refugee status *sur place* so that the claimant is left in the position of facing imputations on his or her credibility whatever is done.

Later, in *GP & Ors (South Korean citizenship) North Korea CG* [2014] UKUT 391, the Upper Tribunal (Mr Ockelton, UTJ Gleeson), affirmed the existence of a 'general duty' to approach the relevant authorities, the context being contemplated reference by the North Korean appellant to the South Korean authorities in relation to whom there was no basis for fear of persecution or retribution, so a general duty actually applicable in particular circumstances, as for instance where no danger to any person could be created by the making of the approach. Whilst there is in general good reason why an individual should be expected to make good a claim he or she raises as regards nationality status, any 'general duty' is in fact logically circumscribed by the particular considerations such as practicality (there may be no diplomatic representation in the receiving State), whether the evidence is in any event clear so that enquiry would be nugatory, and the avoidance of risk to an applicant or to third parties, as identified by the Tribunal in *YL* and by Elias LJ in *MA (Ethiopia)*. In relation to such enquiries the UNHCR *Handbook on Protection of Stateless Persons* provides that: **1.188**

> (7) Enquiries with and responses from foreign authorities
>
> 96. Information provided by foreign authorities is sometimes of central importance to statelessness determination procedures, although not necessary in cases where there is otherwise adequate proof. Under no circumstances is contact to be made with authorities of a State against which an individual alleges a well-founded fear of persecution unless it has definitively been concluded that he or she is neither a refugee nor entitled to a complementary form of protection.
>
> ...
>
> 98. Where statelessness determination authorities make enquiries with foreign authorities regarding the nationality or statelessness status of an individual, they must consider the weight to be attached to the response or lack of response from the State in question.

In *SSHD v SP (North Korea) & Ors* [2012] EWCA Civ 114, the Court of Appeal in England and Wales (Maurice Kay VP, McFarlane and Davis LJJ) rejected the appeal of the Secretary of State from the decision in *KK and others*. One of the grounds of appeal was built upon the suggestion that, although no adjournment of the hearing below had been sought by the Secretary of State, the Tribunal had **1.189** proceeded prematurely because the South Korean authorities had not already refused by that time to acknowledge as their nationals the North Korean applicants, and the Tribunal had relied upon estimates of probability or possibility by experts rather than on definitive official statements. The Court rejected this. It noted that the applicants were accepted as having approached the Embassy of South Korea in good faith, in contrast to *MA (Ethiopia)* where the contrary was found, and that the Tribunal had been entitled to decide the question on the basis of the evidence put before it by the parties. According to Maurice Kay VP, with whom McFarlane and Davis LJJ concurred:

> 29. Two points arise from this. First, in terms of *MA (Ethiopia)*, the appellants have acted *bona fide* and taken all reasonably practicable steps to seek to obtain the requisite documents to enable them to be recognized as nationals of South Korea. Secondly, they instituted appeals which, in principle, fell to be determined in accordance with all the circumstances at the time of the hearing in the Tribunal. It seems to me that, in the light of all this, the Tribunal was entitled to reach the conclusions it reached at the time when it reached them. Mr Manjit Gill [QC] makes a further point which also has some significance. Faced with these cases, the Secretary of State did little on a diplomatic level to try to force the issue with the Embassy. On the evidence, all that was done was to write a last minute letter which, in the event, asked the wrong question, focusing on the Protection Act. No adjournment was sought. This approach left the Tribunal to determine the cases on the material before it which, in my judgment, justified the conclusions. They were, in *MA (Ethiopia)* terms, 'brick wall' cases which the appellants were entitled to have determined in the light of current circumstances.

1.190 In summary, there is good reason why in general a country considering a claim to protection under CSR51 should be able to expect active co-operation from a claimant in ascertaining his or her nationality, including in appropriate circumstances approach to the authorities of a country nationality of which is in question. A claimant might well expect that an unreasonable refusal to provide such co-operation could lead to application of a summary procedure, or support a negative inference as to credibility. However, this should be seen in the context of the 'shared duty' in ascertainment and evaluation of relevant facts, in which context the UNHCR *Handbook* has stated specifically that 'Indeed, in some cases, it may be for the examiner to use all the means at his disposal to produce the necessary evidence in support of the application'. Just as appropriate co-operation may be expected of the applicant, it is inappropriate, given the object of CSR51, that the State responsible for the claim should fail to assist adequately, especially in those respects in which it has a capacity not accessible to, or much greater than, that of the applicant. Further, there remains a need not to escalate any perceived duty beyond its obvious justification in some cases. Insofar as a 'requirement' exists, this is almost certainly a matter potentially going to credibility or evidence, rather than a positive legal obligation in all circumstances, and the relevant situation requires assessment on a case by case basis.

B. Nationality and Citizenship

B1. Distinction of Nationality from, and Relation to, Citizenship and Equivalent Status

The concept of citizenship (the term is adopted here as also covering other terms used for the same concept, such as subject status) is parallel but not identical to nationality. Each denotes legal affiliation to, or membership of, a State. Nationality identifies a person's relationship with a State for purposes of international law, whilst citizenship identifies the relationship of membership, created by national laws, between a particular person and his or her State. As Weis has said: 'Conceptually and linguistically, the terms "nationality" and "citizenship" emphasise two different aspects of the same notion: State membership. "Nationality" stresses the international, "citizenship" the national, municipal, aspect'.[216] Despite this the terms are often used interchangeably. This is understandable, because in the vast majority of cases citizenship and nationality co-exist, and the existence of nationality follows from the possession of citizenship. The removal of citizenship generally constitutes a withdrawal of nationality as well: though the Nazi law of 1935 provides an illustration of the possibility that it may not do so in a specific case. 1.191

Citizenship, which arises under domestic law, therefore is not defined in international law. In most States possession of citizenship connotes full membership, including the possession of political rights. Hirsch Ballin emphasises the importance of citizenship as a standard for legal membership which is at least potentially free of tribal or ethnic colouring: '[an epochal change] is that citizenship marks the end of the subjection of people to the political, tribal, ethnic, or religious entities to which they have been subordinated for centuries, based upon a specific single identity'.[217] 1.192

Some States have distinguished amongst different classes of membership, treating some classes as bound by duties to the State but as having diminished entitlements as holders of a less favoured form of citizenship or as non-citizen subjects.[218] 1.193

The rights and duties of citizenship are defined by national law. The right of citizens to enter into and remain in the territory of a State is a universal or virtually universal practice now promoted at the international level by IHRL provisions such as article 12(4) ICCPR66 ('No one shall be arbitrarily deprived of the right to enter his own country'). Other important rights assigned to citizens under domestic law may include those connected to political participation. Citizens may also have duties under domestic law: for instance that of performing military service. 1.194

---

[216] Weis (n 2 above) 5.
[217] Hirsch Ballin (n 76 above) 83.
[218] Weis (n 2 above) 5.

B2. Acquisition and/or Loss of Citizenship

1.195 Acquisition and/or loss of citizenship is provided for by national law. International standards apply to attribution of nationality, but these do not go to the validity in national law of conduct concerning citizenship. Such conduct may however breach human rights instruments at the domestic, regional, or international level.

B3. Regional Citizenship

1.196 In recent decades some regional organisations have moved to create a collective citizenship. In each case so far the possession of that citizenship is secondary to citizenship of a Member State, and the rights and duties accruing to citizenship are established either in international law or in domestic provisions built to enact a common scheme State by State. The 1975 Treaty Establishing the Economic Community of West African States (ECOWAS) created the first such scheme, article 27(1) thereof ('visa and residence') providing that 'Citizens of Member States shall be regarded as Community citizens and accordingly Member States undertake to abolish all obstacles to their freedom of movement and residence within the Community'. Article 27(2) provides that 'Member States shall by agreements with each other exempt Community citizens from holding visitors' visas and residence permits and allow them to work and undertake commercial and industrial activities within their territories'.

1.197 The most advanced regime of regional citizenship currently is that in place in the European Union. The 1992 Treaty on European Union created 'citizenship of the Union', which like ECOWAS citizenship is not free-standing, but secondary to possession of the nationality of a Member State. After consolidation the relevant provision is now at article 20 of the Treaty on the Functioning of the European Union:

> 1. Citizenship of the Union is hereby established. Every person holding the nationality of a Member State shall be a citizen of the Union. Citizenship of the Union shall be additional to and not replace national citizenship.
> 2. Citizens of the Union shall enjoy the rights and be subject to the duties provided for in the Treaties … These rights shall be exercised in accordance with the conditions and limits defined by the Treaties and by the measures adopted thereunder.

1.198 The Court of Justice of the European Union (CJEU) has found it to be for each Member State, 'having due regard to Community law, to lay down the conditions for the acquisition and loss of nationality': Case C-369/90 *Mario Vicente Micheletti and others v Delegacion del Gobierno en Cantabria* [1992] ECR I-4239. In Case C-192/99 *R (Kaur) v SSHD* [2001] ECR I-1237, the CJEU reaffirmed this, ruling that national citizenship laws determined the scope of the Treaty *ratione personae*. The Court has since held that the loss of the nationality of a Member State may be subject to procedural guarantees of EU law: Case C-135/08 *Rottmann v*

Freistaat Bayern [2010] ECR I-1449, [2010] QB 761. At [39] the Court observed that 'according to established case-law, it is for each Member State, having due regard to Community law, to lay down the conditions for the acquisition and loss of nationality', but it went on to note at [45] that 'the Member States must, when exercising their powers in the sphere of nationality, have due regard to European Union law', so that EU law procedural standards come to bear.[219]

It is not clear that the institution of regional citizenship has any effect as regards nationality on the international law plane. 1.199

C. Statelessness

C1. Definition of Statelessness

To be stateless in general terms is to be without an attachment to a State as a national. Because nationality arises from the domestic law of States, the absence of such attachment has to be determined by reference to national laws. Weis has said that 'a person not having a nationality under the law of any State is called stateless, *apatride*, *apolide*, or *heimatlos*'.[220] An individual may become stateless in any of several ways, for example, being born in circumstances in which he or she does not acquire nationality under national laws either by birth on the territory (*ius soli*) or by descent (*ius sanguinis*), or conversely by having one or more nationalities which are removed by the State or States of nationality. 1.200

As Edwards and van Waas have noted, 1.201

> [t]he phenomenon of statelessness, or the lack of recognition as a national of any State, is intrinsically linked to broader questions surrounding the regulation and content of nationality. The study of statelessness... goes hand in hand with an exploration of nationality law.[221]

Statelessness has been a substantial concern of the international community almost continuously since the aftermath of the First World War and the large-scale denationalisations which occurred thereafter. Through much of this period there was a broad identification of statelessness with the term 'refugee', the underlying commonality being the inability to look to a country of nationality for protection. At its Sixth Session, in 1948, the United Nations Economic and Social 1.202

219 This has been rejected in England and Wales by the Court of Appeal in *G1 (Sudan) v SSHD* [2012] EWCA Civ 867, [2013] QB 1008. In *Pham v SSHD* [2015] UKSC 19, [2015] 1 WLR 1591 the United Kingdom Supreme Court declined to come to any conclusive view prior to adjudication of the points by a junior appellate body.

220 Weis (n 2 above) 161.

221 Edwards and van Waas (n 118 above) 2.

Council adopted a resolution requesting the Secretary-General, in consultation with interested commissions and specialised agencies to:

> [U]ndertake a study of the existing situation in regard to the protection of stateless persons by the issuance of necessary documents and other measures, and to make recommendations to an early session of the Council on the interim measures which might be taken by the United Nations to further this object' in conjunction with a survey of national legislation and international agreements and conventions relevant to statelessness, and recommendations as to the advisability of a new convention on the subject.[222]

The resultant 1949 *Study of Statelessness* of the United Nations Ad Hoc Committee on Refugees and Stateless Persons, was broadly focused on the extant problem, of large numbers of persons in and around Europe left either without a nationality or unable or unwilling to return to or rely upon the protection of a country of nationality. The *Study* divided those referred to as 'stateless' into two 'categories': *de jure* and *de facto*:

> III *DE JURE* and *DE FACTO* STATELESS PERSONS
>
> ...
>
> i. Stateless persons *de jure* are persons who are not nationals of any State, either because at birth or subsequently they were not given any nationality, or because during their lifetime they lost their own nationality and did not acquire a new one.
> ii. Stateless persons *de facto* are persons who, having left the country of which they were nationals, no longer enjoy the protection and assistance of their national authorities, either because these authorities refuse to grant them assistance and protection, or because they themselves renounce the assistance and protection of the countries of which they are nationals. The Constitution of the IRO in its Annex I (First part—Section A.2) uses this formula: 'a person ... who ... is unable or unwilling to avail himself of the protection of the Government of his country of nationality or former nationality'.

1.203 The *Study of Statelessness* noted an essential commonality between the two groups (inability to rely upon national protection and assistance). In the case of *de jure* stateless persons this was by reason of the absence of any State of nationality. In the case of the *de facto* stateless this was because protection and assistance were not relevantly available from a State of nationality. A major step in seeking to address the problems it identified was the creation of a new international refugee law convention, CSR51, albeit this focused upon a subset of those then termed refugees—in essence retaining in the protected class only those identified as refugees under earlier instruments (article 1A(1)) and those outside countries of nationality (of former habitual residence, if stateless) and unable or unwilling to avail themselves of the protection of those countries by reason of well-founded

---

[222] United Nations Economic and Social Council Resolution 116(VI)D, dated 1 and 2 March 1948 (Resolutions adopted by the Economic and Social Council during its Sixth Session (2 February to 11 March 1948) 18).

fear of persecution for a relevant reason (article 1A(2)). Those identified as refugees under article 1A(2) CSR51 are in effect a selective subset of part of each of the categories noted in the *Study*, the core characteristic now being alienage and inability or unwillingness to return due to well-founded fear of persecution for a relevant reason.

In 1952 the ILC examined the international law of nationality, expressly including statelessness. The Special Rapporteur, Manley O Hudson, noted an essential distinction between the classes of case distinguished in the *Study of Statelessness*: **1.204**

> In a 'Study of Statelessness' prepared by the Secretariat a distinction is made between stateless persons *de jure* and stateless persons *de facto* (pp 8, 9). The former are described as 'persons who are not nationals of any State'.
>
> ...
>
> Such a distinction may have been useful for the purpose for which the study was made; it has, however, no place in the present paper. *Stateless persons in the legal sense of the term are persons who are not considered as nationals by any State according to its law.* The so-called stateless persons are *de facto* nationals of a State who are outside of its territory and devoid of its protection; they are, therefore, not stateless: it might be better to speak of '*unprotected persons*' and to call this group '*de facto unprotected persons*', in distinction to '*de jure unprotected persons*', *ie*, stateless persons. Refugees may be stateless or not; in the first case they are *de jure* unprotected persons; in the latter, *de facto* unprotected. The present paper deals exclusively with statelessness in the strict, legal sense of the term.[223]

Hudson's observation remains true, in that *de jure* statelessness is a concept of law (statelessness) possessing a long provenance and based upon the absence of nationality. By contrast the term '*de facto* statelessness' may be used as a descriptive term identifying a category of cases, as in the 1949 *Study*. But it is more generally employed in a somewhat wider sense to denote a situation in which the individual is not *de jure* stateless (not, that is, stateless at all), but is perceived as deprived of incidents otherwise attached to nationals, notably diplomatic protection and/or entry or return to the state of nationality. **1.205**

The term 'stateless person' is defined at article 1(1) of CSSP54 ('For the purpose of this Convention, the term "stateless person" means a person who is not considered as a national by any State under the operation of its law') in terms which closely resemble those used by Hudson as Special Rapporteur ('Stateless persons in the legal sense of the term are persons who are not considered as nationals by any State according to its law'). CSSP54 shares many features with CSR51, and was originally conceived, after the decision to proceed with a narrow refugee convention rather than a broader instrument addressing the position of all other persons without national protection or assistance, as a draft Protocol to CSR51. However, when CSR51 was adopted, the draft Protocol was referred to a separate negotiating **1.206**

223 MO Hudson, 'Report on Nationality, Including Statelessness' (UN Doc A/CN.4/50). Extract from the *Yearbook of the International Law Commission*, vol II (1952) 17.

conference where it was transformed into a self-standing treaty concerning stateless persons. Most importantly for present purposes, CSSP54 established the definition of a 'stateless person' in its article 1(1). This is in essence the *de jure* stateless definition identified in the *Study*, though the addition of the phrase 'the operation of its law' potentially admits not only particular forms of law such as statute or decree, but also a somewhat broader range of factors arising from state practice. It is not clear to what degree the possibility of arbitrariness is accommodated in the CSSP54 definition by the phrase 'the operation of its law', though as set out below the United Kingdom Supreme Court has had to consider this.

1.207 In May 2010 an Expert Meeting organised by the Office of the UNHCR was held at Prato in Italy. The conclusions published subsequently, broadly reflecting the understandings emerging from discussion amongst experts, included the following 'General Considerations' as regards the CSSP54 definition:

> 3. The issue under Article 1(1) is not whether or not the individual has a nationality that is effective, but whether or not the individual has a nationality at all. Although there may sometimes be a fine line between being recognized as a national but not being treated as such, and not being recognized as a national at all, the two problems are nevertheless conceptually distinct: the former problem is connected with the rights attached to nationality, whereas the latter problem is connected with the right to nationality itself.[224]

1.208 The Prato conclusions represent an important body of opinion relating to statelessness, understood conclusively as *de jure* statelessness. As to the meaning of the phrase 'not considered as a national ... under the operation of its law' they record:

> 9. For the purposes of the 1954 Convention, 'national' is to be understood by reference to whether the State in question regards holders of a particular status as persons over whom it has jurisdiction on the basis of a link of nationality. Several participants were of the view that in practice it is difficult to differentiate between the possession of a nationality and its effects, including, at a minimum, the right to enter and reside in the State of nationality and to return to it from abroad, as well as the right of the State to exercise diplomatic protection. Otherwise, according to this view, nationality is emptied of any content.
>
> 10. Article 1(1) does not require a 'genuine and effective link' with the State of nationality in order for a person to be considered as a 'national'. The concept of 'genuine and effective link' has been applied principally to determine whether a State may exercise diplomatic protection in favour of an individual with dual or multiple nationalities, or where nationality is contested. It is therefore possible to be a 'national' even if the State of nationality is one in which the individual was neither born nor habitually resides. The relevant criterion is whether the State in question considers a person to be its national.
>
> ...
>
> 15. 'Under the operation of its law' should not be confused with 'by operation of law', a term which refers to automatic (*ex lege*) acquisition of nationality. Thus, in interpreting

[224] UNHCR, *Expert Meeting* (n 56 above) 2.

the term 'under the operation of its law' in Article 1(1), consideration has to be given to non-automatic as well as automatic methods of acquiring and being deprived of nationality.

...

20. The definition in Article 1(1) refers to a factual situation, not to the manner in which a person became stateless. Voluntary renunciation of nationality does not preclude an individual from satisfying the requirements of Article 1(1) as there is no basis for reading in such an implied condition to the definition of 'stateless person'. Nonetheless, participants noted that diverging approaches have been adopted by States. It was also noted that the manner in which an individual became stateless may be relevant to his or her treatment following recognition and for determining the most appropriate solution.

21. The consequences of a finding of statelessness for a person who could acquire nationality through a mere formality are different from those for a person who cannot do so and a distinction should be drawn in the treatment such persons receive post-recognition. On the one hand, there are simple, accessible and purely formal procedures where the authorities do not have any discretion to refuse to take a given action, such as consular registration of a child born abroad. On the other hand, there are procedures in which the administration exercises discretion with regard to acquisition of nationality or where documentation and other requirements cannot reasonably be satisfied by the person concerned.

The UNHCR subsequently published three sets of Guidelines concerning statelessness. These were superseded in June 2014 by a new UNHCR *Handbook on Protection of Stateless Persons*.[225] **1.209**

The CSSP54 definition has in recent years been examined in litigation in the United Kingdom, where section 40 of the British Nationality Act 1981 (BNA 1981) as amended provides that individuals may be derived of nationality on the basis that 'the Secretary of State is satisfied that deprivation is conducive to the public good' (section 40(2) BNA 1981) but the Secretary of State is prevented from doing so where satisfied that the order would make a person stateless (section 40(4) BNA 1981). In *SSHD v Al-Jedda* [2013] UKSC 62, [2014] 1 AC 253 Lord Wilson, with whom Lord Neuberger, Lady Hale, Lord Mance and Lord Carnwath agreed, rebuffed in strong terms the submission that an individual might be identified as not stateless because the cause of loss of, or failure to acquire, nationality was argued as resulting from unhelpful conduct or omission by the subject: **1.210**

32. I reject this argument. Section 40(4) does not permit, still less require, analysis of the relative potency of causative factors. In principle, at any rate, the inquiry is a straightforward exercise both for the Secretary of State and on appeal: it is whether the person holds another nationality at the date of the order. Even that inquiry may prove complex, as the history of these proceedings demonstrates. But a facility for the Secretary of State to make an alternative assertion that, albeit not holding another nationality at the date of the order, the person could, with whatever degree of ease and speed, re-acquire another

[225] UNHCR, *Handbook on Protection of Stateless Persons* (n 119 above).

> nationality would mire the application of the subsection in deeper complexity. In order to make his argument less unpalatable to its audience, Mr Swift, as already noted, limited it to the re-acquisition of a former nationality, as opposed to the acquisition of a fresh nationality. But, with respect, the limitation is illogical; if valid, his argument would need to extend to the acquisition of a fresh nationality. Yet a person might have good reason for not wishing to acquire a nationality available to him (or possibly even to re-acquire a nationality previously held by him).

1.211 As already noted, it is not clear to what degree the possibility of arbitrariness is accommodated in the CSSP54 definition by the phrase 'the operation of its law', though as set out below the United Kingdom Supreme Court has had to consider this in *Pham v SSHD* [2015] UKSC 19, [2015] 1 WLR 1591, another nationality deprivation case. In *Pham*, Lord Carnwath, with whom Lord Neuberger, Lady Hale and Lord Wilson agreed, found that:

> 38. I would accept that the question arising under article 1(1) of the 1954 Convention in this case is not necessarily to be decided solely by reference to the text of the nationality legislation of the state in question, and that reference may also be made to the practice of the government, even if not subject to effective challenge in the courts. However, there is in my view no evidence of a decision made or practice adopted by the Vietnamese government, which treated the appellant as a non-national 'by operation of its law', even adopting the broadest view of those words as interpreted by the UNHCR; nor in any event of one which was effective at the date of the Secretary of State's decision. The appeal under this ground must accordingly be dismissed.

Views of other members of the Court differed in emphasis, as set out at paragraph 1.81 above, and the question cannot be regarded as having been finally resolved even in the United Kingdom, where the adoption of the article 1(1) CSSP54 definition into domestic law has sharply increased the degree of judicial attention it receives.

1.212 In *Pham* the UNHCR guidance was before the Court. Lord Carnwath, with whom Lord Neuberger, Lady Hale and Lord Wilson agreed, noted some reservation as to the degree to which the guidance was supported by CSSP54 in relation to the phrase 'under the operation of its law':

> 28. I do not with respect find some of the UNHCR guidance easy to reconcile with the wording of the article itself, especially when regard is had to the equivalent expressions in the French or Spanish versions. The Spanish version in particular seems to indicate, perhaps even more clearly than the English or French versions, the need for 'conformity' with a law of some kind. Furthermore, the reference to 'its' law seems to imply that the starting point, at least, is the relevant national law where one exists … It is difficult to see how a process of consideration by the state which pays no regard at all to this legal framework could be said to be 'by operation' of 'its' law.

The matter did not require resolution because the guidance was not challenged. Lord Carnwath considered therefore that 'It is appropriate therefore to take the guidance into account in considering the facts of the present case, without necessarily expressing a concluded view on its accuracy as a legal interpretation of the article'.

There may be some question as to whether the CSSP54 definition has in every respect come to be applicable for all purposes in international law, rather than a special one, particular to CSSP54 and to other instruments invoking it. In 2006 the ILC in its 'Draft Articles on Diplomatic Protection with Commentaries' stated, referring to provision in the 'Draft Articles for Diplomatic Protection by States' of 'lawfully and habitually resident' stateless persons, that the article 1(1) CSSP54 definition 'can no doubt be considered as having acquired a customary nature'.[226] 1.213

i. De Facto *Statelessness*

The Prato meeting also set out conclusions as regards a definition of *de facto* statelessness. The role of this part of the conclusions is much more tentative than that relating to statelessness (*de jure*), because *de facto* statelessness lacks any substantial footing in international law, and is used in different senses as a term descriptive of a condition which in one or more respects is considered to be parallel to, but different from, statelessness: 1.214

1. *De facto* statelessness has traditionally been linked to the notion of effective nationality[227] and some participants were of the view that a person's nationality could be ineffective inside as well as outside of his or her country of nationality. Accordingly, a person could be *de facto* stateless even if inside his or her country of nationality. However, there was broad support from other participants for the approach set out in the discussion paper prepared for the meeting which defines a *de facto* stateless person on the basis of one the principal functions of nationality in international law, the provision of protection by a State to its nationals abroad.
2. The definition is as follows: *de facto* stateless persons are persons outside the country of their nationality who are unable or, for valid reasons, are unwilling to avail themselves of the protection of that country. Protection in this sense refers to the right of diplomatic protection exercised by a State of nationality in order to remedy an internationally wrongful act against one of its nationals, as well as diplomatic and consular protection and assistance generally, including in relation to return to the State of nationality.

This definition in substantial part echoes the *Study of Statelessness* definition of 1949. It focuses upon inability or justified unwillingness to rely upon 'the protection of that country' as the incident of nationality, the absence of which creates *de facto* statelessness. It adds a requirement, in cases of unwillingness to avail of protection, for 'valid reason', something not present in the formula 1.215

---

[226] ILC, 'Draft Articles on Diplomatic Protection with Commentaries' *Yearbook of the International Law Commission*, vol II(2) (2006) 48–49.

[227] This is a reference to the Final Act of the conference which concluded CRS61, which recommends that 'persons who are stateless *de facto* should as far as possible be treated as stateless *de jure* to enable them to acquire an effective nationality'.

employed in the *Study of Statelessness*, and tending to highlight the malleability of the term and uncertainty as to the existence of a cohesive underlying concept. But the value of definition of *de facto* statelessness is in general much less than that of *de jure* statelessness. There is but a single use of the term '*de facto* statelessness' in the Final Act to the conference which concluded CSR61, and the term there is not defined, nor is the Act binding upon States Parties. The Prato guidance may be seen as enlarging upon the meaning to be given to *de facto* statelessness in the context of that Act, using language which partly ('unable or … unwilling') mirrors that of CSR51, though lacking the unifying elements of CSR51 (well-founded fear of persecution for a relevant reason) and adding the express qualification of valid reasons for unwillingness. This effort of definition could over time be developed through further international action. It is difficult to see that the paper provides a definition viable for wider purposes or consistent with the ordinary meaning of the term. If a general definition were to be sought it is difficult to see on what basis, without creating an entirely new definition reflecting particular policy factors, this could exclude those who were in a position not amounting to but parallel to statelessness, but without 'valid reasons' for international protection—for instance those who have destroyed their documents or withheld co-operation so that nationality cannot be proven. This in turn would highlight the difference between statelessness *de jure*—delineated by the absence of a legal relationship of nationality, without regard to the reasons for this—and what would then be called statelessness *de facto.*

2

The Law of Refugee Status

The interwar refugee regimes which mark the first stage in development of international refugee law responded to phenomena closely limited to nationality, most particularly mass denationalisation. The cornerstone of the modern international law of refugee status is the 1951 Convention relating to the Status of Refugees (CSR51). Nationality is important to the delineation of entitlement at article 1A(2) CSR51, and of provision for cessation at article 1C CSR51 and exclusion at article 1E CSR51 respectively.

Contents

A. The Formation of Modern International Refugee Law

A1. The Interwar Period

2.1 Prior to the First World War there was no developed international law regime concerned with refugee status. There was indeed no authoritative international definition of the term 'refugee'. In common parlance, as Jacques Vernant noted, it simply meant someone compelled to abandon his or her home, including persons driven from home by an earthquake or environmental disaster as well as those deprived of membership in and driven from a community, or forced to leave by fear of political or ethnic violence.[1] The earliest period in which the international community sought to create an international law regime concerning refugees was therefore also one in which both the definition of that term, and the scope of any protective regime in international law, had to be settled.

2.2 The immediate ancestor of the current international refugee law regime is the developing system for assistance to refugees seen in the years between the close of the First World War and the outbreak of the Second. Until well into the 1930s denationalisation, in the sense of withdrawal of nationality or citizenship, was perceived as the paradigm refugee-creating situation confronting the international community. Given the scale of the problem in that period, outlined in greater detail in chapter one, section A4.iii, this is understandable, as Plender noted:

> In the 1920s, between one and two million people were deprived of their Soviet citizenship by the Bolsheviks. The German Reich followed a similar policy in respect of Jews in the 1930s. Measures of a comparable character (although on a smaller scale) were adopted during the same decade by the Italian and Turkish authorities.[2]

2.3 The consequences of measures of this type motivated the creation during the interwar period of the earliest modern regimes of international refugee law. This was necessitated because of other changes which had reduced or removed the scope for migration and the acquisition of new national identities. In the course of the First World War opportunities for migration had slowed, and States erected much stronger regimes of border control than had existed previously. After the end of the war the maintenance of more stringent migration regimes than those of the pre-war years was perpetuated by social, economic and political concerns. Skran notes the effect during the 1920s and 1930s:

> Immigration restrictions made movement more difficult for those looking to improve their lives for economic reasons, but they created real hardship for refugees, those forced to flee their home countries because of war or persecution. These refugees included the millions uprooted during and shortly after the First World War, including over one

1 J Vernant, *The Refugee in the Post-War World* (George Allen & Unwin, 1953) 3.
2 R Plender, *International Migration Law* (2nd edn, Martinus Nijhoff, 1988) 144.

million Russians, 300,000 Magyars, over one million Greeks, and in the 1930s, 500,000 fleeing Nazi Germany and 400,000 Spanish Republicans. More than anything else, the development of refugee law represents an attempt to provide legal status and personal security to those forced to flee their home countries but unable to establish new lives fully elsewhere.[3]

In the aftermath of the First World War the newly established League of Nations in 1921 appointed Fridtjof Nansen as High Commissioner for Russian Refugees. The Russian refugees, broadly identified as those persons originating from the former Russian Empire without Russian diplomatic or other protection, faced numerous problems including the absence of secure evidence of identity and nationality for travel or residence purposes. The Soviet decree of 15 December 1921 exacerbated the situation, rendering stateless a large majority of the displaced Russians. In July 1922 an intergovernmental conference in Geneva accepted Nansen's proposal that States issue identity documents in common form to Russian refugees on their territories, agreeing an Arrangement with respect to the issue of certificates of identity to Russian Refugees.[4] This process would in effect create a census of the Russian refugee population, whilst refugees benefited from possession of a document which could be used for travel or residence purposes. Mutual recognition of the so-called 'Nansen passports' meant that States were less reluctant than hitherto to grant visas to affected Russians. In 1924 the idea was extended to another group, by a Plan for the Issue of a Certificate of Identity to Armenian Refugees. Each of the schemes attracted widespread participation by States. By August 1929, 52 States accepted the 1922 Arrangement and 39 the 1924 Plan. 2.4

The longer-term objective of the international community as regards the stateless Russians had been repatriation. However, Nansen was unsuccessful in negotiations seeking acceptance by the Soviet Union of its obligation to accept repatriation of denationalised Russians, and the League of Nations adopted a further Arrangement of 12 May 1926 relating to the Issue of Identity Certificates to Russian and Armenian Refugees.[5] This contained the first modern refugee definition: 2.5

2. The Conference adopts the following definitions of the term 'refugees':

'Russian': Any person of Russian origin who does not enjoy or who no longer enjoys the protection of the Government of the Union of Socialist Soviet Republics and who has not acquired another nationality.

---

[3] C Skran, 'Historical Development of International Refugee Law' in A Zimmermann (ed), *The 1951 Convention Relating to the Status of Refugees and its 1967 Protocol: A Commentary* (OUP, 2011) 6, §2 The same author's *Refugees in Interwar Europe: The Emergence of a Regime* (OUP, 1995) provides an excellent fuller account.

[4] League of Nations, *Arrangement with respect to the issue of certificates of identity to Russian Refugees*, 5 July 1922, League of Nations, Treaty Series Vol XIII No 355, available at: www.refworld.org/docid/3dd8b4864.html.

[5] League of Nations, *Arrangement Relating to the Issue of Identify Certificates to Russian and Armenian Refugees*, 12 May 1926, League of Nations, Treaty Series Vol LXXXIX, No 2004, available at: www.refworld.org/docid/3dd8b5802.html.

'Armenian': Any person of Armenian origin formerly a subject of the Ottoman Empire who does not enjoy or who no longer enjoys the protection of the Government of the Turkish Republic and who has not acquired another nationality.

This Arrangement was recognised by 22 States or entities by August 1929.

2.6 In 1928 an Arrangement relating to the Legal Status of Russian and Armenian Refugees, was made following agreement 'that it is necessary to define more clearly the legal status of Russian and Armenian refugees'. Subsequently by the 1933 League of Nations Convention relating to the International Status of Refugees, States Parties for the first time undertook real obligations on behalf of Russian, Armenian and assimilated refugees. It addressed administrative measures, *refoulement* and other matters, also providing for the creation of supervisory committees for refugees. By 1937 eight countries had ratified the 1933 Convention, another had signed but not ratified it, and a further eight stated that they applied its standards in practice.[6]

2.7 By the time the 1933 Convention was signed, however, new refugee-producing situations were coming into being. The most significant was created by the coming to power in Germany of the Nazi regime in that year. The League of Nations declined to act to aid refugees further by international convention or even as a 'purely technical matter', though agreeing to the appointment of a High Commissioner for Refugees (Jewish and Other), whose office was to remain underfunded and relatively unsupported. James G Macdonald was appointed to the post, but made minimal progress and resigned publicly in 1935 as a protest against inaction, pleading that the League of Nations realistically address what he called the 'current and impending tragedies' being caused by German actions against its population. Early in 1936, in the wake of Macdonald's public resignation, the League of Nations created the post of High Commissioner for Refugees coming from Germany and appointed to it Sir Neill Malcolm, with instructions to convene an international conference to address the question of refugees coming from Germany.

2.8 This resulted in a 1936 Provisional Arrangement Concerning the Status of Refugees Coming from Germany, which took some elements from the earlier interwar schemes. It deemed the term 'refugee coming from Germany' to apply:

to any person who was settled in that country, who does not possess any nationality other than German nationality, and in respect of whom it is established in law or in fact he or she does not enjoy the protection of the Government of the Reich.

This definition, as Skran has pointed out, on one possible reading actually required present possession of German nationality (and no other nationality). The Provisional Arrangement made allowance for travel and identity certificates and for a very limited temporary protection against expulsion or *refoulement*, including

[6] Skran (n 3 above) 8–31 [63].

some procedural safeguards for those affected by contemplated expulsion. Despite the weakness of the demands upon States made by the instrument, only seven ultimately signed it.

The Provisional Arrangement had been intended as a temporary measure. In 1936 **2.9**
the number of refugees coming from Germany in High Commissioner Malcolm's estimation considerably exceeded 100,000, but only a relatively small number, around 15,000, were considered to be in a precarious situation, and the number of new arrivals appeared to be relatively low.[7] Governments sought to develop a more durable framework. This was provided, albeit again with minimal international support, by the 1938 Convention concerning the Status of Refugees Coming from Germany. The 1938 Convention was concluded in February 1938, only a month before the *Anschluss* brought Austria under German control and extended Nazi persecutions to its territory. By article 1 the 1938 Convention provided that:

> Article 1
>
> 1. For the purposes of the present Convention, the term 'refugees coming from Germany' shall be deemed to apply to:
>
> (a) Persons possessing or having possessed German nationality and not possessing any other nationality who are proved not to enjoy, in law or in fact, the protection of the German Government.
> (b) Stateless persons not covered by previous Conventions or Agreements who have left Germany territory after being established therein and who are proved not to enjoy, in law or in fact, the protection of the German Government.
>
> 2. Persons who leave Germany for reasons of purely personal convenience are not included in this definition.[8]

The Convention was signed by seven States, which like the 1936 Provisional Arrangement contained some restrictions on expulsion and *refoulement*. Only two of the signatories, Belgium and the United Kingdom, had ratified it by the outbreak of the Second World War in Europe in September 1939. Its Additional Protocol of 14 September 1939 extended the Convention to refugees from post-*Anschluss* Austria.[9]

[7] League of Nations, *Report submitted to the Seventeenth Ordinary Session of the Assembly of the League of Nations by the High Commissioner*, 1 September 1936, LN Doc A.19.1936.XII (1936) 2.

[8] League of Nations, *Convention concerning the Status of Refugees Coming From Germany*, 10 February 1938, League of Nations Treaty Series, Vol CXCII, No 4461, 59, available at: www.refworld.org/docid/3dd8d12a4.html.

[9] League of Nations, *Additional Protocol to the Provisional Arrangement and to the Convention Concerning the Status of Refugees Coming from Germany*, 14 September 1939, League of Nations Treaty Series, Vol CXCVIII, No 4634, 141, available at: www.refworld.org/docid/3dd8d1fb4.html.

2.10 The instruments created by the League of Nations in the 1920s and early 1930s generally regarded (and from the 1926 Arrangement onward expressly defined) as refugees those persons of a particular national origin recognised by the international community as without the protection of a country of nationality and therefore requiring international assistance.[10] Neither the 1933 Convention relating to the International Status of Refugees nor the 1938 Convention concerning the Status of Refugees coming from Germany employed any test aimed at an individual's particular situation beyond origin and absence of national protection, save that, as seen above, the 1938 Convention provided for exclusion of persons who had left Germany for reasons 'of purely personal convenience', an important precursor of individualised decision-making concerned with the merit of particular individuals' need for protection.

2.11 Sir John Hope Simpson noted in 1939 that the refugee definitions adopted in preceding instruments were 'technical definitions framed for legal and administrative purposes'. For his own 1939 study he adopted 'a wider and less technical explanation':

> The refugee finds himself deprived of legal protection, mutual support, the access to employment, and the measure of freedom of movement which happier mortals take as a matter of course. In an ordered world this legal protection and mutual support … is enjoyed by the nationals of a sovereign State. Security is extended to them, not only at home, but when they move about the world in other countries. The refugee, unless special means are taken for his protection, has no such security, but exists in any country on sufferance. His defencelessness lies in his inability to demand the protection of any State. For practical purposes he is outlawed by his country of origin; in his country of refuge, he has a measure of ordinary legal protection in any decently governed State, but he suffers under all sorts of disabilities, as is shown in later chapters of this book; above all, he has no claim as of right to continued residence, and he is liable to expulsion of his presence for any reason is no longer desired. The essential quality of a refugee therefore may be said to be that he has left his country of regular residence, of which he may or may not be a national, as a result of political events in that country which render his continued residence impossible or intolerable, and has taken refuge in another country, or, if already absent from his home, is unwilling or unable to return, without danger to life or liberty, as a direct consequence of the political conditions there.[11]

Simpson's examination of the problem of definition was remarkably prescient, and is important for itself and also because of what can be seen as close parallels between his reasoning and concepts which are central to the definition now contained at article 1A(2) of the Convention relating to the Status of Refugees 1951 (CSR51).

[10] Skran (n 3 above) 8–31 [10]–[82].

[11] J Hope Simpson, *The Refugee Problem, Report of a Survey* (OUP, 1939) 3–4.

A2. Wartime and the Immediate Post-War Period

The interwar regimes did not employ any concept of 'persecution' as a condition for refugee status. During the Second World War this term, later central to the CSR51 regime, was not employed specifically as regards refugees. But it did acquire a place both in the ordinary language used by people in Allied and neutral countries to refer to actions of Germany and Japan, and in the language used in relation to the concept of human rights, the place of which in international law was being actively debated. During the course of the Second World War the term 'persecution' came to denote the targeted infliction upon particular persons or groups of persons of serious violations of human rights, a notable example of this use being its employment in conjunction with the 1942 United Nations Declaration on the Persecution of the Jews.[12] **2.12**

By 15 December 1946, when the Constitution of the International Refugee Organisation (IRO) was adopted by a resolution of the United Nations General Assembly, with refugees being defined at Annexe 1, Part A, Section 1, the concept of persecution, linked specifically to the Nazis in Germany and Austria, had evidently achieved some currency within the nascent regime of international refugee law as part of a ground of entitlement to protection (para 3), but remained distinctly secondary to being a victim of specified historical circumstances (para 1) or inability or unwillingness to obtain recourse to the protection of 'the Government of his country of nationality or former nationality' (para 2), unaccompanied children being another category (para 4): **2.13**

> SECTION A—DEFINITION OF REFUGEES
>
> 1. Subject to the provisions of sections C and D and Part II of this Annex, the term 'refugee' applies to a person who has left, or who is outside of, his country of nationality or of former habitual residence, and who, whether or not he had retained his nationality, belongs to one of the following categories:
>
> (a) Victims of the nazi or fascist régimes or of régimes which took part on their side in the second world war, or of the quisling or similar régimes which assisted them against the United Nations, whether enjoying international status as refugees or not;
> (b) Spanish Republicans and other victims of the Falangist regime in Spain, whether enjoying international status as refugees or not;
> (c) Persons who were considered refugees before the outbreak of the second world war, for reasons of race, religion, nationality or political opinion.
>
> 2. Subject to the provisions of sections C and D and of Part II of this Annex regarding the exclusion of certain categories of persons, including war criminals, quislings and

[12] For instance see 'Persecution of the Jews: Allies' Declaration', HL Deb 17 December 1942, vol 125, cols 607–12.

> traitors, from the benefits of the Organization, the term 'refugee' also applies to a person, other than a displaced person as defined in section B of this Annex, who is outside of his country of nationality or former habitual residence, and who, as a result of events subsequent to the outbreak of the second world war, is unable or unwilling to avail himself of the protection of the Government of his country of nationality or former nationality.
>
> 3. Subject to the provisions of section D and of Part II of this Annex, the term 'refugee' also applies to persons who, having resided in Germany or Austria, and being of Jewish origin or foreigners or stateless persons, were victims of nazi persecution and were detained in, or were obliged to flee from, and were subsequently returned to, one of those countries as a result of enemy action, or of war circumstances, and have not yet been firmly resettled therein.
>
> 4. The term 'refugee' also applies to unaccompanied children who are war orphans or whose parents have disappeared, and who are outside their countries of origin. Such children, 16 years of age or under, shall be given all possible priority assistance, including, normally, assistance in repatriation in the case of those whose nationality can be determined.[13]

The IRO Constitution thus identified persons as refugees by specific categories, such as 'victims of the Nazi or fascist regimes or of the quisling or similar regimes which assisted them against the United Nations' and 'Spanish Republicans and other victims of the Falangist regime in Spain'. It also cited 'persecution, or fear, based on reasonable grounds of persecution because of race, religion, nationality or political opinions, provided these opinions are not in conflict with the principles of the United Nations, as laid down in the Preamble of the Charter of the United Nations' as a valid reason for a refugee objecting to repatriation.[14] The term 'persecution' was otherwise then chiefly employed by the United Nations Relief and Rehabilitation Administration and by the military authorities in occupied Europe, though Grahl-Madsen noted later that the term 'persecution' in this period could be said to have been 'in the air'.[15] And in 1948, article 14 of the new Universal Declaration of Human Rights 1948 (UDHR48) enjoined that 'Everyone has the right to seek and to enjoy in other countries asylum from persecution'. Although the term 'persecution' was employed at article 14 UDHR48, it was not further defined in that instrument, and the article 14 UDHR48 right ultimately did not lead to a similar provision within the International Covenant on Civil and Political Rights 1966 (ICCPR66). The imminent development of international refugee law was by an instrument which established a distinct refugee regime related to but not immediately part of a contemplated body of international law dedicated to the identification of fundamental rights and freedoms of individuals.

---

[13] United Nations, Constitution of the International Refugee Organisation 1946, Annexe 1, part 1, section A, 15 December 1946, United Nations, Treaty Series, vol 18, available at: www.unhcr.org/3ae69ef14.html.

[14] Ibid, Annexe 1, part 1, section C.

[15] A Grahl-Madsen, *The Status of Refugees in International Law*, vol I (AW Sijthoff, 1966) 189, §80.

A3. The Creation of the 1951 Convention Relating to the Status of Refugees

In 1947 the United Nations Commission on Human Rights, itself created only a year earlier, adopted a resolution by which it expressed the wish that: 2.14

> early consideration be given by the United Nations to the legal status of persons who do not enjoy the protection of any government, in particular pending the acquisition of nationality as regards their legal and social protection and their documentation.[16]

In response, the United Nations Economic and Social Council in March 1948 requested the Secretary-General of the United Nations to 'undertake a study of the existing situation in regard to the protection of stateless persons … and … make recommendations to an early session of the Council on the interim measures which might be taken by the United Nations to further this object', to undertake a study of national legislation relevant to statelessness, and to submit recommendations to the Council as to desirability of an international treaty regime addressing statelessness.[17]

The outcome of the work by the Secretary-General was published in 1949 by the United Nations Department of Social Affairs, under the title *A Study of Statelessness.*[18] It recommended the conclusion of an international convention concerning the legal status of stateless persons, whether *de jure* or *de facto*, the latter category being loosely defined by the absence of national protection generally associated with refugees as then defined (see chapter one section C above). On 8 August 1949 the Economic and Social Council issued Resolution 248(IX)B which, *inter alia*, appointed an Ad Hoc Committee consisting of representatives of 13 governments, and instructed this to prepare draft agreements in the light of comments of governments and specialised agencies. On 3 January 1950 the Secretary-General by a Memorandum indicated that in his view it was desirable to create a new treaty, and provided a brief account of the reasoning for this: 2.15

> In point of fact:
>
> (a) No Government will be willing to take the first step in this direction for fear of being the only one to improve the status of stateless persons, thus causing an influx of them into its territory.
> (b) Action on these lines, if taken by a single Government alone, might appear to be inspired by certain political views. Simultaneous action is the only means of avoiding such suspicion.

---

[16] UNCHR document E/600 [46].

[17] UN Economic and Social Council (ECOSOC), Sixth Session, Resolution 116(VI)D.

[18] UN Ad Hoc Committee on Refugees and Stateless Persons, *A Study of Statelessness, United Nations, August 1949, Lake Success—New York*, 1 August 1949, E/1112; E/1112/Add.1, available at: www.refworld.org/docid/3ae68c2d0.html.

(c) A law designed to improve the status of stateless persons would have to contain a whole body of provisions impinging on the most varied branches of internal legislation. It would be difficult to get parliaments, habitually overburdened with work as they are, to adopt such a law, of an unwonted nature and content, which would require prior study by a number of Commissions.

(d) Ratification of a convention in which all these provisions find their natural place gives rise to less difficulty.

(e) Experience in this field shows that nothing was done in the field of internal legislation to give effect to the recommendations contained in the Arrangement of 30 June 1928[4] although these recommendations, which were adopted after exhaustive discussion, answered to the intentions of numerous Governments. However, when they had been inserted in the 1933 and 1938 Convention, these same provisions were incorporated in the law of the contracting countries.

(f) A general convention is a lasting international structure; being open to the accession of States which have not signed it, it encourages governments to associate themselves with the work of their forerunners; even if those governments are not in a position to accede to it, such a convention sometimes exerts a direct influence on the administrative and legal practice of their countries.[19]

2.16 The Memorandum of the UN Secretary-General of 3 January 1950 invited the Ad Hoc Committee to consider how entitlement to protection as a refugee could be delineated. It cited as alternative approaches first a continuation of the historical practice of identification through membership in a particular category of persons without national protection, further limited by reference to specified geographical origin and circumstances. The alternative was the novel option of a general definition free from more specific requirements such as a particular place of origin. The Ad Hoc Committee opted for the second alternative. It took the decision not to include in the definition all persons lacking the protection of their State of origin or of any State, but rather to protect as refugees only a subclass of that group it perceived as warranting more immediate protection.[20]

2.17 The Ad Hoc Committee met again in New York between 16 January and 16 February 1950, preparing a draft Convention relating to the Status of Refugees intended to create a new framework for international protection of those enumerated as refugees. The Council at its Eleventh Session considered the work of the Ad Hoc Committee and the draft Preamble and refugee definition at article 1, and on 16 August 1950 adopted a resolution and requested the Secretary-General to reconvene the Ad Hoc Committee to prepare revised drafts after consultation

---

[19] Ad Hoc Committee on Statelessness and Related Problems, 'Status of Refugees and Stateless Persons—Memorandum by the Secretary-General' (Statelessness conference, 3 January 1950), available at: www.unhcr.org/3ae68c280.html.

[20] T Einarson, 'Drafting History of the 1951 Convention and the 1967 Protocol' in A Zimmermann (ed), *The 1951 Convention Relating to the Status of Refugees and its 1967 Protocol: A Commentary* (OUP, 2011) 54–57, [33]–[38].

with States and a range of other relevant bodies, incorporating the Preamble and definition adopted by the Council.[21] The Ad Hoc Committee held a second session in Geneva in August 1950 and revised the articles of the draft Convention excepting draft article 1.

Thereafter the Council adopted a resolution requesting submission of the draft to the General Assembly. This body on 14 December 1950 adopted its Resolution 429(V) adopting the draft for further consideration at a Conference of Plenipotentiaries. The Conference took place in Geneva between 2 and 25 July 1951, adopting the new CSR51 on 25 July 1951. The Final Act of the Conference was signed on 28 July 1951. The new instrument entered into force on 12 April 1954. The application of CSR51 was then modified in 1967, for signatories to both instruments, by the 1967 Protocol relating to the Status of Refugees (PSR67). **2.18**

As at April 2015 the United Nations High Commissioner for Refugees (UNHCR) reported that there were 145 States Parties to CSR51 and 146 to PSR67, a total of 148 States being a State Party in respect of at least one instrument.[22] As the figures above suggest there is a high degree of adherence to the regime of international refugee law. An idea of regional disparities regarding membership can be seen from the map published by the UNHCR showing this. Particular regional exceptions exist however in the Arabian Peninsula and around the Persian Gulf (except Yemen and Iran, both States Parties to CSR51 and PSR67), and in South and South-East Asia from Pakistan through India as far as Indonesia.[23] **2.19**

B. The 1951 Convention Relating to the Status of Refugees

B1. Article 1A(2) of the Convention Relating to the Status of Refugees 1951

i. Text of Article 1A(2)

By article 1A(2) CSR51, as modified in application by PSR67, a refugee is defined in the following terms: **2.20**

Article 1

Definition of the term 'Refugee'

[21] UN Economic and Social Council (ECOSOC), *UN Economic and Social Council Resolution 319 (XI): Refugees and stateless persons Resolutions of 11 and 16 August 1950*, 16 August 1950, E/RES/319 (XI), available at: www.refworld.org/docid/3ae69efd2.html.

[22] See: www.unhcr.org/3b73b0d63.html.

[23] See: reliefweb.int/sites/reliefweb.int/files/resources/505187992.pdf.

A For the purposes of the present Convention, the term 'refugee' shall apply to any person who:

...

(2) Owing to well-founded fear of being persecuted for reasons of race, religion, nationality, membership of a particular social group or political opinion, is outside the country of his nationality and is unable or, owing to such fear, is unwilling to avail himself of the protection of that country; or who, not having a nationality and being outside the country of his former habitual residence as a result of such events, is unable or, owing to such fear, is unwilling to return to it.

In the case of a person who has more than one nationality, the term 'the country of his nationality' shall mean each of the countries of which he is a national, and a person shall not be deemed to be lacking the protection of the country of his nationality if, without any valid reason based on well-founded fear, he has not availed himself of the protection of one of the countries of which he is a national.

ii. Relationship to Other Provisions

2.21 Article 1A(2) CSR51 provides the primary modern definition of 'refugee'. An individual who is a refugee as defined at article 1A(2) is entitled to the benefit of CSR51 unless one of the exclusion clauses (articles 1D, 1E, 1F) applies, until or unless cessation arises (article 1C).

2.22 A refugee is subject to the positive duty at article 2 CSR51 to conform to the laws of the country in which he or she is present. The State Party, in the territory of which the refugee is sojourning, is subject to a large number of duties essentially contained at articles 3 to 31. This leaves three substantive provisions of particular present importance. By article 32 ('Expulsion') a refugee who is lawfully present in the territory of a contracting State is protected from expulsion save on grounds of national security or public order, and even in one of those cases benefits from procedural safeguards.

2.23 Article 33(1) provides that:

> 33(1) No Contracting State shall expel or return ('*refouler*') a refugee in any manner whatsoever to the frontiers of territories where his life or freedom would be threatened on account of his race, religion, nationality, membership of a particular social group or political opinion.

This provision is likely, with the refugee definition at article 1 CSR51, one of the two most critical provisions in the Convention. The benefit of article 33(1) is however denied by CSR51 in either of two circumstances identified at article 33(2):

> 2. The benefit of the present provision may not, however, be claimed by a refugee whom there are reasonable grounds for regarding as a danger to the security of the country in which he is, or who, having been convicted by a final judgment of a particularly serious crime, constitutes a danger to the community of that country.

By the interaction of article 1 CSR51 and article 33(1) thereof, a refugee as defined by the former provision is protected from *refoulement* to a territory where a relevant threat arises. Despite some difference in language, 'the threat to life or freedom' in article 33(1) has been identified with the source of 'well-founded fear of being persecuted for reasons of race, religion, nationality, membership of a particular social group or political opinion' in article 1A(2).

Article 34 provides a provisional commitment to facilitate assimilation and naturalisation of refugees including in particular 'every effort' to expedite naturalisation and to reduce so far as possible the costs thereof. 2.24

iii. Nationality, Statelessness and Article 1A(2)

Article 1A(2) CSR51 is critical to the initial application or otherwise of CSR51. 2.25
In its two paragraphs the term 'nationality' is used a total of six times. The term is also referenced in the first paragraph ('that country', referring to the earlier formula, 'the country of his nationality'). These usages may be separated into the following:

i. 'Nationality' is given as one of the reasons, often referred to as 'Convention reasons', which must jointly or severally represent the basis for an individual's well-founded fear of being persecuted, if that person is to be a refugee.
ii. Wherever an individual possesses a nationality for relevant purposes, the term 'nationality', in the phrases 'the country of his nationality' and 'that nationality', denotes the reference country—to be a refugee that person must be 'outside the country of his nationality' and also 'unable or, owing to [well-founded fear of being persecuted for Convention reason], unwilling to avail himself of the protection of that country'.
iii. By the interpretive gloss added by the second paragraph of article 1A(2), if a person has more than one nationality, then the term 'the country of his nationality' means each of the countries of nationality. In such a case 'a person shall not be deemed to be lacking the protection of the country of his nationality if, without any valid reason based on well-founded fear, he has not availed himself of the protection of one of the countries of which he is a national'.
iv. If the individual is without a nationality, or stateless ('not having a nationality') this identifies the need to substitute a reference State on a basis (habitual residence) which is alternative to nationality ('being outside the country of his former habitual residence as a result of such events, is unable or, owing to such fear, is unwilling to return to it').

iv. Nationality as Convention Reason

The reference to nationality at article 1A(2) CSR51 coincides with the later reference, in an identical list of prohibited causes, at article 33(1) CSR51. The concept of nationality applied in this context is examined in chapter four. 2.26

v. Identifying 'the Country of His [or Her] Nationality' or Each Such Country

2.27 The reference in the first paragraph of article 1A(2) CSR51 to 'the country of his nationality' is supplemented by the reference in the second paragraph as regards plural nationality, that is, the condition of having more than one relevant nationality. The meaning of 'the country of his nationality', and within this the way in which plural national is treated, will be examined in chapter five.

vi. Persecution in the Form of Loss or Denial of Nationality (or Citizenship)

2.28 The concept of 'persecution' is critical to identifying the extent of the definition at article 1A(2) and hence to the extent of protection afforded by CSR51. The delineation of the range of conduct covered as 'persecution' has been authoritatively considered as aided by reference to established standards for the protection of human rights under international law. The boundary of the range of conduct related to nationality covered by 'persecution' is considered in chapter six.

B2. Article 1C of the Convention Relating to the Status of Refugees 1951

i. Text of Article 1C

2.29 Article 1C delineates circumstances in which someone who met the refugee definition ceases to be covered by CSR51:

> C This Convention shall cease to apply to any person falling under the terms of section A if:
>
> (1) He has voluntarily re-availed himself of the protection of the country of his nationality; or
> (2) Having lost his nationality, he has voluntarily re-acquired it; or
> (3) He has acquired a new nationality, and enjoys the protection of the country of his new nationality; or
> (4) He has voluntarily re-established himself in the country which he left or outside which he remained owing to fear of persecution; or
> (5) He can no longer, because the circumstances in connection with which he has been recognized as a refugee have ceased to exist, continue to refuse to avail himself of the protection of the country of his nationality;
> (6) Being a person who has no nationality he is, because of the circumstances in connection with which he has been recognized as a refugee have ceased to exist, able to return to the country of his former habitual residence;
>
> Provided that this paragraph shall not apply to a refugee falling under section A(1) of this article who is able to invoke compelling reasons arising out of previous persecution for refusing to avail himself of the protection of the country of nationality.

Article 1C CSR51 mirrors article 1A(2) in the important role given to nationality and related concepts. Five of the six bases for cessation refer to 'nationality' and/or the related term 'protection'. By article 1C, cessation follows if an individual 'has voluntarily re-availed himself of the protection of the country of his nationality' (article 1C(1)), if he or she has lost a nationality but 'has voluntarily re-acquired it' (article 1C(2)), or has acquired a new nationality and enjoys 'the protection of the country of his new nationality' (article 1C(3)), or if the individual in question 'can no longer, because the circumstances in connection with which he has been recognized as a refugee have ceased to exist, continue to refuse to avail himself of the protection of the country of his nationality' (article 1C(5)), or a person with no nationality who 'is, because of the circumstances in connexion with which he has been recognized as a refugee have ceased to exist, able to return to the country of his former habitual residence' (article 1C(6)).

ii. Cessation Provisions

The application of these cessation provisions related to nationality is considered in chapter seven. **2.30**

B3. Article 1E of the Convention Relating to the Status of Refugees 1951

i. Text of Article 1E

Article 1E CSR51 provides that: **2.31**

> 1E This Convention shall not apply to a person who is recognized by the competent authorities of the country in which he has taken residence as having the rights and obligations which are attached to the possession of the nationality of that country.

ii. Exclusion under Article 1E

The application of article 1E CSR51 is considered in chapter eight. **2.32**

C. Regional Regimes

C1. The Organisation of African Unity/African Union

The Organisation of African Unity Convention Governing the Specific Aspects of **2.33**
Refugee Problems in Africa adopted on 10 September 1969 by the OAU Assembly

of Heads of State and Government came into force on 20 June 1974. In article 1 ('Definition of the term "refugee"'), article 1(1) effectively reproduces the formula for qualification at article 1A(2) CSR51 including reference to 'the country of his nationality' as the reference country where a nationality exists and 'the country of his former habitual residence' as its analogue in the case of a person without nationality. Article 1(3) reproduces the second paragraph of article 1A(2) CSR51. Between these provisions at article 1(2) is a supplementary category extending beyond the protective limit of CSR51 which uses the dual phrase 'country of origin or nationality', to identify the reference country:

> Article 1
>
> . . .
>
> 2. The term 'refugee' shall also apply to every person who, owing to external aggression, occupation, foreign domination or events seriously disturbing public order in either part or the whole of his country of origin or nationality, is compelled to leave his place of habitual residence in order to seek refuge in another place outside his country of origin or nationality.

The term 'country of origin' is not defined in the Convention, but would on the face of it include at least a country from which a person has come, where he or she either has never held or no longer holds the nationality of that State.

2.34 Article 2 ('Asylum') provides that:

> Article 2
>
> . . .
>
> 1. Member States of the OAU shall use their best endeavours consistent with their respective legislation to receive refugees and to secure the settlement of those refugees who, for well-founded reasons, are unable or unwilling to return to their country of origin or nationality.
>
> . . .
>
> 4. Where a Member State finds difficulty in continuing to grant asylum to refugees, such Member State may appeal directly to other Member States and through the OAU, and such other Member States shall in the spirit of African solidarity and international co-operation take appropriate measures to lighten the burden of the Member State granting asylum.
>
> 5. Where a refugee has not received the right to reside in any country of asylum, he may be granted temporary residence in any country of asylum in which he first presented himself as a refugee pending arrangement for his re-settlement in accordance with the preceding paragraph.

The term 'country of asylum' in article 2(5) is not defined, but on its face appears to mean 'potential country of asylum' because a 'country of asylum' may specifically be a country which has not afforded the refugee a right to reside. This formula also distinguishes 'temporary residence' from 'asylum', albeit the former presumably affords protection, even if temporary, from *refoulement*, treating asylum as a more established protective status.

C2. The Americas

The Colloquium on Asylum and International Protection of Refugees in Latin America held in Mexico City from 11 to 15 May 1981 under the auspices of the Mexican Ministry of Foreign Affairs in collaboration with UNHCR experts examined the Latin American institution of asylum in relation to the international refugee law regime and adopted a series of conclusions: **2.35**

> 3. To indicate the necessity in Latin America for the protection of the universal [international] and inter-American provisions for refugees and asylum cases to be extended to all persons who flee their country because of foreign aggression, occupation or domination, massive human rights violations, or occurrences that seriously alter public order in all or part of the country of origin.

This was followed by the Cartagena Declaration on Refugees adopted by the Colloquium on the International Protection of Refugees in Central America, Mexico and Panama, held at Cartagena, Colombia from 19 to 22 November 1984: **2.36**

> I
>
> *Recalling* the conclusions and recommendations adopted by the Colloquium held in Mexico in 1981 on Asylum and International Protection of Refugees in Latin America, which established important landmarks for the analysis and consideration of this matter;
>
> III
>
> The Colloquium adopted the following conclusions:
>
> ...
>
> 3. To reiterate that, in view of the experience gained from the massive flows of refugees in the Central American area, it is necessary to consider enlarging the concept of a refugee, bearing in mind, as far as appropriate and in the light of the situation prevailing in the region, the precedent of the OAU Convention (article 1, paragraph 2) and the doctrine employed in the reports of the Inter-American Commission on Human Rights. Hence the definition or concept of a refugee to be recommended for use in the region is one which, in addition to containing the elements of the 1951 Convention and the 1967 Protocol, includes among refugees persons who have fled their country because their lives, safety or freedom have been threatened by generalized violence, foreign aggression, internal conflicts, massive violation of human rights or other circumstances which have seriously disturbed public order.

This adds the recommendation that Latin American states provide refugee protection not only to those meeting the requirements of CSR51 and PSR67, but also to others who have fled from one of a list of enumerated considerations. The language defining the extent of the supplementary class (who have fled 'their country') does not specify a 'country of nationality' and might be taken as a wider formula. Such an inference gains some support from the express aim of producing a wider supplementary class of beneficiary beyond CSR51/PSR67.

C3. The European Union

2.37 The European Union has taken steps to create a common policy on asylum, including a Common European Asylum System. The European Council at a special meeting in Tampere on 15–16 October 1999 agreed to work towards the establishment of that Common European Asylum System, based on 'the full and inclusive application of [CSR51], as supplemented by [PSR67] thus affirming the principle of non-*refoulement* and ensuring that nobody is sent back to persecution'. The primary European Union instrument regarding refugee status is Council Directive 2004/83/EC of 29 April 2004 on minimum standards for the qualification and status of third-country nationals or stateless persons as refugees or as persons who otherwise need international protection and the content of the protection granted (the Qualification Directive). Paragraphs 3 and 4 of the Preamble record respectively that '[CSR51 and PSR67] provide the cornerstone of the international legal regime for the protection of refugees' and 'the Tampere conclusions provide that a Common European Asylum System should include, in the short term, the approximation of rules on the recognition of refugees and the content of refugee status'.

2.38 Article 2(c) Qualification Directive defines 'refugee', for purposes of the Directive, as:

> 2(c) a third country national who, owing to a well-founded fear of being persecuted for reasons of race, religion, nationality, political opinion or membership of a particular social group, is outside the country of nationality and is unable or, owing to such fear, is unwilling to avail himself or herself of the protection of that country, or a stateless person, who, being outside of the country of former habitual residence for the same reasons as mentioned above, is unable or, owing to such fear, unwilling to return to it, and to whom Article 12 ['exclusion'] does not apply.

The phrase 'a third-country national' is not expressly defined in the Qualification Directive but had been defined earlier as meaning 'anyone who is not a citizen of the Union within the meaning of Article 17(1) of the Treaty establishing the European Community' at article 2(a) of Council Regulation (EC) No 343/2003 of 18 February 2003 establishing the criteria and mechanisms for determining the Member State responsible for examining an asylum application lodged in one of the Member States by a third-country national (the Dublin II Regulation). Accordingly the Qualification Directive would not apply in respect of a claim to protection made by a national of another European Union Member State—such a claim would fall to be dealt with by alternative national procedures.[24] The Dublin II Regulation has now been reconstituted as Regulation (EU) No 604/2013 of the European Parliament and of the Council of 26 June 2013 establishing the criteria and mechanisms for determining the Member State responsible for examining an application for international protection lodged in one of the Member States by a third-country national or a stateless person (recast) (the Dublin III Regulation). The Republic of Ireland and United Kingdom have chosen to take part in the adoption of the amended instrument. Only Denmark has chosen not to take part. Article 2(a) of the Dublin III Regulation provides that 'third-country national' means any person who is not a citizen of the Union within the meaning of Article 20(1) of the Treaty on the Functioning of the European Union and who is not national of a State which participates in this Regulation by virtue of an agreement with the European Union.

Elsewhere in the Qualification Directive the text frequently refers to 'country of origin', a phrase defined for relevant purposes at article 2(k) of the Directive: **2.39**

> 2(k) 'country of origin' means the country or countries of nationality or, for stateless persons, of former habitual residence.

Chapter II of the Qualification Directive ('Assessment of applications for international protection') provides guidance concerning the design of assessment processes and the relevant responsibilities of States and applicants. By article 4 ('Assessment of facts and circumstances') this provides as follows: **2.40**

> Chapter II
>
> Article 4
>
> ...
>
> 1. Member States may consider it the duty of the applicant to submit as soon as possible all elements needed to substantiate the application for international protection. In cooperation with the applicant it is the duty of the Member State to assess the relevant elements of the application.
>
> 2. The elements referred to in of paragraph 1 consist of the applicant's statements and all documentation at the applicant's disposal regarding the applicant's age, background, including that of relevant relatives, identity, nationality(ies), country(ies) and place(s) of previous residence, previous asylum applications, travel routes, identity and travel documents and the reasons for applying for international protection.
>
> 3. The assessment of an application for international protection is to be carried out on an individual basis and includes taking into account:
>
> ...

[24] In the United Kingdom the statutory instrument transposing the Qualification Directive into domestic law does not use the concept of 'third-country nationals', effectively treating nationals of other EU States identically to nationals of other States: see Refugee or Person in Need of International Protection (Qualification) Regulations 2006, SI 2006/2525, regs 1 and 2.

(e) whether the applicant could reasonably be expected to avail himself of the protection of another country where he could assert citizenship.

Article 4(e) might be consistent with CSR51 if the assessment of the application treats *as a question going to credibility* the enquiry as to whether the applicant is presenting himself or herself rather than 'assert citizenship' in another State. Only in this interpretation is the provision consistent with CSR51. Article 1A(2) of the latter, as already seen, refers only to 'the country of his nationality' (or each country of nationality in the case of a plural national) or the country of former habitual residence of an individual without a nationality, as identifying the reference country(ies) for purposes of ascertaining status. A reading of article 4(3) of the Qualification Directive which treated the existence of a country of potential citizenship as undermining qualification as a refugee even where the article 1A(2) rubric is met, by treating such a country as a country of reference for status determination itself, would be indefensible as a translation of article 1A(2) CSR51. The statement at paragraph 3 of the Preamble that CSR51 and PSR67 'provide the cornerstone of the international legal regime for the protection of refugees' strongly suggests that a fully compatible reading of article 4(3)(e) should be preferred.

2.41 Chapter III of the Qualification Directive ('Qualification for being a refugee') sets out guidance to aid application of the rubric for qualification as a refugee. By article 9 ('Acts of persecution') this provides as follows:

Article 9

...

1. Acts of persecution within the meaning of article 1A [CSR51] must:

(a) be sufficiently serious by their nature or repetition as to constitute a severe violation of basic human rights, in particular the rights from which derogation cannot be made under Article 15(2) of the European Convention for the Protection of Human Rights and Fundamental Freedoms; or
(b) be an accumulation of various measures, including violations of human rights which is sufficiently severe as to affect an individual in a similar manner as mentioned in (a).

2. Acts of persecution as qualified in paragraph 1, can, *inter alia*, take the form of:

...

(b) legal, administrative, police, and/or judicial measures which are in themselves discriminatory or which are implemented in a discriminatory manner.

Article 10 ('Reasons for persecution') is also within Chapter III, and provides that:

Article 10

...

1. Member States shall take the following elements into account when assessing the reasons for persecution:

...

(c) the concept of nationality shall not be confined to citizenship or lack thereof but shall in particular include membership of a group determined by its cultural, ethnic, or linguistic identity, common geographical or political origins or its relationship with the population of another State.

A material difference between CSR51 and the Qualification Direction lies in the content of international protection provided by the latter. In Chapter VII ('Content of international protection'), article 20(1) Qualification Directive states that it is a general rule that: 2.42

Article 20

1. This Chapter shall be without prejudice to the rights laid down in the Geneva Convention.

Article 21 Qualification Directive adumbrates the protection provided to a refugee under that instrument in relation to *refoulement*:

Article 21

Protection from refoulement

1. Member States shall respect the principle of non-refoulement in accordance with their international obligations.

2. Where not prohibited by the international obligations mentioned in paragraph 1, Member States may refoule a refugee, whether formally recognised or not, when:

(a) there are reasonable grounds for considering him or her as a danger to the security of the Member State in which he or she is present; or
(b) he or she, having been convicted by a final judgement of a particularly serious crime, constitutes a danger to the community of that Member State.

3. Member States may revoke, end or refuse to renew or to grant the residence permit of (or to) a refugee to whom paragraph 2 applies.

Article 24 ('Residence permits') provides that:

Article 24

...

1. As soon as possible after their status has been granted, Member States shall issue to beneficiaries of refugee status a residence permit which must be valid for at least three years and renewable unless compelling reasons of national security or public order otherwise require, and without prejudice to Article 21(3).

The Qualification Directive has now been partially reformulated as Directive 2011/95/EU of the European Parliament and of the Council of 13 December 2011 on standards for the qualification of third-country nationals or stateless persons as beneficiaries of international protection, for a uniform status for refugees or for persons eligible for subsidiary protection, and for the content of the protection 2.43

granted (recast) (the Qualification Directive Recast). Denmark, the Republic of Ireland and the United Kingdom have chosen not to take part. Most of the provisions of the Qualification Directive referred to above recur with no change save in some cases renumbering—paragraphs 3 and 4 in the original Preamble are now paragraphs 4 and 5 in the Recast, article 2(c) in the Qualification Directive is article 2(d) in the Qualification Directive Recast, and so on.

C4. The Arab World

2.44 Although the Gulf Cooperation Council countries represent one of the main group exceptions to the substantial pattern of participation in the CSR51/PSR67 regime, a substantial number of Arab States elsewhere are States Parties including Algeria, Egypt, Tunisia, Sudan and Yemen. There is no separate regime, but attention has been given to particular issues of concern to States in the Arab world. In 1992 a Group of Arab Experts, meeting in Cairo at the Fourth Arab Seminar on 'Asylum and Refugee Law in the Arab World', finalised a Declaration on the Protection of Refugees and Displaced Persons in the Arab World. This recognised CSR51 and PSR67 as 'the basic universal instruments governing the status of refugees'. Article 1 declaration of the 'Reaffirms the fundamental right of every person to the free movement within his own country, or to leave it for another country and to return to his country of origin'.[25]

2.45 Two years later the League of Arab States adopted the 1994 Arab Convention on Regulating the Status of Refugees in the Arab Countries. This includes a widened refugee definition at article 1:

> Article 1
>
> For the purposes of this present Convention, a refugee means:
>
> Any person who is outside the country of his nationality or outside his habitual place of residence in case of not having a nationality and owing to well-grounded fear of being persecuted on account of his race, religion, nationality, membership of a particular social group or political opinion, unable or unwilling to avail himself of the protection of or return to such country.
>
> Any person who unwillingly takes refuge in a country other than his country of origin or his habitual place of residence because of sustained aggression against, occupation and foreign domination of such country or because of the occurrence of natural disasters or grave events resulting in major disruption of public order in the whole country or any part thereof.[26]

---

[25] Group of Arab Experts, *Declaration on the Protection of Refugees and Displaced Persons in the Arab World*, 19 November 1992, available at: www.refworld.org/docid/452675944.html.

[26] League of Arab States, *Arab Convention on Regulating Status of Refugees in the Arab Countries*, 1994, available at: www.refworld.org/docid/4dd5123f2.html.

As can be seen, the widened definition in the second paragraph consciously departs from the original emphasis on nationality, adopting instead an alternative formulation ('country of origin or his habitual place of residence').

C5. The Organization of the Islamic Conference/Organisation of Islamic Cooperation

The Organization of the Islamic Conference was established in 1969. On 28 June 2011 it changed its name to 'Organisation of Islamic Cooperation'. **2.46**

In 1990 at the Nineteenth Islamic Conference of Foreign Ministers, an institution of the Organization of the Islamic Conference established in 1969, 45 foreign ministers of Member States agreed publication of the Cairo Declaration on Human Rights in Islam Article 12 thereof provides that: **2.47**

> Article 12
>
> Every man shall have the right, within the framework of the Shari'ah, to free movement and to select his place of residence whether within or outside his country and if persecuted, is entitled to seek asylum in another country. The country of refuge shall be obliged to provide protection to the asylum-seeker until his safety has been attained, unless asylum is motivated by committing an act regarded by the Shari'ah as a crime.

Resolution No 15/10-P (IS) on the Problem of Refugees in the Muslim World, adopted at the Tenth Session of the Islamic Summit Conference in Malaysia expressed appreciation for the CSR51 regime calling on Member States to co-ordinate actions at international level with the UNHCR and, if not States Parties to CSR51, to consider accession 'given its continued relevance as the main universal instrument of refugees protection'. **2.48**

3

Interpretation

There is in principle only one correct interpretation of the Convention relating to the Status of Refugees 1951 (CSR51). Interpretation follows principles established in international law now expressed at articles 31–33 of the Vienna Convention on the Law of Treaties 1969 (VCLT69).

Contents

A. In Principle, One Interpretation

3.1 In principle there is only one true interpretation of the Convention relating to the Status of Refugees 1951 (CSR51), and the task of any international organisation, national court, or other interpreter is, as Lord Steyn has stated in *R v SSHD ex Adan; R v Secretary of State for the Home Department, ex p Aitseguer* [2000] UKHL 67, [2001] 2 AC 477, 516H–517A, to search, 'untrammelled by notions of its national legal culture, for the true autonomous and international meaning'. The delineation of the 'true and autonomous' meaning has however not been wholly free from difficulty in relation to CSR51.[1]

[1] See for instance G Goodwin-Gill, 'The Search for the One, True Meaning...' in G Goodwin-Gill and H Lambert, *The Limits of Transnational Law: Refugee Law, Policy Harmonization and Judicial Dialogue in the European Union* (CUP, 2010); and J McAdam, 'Interpretation of the 1951 Convention' in A Zimmermann (ed), *The 1951 Convention Relating to the Status of Refugees and its 1967 Protocol: A Commentary* (OUP, 2011).

B. The Vienna Convention on the Law of Treaties 1969

It is trite that CSR51 is an international instrument and that interpretation follows the rules of interpretation set out at articles 31–33 of the Vienna Convention on the Law of Treaties 1969 (VCLT69), including the 'General Rule of Interpretation' at article 31 VCLT69.[2] VCLT69 is likely to be enlarged in due course by the Vienna Convention on the Law of Treaties between States and International Organizations or between International Organizations 1986, but this has not yet come in to force (by article 85 it is to enter into force on the thirtieth day following the date of deposit of the thirty-fifth instrument of ratification or accession by a State or by Namibia, represented by the United Nations Council for Namibia: to date 31 such instruments have been filed). The 1986 Convention reproduces rather than altering or enlarging the VCLT69 provisions as regards treaty interpretation.[3] 3.2

B1. The General Rule of Interpretation

i. General Features

The 'General Rule of Interpretation' at article 31 provides as follows: 3.3

> Article 31
>
> General rule of interpretation
>
> 1. A treaty shall be interpreted in good faith in accordance with the ordinary meaning to be given to the terms of the treaty in their context and in the light of its object and purpose.
>
> 2. …
>
> 3. There shall be taken into account, together with the context:
>
> (a) any subsequent agreement between the parties regarding the interpretation of the treaty or the application of its provisions;
> (b) any subsequent practice in the application of the treaty which establishes the agreement of the parties regarding its interpretation;
> (c) any relevant rules of international law applicable in the relations between the parties.
>
> 4. A special meaning shall be given to a term if it is established that the parties so intended.

---

[2] Only a shorter account of general principles may be provided here. For a fuller account addressing both general principles and particular characteristics with particular regard to CSR51, see McAdam (above n 1); for another account by leading commentators, see J Hathaway and M Foster, *The Law of Refugee Status* (2nd edn, CUP, 2014) 5–13.

[3] See the relevant chapters in O Corten and P Klein (eds), *The Vienna Conventions on the Law of Treaties: A Commentary*, vol 1 (OUP, 2011).

3.4 Crawford has observed that VCLT69 represents the adoption of a particular approach, against a history in which multiple approaches had previously been advanced:

> Various 'rules' for interpreting treaties have been put forward over the years. These include the textual approach, the restrictive approach, the teleological approach, and the effectiveness principle. Of these only the textual approach is recognized in VCLT: Article 31 emphasizes the intention of the parties as expressed in the text, as the best guide to their common intention. The jurisprudence of the International Court likewise supports the textual approach.[4]

The VCLT69 approach is now applied almost universally by international courts and tribunals, including the International Court of Justice (ICJ) itself. The main exception is the Court of Justice of the European Union which tends to adopt a teleological, or purposive, approach at least in relation to European Union treaties: as Sorel and Boré-Eveno observe, 'the ECJ ... very early on developed a teleological interpretation in favour of Community treaties'.[5]

ii. 'Good Faith'

3.5 International courts and tribunals have had little to say concerning the requirement of 'good faith' in treaty interpretation, beyond reiteration of the General Rule at article 31(1) VCLT69 in which it is referred to. It obviously excludes the converse phenomenon: that of 'bad faith' in the sense of dishonest or manifestly unfounded interpretation. It cannot however be invoked to fill lacunae in the body of a treaty in a manner which if accepted would impose additional obligations upon the parties. In *R v Immigration Officer at Prague Airport ex parte European Roma Rights Centre* [2004] UKHL 55, [2005] 2 AC 1, an important issue was whether CSR51 prevented the United Kingdom from stationing immigration officials in the Czech Republic to prevent individuals from travelling to the United Kingdom to seek refugee status. Their Lordships' House cited 'good faith' both as a part of the general approach to interpretation of particular provisions and as a matter raised in submissions in which the action of the United Kingdom was said not to be in line with 'good faith' observation of CSR51, breaching an obligation to perform a treaty to which it is a State Party in good faith. Lord Bingham at 31e–32c reviewed some observations of other senior courts, and in conclusion held that 'there is no want of good faith if a state interprets a treaty as meaning what it says and declines to do anything significantly greater than or different from what it agreed to do':

> 19. In urging a broader and less literal approach to interpretation of the Convention, Lord Lester relied on article 26 of the Vienna Convention, entitled *Pacta sunt servanda*,

---

[4] J Crawford (ed), *Brownlie's Principles of Public International Law* (8th edn, OUP, 2012) 379.

[5] J-M Sorel and V Boré-Eveno, 'Article 31: General Rule of Interpretation' in O Corten and P Klein (eds), *The Vienna Conventions on the Law of Treaties: A Commentary*, vol 1 (OUP, 2011) 822.

which requires that a treaty in force should be performed by the parties to it in good faith and also on the requirement in article 31(1) that a treaty should be interpreted in good faith. Taken together, these rules call for good faith in the interpretation and performance of a treaty, and neither rule is open to question. But there is no want of good faith if a state interprets a treaty as meaning what it says and declines to do anything significantly greater than or different from what it agreed to do. The principle that *pacta sunt servanda* cannot require departure from what has been agreed. This is the more obviously true where a state or states very deliberately decided what they were and were not willing to undertake to do. The important backdrop to the Convention was well described by Hyndman, 'Refugees under International Law with a Reference to the Concept of Asylum' (1986) 60 ALJ 148, 153, in a passage quoted by McHugh and Gummow JJ in *Khawar*, above, para 44:

> 'States the world over consistently have exhibited great reluctance to give up their sovereign right to decide which persons will, and which will not, be admitted to their territory, and given a right to settle there. They have refused to agree to international instruments which would impose on them duties to make grants of asylum.
>
> Today, the generally accepted position would appear to be as follows: States consistently refuse to accept binding obligations to grant to persons, not their nationals, any rights to asylum in the sense of a permanent right to settle. Apart from any limitations which might be imposed by specific treaties, States have been adamant in maintaining that the question of whether or not a right of entry should be afforded to an individual, or to a group of individuals, is something which falls to each nation to resolve for itself'.

While a state party must show good faith in interpreting and performing a treaty obligation, the International Court of Justice made plain in *In re Border and Transborder Armed Actions* (*Nicaragua v Honduras*) [1988] ICJ Rep 69, para 94, and repeated in *In re Land and Maritime Boundary between Cameroon and Nigeria* (*Cameroon v Nigeria*) [1998] ICJ Rep 275, para 39, that

> 'The principle of good faith is, as the Court has observed, "one of the basic principles governing the creation and performance of legal obligations" … ; it is not in itself a source of obligation where none would otherwise exist'.

Lord Steyn at 45d–f echoed in his speech the conclusion that good faith did not entitle the Court to fill gaps left, implicitly intentionally, in the text of an international instrument:

> 43. The appellants never left the Czech Republic and are therefore not 'refugees' under article 1 of the Refugee Convention. They also never presented themselves at the frontier of the United Kingdom and properly construed the non-refoulement obligation under article 33 is not engaged. It is true, of course, that the Refugee Convention is a living instrument and must be interpreted as such. It must also be interpreted in accordance with good faith: article 31 of the Vienna Convention on the Law of Treaties. These are very important principles of interpretation. But they are not capable of filling gaps which were designedly left in the protective scope of the Refugee Convention. In my view there is no answer to the reasoning of Lord Bingham of Cornhill on these points.

Finally Lord Hope at 52a–f reiterated the principle already stated by Lords Bingham and Steyn:

> 62. But it is one thing for good faith to present itself as a principle of general application, as it is in these materials. It is another for it to be appealed to as a source of obligation in itself. It is here that caution is needed. In *In re Border and Transborder Armed Actions (Nicaragua v Honduras)* [1988] ICJ Rep 69, 105, para 94 the International Court of Justice referred to its observations in the *Nuclear Tests* case about the basic principle, adding that good faith 'is not in itself a source of obligation where none would otherwise exist'. This proposition was reaffirmed in *In re Land and Maritime Boundary between Cameroon and Nigeria (Cameroon v Nigeria)* [1998] ICJ Rep, 275, 297, para 39. In his review essay on *La Bonne Foi en Droit International Public* by Elisabeth Zoller (Paris, 1977) Michel Virally criticises her conclusion that, as good faith is not an autonomous source of legal rights and duties, no general obligation to behave in good faith exists in public international law (1983) 77 AJIL 130, 131. The view which he takes, which I for my part would accept, is that good faith really is a principle of international law, that all the actors in the international legal order are subjected to it and that they must endure its consequences, since good faith will serve to determine both the legal effects of their declarations and behaviour and the extent of their duties: p 133. But he also accepts it as true that, in practice, this general principle of law has only marginal value as an autonomous source of rights and duties and that, on this point, M Zoller's conclusions cannot be faulted. As he puts it, good faith is always related to specific behaviour or declarations. What it does is invest them with legal significance and legal effects: pp 133–134.
>
> 63. The question then is whether the appellants are seeking to do no more by appealing to this principle than insist that the rights and obligations which the 1951 Convention creates are exercised within the law, as Mr Goodwin-Gill put it, or whether they are seeking to enlarge what it provides so as to impose new obligations on the contracting states. In my opinion the answer to this question must be found in the language of the Convention, interpreted in good faith in accordance with the ordinary meaning to be given to the terms of the treaty in their context and in the light of its object and purpose, as article 31 of the Vienna Convention requires. The argument that good faith requires the state to refrain from actions which are incompatible with the object and purpose of the treaty can only be pressed so far. Everything depends on what the treaty itself provides.

The conclusion of Lord Bingham was cited and approved once again by Lord Hope in *R (otao ST Eritrea) v SSHD* [2012] UKSC 12, [2012] 2 AC 135, at [35].

3.6 Looking to the available material it appears that in ordinary cases, in which evidence of bad faith is lacking, the requirement for good faith adds little: in essence it provides a concrete citation of the need to avoid bad faith or egregious error.

iii. 'Ordinary Meaning'

3.7 The formulation of the rule in article 31 VCLT69 as not depending entirely upon 'ordinary meaning' recognises that most general terms possess multiple 'ordinary' meanings and that the most immediately apparent meaning, assuming that one can be agreed, may represent only 'a very fleeting starting point'.[6] An approach which gives precedence to ordinary meaning rather than analysing this in the round with other relevant factors may create intractable conflict between two or more 'ordinary meanings'. As Schwarzenberger pithily observed, 'The difficulty about [focus upon ordinary meaning] is that almost any word has more than one meaning. The word "meaning" itself, has at least sixteen different meanings'.[7] It is for this reason that considerable weight may attach to context and to object and purpose. The invocation of 'ordinary meaning' at article 31(1) VCLT69 does not point to direct reference to dictionary meanings in isolation. But as Gardiner has noted, dictionary or other sources of information concerning meaning may have one or more important uses in the task of interpretation under VCLT69:

> Dictionaries and other sources of definitions play their part in three ways:
>
> (i) The basic discovery of ordinary meanings of a term;
> (ii) The identification of a 'functional' meaning, in the sense of a meaning appropriate to the subject matter be it international law, hydrology, or whatever; and
> (iii) Ascertaining different language meanings, either to seek concepts peculiar to a languag e or as a prelude to comparing texts (in substance, the province of article 33 of the Vienna Convention).[8]

The use of 'ordinary meaning' as a starting point is not an invitation to impose a literal meaning which is not appropriate contextually. In *Polish Postal Service in Danzig (Advisory Opinion)* (1925) PCIJ Ser B No 11, the Permanent Court of International Justice considered the request of the responsible official of the League of Nations regarding the meaning of provisions in the 1919 Versailles Treaty and other instruments providing for the operation by Poland of a 'postal service' extra-territorially in the Free City of Danzig. A building in Danzig had been provided for use by the Polish postal authorities, but the Free City protested against the setting up of post boxes and all activity by Polish postmen on its territory outside the building provided. The Court considered it plain that the term 'Permission to establish a private local postal and telegraph service in the port of Danzig' implied liberty to extend the 'normal functions' of a postal service including the collection and delivery of post outside the main Post Office building: **3.8**

> It will be seen that there is no trace of any provision confining the operation of the Polish postal authorities to the inside of its postal building. The postal service which Poland is entitled to establish in the port of Danzig must be interpreted in its ordinary sense so as to include the normal functions of a postal service as regards the collection and distribution of postal matter outside the post-office. Indeed, any limitations or

[6] R Gardiner, *Treaty Interpretation* (2nd edn, OUP, 2015) 181.

[7] G Schwarzenberger, 'Myths and Realities of Treaty Interpretation: Articles 27–29 of the Vienna Draft Convention on the Law of Treaties' (1968) 9 *Virginia Journal of International Law* 1, 13.

[8] See Gardiner (n 6 above) 183–84 and 186.

> restrictions in this respect would be of so exceptional a character that they cannot, in the absence of express reservations, be read into the text of treaty stipulations.[9]

3.9 Ordinary meaning 'is immediately and intimately linked with context, and then to be taken in conjunction with all other relevant elements of the Vienna rules', that is, object and purpose.[10] Crawford has said that

> A corollary of the principle of ordinary meaning is the principle of integration: the meaning must emerge in the context of the treaty as a whole (including the text, its preamble and annexes, and any agreement or instrument related to the treaty and drawn up in connection with its conclusion) and in the light of its object and purpose.[11]

The same point has been frequently made by the International Court of Justice. In its decision concerning the *Arbitral Award of 31 July 1989 (Guinea-Bissau v Senegal)* [1991] ICJ Reports 53, the Court reiterated and endorsed observations concerning the correct approach to 'ordinary meaning' in treaty interpretation. The question before it had been earlier defined as whether 'by rendering the disputed Award the Tribunal acted in manifest breach of the competence conferred on it by the Arbitration Agreement, either by deciding in excess of, or by failing to exercise, its jurisdiction'. The Court's judgment then moved to consider the rules of interpretation which bound the arbitration:

> 48. Such manifest breach might result from, for example, the failure of the Tribunal properly to apply the relevant rules of interpretation to the provisions of the Arbitration Agreement which govern its competence. An arbitration agreement (compromis d'arbitrage) is an agreement between States which must be interpreted in accordance with the general rules of international law governing the interpretation of treaties. In that respect
>
> > 'the first duty of a tribunal which is called upon to interpret and apply the provisions of a treaty, is to endeavour to give effect to them in their natural and ordinary meaning in the context in which they occur. If the relevant words in their natural and ordinary meaning make sense in their context, that is an end of the matter. If, on the other hand, the words in their natural and ordinary meaning are ambiguous or lead to an unreasonable result, then, and then only, must the Court, by resort to other methods of interpretation, seek to ascertain what the parties really did mean when they used these words'. (*Competence of the General Assembly for the Admission of a State to the United Nations, Advisory Opinion, ICJ Reports 1950*, P 8.)
>
> The rule of interpretation according to the natural and ordinary meaning of the words employed
>
> > 'is not an absolute one. Where such a method of interpretation results in a meaning incompatible with the spirit, purpose and context of the clause or instrument in which the words are contained, no reliance can be validly placed on it'. (*South West Africa, Preliminary Objections, Judgment, ICJ Reports 1962*, p 336.)

---

[9] At 37.
[10] Gardiner (n 6 above) 181.
[11] Crawford (n 4 above) 381.

These principles are reflected in Articles 31 and 32 of the Vienna Convention on the Law of Treaties, which may in many respects be considered as a codification of existing customary international law on the point.

iv. 'Context'

'Context' requires that account be taken of the whole structure, content and syntax, including Preamble, text and annexes, and also the matters invoked at article 31(2) VCLT69.[12] 3.10

v. 'Object and Purpose'

'Object' and 'purpose' often appear as a single dual citation, reflecting the closeness of meaning the two terms possess in English. However, in French (the Treaty texts in the two languages are by the Treaty itself made equally authentic) the parallel language makes the two terms '*l'objet*' and '*le but*' somewhat more mutually distinctive, which is of some assistance in interpreting the intention embedded in the English terms. Gardiner cites Buffard and Zemanek on the French public law underlying the language, by which '*l'objet*' means what a legal instrument 'does in the sense of creating a particular set of rights and obligations' and '*le but*', as the reason or motivation for enacting the instrument and its *objet*:[13] 3.11

> According to this French doctrine the term 'object' indicates the substantial content of the norm, the provisions, rights, and obligations created by the norm. The object of a treaty is the instrument for the achievement of the treaty's purpose, and this purpose is, in turn, the general result which the parties want to achieve by the treaty. While the object can be found in the provisions of the treaty, the purpose may not always be explicit and be prone to a more subjective understanding.[14]

An important source of guidance regarding the object and purpose of a convention is its Preamble. Some modern treaties also have express accompanying guidance. The *travaux préparatoires*, or records of the negotiation and drafting history, do not have any relevance for purposes of article 31 VCLT69—they are expressly a secondary source under article 32 VCLT69. 3.12

Article 31(3)(c) VCLT69 requires the taking into account 'together with the context' of 'any relevant rules of international law applicable in the relations between the parties'. The question of what international law rules are relevant of course depends upon the context, so that the direct linkage of these two matters 3.13

[12] Gardiner (n 6 above) 197–210.

[13] Ibid, 213.

[14] I Buffard and K Zemanek, 'The "Object and Purpose" of a Treaty: An Enigma?' (1998) 3 *Austrian Review of International and European Law* 311, 326.

reflects the relationship. An example of application of such rules is the decision of the ICJ in the case of *Oil Platforms (Islamic Republic of Iran v United States of America)* (Judgment) [2003] ICJ Reports 161, in which the application of relevant international rules was affirmed as 'an integral part of the task of interpretation' of the 1955 Treaty of Amity, Economic Relations and Consular Rights between Iran and the United States:

> 41. Moreover, under the general rules of treaty interpretation, as reflected in the 1969 Vienna Convention on the Law of Treaties, interpretation must take into account 'any relevant rules of international law applicable in the relations between the parties' (Art 31, para 3 (c)). The Court cannot accept that Article XX, paragraph 1(d), of the 1955 Treaty was intended to operate wholly independently of the relevant rules of international law on the use of force, so as to be capable of being successfully invoked, even in the limited context of a claim for breach of the Treaty, in relation to an unlawful use of force. The application of the relevant rules of international law relating to this question thus forms an integral part of the task of interpretation entrusted to the Court by Article XXI, paragraph 2, of the 1955 Treaty.

3.14 Article 31(3)(c) VCLT69 has been frequently referred to in adjudications of other international tribunals, for instance the Dispute Settlement Body of the World Trade Organization (WTO) in a line of panel reports. In *Korea: Measures Affecting Government Procurement*, for example, the panel affirmed that customary international law applies generally to the economic relations between WTO Members, and can be excluded in WTO arrangements only by specifically opting out:

> 7.96 Customary international law applies generally to the economic relations between the WTO Members. Such international law applies to the extent that the WTO treaty agreements do not 'contract out' from it. To put it another way, to the extent there is no conflict or inconsistency, or an expression in a covered WTO agreement that implies differently, we are of the view that the customary rules of international law apply to the WTO treaties and to the process of treaty formation under the WTO.[15]

3.15 Article 31(3)(c) VCLT69 has also been important in decisions of the European Court of Human Rights.[16] In *Golder v United Kingdom* 4451/70 [1975] ECHR 1 the Court established a pattern of relating 'relevant rules of international law' under article 31(3)(c) VCLT69 to the 'general principles of law recognized by civilized nations' envisaged under article 38(1)(c) of the 1945 Statute of the International Court of Justice.

> 35. Article 31 para 3(c) of the Vienna Convention indicates that account is to be taken, together with the context, of 'any relevant rules of international law applicable in the

[15] World Trade Organization Dispute Settlement Body, *Korea, Measures Affecting Government Procurement*, 1 May 2000, WTO Doc WT/DS163/R, 7.96.

[16] Further iterations of the principle may be found at *Soering v United Kingdom*: 14038/88 (1989) 11 EHRR 439 [88]; *Al-Adsani v United Kingdom*: 35763/97 [2001] ECHR 761, (2001) 34 EHRR 273 [55]; *Mamatkulov and Askarov v Turkey*: 46827/99, 46951/99 (2005) 41 EHRR 25 [52], [99]; *Bosphorus Hava Yollari Turizm ve Ticaret Anonim Şirketi v Ireland*: 45036/98 [2005] ECHR 440, (2005) 42 EHRR 1 [100], [150]; *Saadi v United Kingdom*: 13229/03, [2008] ECHR 80' (2008) 47 EHRR 17 [26], [62].

> relations between the parties'. Among those rules are general principles of law and especially 'general principles of law recognized by civilized nations' (Article 38 para 1(c) of the Statute of the International Court of Justice). Incidentally, the Legal Committee of the Consultative Assembly of the Council of Europe foresaw in August 1950 that 'the Commission and the Court must necessarily apply such principles' in the execution of their duties and thus considered it to be 'unnecessary' to insert a specific clause to this effect in the Convention (Documents of the Consultative Assembly, working papers of the 1950 session, Vol III, no 93, p 982, para 5).[17]

The rules of international law within the scope of article 31(3)(c) VCLT69 are not restricted, in the case of an instrument such as CSR51, to those extant at the time of its original agreement. As *Oppenheim's International Law* acknowledges, general concepts embodied in a treaty may be read as intended to evolve accommodating changing circumstances rather than to remain static.[18] In its Advisory Opinion in *Legal Consequences for States of the Continued Presence of South Africa in Namibia (South West Africa) notwithstanding Security Council Resolution 276* [1971] (Advisory Opinion) ICJ Reports 16, at 31 [53], the Court with reference to the issue of whether principles concerning self-determination international law should be considered in interpreting earlier instruments, said that: 3.16

> 53. That is why, viewing the institutions of 1919, the Court must take into consideration the changes which have occurred in the supervening half-century, and its interpretation cannot remain unaffected by the subsequent development of law, through the Charter of the United Nations and by way of customary law. Moreover, an international instrument has to be interpreted and applied within the framework of the entire legal system prevailing at the time of the interpretation. In the domain to which the present proceedings relate, the last fifty years, as indicated above, have brought important developments.

Other ICJ decisions and Advisory Opinions have referred to the same principle.[19] The *Namibia* case shows the degree to which interpretation of the terms of a treaty 'in their context and in the light of its object and purpose' may itself militate towards development in line with the state of the wider international law, at least in the absence of express limitation in the treaty's terms. Interpretation of CSR51 follows this approach.[20] In the House of Lords, Lord Bingham in *Sepet v SSHD* [2003] UKHL 15 [2003] 1 WLR 856 [6] cited with approval earlier conclusions of two greatly respected judges, each concluding separately that CSR51 was 'a living instrument' in the sense of anticipating onward development in surrounding international law norms: 3.17

> 6. It is plain that the Convention has a single autonomous meaning, to which effect should be given in and by all member states, regardless of where a decision falls to be

[17] *Golder v United Kingdom* app no 4451/70 [1975] ECHR 1 [35].

[18] R Jennings and A Watts (eds), *Oppenheim's International Law*, vol 1 ('Peace') (9th edn, OUP, 1992) 1282, §633.

[19] For instance see *Aegean Sea Continental Shelf (Greece v Turkey)* [1978] ICJ Rep 3, 33.

[20] McAdam (n 1 above) 103–04.

made ... It is also, I think, plain that the Convention must be seen as a living instrument in the sense that while its meaning does not change over time its application will. I would agree with the observation of Sedley J in *R v Immigration Appeal Tribunal, Ex p Shah* [1997] Imm AR 145, 152:

> 'Unless it [the Convention] is seen as a living thing, adopted by civilised countries for a humanitarian end which is constant in motive but mutable in form, the Convention will eventually become an anachronism'.

I would also endorse the observation of Laws LJ in [*R v SSHD ex p Adan; R v SSHD ex p Aitsegeur* [1999] EWCA Civ 1948, [1999] 4 All ER 774, 795]:

> 'It is clear that the signatory states intended that the Convention should afford continuing protection for refugees in the changing circumstances of the present and future world. In our view the Convention has to be regarded as a living instrument: just as, by the Strasbourg jurisprudence, the European Convention on Human Rights is so regarded'.

3.18 Article 31(4) VCLT69 provides that 'A special meaning shall be given to a term if it is established that the parties so intended'. This represents an avenue in relation to which the intention of the parties, which is not specifically admitted by article 31 VCLT69 for any other purpose, is particularly significant. Sorel and Boré-Eveno observe that

> The Vienna Convention places priority on textual interpretation. Nevertheless, as reflected by the history of the [International Law Commission] *travaux*, proponents of interpretation based on the intention of the parties (or 'subjective' interpretation) have not surrendered. Moreover, it is not always obvious in practice to distinguish between the 'declared' intention of the parties resulting from a reading of the text, and the search for the true intention of the parties, a much more subjective exercise. The compromise represented by Article 31 therefore makes space for the intention of the parties in a somewhat subsidiary manner, but that space has proven crucial for certain courts. Indeed, while logic may imply that the discovery of a 'special meaning' should lead to an analysis of the intention of the parties, the reality is sometimes limited to affirming the existence of 'special meaning' to privilege this intention, without always paying attention to the veracity of this specificity.[21]

The most obvious evidence of the intention to apply a special meaning is a special definition provided within the treaty: so, in familiar contexts, the definitions of 'refugee' for purposes of CSR51 provided at article 1A CSR51 and of 'stateless person' at article 1(1) of the Convention relating to the Status of Stateless Persons 1954.

B2. Supplementary Means of Interpretation

3.19 Article 32 VCLT69 identifies two further potential sources—the *travaux préparatoires* and circumstances of conclusion of the treaty—as secondary

[21] Sorel and Boré-Eveno (n 5 above) 829.

sources, admissible only to confirm the result of article 31 VCLT69 analysis or to determine meaning when interpretation according to article 31 VCLT69 '(a) leaves the meaning ambiguous or obscure; or (b) leads to a result which is manifestly absurd or unreasonable'.

C. Fragmentation and *Lex Specialis*

As early as 1953, C Wilfred Jenks noted the absence of a general legislative body of the international community as a result of which international law remained a highly decentralised system. He envisaged the potential need to act to address both the possibility of conflict between treaty regimes and the risk of isolation of regimes from general international law: **3.20**

> In the absence of a world legislature with a general mandate, law-making treaties are tending to develop in a number of historical, functional and regional groups which are separate from each other and whose mutual relationships are in some respects analogous to those of separate systems of municipal law.[22]

More recently, following an extensive debate amongst commentators, the International Law Commission has focused upon the subject of 'fragmentation', motivated by concerns on the part of some international lawyers and judges that the isolation of certain regimes within international law from others and from the wider body of international law creates a risk of conflict or incoherence. The topic is most fully addressed in 2006 by the Report of the Study Group of the International Law Commission on *Fragmentation of International Law: Difficulties arising from the Diversification and Expansion of International Law* chaired by Martii Koskenniemi.[23] The Study Group identified fragmentation as having attained significance through an increasing specialisation of separate international law regimes in line with functional differentiation in many other aspects of modern society: **3.21**

> 7. One of the features of late international modernity has been what sociologists have called 'functional differentiation', the increasing specialization of parts of society and the related autonomization of those parts. This takes place nationally as well as internationally. It is a well-known paradox of globalization that while it has led to increasing uniformization of social life around the world, it has also lead to its increasing fragmentation—that is, to the emergence of specialized and relatively autonomous spheres of social action and structure.

[22] CW Jenks, 'The Conflict of Law-Making Treaties' in *British Yearbook of International Law* 1953 (OUP, 1954) 401–53, 403.

[23] ILC, Report of the International Law Commission, Fifty-eighth Session (1 May–9 June and 3 July–11 August 2006) Ch 12, Conclusions of the work of the Study Group on the Fragmentation of International Law: Difficulties arising from the Diversification and Expansion of International Law (UN Doc A/61/10). Fragmentation of International Law: Difficulties Arising from the Diversification and Expansion of International Law, Report of the Study Group of the International Law Commission Finalized by Martti Koskenniemi (ILC Doc A/CN.4/L.682) (13 April 2006).

8. The fragmentation of the international social world has attained legal significance especially as it has been accompanied by the emergence of specialized and (relatively) autonomous rules or rule-complexes, legal institutions and spheres of legal practice. What once appeared to be governed by 'general international law' has become the field of operation for such specialist systems as 'trade law', 'human rights law', 'environmental law', 'law of the sea', 'European law' and even such exotic and highly specialized knowledges as 'investment law' or 'international refugee law' etc—each possessing their own principles and institutions. The problem, as lawyers have seen it, is that such specialized law-making and institution-building tends to take place with relative ignorance of legislative and institutional activities in the adjoining fields and of the general principles and practices of international law. The result is conflicts between rules or rule-systems, deviating institutional practices and possibly, the loss of an overall perspective on the law.

3.22 The Study Group acknowledged the existence of a system of international law containing norms and systems of norms which potentially interacted on a number of different levels, which might severally relate to each other through interpretation or might conflict:

2. CONCLUSIONS OF THE WORK OF THE STUDY GROUP

251. The conclusions reached in the work of the Study Group are as follows:

(a) *General*

(1) International law is a legal system. Its rules and principles (ie its norms) act in relation to and should be interpreted against the background of other rules and principles. As a legal system, international law is not a random collection of such norms. There are meaningful relationships between them. Norms may this exist at higher and lower hierarchical levels, their formulation may involve greater or lesser generality and specificity and their validity may date back to earlier or later moments in time.

(2) In applying international law, it is often necessary to determine the precise relationship between two or more rules and principles that are both valid and applicable in respect of a situation. For that purpose the relevant relationships fall into two general types:

- *Relationships of interpretation.* This is the case where one norm assists in the interpretation of another. A norm may assist in the interpretation of another norm for example as an application, clarification, updating, or modification of the latter. In such situation, both norms are applied in conjunction.
- *Relationships of conflict.* This is the case where two norms that are both valid and applicable point to incompatible decisions so that a choice must be made between them. The basic rules concerning the resolution of normative conflicts are to be found in the VCLT.[24]

(3) *The VCLT.* When seeking to determine the relationship of two or more norms to each other, the norms should be interpreted in accordance with or analogously to the VCLT and especially the provisions in its articles 31–33 having to do with the interpretation of treaties.

---

[24] Ibid, §252.

(4) *The principle of harmonization.* It is a generally accepted principle that when several norms bear on a single issue they should, to the extent possible, be interpreted so as to give rise to a single set of compatible obligations.

The term *lex specialis*, which is employed in many contexts in international law, including in relation to questions of conflict or overlapping of different norms in relation to particular subject matter, also identifies the relationship by which open-ended norms of international law may be interpreted by reference to other norms of international law concerning particular subject matter. In 2006 the Report of the Study Group, chaired by Martii Koskenniemi, sought to clarify the core meaning of the term: **3.23**

2. The maxim *lex specialis derogat legi generali*

(5) *General principle.* The maxim *lex specialis derogat legi generali* is a generally accepted technique of interpretation and conflict resolution in international law. It suggests that whenever two or more norms deal with the same subject matter, priority should be given to the norm that is more specific. The principle may be applicable in several contexts: between provisions within a single treaty, between provisions within two or more treaties, between a treaty and a non-treaty standard, as well as between two non-treaty standards. The source of the norm (whether treaty, custom, or general principle of law) is not decisive for the determination of the more specific standard. However in practice treaties often act as *lex specialis* by reference to the relevant customary law and general principles.

(6) *Contextual appreciation.* The relationship between the *lex specialis* maxim and other norms of interpretation or conflict solution cannot be determined in a general way. Which consideration should be predominant—ie whether it is the speciality or the time of emergence of the norm—should be decided contextually.

An illustration is provided by the ICJ in the *Legality of the Threat or Use of Nuclear Weapons* Advisory Opinion of 8 July 1996, [1996] ICJ Reports 226, wherein the majority found that international humanitarian law (the law particularly concerned with the conduct of warfare) did not have to be looked to independently where it was in any event relevant as *lex specialis* informing open-ended norms of international human rights law, in that case article 6 of the International Covenant on Civil and Political Rights 1966:

25. The test of what is an arbitrary deprivation of life, however, then falls to be determined by the applicable *lex specialis*, namely, the law applicable in armed conflict which is designed to regulate the conduct of hostilities. Thus whether a particular loss of life, through the use of a certain weapon in warfare, is to be considered an arbitrary deprivation of life contrary to Article 6 of the Covenant, can only be decided by reference to the law applicable in armed conflict and not deduced from the terms of the Covenant itself.

The concerns expressed by commentators in relation to fragmentation—of collective incoherence and mutual conflict amongst international law norms, are mitigated by correct application of *lex specialis* principles as an interpretive technique where this is otherwise consistent with VCLT69. **3.24**

Part II

Interpretation of Relevant Provisions

4

Well-Founded Fear of Being Persecuted 'for Reasons of ... Nationality'

'Nationality' as one of the Convention reasons enumerated at article 1A(2) of the Convention relating to the Status of Refugees (CSR51) may overlap other Convention reasons such as race. It includes both nationality or citizenship status in the legal sense, including the absence of nationality (statelessness), and nationality as a historico-biological term denoting membership of a nation.

Contents

A. Nationality: Use of the Term in Different Senses in the 1951 Convention Relating to the Status of Refugees

The term 'nationality' is employed at article 1A(2) of the Convention relating to the Status of Refugees 1951 (CSR51) in two distinct contexts. When first employed, in the phrase 'owing to well-founded fear of being persecuted for reasons of ... nationality', it identifies one of the five enumerated reasons for 'fear of being persecuted' necessary for qualification as a refugee. This usage is repeated later at article 33(1) where it delineates one of the reasons for relevant threat which engage the prohibition of *refoulement*. The term is also used elsewhere in article 1A(2) in relation to the determination of the country or countries of reference, in respect of which an individual must show inability or unwillingness to return due to well-founded fear of persecution for a relevant reason. This chapter 4.1

addresses the interpretation of 'nationality' in the first sense, that of nationality as one of the five qualifying reasons for persecution often referred to collectively as 'Convention reasons'.

B. Earlier Citation of Nationality as a Qualifying Reason

4.2 The very requirement that persecution be motivated by one (or more) of the factors identified at article 1A(2) CSR51 indicates the importance of discrimination to the international refugee law regime. By the time CSR51 was drafted, protection from discrimination on the basis of nationality had already attracted some notice in international law. The United Nations Charter, signed in June 1945, contains no specific declaration identifying nationality as a prohibited basis for discrimination. But the Constitution of the International Refugee Organisation (IRO) 1946, at Annex 1, Part 1, section A, paragraph 1, whilst not referring to nationality-based discrimination as part of the refugee definition, cited 'Persons who were considered refugees before the outbreak of the second world war, for reasons of race, religion, nationality or political opinion' as entitled to protection (see quotation at para 2.13 above). At section C the Constitution provided as valid reasons for objection to repatriation on the part of a refugee (then a primary aim of a legal regime based largely upon absence of national protection or displacement rather than fear of return to a home country) 'Persecution, or fear, based on reasonable grounds of persecution because of race, religion, nationality or political opinions, provided these opinions are not in conflict with the principles of the United Nations, as laid down in the Preamble of the Charter of the United Nations'.[1]

4.3 Later, article 2 of the Universal Declaration of Human Rights 1948 (UDHR48) provided that 'Everyone is entitled to all the rights and freedoms set forth in this declaration, without distinction of any kind, such as race, colour, sex, language, political or other opinion, national or social origin, property, birth, or other status', 'national origin' including and extending beyond nationality in the wider sense, and the 1950 Statute of the Office of the United Nations High Commissioner for Refugees (UNHCR) at article 6A(ii), an important precursor of article 1A(2) CSR51, defined as a refugee a person 'outside the country of his nationality' by reason of a well-founded fear of being persecuted 'for reasons of race, religion, nationality, or political opinion'– the changed definition reflecting the significant developments in the calculation of protection entitlement since the IRO Constitution only four years before. Nationality was included amongst the grounds for persecution identified in CSR51 from almost the start of the drafting process, being part of the provisional draft before the Ad Hoc Committee on Statelessness

[1] United Nations, Constitution of the International Refugee Organisation 1946, 15 December 1946, United Nations, Treaty Series, vol 18, available at www.unhcr.org/3ae69ef14.html.

and Related Problems on 23 January 1950: article 1A(2) of the draft identified as a refugee:

> Any person who (i) is and remains outside the countries of his nationality, former nationality or former habitual residence owing to persecution, or well-founded fear of persecution, for reasons of race, religion, nationality or political opinion, (ii) is unable or for valid reasons unwilling to avail himself of the protection of any one of the said countries, and (iii) belongs to one of the following categories:
>
> (a) victims of the Nazi regime in Germany or in territory purported to have been incorporated in Germany, or of a regime which took part on its side in Second World War, or of a regime in a country occupied by Germany which assisted Germany against the United Nations;
> (b) victims of the Falangist regime in Spain;
> (c) persons whose persecution or fear of persecution is due to events in Europe after the outbreak of the Second World War and before July 1, 1950.[2]

Accordingly the citation of nationality as a basis for well-founded fear of persecution capable of giving rise to refugee status entitlement was not novel—a route of descent can be seen leading in particular from the IRO Constitution and UDHR48 to CSR51. More generally, nationality is frequently cited in relation to the growth of non-discrimination into an important principle of international law. In *Canada (Attorney General) v Ward* [1993] 2 SCR 689 (1993) 103 DLR (4th) 1, La Forest J delivering the judgment of the Court cited at 33h, with evident approval, a conclusion of Goodwin-Gill quoted earlier at 30d: **4.4**

> The references to 'race, religion, nationality, membership of [*sic*] a particular social group or political opinion' illustrate briefly the characteristics of individuals and groups which are considered worthy of special protection. These same factors have figured in the development of the fundamental principle of non-discrimination in general international law, and have contributed to the formulation of other fundamental human rights.[3]

C. Meaning

i. Definition of 'Nationality'

As already seen in chapter one, the term 'nationality' has long had at least two distinct general meanings relevant for present purposes. These were delineated in 1956 and again in 1979 by Weis: **4.5**

> The term 'nationality'... is a politico-legal term denoting membership of a State. It must be distinguished from nationality as a historico-biological term denoting membership

---

[2] UN Ad Hoc Committee on Refugees and Stateless Persons, *Ad Hoc Committee on Statelessness and Related Problems, Provisional Draft of Parts of the Definition Article of the Preliminary Draft Convention Relating to the Status of Refugees, Prepared by the Working Group on This Article*, 23 January 1950, E/AC.32/L.6, available at: http://www.refworld.org/docid/3ae68c1814.html.

[3] The quotation is from G Goodwin-Gill, *The Refugee in International Law* (Clarendon Press, 1983) 39.

> of a nation. In the latter sense it means the subjective corporate sentiment of unity of members of a specific group forming a 'race' or 'nation' which may, though not necessarily, be possessed of a territory and which, by seeking political unity on that territory, may lead to the formation of a State.[4]

The 'historico-biological' part of the definition requires a quality properly highlighted by Weis, that is, the attachment of some 'national', or 'political', character to the group. An expansive ethnic or linguistic group, such as speakers of English or of Swahili, which has no sufficiently shared political history or destiny, is not *per se* a 'nationality', though it may be a race or social group.

ii. Interpretation of 'Nationality' as a Convention Reason

4.6 Whilst difficult issues may arise in considering the application of the term 'nationality' to particular situations, the relevance and basic scope of nationality as a reason for persecution is relatively clear. Although the early commentator Robinson ventured that 'It is rather difficult to understand how a national of a country could be persecuted by his own government because of his nationality',[5] the objection itself is, with respect, one which can be seen to be unsound. There is obvious potential for persecution of people by reason of their nationality where the country is dominated by non-nationals, with those possessing or thought to possess nationality or citizenship or some of them as targets of persecution for this reason. Military occupation or political domination by a foreign State or group represents a potential context for this. It also seems patently clear that nationality could be a reason for persecution where the nationality in question is a dual nationality—so that a person who is a national both of country A and of country B fears persecution in country A because of a nationality of country B (though refugee status might then also depend upon the situation as regards that person and country B and any other country of nationality, as explored in chapter five). Further, the language of persecution 'for reasons of … nationality' seems capable of extending to the situation in which an individual is persecuted for lacking a nationality—as for distance where a section of the population has been denationalised or is denied the benefits of nationality or citizenship.

4.7 Other possibilities include a State having more than one class of national, with one or more classes of national oppressed by the authorities or by agents of

---

[4] P Weis, *Nationality and Statelessness* (2nd edn, Brill, 1979) 3.

[5] N Robinson, *Convention relating to the Status of Refugees, its History, Contents, and Interpretation* (Institute of Jewish Affairs, 1953) 53.

persecution,[6] or oppression in the context of an attempt to remove rights by the creation of a false situation of state succession, as when South Africa created 'bantustan' territories whose nationality it assigned to black South Africans to deny them their rights as South African citizens—here the 'reasons of ... nationality' are tied to the delineation of a group by the State and its discriminatory manipulation of its laws.[7]

Further, whilst commentators have differed in the language they have used, and some have dealt relatively shortly with this issue, there is virtually complete agreement that nationality in the context of well-founded fear of being persecuted 'for reasons of ... nationality' extends both to nationality in the sense of linkage to a State for purposes of international law, and also to nationality in a wider cultural or political sense.[8] Reasons for this include the absence of any explicit justification for limitation to the international law definition of nationality (by distinction with 'nationality' as used in the other sense in article 1A(2) CSR51, in direct relationship with the term 'country' and the concept of 'protection of that country') and also the wide employment of the other definition in ordinary language. This consensus recognises the meaning of nationality in the Convention reason context as taking in both of the meanings delineated by Weis. As a Convention reason, 'nationality' includes the politico-legal term denoting membership of a State and the separate historico-biological notion of members of a non-State 'nation'.[9] **4.8**

This dual definition is supported by possibly the earliest commentator to have substantial authority as a specialist in international refugee law, Grahl-Madsen. As early as 1966 he identified the extension of nationality both to legal nationality or citizenship and to a wider concept he linked to ethnicity: **4.9**

> 'Nationality' may mean citizenship (nationality in a formal sense, *Staatsangehörigkeit*) as well as membership of an ethnic group. In the present context [Convention reason] the term means both. There is no doubt that persons persecuted because of their citizenship as well as persons persecuted because of their ethnic affiliation may benefit under the present provision.[10]

---

[6] Anker cites Palestinians in Israel: D Anker, *The Law of Asylum in the United States* (7th edn, Thomson Reuters, 2014) 538, §5.85.

[7] L Waldman, *The Definition of Convention Refugee* (Butterworths Canada, 2001) §8.180, §8.271; J Hathaway and M Foster, *The Law of Refugee Status* (2nd edn, CUP, 2014) 398; Anker (n 6 above) 538, §5.85.

[8] For instance Waldman (n 7 above) 8.180–8.181; G Goodwin-Gill and J McAdam, *The Refugee in International Law* (3rd edn, OUP, 2007) 72–73; M Symes and P Jorro, *Asylum Law and Practice* (2nd edn, Bloomsbury Professional, 2010) 207, §4.6t; A Zimmermann and C Mahler in A Zimmermann (ed), *The 1951 Convention Relating to the Status of Refugees and its 1967 Protocol: A Commentary* (OUP, 2011) 388–90, §§384–94 and 442, §583 respectively; Hathaway and Foster (n 7 above) 397–99; Anker (n 6 above) 537–40, §5.85–5.86.

[9] See for instance the *Oxford English Dictionary* entry for 'nation', quoted in relevant part in ch 1, para 1.1, above.

[10] A Grahl-Madsen, *The Status of Refugees in International Law*, vol I (AW Sijthoff, 1966) 218–19, §89.

4.10 This dual definition—encompassing nationality in a legal sense on one hand and a broader 'historico-biological' meaning, in the words of Weis, is made explicit in the UNHCR *Handbook*, first published in 1979, which states that:

> 74. The term 'nationality' in this context is not to be understood only as 'citizenship'. It refers also to membership of an ethnic or linguistic group and may occasionally overlap with the term 'race'. Persecution for reasons of nationality may consist of adverse attitudes and measures directed against a national (ethnic, linguistic) minority and in certain circumstances the fact of belonging to such a minority may in itself give rise to well-founded fear of persecution.[11]

4.11 This was echoed in 1988 by Plender, citing early Dutch decisions regarding Eritreans in Ethiopia: 'The term "nationality" [in the context of Convention reason] is to be understood in a broad sense, to embrace not only citizenship but also membership of an ethnic or linguistic group'.[12] In 2001 Waldman also contrasted these two concluding that 'nationality' as a Convention reason possessed a broader definition than elsewhere.[13] And more recently the conclusion of Haines has been similar. He wrote that nationality 'should be understood not simply as citizenship but, in its broadest sense, to include membership of an ethnic or linguistic group'.[14]

4.12 The UNHCR *Handbook* entry endorsing a compound significance for 'nationality' in the Convention reason sense is referred to with apparent approval in the Immigration and Refugee Board of Canada Interpretation of the Convention Refugee Definition in the Case Law of 2010.[15] In the United States, too, a dual definition appears to be accepted. The current United States Citizenship and Immigration Services (USCIS) Asylum Officer Basic Training Course refers to nationality in the Convention reason context as 'the second part of the refugee definition' expressly including both nationality as legal membership and nationality in the historico-biological sense:

> Contrast this with the definition of 'nationality' in the second part of the refugee definition—'on account of nationality'. In the second part of the definition, 'nationality' is *not* to be understood only as 'citizenship', but also refers to ethnic or linguistic groups.[16]

---

[11] UNHCR, *Handbook and Guidelines on Procedures and Criteria for Determining Refugee Status under the 1951 Convention and the 1967 Protocol relating to the Status of Refugees*, Reissued, Geneva, December 2011, §§74–76.

[12] R Plender, *International Migration Law* (2nd edn, Martinus Nijhoff, 1988) 421.

[13] Waldman (n 7 above) §8.333.

[14] R Haines, 'Gender-related Persecution' in E Feller, V Türk and F Nicholson (eds), *Refugee Protection in International Law* (CUP, 2003) 344.

[15] Immigration and Refugee Board of Canada, *Interpretation of the Convention Refugee Definition in the Case Law, 31 December 2010, 4.3*, available at: www.irb-cisr.gc.ca/Eng/BoaCom/references/LegJur/Pages/RefDef.aspx.

[16] USCIS Asylum Officer Basic Training Course, *Asylum Eligibility Part I: Definitions; Past Persecution* 8–9, available at: www.uscis.gov/sites/default/files/USCIS/Humanitarian/Refugees%20%26%20Asylum/Asylum/AOBTC%20Lesson%20Plans/.

4.13 By contrast, Zimmermann and Mahler have also pointed to a wider definition, though focusing on ethnic origin apparently to the exclusion of status, rather than to a definition including both:

> As part of the relevant grounds of persecution eventually leading to a well-founded fear of persecution listed in Art 1A para 2, the notion of 'nationality', as demonstrated above, does *not* refer to the technical term of 'nationality', *ie* the legal bond between a person and a State in the sense of citizenship, but rather to a person's ethnic origin.[17]

4.14 Insofar as Zimmermann and Mahler advance a more restrictive view than other commentators, the balance of authority and comment seems to weigh against this. In addition to the considerable weight of official material and commentary already referred to, Goodwin-Gill and McAdam cite both nationality as a legal status and the application in this context of an extension beyond this: 'Nationality [in the Convention reason sense] is usually interpreted more loosely, to include origins and the membership of particular ethnic, religious, cultural and linguistic communities'.[18] And Hathaway and Foster, in their extremely detailed and careful study, have come to a view congruent with that of earlier experts and the *Handbook* and official guidance:

> In sum, the Convention ground of nationality is appropriately invoked both by reference to legal notions of nationality such as statelessness, as well as when a risk of being persecuted is due to a person's identification as a member of a culturally, ethnically, linguistically, or otherwise distinct 'national' group.[19]

4.15 Symes and Jorro refer to earlier writings of Hathaway but find a particular pointer towards a dual meaning in article 10(1)(c) of Council Directive 2004/83/EC of 29 April 2004 on minimum standards for the qualification and status of third country nationals or stateless persons as refugees or as persons who otherwise need international protection and the content of the protection granted (the Qualification Directive), which as seen in chapter two (at para 2.41) provides that:

> the concept of nationality shall not be confined to citizenship or lack thereof but shall in particular include membership of a group determined by its cultural, ethnic, or linguistic identity, common geographical or political origins or its relationship with the population of another State.[20]

4.16 There is a paucity of express judicial precedent, perhaps because there is such uniformity of view that points are rarely taken, or because the presence of other overlapping Convention reasons such as race or social group in most cases reduces the materiality of any dispute as to the meaning of nationality as a Convention reason. In *Hanukashvili v Canada (MCI)* [1997]129 FTR 216, 1997 CanLII 6020 (FC), Pinard J in the Federal Court of Canada cited with approval commentary by

---

[17] Zimmermann and Mahler (n 7 above) 442, §583.
[18] Goodwin-Gill and McAdam (n 8 above) 73.
[19] Ibid, 399.
[20] Symes and Jorro (n 8 above) 207, §4.6 and 307, §4.6.

Waldman[21] distinguishing 'nationality' in the context of Convention reason from the narrower definition applicable in relation to identification of the reference state(s).

4.17 The definition of nationality in the Convention reason sense therefore includes the possibility of nationality in the sense of citizenship or legal membership at the level of international law as well as membership in a broader 'historico-biological' group. Whether 'nationality' as a reason for fear of persecution encompasses citizenship in the absence of nationality is likely a moot point given that a group defined by a particular form of status, such as an inferior class of citizenship, is likely to come within the 'historico-biological' dimension to nationality, or other enumerated reasons for fear of persecution, most obviously 'social group' or 'race'.

iii. Nationality as a Convention Reason Includes Statelessness

4.18 There is a substantial basis for the conclusion that nationality extends to forms of 'national status' *including the absence thereof*, whether in the sense of absence of possession of a particular nationality, or in the sense of possessing no nationality at all, that is, of statelessness. Although Robinson suggested that a person having no nationality could not be persecuted by reason of statelessness,[22] that conclusion is unsupported by substantial reasoning and may be considered wrong. Grahl-Madsen, a commentator whose work shows considerably greater depth, categorically disagreed, concluding that 'Persecution for "reasons of nationality" is also understood to include persecution for lack of nationality', referring to persecution by reason of statelessness, which he considered might also support a claim based on membership of a social group.[23] Subsequent commentators have consistently (and, it is suggested, correctly) preferred Grahl-Madsen's view. Hathaway and Foster enlarge this somewhat, reaching a conclusion in part by reference to Convention protection as a matter of principle encompassing both possessors of relevant attributes (race, religion, political opinion) and those possessing a relevant fear by reason of the absence of that characteristic:

> First, resident internationally unprotected persons, such as stateless persons, are sometimes the object of human rights abuse by reason of their status as 'foreigners' or 'non-national'. Recognition that non-nationals are protected under the Refugee Convention is consistent with the general proposition that Convention grounds extend both to persons who do, and those who do not, have the relevant attributes set by the Convention.[24]

---

21 Waldman (n 7 above) §8.126.
22 Robinson (n 5 above) 53.
23 Grahl-Madsen (n 10 above) 219, fn 99, §89.
24 Hathaway and Foster (n 7 above) 397.

The views of Grahl-Madsen and Hathaway and Foster, grounded in each case in deeper study and observation of the international refugee regime in operation, possess greater logical force and should be preferred to the view of Robinson.

iv. Intersection with Other Convention Reasons

Assessing the existence and causative relevance of a relevant group of course may require close attention to the factual background (including in this the treatment of individuals and groups under the nationality or citizenship law of reference countries). It is inherent in the nature of the definition of nationality as a Convention reason that it may overlap with other such reasons. As Anker notes: **4.19**

> Nationality may be imbued with political significance, and, in such cases, asylum claims may be based on both the political opinion and nationality grounds. Ethnicity or tribal membership, for example, is a common indicator of distinct nationality within a nation-state … ethnicity or national origin is considered indistinguishably as race or nationality.[25]

A useful conjectural example of this is provided in the USCIS Asylum Officer Basic Training Course: **4.20**

> Consider a Quiche applicant from Guatemala The characteristic of being Quiche may be perceived by the persecutor or feared persecutor as a racial characteristic, an ethnic characteristic (nationality), an immutable characteristic shared with other members of a distinct group (particular social group), a religious characteristic (some communities still practice indigenous religions), or a political characteristic (indigenous communities were often linked with guerrilla organizations).The important inquiry is whether the persecutor is motivated to harm the applicant on account of his or her being Quiche; if so, any one of the protected characteristics would likely apply.[26]

In *Refugee Appeal No 73861* [2005] NZRSAA 228 the New Zealand Refugee Status Appeals Authority found that a stateless Palestinian born in Saudi Arabia was entitled to protection as a refugee: at §113 'As well as imputed political opinion the Authority also finds that the appellant's Palestinian race/nationality was also a contributing factor to his ill-treatment'. **4.21**

The US Court of Appeals for the Sixth Circuit in *Almuhtaseb v Gonzales*, 453 F 3d 743 (6th Cir 2006) concluded that it did not have jurisdiction to review an appeal of the denial of asylum because of delay, and so could not consider the correctness **4.22**

---

[25] Anker (n 6 above) 539, §5.86.

[26] USCIS Asylum Officer Basic Training Course, *Asylum Eligibility Part III: Nexus and the Five Protected Characteristics* 17, available at: www.uscis.gov/sites/default/files/USCIS/Humanitarian/Refugees%20%26%20Asylum/Asylum/AOBTC%20Lesson%20Plans/Nexus-the-Five-Protected-Characteristics-31aug10.pdf.

of rejection by the immigration judge of the proposition that the situation for Palestinians in the West Bank had altered so that Convention reason of nationality or political opinion arose:

> Almuhtaseb argues that the circumstances in the West Bank had changed such that the conditions were not just those associated with generalized violence, but rather that violence was now directed specifically at Palestinians on the basis of their nationality and political views. '[T]he existence of "changed circumstances" that materially affect eligibility for asylum is a predominantly factual determination, which will invariably turn on the facts of a given case' *Ramadan*, 427 F 3d at 1221–22; *accord Mehilli*, 433 F 3d at 93. In this case, an assessment of Almuhtaseb's argument regarding changed circumstances would require us to consider evidence regarding the nature of the violence in the West Bank to determine whether, as a matter of fact, Palestinians had become targets of violence on the basis of their nationality and political views.

4.23 In *Bah v Mukasey*, 529 F 3d 99 (2nd Cir 2008) the US Court of Appeals for the Second Circuit treated nationality together with gender as a potential Convention reason defining a relevant social group, in a case involving women from the Fulani ethic group in Guinea and female genital cutting: 'As some of our sister circuits have found in cases involving claims of female genital mutilation, it appears to us that petitioners' gender combined with their ethnicity, nationality, or tribal membership satisfies the social group requirement'.

4.24 In the United Kingdom issues concerning nationality as a Convention reason have been contested relatively infrequently, and where issues do arise, nationality is frequently one of a set of potentially interlocking Convention reasons. In *AB and DM (Risk categories reviewed, Tutsis added) Democratic Republic of Congo CG* [2005] UKIAT 00118 a panel including two Vice Presidents of the Immigration and Asylum Tribunal treated nationality as a Convention reason as including both nationality in the international law sense and a nationality which might be falsely perceived by reason of tribal origin or appearance. In *ST (Ethnic Eritrean—nationality—return) Ethiopia CG* [2011] UKUT 252 (IAC), a country guidance decision of the Upper Tribunal (Immigration and Asylum Chamber) concerning the denationalisation of persons of Eritrean background by Ethiopia, the Upper Tribunal (Immigration and Asylum Chamber) found nationality to be one of four potentially interlocking Convention reasons:

> 78. I have to say that I find it difficult to decide whether the mere removal of the appellant's ID card crossed the threshold of persecution. What I am sure about, however, is that when one puts that act in the context of what was happening to ethnic Eritreans in the summer of 1998 and views it by reference to the attitude evinced by the Ethiopian authorities since that time towards persons in the appellant's position, the removal of the card is part of an ongoing deprivation of nationality that has had a very serious effect upon the appellant. Seen in that light, which is the only sensible way in which it can be seen, the action was persecutory … The persecution was for a Convention reason, namely, race, nationality, membership of a particular social group and political opinion (actual or imputed).

4.25 An illustration touching on several important aspects of nationality as a basis for 'fear of being persecuted' is the decision of the New Zealand Refugee Status Appeals Authority in *Refugee Appeal No 74467* [2004] NZRSAA 283. The appellant, a Kuwaiti Bidoon, had initially been refused asylum because the reason for his fear of persecution was found to be his statelessness rather than because of one of the five Convention grounds. That decision was overturned by the Authority, the appellant being accepted as possessing a well-founded fear of persecution on the basis of nationality (beduin-descended Bidoon or stateless Kuwaiti) or social group (Bidoon). The decision addressed this as follows:

> 94. Once this pattern of historical discrimination is appreciated and in particular, the manner in which citizenship has been used by the ruling elite 'to organise and define the internal power relationships', the historical nexus between the status of bidoon and one or more Convention grounds is apparent. These grounds embrace race and nationality (tribe/clan/geographical origins/settled/nomadic, religion (Sunni/Shia) and gender (social group).
>
> …
>
> 103. Summarising my conclusions in respect of the present appellant, he is descended from beduin who lived and grazed their flocks of sheep outside Kuwait city in the Jahra-Al Ahmedi area. He knows of no ancestral connection to any country other than Kuwait. He regards himself as a Kuwaiti. His background is typical of that of many bidoons. The cumulative harm of the past discriminatory measures against him—which effectively rendered him a non-person in his own country—reached such a serious degree as to amount to persecution. If returned to Kuwait his circumstances would be little changed. His fears of being persecuted are therefore well-founded.
>
> 104. The persecution feared by the appellant is by reason of the Convention grounds of nationality and his membership of the social group of bidoons.

v. Absence of Requirement for Minority Status

4.26 Fear of persecution by reason of nationality does not require that the national group be a minority. This is expressly stated in the UNHCR *Handbook*:

> Whereas in most cases persecution for reason of nationality is feared by persons belonging to a national minority, there have been many cases in various continents where a person belonging to a majority group may fear persecution by a dominant minority.[27]

4.27 Eminent commentators have echoed this conclusion: for example, Goodwin-Gill and McAdam state that '[it] is not necessary that those persecuted should constitute a minority in their own country, for oligarchies traditionally tend to

[27] UNHCR, *Handbook and Guidelines on Procedures and Criteria for Determining Refugee Status* (n 9 above) §76.

resort to oppression'.[28] This is supported by interpretation of article 1A(2) CSR51 on VCLT69 principles taking into account the absence of any implicit or express requirement to the contrary. There simply is no reason why membership in a group forming a national majority should be discounted as an admissible basis for protection under CSR51, if members of that group possess a well-founded fear of suffering relevantly serious adverse treatment by reason of one or more relevant matters.

D. 'Imputed Nationality'

4.28 A Convention reason for well-founded fear of persecution arises where the relevant reason is imputed to the potential victim, even if the perception is unfounded. As Anker notes:

> Asylum claims may also be presented on the basis of perceived nationality. Applicants who have the accent, name, or appearance of an ethnic minority or a parent who is a member of an ethnic minority group, may be targeted for persecution on account of nationality, even where they do not self-identify with that nationality ... interethnic or interreligious marriages can also form the basis of an asylum claim for reasons of nationality.[29]

4.29 In *Miljkovic v Ashcroft*, 376 F 3d 754 (7th Cir 2004), the applicant before the United States Court of Appeals for the Seventh Circuit, whose claim to persecution hinged on the claim that he had been selected for hazardous military duties by reason of perceived nationality, was born in Croatia, at the time part of Yugoslavia, to Serbian parents. Although both his parents were originally from Serbia and moved back to Serbia and he grew up in Serbia, it was accepted that he was perceived by Serbians to be Croatian because born in Croatia and speaking Serbo-Croat with a Croatian accent.

4.30 In *AB and DM (Risk categories reviewed, Tutsis added) Democratic Republic of Congo CG* [2005] UKIAT 00118 the United Kingdom Immigration and Asylum Tribunal found that persons of 'a nationality or perceived nationality of a state regarded as hostile' including those of actual or perceived Tutsi or Banyamulenge origin faced relevant risk in the Democratic Republic of Congo:

> 51. (i) We confirm as continuing to be a risk category those with a nationality or perceived nationality of a state regarded as hostile to the DRC and in particular those who have or presumed to have Rwandan connections or are of Rwandan origins.

4.31 In *EB (Ethiopia) v SSHD* [2007] EWCA Civ 809 [2009] QB 1 the Court of Appeal, Civil Division, noted the finding of the Eritrean Ethiopian Claims Commission

---

[28] Goodwin-Gill and McAdam (n 8 above) 73.
[29] Anker (n 6 above) 540 §5.87.

that Ethiopia had erroneously ascribed Eritrean nationality to some persons who were then deprived of Ethiopian nationality, becoming stateless.[30] According to Pill LJ (with whom Longmore and Jacob LJJ concurred):

> 5. Amongst the findings on liability, it was held that Ethiopia was liable to Eritrea for a violation of international laws in 'erroneously depriving at least some Ethiopians who were not dual nationals of their Ethiopian nationality'.

The Court appears to have treated the deprivation as being by reason of race, though it might equally have been treated as being on the basis of nationality in the sense of national association or origin.

[30] *Eritrea Ethiopia Claims Commission, Partial Award: Civilians Claims—Eritrea's Claims 15, 16, 23 & 27–32*, Permanent Court of Arbitration, The Hague, 17 December 2004, §62, available at www.pca-cpa.org/ER%20Partial%20Award%20Dec%20048515.pdf?fil_id=148: 'Perhaps more likely, statelessness would result if Ethiopia erroneously determined that one of its nationals had acquired Eritrean nationality when, in fact, he or she had not done so. Such an unfortunate result might be most likely to occur with respect to Ethiopian nationals not resident in Ethiopia, but it could occur even with respect to Ethiopians resident in Ethiopia. The evidence indicates that Ethiopia appears to have made at least a few errors in this process. While Eritrea cannot claim for the loss suffered by the persons who were the victims of those errors, Ethiopia is liable to Eritrea for any damages caused to it by those errors'.

5

Nationality and the Identification of a Reference Country (or Countries)

'The country of his nationality' refers to a State and 'nationality' means current nationality. 'Nationality' remains relevant for this purpose if it is said to be 'ineffective'. The subjective attitude of an individual to a State of nationality is irrelevant. Nationality may exist where it is not already evidenced as by possession of relevant documentation, but nationality at article 1A(2) of the Convention relating to the Status of Refugees 1951 (CSR51) does not include a nationality for which an application might be made but not already possessed by a claimant. Nationality in this context means nationality recognised on the international plane. In plural nationality cases interpretation points to the need, once a well-founded fear of persecution for relevant reason is found in at least one country of nationality, to examine whether another country of nationality does or does not provide a 'national protection alternative' on principles parallel to those applied in relation to internal protection alternative. 'Not having a nationality' means being without a nationality applying the approach to nationality established in international law.

Contents

A. Introduction

A1. Text of Article 1A(2) of the Convention Relating to the Status of Refugees 1951

Article 1A(2) of the Convention relating to the Status of Refugees 1951 (CSR51), as modified post the 1967 Protocol relating to the Status of Refugees (PSR67), defines a refugee as 'any person' who: 5.1

> 1A(2) [o]wing to well-founded fear of being persecuted for reasons of race, religion, nationality, membership of a particular social group or political opinion, is outside the country of his nationality and is unable or, owing to such fear, is unwilling to avail himself of the protection of that country; or who, not having a nationality and being outside the country of his former habitual residence ..., is unable or, owing to such fear, is unwilling to return to it.
>
> In the case of a person who has more than one nationality, the term 'the country of his nationality' shall mean each of the countries of which he is a national, and a person shall not be deemed to be lacking the protection of the country of his nationality if, without any valid reason based on well-founded fear, he has not availed himself of the protection of one of the countries of which he is a national.

One note regarding the French text is justified. The term '*ressortissant*' is frequently used in the French text of treaties where the term 'national' is employed in the English text. Weis concluded, in the light of the decision of the French Cour de Cassation in *Prince Elie de Bourbon-Parma v Auroux es qualité ministère public* (1923) *Clunet* 904–30, that the French term had a somewhat wider meaning than 'national', also including other protected persons ('*protégés*') and perhaps resident aliens under temporary protection. The French and English texts of CSR51 are equally authoritative, and the French text at article 1 uses the term '*nationalité*' where the English text employs 'nationality'. By contrast, the term '*ressortissant*' is employed in the French text in four other articles (8, 15, 16 and 17) where the English word chosen is 'national'. Both terms ('*nationalité*' and '*ressortissant*') appear to be employed generally to denote protective linkage at the level of international law, rather than any broad linkage to a location ('*pays*').

A2. Article 1A(2) of the Convention Relating to the Status of Refugees 1951 and Identification of a Reference Country (or Countries)

5.2 By article 1A(2) a primary question, determining the country of reference for purposes of the definition, is whether an individual is 'outside the country of his nationality and … unable, or owing to [relevant fear] unwilling to avail himself of the protection of that country'. Where an individual is a national of more than one State, the position as regards each State may have to be examined: the second paragraph of article 1A(2) CSR51 points to a requirement for examination of each country of nationality. In contrast an individual with no nationality, that is, who is stateless, must show relevant characteristics as regards his or her country of former habitual residence. The requirements of article 1A(2) might therefore be drawn out as below:

i. Wherever an individual possesses a nationality for relevant purposes, the term 'nationality', in the phrases 'the country of his nationality' and 'that nationality', identifies the reference country—to be a refugee that person must be 'outside the country of his nationality' and also 'unable or, owing to such fear [of well-founded fear of being persecuted for reasons of race, religion, nationality, membership of a particular social group or political opinion], … unwilling to avail himself of the protection of that country.
ii. If a person has more than one nationality, then the second paragraph of article 1A(2) CSR51 makes it clear that the term 'the country of his nationality' in the first paragraph must be taken as meaning each country of nationality. In such a case 'a person shall not be deemed to be lacking the protection of the country of his nationality if, without any valid reason based on well-founded fear, he has not availed himself of the protection of one of the countries of which he is a national'.

iii. Where the individual in question is stateless ('not having a nationality') the first paragraph identifies the need to substitute a reference State on a basis alternative to nationality. In such cases the place of reference is 'the country of his former habitual residence'. The individual must be outside it, and unable or, owing to such fear, unwilling to return to it.

The preceding chapter examined the use of the term 'nationality' in the context of Convention reason. This chapter examines the other important context in which the term is employed in article 1A(2) CSR51. This provision contains a series of interconnected references to nationality or the absence thereof (statelessness) which are critical to the operation of the CSR51 scheme, because they determine the country or countries in respect of which the other criteria in article 1A(2) CSR51 must be satisfied. 5.3

A3. 'Protection'

In the article 1A(2) formula there is a particularly close link between two concepts: first 'the country of his nationality' and thereafter 'protection' in the sense of 'the protection of that country'. The *Oxford English Reference Dictionary* offers, as the primary meaning of 'protection', 'the act or an instance of protecting' and 'the state of being protected; defence', further defining the verb 'protect' as 'keep (a person, thing, etc) safe; defend; guard'.[1] This provides an instance in which, as the 'General Rule' of interpretation at article 31 of the Vienna Convention on the Law of Treaties 1969 (VCLT69) anticipates (see chapter three, section B1.iii), the ordinary meaning of the term indicates a starting point, but substantial further interpretation is needed to ascertain the correct interpretation in context and in the light of object and purpose. In ordinary use the terms 'protect' or 'protection' are modified by the context, and in particular by the threat against which the need for protection is contemplated. Someone may protect herself from rain by the use of an umbrella or by remaining indoors, or from bullets by hiding in a ditch or behind a wall (or by paying 'protection money' to a potential assassin). Changing the nature of the thing against which protection is contemplated alters the sense of the situation dramatically. 'Protection' is a term possessing a wide range of meanings, but the common link is some threat against which protection is sought. Even in international law and legal theory, the term protection is used in several distinct senses. In particular, it is used in the context of international or diplomatic protection to denote the right of a State of nationality to intervene as against another State in relation to harm done to the national, and in legal theory it has 5.4

[1] J Pearsall and B Trumble (eds), *The Oxford English Reference Dictionary* (2nd edn, OUP, 1996) 1160.

been employed to advance the concept of a duty *internally* on the part of a State, to protect its citizens and perhaps others on its territory (see chapter one, section A6).

5.5 The general rule at article 31(1) of VCLT69 is that a treaty 'shall be interpreted in good faith in accordance with the ordinary meaning to be given to the terms of the treaty in their context and in the light of their object and purpose'.

5.6 The conclusion underlying this work, in line with the conclusions of most informed commentators, is that 'protection' in article 1A(2) refers to a form of internal protection which is particular to the context in question. Protection in article 1A(2) means protection from persecution or protection from well-founded fear of being so persecuted: it is universally accepted that there does not have to be a certainty of such persecution for qualification as a refugee, it being sufficient that the situation in the country in question is such that a fear of persecution for relevant reasons is well founded. As Zimmermann and Mahler have judged, 'It is … only when the respective country of origin does *de facto* provide protection from such persecution that the need for surrogate international protection by the community of contracting parties of [CSR51] does not arise'.[2] This is consistent with the United Nations High Commissioner for Refugees (UNHCR) *Handbook*, which does not isolate the term 'protection' but links it to relevant fear of persecution:

> As long as he has no fear in relation to the country of his nationality, he can be expected to avail himself of that country's protection. He is not in need of international protection and is therefore not a refugee.[3]

A later reference alludes to refusal of documentation or of respect for the right to return as potentially indicative of absence of protection ('If it appears that the applicant has been denied services (eg, refusal of a national passport or extension of its validity, or denial of admittance to the home territory) normally accorded to his co-nationals, this may constitute a refusal of protection within the definition')[4] but the reference to discrimination as compared with 'co-nationals' illuminates that *de facto* or *de jure* denationalisation for a relevantly discriminatory reason may itself constitute persecution and hence coincide with absence of protection. The conclusion of Zimmermann and Mahler is generally consistent with the treatment of this issue by Goodwin-Gill and McAdam[5] and by Hathaway and Foster.[6]

---

[2] C Mahler and A Zimmermann 'Article 1A para 1 1951 Convention' in A Zimmerman (ed), *The 1951 Convention Relating to the Status of Refugees and its 1967 Protocol: A Commentary* (OUP, 2011) 445–46, §§596–600.

[3] UNHCR, *Handbook and Guidelines on Procedures and Criteria for Determining Refugee Status under the 1951 Convention and the 1967 Protocol relating to the Status of Refugees*, Reissued, Geneva, December 2011, §90.

[4] Ibid, §99.

[5] G Goodwin-Gill and J McAdam, *The Refugee in International Law* (3rd edn, OUP, 2007) s 2.6.

[6] J Hathaway and M Foster, *The Law of Refugee Status* (2nd edn, CUP, 2014) ch 4, esp sections 4.1–4.2.

B. 'The Country of His Nationality' and 'Unable or Unwilling to Avail Himself of the Protection of that Country'

As already seen, Weis identified two significant meanings of the term 'nationality': **5.7**

> The term 'nationality' ... is a politico-legal term denoting membership of a State. It must be distinguished from nationality as a historico-biological term denoting membership of a nation. In the latter sense it means the subjective corporate sentiment of unity of members of a specific group forming a 'race' or 'nation' which may, though not necessarily, be possessed of a territory and which, by seeking political unity on that territory, may lead to the formation of a State.[7]

In the present context 'the country of his nationality' means a State. Under international law the primary link of protection is not with any non-state entity, but with the State. Under international law, which represents the context for CSR51, only a State, rather than a 'historico-biological' unit such as a 'race' or 'nation', in Weis' description, is competent to create nationality in the sense of the word valid in international law.[8] One recent restatement by the African Commission on Human and Peoples' Rights Special Rapporteur on the Rights of Refugees, Asylum Seekers, and Internally Displaced Persons noted that 'the first obvious fact is that the concept of nationality is consubstantial with the concept of the State. The existence of a nationality presupposes the existence of a sovereign State'.[9] On a VCLT69 approach therefore it seems clear that in the passages 'the country of his nationality' and 'the protection of that country' in article 1A(2) CSR51, the meaning to be assigned to 'nationality' is nationality as 'a politico-legal term denoting membership of a State'. This is clear from the phrase 'country of his nationality' given the link between State and nationality. Both international protection and internal protection (see chapter one, section A6) look exclusively to a State. The conclusion that 'the country of his nationality' means a State is supported by significant factors of clarity and utility. In addition, attempting to widen the definition of nationality applied in the present context, to include a non-state entity, would lead to incoherence or ineffectiveness: the first because of the difficulty in many cases of deciding whether a non-state group possessed 'national' characteristics, and answering other questions such as what if any territory attaches to a non-state group, and the latter because an individual would potentially meet the CSR51 definition on the basis of unwillingness or inability to return to a small part of the State's territory (that occupied by the non-state **5.8**

---

[7] P Weis, *Nationality and Statelessness* (2nd edn, Brill, 1979) 3.

[8] Ibid.

[9] African Commission on Human and Peoples' Rights, *The Right to Nationality in Africa* (Study undertaken by the Special Rapporteur on the Rights of Refugees, Asylum Seekers, Migrants and Internally Displaced Persons in Africa (Maya Sahli Fadel)) (Banjul, ACHPR, 2015) 13.

entity) even though unquestionably protected by the State itself over other parts of its territory.

B1. Nationality Means Nationality of a State as Defined in International Law

i. Establishment under Domestic Law

5.9 In practice the basic interpretation, by which 'nationality' means nationality in the sense of international law, appears to have been uncontroversial, though certain complications which have arisen in practice will be examined later in this chapter.

5.10 There is a substantial consensus that nationality in this context denotes legal membership of a State for purposes of international law. The UNHCR *Handbook* in its original version and through subsequent revisions has consistently treated 'the country of his nationality' as meaning 'the country of citizenship', using that term as synonymous with nationality:

> 87. In this context, 'nationality' refers to 'citizenship'. The phrase 'is outside the country of his nationality' relates to persons who have a nationality, as distinct from stateless persons. In the majority of cases, refugees retain the nationality of their country of origin.[10]

5.11 In its *Interpretation of the Refugee Definition in the Case Law* the Immigration and Refugee Board of Canada states that:

> A claimant must establish that he or she is a Convention refugee from the country of their nationality. In this context, nationality means citizenship of a particular country. If the claimant has a country of nationality, the claim should be assessed only against that country and not against some other country where the claimant may have residency status.[11]

5.12 The United States Citizenship and Immigration Services (USCIS) Asylum Officer Basic Training Course also identifies 'country of nationality' as denoting exclusively citizenship of a State:

> A. Definition of Nationality
>
> For purposes of the first part of the refugee definition—'outside any country of such person's nationality'—nationality refers to 'citizenship'.
>
> Contrast this with the definition of 'nationality' in the second part of the refugee definition—'on account of nationality'. In the second part of the definition,

[10] UNHCR, *Handbook and Guidelines on Procedures and Criteria for Determining Refugee Status* (n 3 above) §87.

[11] Available at: www.irb-cisr.gc.ca/Eng/BoaCom/references/LegJur/Pages/RefDef02.aspx#n21.

'nationality' is not to be understood only as 'citizenship', but also refers to ethnic or linguistic groups.

The INA defines 'national' as a citizen or a person owing permanent allegiance to a State. The Court of Appeals for the Second Circuit has noted that '[n]ationality is a status conferred by a state, and will generally be recognized by other states provided it is supported by a "genuine link" between the individual and the conferring state'. Asylum officers must consider how the State views the applicant to determine whether the applicant is a national of the State or is stateless. See discussion below on statelessness.[12]

All leading modern commentators who have given attention to the question have differentiated between the two contexts in which 'nationality' is invoked at article 1A(2), applying a narrower meaning in the context of 'country of nationality'. In 2001 Waldman concluded that: 5.13

While it was suggested [in relation to Convention reason] that the context required a broad definition of nationality, such is not the case here. As will be argued in the next section, in the present context, nationality means citizenship. This is so particularly because the definition distinguishes between persons who have a country of nationality, and individuals who do not.[13]

More recently Zimmermann and Mahler have echoed this: 5.14

As part of the relevant grounds of persecution eventually leading to a well-founded fear of persecution listed in Art 1A para 2, the notion of 'nationality', as demonstrated above, does *not* refer to the technical term of 'nationality', *ie* the legal bond between a person and a State in the sense of citizenship, but rather to a person's ethnic origin. In contrast thereto, in the two other instances the term 'nationality', given the respective context, is used in its technical meaning, *ie* refers to citizenship.[14]

Goodwin-Gill and McAdam refer to the requirement of being outside 'his or her country of origin' without specifically considering the meaning of 'the country of his nationality' but appear to treat nationality as state membership.[15] Hathaway and Foster specifically cite nationality in this sense as membership in a State: 5.15

The plain language of the Convention requires the substantive evaluation of refugee status to be undertaken by reference to conditions in the refugee claimant's state of nationality. Whatever her relationship with other countries, the basic inquiry into the existence of a relevant well-founded fear focuses squarely on … the country of which the individual is a citizen.[16]

They set out a detailed and clear account of the reasons for this judgement, citing the particular function of nationality in international law, which has been 5.16

---

[12] USCIS Asylum Officer Basic Training Course, *Asylum Eligibility Part I: Definitions; Past Persecution* 8–9, available at: www.uscis.gov/sites/default/files/USCIS/Humanitarian/Refugees%20%26%20Asylum/Asylum/AOBTC%20Lesson%20Plans/.

[13] L Waldman, *The Definition of Convention Refugee* (Butterworths Canada, 2001) §8.333.

[14] Mahler and Zimmermann (n 2 above) 442, §583.

[15] Goodwin-Gill and McAdam (n 5 above) 72–73.

[16] Hathaway and Foster (n 6 above) 49–50.

described in chapter one, and the genesis of refugee protection as intended to provide surrogate protection in the absence of national protection:

> The choice of the state of nationality as the country of reference for risk analysis was driven by the Convention's overarching goal of responding to the need to provide a new national home to persons driven from their own country by the risk of persecution. The commitment of international law to individuals having a nationality in the legally recognized form of citizenship, and hence being 'allocated' to a state, follows in part from the logic of the interstate system. The jurisdiction over individuals afforded by nationality is critical to the community of states as a whole since the state of nationality 'has a certain responsibility for the acts of its citizens ... of which its agents know or ought to know and which cause harm to the legal interest of another state'. Citizenship is a universally recognized basis for jurisdiction over individuals, who are subject to a duty of allegiance to their country of nationality. Nationality thus provides a default means by which individuals may be brought under the authority of the interstate system.
>
> At least as important, and of greater immediate relevance in the context of refugee protection, nationality provides the essential means by which individuals are able to avail themselves of the protection of international law. Under international law, injury to a citizen is treated as an injury to the state of citizenship. It is the state of citizenship that is entitled to exercise diplomatic protection to aid its citizen and to seek a remedy for harms suffered.[17]

The judgement of the UNHCR, of national authorities and commentators, that nationality in 'the country of his nationality' means nationality in the sense of linkage to a State for purposes of international law, is firmly based in the international law background to CSR51. As will be seen below, it is only in a small number of relatively unusual cases concerning entities with some state-like characteristics that any doubt has arisen.

5.17 The views of the UNHCR and of authoritative commentators, reviewed above, are bolstered by judicial decisions on the point. In *Tjhe Kwet Koe v MIEA* [1997] 912 FCA, the appeal before Tamberlin J in the Federal Court of Australia focused upon whether Hong Kong, at the time a colony of the United Kingdom, constituted 'the country of his former habitual residence' in relation to a stateless claimant. The Court distinguished between what it found to be a more flexible usage of the term 'country' in the formula 'country of former habitual residence' as opposed to strict definition of 'country of nationality' as a State in being under international law:

> The language of Article 1A of the Convention itself draws a distinction between 'the country of nationality' and 'the country of former habitual residence'. The word 'country' in each of these expressions is used in a different sense. In the first phrase it is used to designate a country capable of granting nationality. In the second it is used to denote a country which need not have this capability but in which the individual resides. The concept of 'country' is broader than the concept of a State.

[17] Ibid, citing (first para) I Brownlie, *Principles of Public International Law* (7th edn, OUP, 2008) 519.

In the same year Pinard J in the Canadian Federal Court held in *Hanukashvili v Canada (MCI)* (1997) 129 FTR 216, that in relation to claimants from the former USSR who had later taken nationality in Israel, the sole reference country was Israel, unless another nationality subsisted. In *Yah Abedalaziz v Canada (MCI)* [2011] FCJ 1271 (QL), a later decision of the same Court, the claimant had been born in Jordan but asserted that he was a stateless Palestinian. Shore J reiterated that 'country of nationality' meant a country capable of affording citizenship: **5.18**

> [28] Moreover, the question of the applicant's citizenship is not a temporary issue, as he claims, but an important one because, if the RPD found that the applicant is a Jordanian citizen and did not seek protection in that country, his refugee claim collapses.
>
> [29] This is a fundamental element that the applicant must demonstrate. In fact, the refugee claimant must demonstrate that he or she is a 'Convention refugee' or a 'person in need of protection' in his or her country of nationality. In this context, nationality means citizenship in a particular country (sections 96 and 97 of the [*Immigration and Refugee Protection Act*, SC 2001, c 27]; *Hanukashvili v Canada (MCI)* (1997), 1997 CanLII 6020 (FC), 129 FTR 216, 72 ACWS (3d) 914; *Ward*, above).

In *Veysi Dag v SSHD* also known as *Dag (Nationality—Country of Habitual Residence—TRNC) Cyprus * CG* [2001] UKIAT 00002, [2001] Imm AR 587, a decision marked as having 'starred' status and thus as binding other tribunal panels and adjudicators, the Immigration and Asylum Tribunal in the United Kingdom (Mr Ockelton, Mr Fox, and Mr Warr) squarely rejected the proposition that the so-called Turkish Republic of Northern Cyprus could be treated as 'the country of his nationality' in respect of an asylum seeker, and set out cogent reasons why this could not be the case: **5.19**

> 29. No authority cited to us favours Mr Tam's argument and [*Tjhe Kwet Koe v MIEA* [1997] 912 FCA] is against it. Quite apart from authority we should not have accepted it, for a number of reasons. It appears to us to be self-evident that a distinction is being drawn in Article 1A(2) between persons who have a nationality and persons who do not have a nationality. (It also goes without saying that 'nationality' is to be taken in a different sense where it occurs, later in the definition of a refugee, as one of the 'Convention reasons').
>
> 30. Our first impression was that nationality is a concept in international law recognising the relationship between a person and a State. We have not been persuaded to change our initial view and we therefore hold that nationality can be granted only by a State recognised as such by the international community.
>
> 31. In the context of the Refugee Convention there are in fact at least two reasons why we should prefer this, albeit formal, interpretation of the phrase 'country of … nationality'. One is that, being formal, it tends to promote consistency in interpreting the Convention between various jurisdictions. If a particular territory is not a State, then none of the parties to the Convention will treat it as the country of anybody's nationality for the purposes of the Convention.

32. The other reason lies in the function of the Convention to provide protection for those who need it. Here particularly we do invoke the purposive interpretation of Article 31 of the Vienna Convention. A territory that has no formal or legal existence as a State (particularly one whose existence, or whose government, has been declared illegal) cannot be a signatory to an international convention, and it may be more than a little difficult to secure its compliance with internationally recognised or prescribed norms of conduct. It is surely not right to regard such an entity as equivalent to a State for the purposes of defining and, more to the point, returning refugees. Of course, if a person has no nationality, it is necessary to consider him by reference to his country of former habitual residence. No country owes him duties as its citizen, and, against that background, the contrast between returning him to a State and to a territory that is not a State is less damaging. But for a person who has a nationality it cannot be appropriate to treat a State on the one hand and a power illegally occupying a territory on the other as equal partners or parallel alternative guardians of his future safety.[18]

5.20 Later the Court of Appeal in England and Wales was asked to consider whether the then Kurdish Autonomous Region in northern Iraq could be treated as 'the country of his nationality' and therefore the entity competent to provide 'the protection of that country'. The case was considered soon after a decision in *R (otao Vallaj) v Special Adjudicator* [2000] EWHC Admin 438, [2002] Imm AR 16, [2001] INLR 455 accepting that the authorities functioning under an international mandate might be taken as providing protection 'of that country'. In *Gardi v SSHD* [2002] EWCA Civ 750, [2002] 1 WLR 2755 Keane LJ, with whom Ward LJ and Sir Martin Nourse concurred, set out the following conclusion in relation to state protection, in the context of Iraq prior to the fall of the Ba'athist regime:

37. The reference in Article 1A(2) is to an asylum seeker being unable or unwilling to avail himself 'of the protection of that country', a reference to the earlier phrase 'the country of his nationality'. That does seem to imply that the protection has to be that of an entity which is capable of granting nationality to a person in a form recognised internationally. That indeed was a point made in [the decision of the Federal Court of Australia in *Tjhe Kwet Koe—v- Minister for Immigration and Ethnic Affairs* [1997] 912 FCA] at page 11. The KAR does not meet that criterion. I see force also in the point made by Hathaway and Foster in their paper at page 46, that protection can only be provided by an entity capable of being held responsible under international law. The decision in [*R (otao Vallaj) v Special Adjudicator*] is not inconsistent with that proposition, since the UNMIK regime in Kosovo had the authority of the United Nations plus the consent of the Federal Republic of Yugoslavia. Yet no-one suggests that the KAR or any part of it is such an entity under international law.

5.21 The *Gardi* decision was subsequently found to have been taken without jurisdiction; given the particular circumstances of the appellant the appeal

[18] *Veysi Dag v SSHD*, 01TH00075, [2001] Imm AR 587 United Kingdom: Asylum and Immigration Tribunal/Immigration Appellate Authority, 14 March 2001, available at: www.refworld.org/docid/404879d74.html. A somewhat similar and equally unsuccessful argument, relating to Kosovo, was rejected in another 'starred' decision by the same Tribunal: *Dyli v SSHD*, 00TH02186, [2000] Imm AR 652, [2000] INLR 372, available at: www.refworld.org/docid/3dec84942.html.

should have been brought in Scotland, not in England: *Gardi v SSHD (No 2)* [2002] EWCA Civ 1560 [2002] 1 WLR 3282. In *Saber v SSHD* [2003] ScotCS 360 [2004] INLR 222 the Inner House of the Court of Session, albeit in the further alternative, and therefore *obiter*, rejected the submission that the Tribunal was entitled to conclude that the then KAR could be treated as a reference country. Those cases sparked a prolonged dissention by the United Kingdom Asylum and Immigration Tribunal on the point of whether 'the protection of that country' could be provided by a non-state body: see for example *DM (Majority Clan Entities Can Protect) Somalia* [2005] UKAIT 00150 (27 July 2005). Article 1A(2) CSR51 does require a refugee to possess inability or unwillingness to go to the country of nationality by reason of a current well-founded fear of persecution for a relevant reason, and that without this, it is academic whether on the ground the State, or other States acting under an international mandate (as in Kosovo in the period of the *Vallaj* case), or anyone else, provides protection—it was on this basis that the claimant can be seen to have failed in the *Vallaj* case (Dyson J at [71]). But where protection is relevant it must in general be the protection of the State itself, potentially extended to 'international organisations controlling the State or a substantial part of the territory of the State, including by means of the presence of a multinational force in that territory'– the conclusion of the Court of Justice of the European Union in *Salahadin Abdulla (Area of Freedom, Security and Justice)* [2010] EUECJ C-175/08 [2011] 1 QB 46 [76], mirroring the earlier United Kingdom decision in *R (otao Vallaj) v Special Adjudicator.* However, it is important that these cases go to a particular question, that of 'protection of that country'. They indicate that in some cases a country may assign its protective function to, or it may temporarily be assumed by, organisations delegated by the international community. They do not extend the initial definition of 'the country of his nationality'.

In *Dhoumo v Board of Immigration Appeals*, 416 F 3d 172, 175 (2nd Cir 2005) the US Court of Appeals for the Second Circuit (Pooler and Sotomayor CJJ, Chin DJ) considered the application for review of a decision below, in which an ethnic Tibetan claimant had given evidence that he held Tibetan nationality by descent, and the evidence had been ignored, the conclusion instead being drawn that he had been relevantly settled in India which became the State of reference. In doing so the Court held affirmatively that 'country of his nationality' meant a State, competent as such to extend nationality: **5.22**

> A 'national' is 'a person owing permanent allegiance to a state'. 8 USC § 1101(a)(21). Nationality is a status conferred by a state, and will generally be recognized by other states provided it is supported by a 'genuine link' between the individual and the conferring state. See Restatement (Third) of Foreign Relations §211.

Accordingly, any putative 'country of … nationality' must meet the requirements of a State under international law as identified in chapter one, section A3: there can be no nationality, for purposes of article 1A(2), save where this is created by the domestic laws of an eligible State in line with the standards reviewed in **5.23** chapter one. Whilst these laws may be understood to include not only statute but also other valid emanations of domestic law, nationality in this sense does not extend to a putative status created by invalid means. As already seen in chapter one, the Convention on Certain Questions Relating to the Conflict of Nationality Laws 1930 defines nationality as status 'under its law' (article 1) and requires questions as to possession of nationality to be dealt with 'in accordance with the law of the State'.

ii. Evidence of Nationality is Declaratory, Not Constitutive

5.24 It also follows, because a State's acknowledgment of the existence of nationality is declaratory rather than constitutive, that a person may be a national even if the State in question is unable or declines to confirm this. So nationality may certainly be extant when not documented by a national passport or a decisive indication of status by the competent authorities of the State in question. In *Bouianova v Canada (MEI)* (1993) 67 FTR 74 the applicant had resided in Latvia prior to filing a claim to refugee status in Canada. The State of which she had been a national, the USSR, had been dissolved in December 1991. Latvia, which had been treated by the USSR as a Soviet republic since soon after its military occupation by the USSR in June 1940 (a status unrecognised by many other States), regained active independence after the dissolution of the USSR. Amongst the various successor States to the USSR was the Russian Federation, whose territory included the birthplace of the applicant. Ms Bouianova was held by the panel at a 'credible basis' hearing to be a citizen of the Russian Federation. The evidence included a letter of the Embassy of the Russian Federation answering questions provided to it. This stated, *inter alia*, that:

> Q: If a person was born in what is now considered the Russian Republic, but at the time was considered the USSR, and has lived in another republic for the majority of their life, is that person considered a citizen of the Russian Republic?
>
> A: This person is a Russian citizen unless he wants to become a citizen of another state.
>
> Q: With regard to the questions I have asked, does a person need to make an application of any sort, or is the acquisition of Russian citizenship automatic?
>
> A: This person has to send us his passport with a letter requesting Russian citizenship and we shall put the necessary stamp in his passport.

5.25 Rothstein J rejected the argument of the applicant that the absence of a current stamp in her passport meant that the panel should not have treated her as a national of the Russian Federation:

> In my view the applicant by simply making a request and submitting her passport to be stamped becomes a citizen of Russia. On the evidence before me, there is no discretion by the Russian officials to refuse her Russian citizenship. I do not think the necessity

of making an application, which in these circumstances is nothing more than a mere formality, means that a person does not have a country of nationality just because they chose not to make such an application. In my view, the decision of *MEI v Akl* (1990), 140 NR 323 (FCA) holding that, if an applicant has citizenship in more than one country, he must demonstrate a well-founded fear of persecution in relation to each country of citizenship before he can seek asylum in a country of which he is not a national, is wide enough to encompass the situation of an applicant who, by reason of her place of birth, is entitled to be a citizen of a particular country, upon compliance with requirements that are mere formalities.

Whilst the language of the judgment is not wholly clear as regards the important question of whether Ms Bouianova was already a national of the Russian Federation or whether she would only become a citizen through the stamping of her passport, reference to the evidence suggests that Ms Bouianova was found already to be a national (citizen) of the Russian Federation. The 'mere formality' was an application, not to be granted nationality by derivative acquisition, but for recognition of an already existing nationality established under the law of the Russian Federation. Writing in 2001, Waldman identified this as a defining feature of the *Bouianova* decision: **5.26**

§8.351 It is clear from the facts of the case that this decision does not stand for the proposition that claimants are required to apply for citizenship and prove a well-founded fear of persecution from each potential country of nationality. The applicant in this case was a citizen of Russia by birth, and, as the result of the operation of Russian law, and the application to the Russian Consulate, was merely asking for recognition of a pre-existing status. Upon application, the Consulate would automatically put a stamp in her passport and this stamp would merely be a declaration or confirmation of the applicant's actual nationality. This situation is clearly different from that of a person who does not have nationality at the time the application for refugee status is made, but who must make an application in order for citizenship to be conferred. The application in the latter case is a necessary step to the obtaining of citizenship and not merely an application for recognition of a pre-existing status.[19]

The principle applies in any situation in which an individual *possesses* a nationality and what is sought is recognition of a pre-existing status as a national. The source of that status—birth, descent, state succession—is in principle irrelevant so long there arises a nationality status recognised on the plane of international law (see section B5 below).

The requirement of nationality, rather than some lesser link, founded an important decision in the Federal Court of Canada by McKeown J in *Katkova v Canada (MCI)* (1997) 130 FTR 192. The issue in the case concerned whether, given the religious or cultural antecedents of a Jewish citizen of the Ukraine, Israel by reason of its Law of Return should be treated as the claimant's second country of nationality. The judgment does not identify as relevant for this purpose any **5.27**

[19] Waldman (n 13 above) §8.351.

other link, such as past admission or residence, to Israel, and treats the Law of Return as not creating Israeli nationality in every Jew prior to migration to Israel.

B2. 'Effectiveness' of Nationality is Irrelevant to Question of Whether Nationality Exists

5.28 There is no consensus that the definition of nationality for purposes of international law implies a minimum content beyond the existence (acknowledged by the individual and/or State in question or otherwise) of a legal relationship of membership extending to the plane of international law (see chapter one section A8). Nor, as indicated in chapter one, section A9, does there exist any single clear or agreed concept of 'effective nationality'. The term may be employed as it is in the context of international protection to identify a 'primary' nationality of reference and to discount any other nationality. It is quite clear that that is not the approach adopted in the citation of the 'country of his nationality' in article 1A(2), because the second paragraph specifically indicates that *every* relevant nationality must be considered: an approach which seems wholly in line with the underlying general aim of CSR51, of providing surrogate protection only where national protection is unavailable. As regards plural nationality cases (that is, claims to refugee status in which the claimant possesses more than one nationality) relevant matters of interpretation are considered in detail in section B7, below.

5.29 Further, 'effective nationality' might be used as a term asserting that a legal status of nationality is 'effective', in that it carries either all characteristics thought to attach to possession of nationality, or a particular characteristic in the mind of the user of the term. Obvious contexts include international or consular protection, internal protection, or recognition or respect by the State for a duty of readmission extending to a national. But all of these separate concepts are qualifications of the concept of nationality, and the term is employed at article 1A(2) without qualification. Nothing in the object or purpose of CSR51 requires the introduction of any qualification.

5.30 Accordingly article 1A(2) CSR51 initially enables a reference country or reference countries to be identified by the existence of nationality (in line with the standards identified in chapter one) alone. Where a nationality exists, this does not have to pass some further qualitative test prior to being treated as identifying a State of reference for purposes of article 1A(2). As seen in chapter one, section A8, there is no authority for the proposition that at some point the attributes attached to nationality may be so thin that the status involved ceases to be a nationality at all. A State may be a reference State for purposes of article 1A(2) even if it has effectively sought to denationalise the applicant for protection and in no circumstance will treat him or her as its national (it will be the reference State if it has only *de facto* excluded the individual from the benefits of citizenship, and even if it has accomplished the termination of nationality effectively for domestic legal purposes, this may, as set out in section B5 below, not be recognised on the plane of international law). However, the absence of a qualitative standard for initial identification as a reference State does not mean that action by a State which goes to nationality itself may not be relevant for the purposes of other aspects of article 1A(2), in relation to such questions as whether an individual possesses a well-founded fear of persecution for a relevant reason. This topic is addressed in chapter six. On the other hand, a nationality may also be 'ineffective' in a way which does not support a claim to refugee status—for instance a State of origin may refuse to acknowledge the legal relationship of citizenship through absence of evidence—because other aspects of the article 1A(2) definition are not met, for instance through the absence of a well-founded fear of persecution for a relevant reason.

There is therefore no implied fetter in the definition of 'the country of his nationality' in article 1A(2) CSR51, which treats a nationality perceived as not 'effective' as not engaging article 1A(2) so as to make the State in question a reference State. To this extent article 1A(2) assumes that a State of nationality will protect. This is consistent with the principle of 'surrogate protection', identified by Hathaway and adopted by the Canadian Supreme Court in *Canada (Attorney General) v Ward* [1993] 2 SCR 689, (1993) 103 DLR (4th) 1. The decision of the four judges who took part in the judgment (La Forest, L'Heureux-Dubé, Gonthier and Iacobucci JJ) was given by La Forest J: 5.31

> At the outset, it is useful to explore the rationale underlying the international refugee protection regime, for this permeates the interpretation of the various terms requiring examination. International refugee law was formulated to serve as a back-up to the protection one expects from the state of which an individual is a national. It was meant to come into play only in situations when that protection is unavailable, and then only in certain situations. The international community intended that persecuted individuals be required to approach their home state for protection before the responsibility of other states becomes engaged. For this reason, James Hathaway refers to the refugee scheme as 'surrogate or substitute protection', activated only upon failure of national protection; see *The Law of Refugee Status* (1991), at p 135.

The members of their Lordships' House in *Horvath v SSHD* [2000] UKHL 37; 1 AC 489 adopted the same expression, which is commonplace in subsequent decisions. Article 1A(2) is substantially based upon the presumption that a State of nationality is the preferred and desirable protector of the individual. It assumes, at the initial stage of assessing the identity of any reference country or countries of nationality, that these are capable of providing protection in the light of which surrogate international protection is not necessary. Against this, it is of course the case that nationality is not always 'effective'. This is a problem which has arisen particularly in conjunction with consideration of the situation in which an individual has more than one nationality, and does not face a relevant risk of persecution in every country of nationality. That situation is considered in section B7 below. But the material considerations applicable in that situation do not vitiate a State being a reference country by reason of an individual holding its nationality.

Instead they fall to be considered at a subsequent stage of the assessment. Particular issues may arise in relation to plural nationality—see section B7 below—but these do not obviate the existence of nationality itself.

B3. Reluctance to Seek Protection of State of Nationality is Irrelevant Once Nationality Exists

5.32 Hathaway and Foster cite, referring to *Lay Kon Tji v Minister for Immigration & Multicultural Affairs* [1998] FCA 1380, (1998) 158 ALR 681, reluctance to treat nationality as available solely because of a 'volition' requirement.[20] It is obviously correct that nationality continues to exist whatever the attitude of the individual to this, so that reliance upon a country of nationality rather than surrogate protection is expected by the CSR51 scheme, rather than being optional. To the extent that the possibility of reference is restricted to nationality already in existence, their reservation appears well founded—the inclusion of a non-persecuting State as a country of reference for article 1A(2) CSR51 purposes cannot depend upon the feelings of the individual. In line with the conceptual framework identified by La Forest J in the *Ward* case (see previous paragraph), CSR51 is adjusted to a higher degree of exigency or need for protection.

B4. Potential Nationality does not Constitute 'Nationality' for Relevant Purposes

5.33 As seen above in paragraphs 5.24–5.26, in *Bouianova v Canada (MEI)* (1993) 67 FTR 74 Rothstein J in the Federal Court of Canada held that an individual was to be treated as a national on the basis of a pre-existing nationality notwithstanding that this was not yet acknowledged by the authorities. Unfortunately, since that decision a body of law has grown—primarily in Canada but also elsewhere, under the influence of the Canadian decisions—which appears to have extended the application of that decision beyond its original rationale, treating 'the country of his nationality' as including a country whose nationality is accepted as one an individual does not possess but which he or she could acquire. This is incorrect as an interpretation of CSR51, even if unavoidable in some jurisdictions as a matter of domestic law rules of precedent. As may also be seen below, this primarily Canadian approach to interpretation is unsupported, or weakly supported, by examination of the comparative jurisprudence, and is contrary to the views of most authorities and commentators. It can be seen to be erroneous as inconsistent with a VCLT69 interpretation of article 1A(2)—indeed some of these cases

[20] Hathaway and Foster (n 6 above) 62.

might be used to illustrate the error of adopting a teleological approach rather than applying VCLT69, which rejects such approaches—see Crawford in chapter three, paragraph 3.4 above. Several cases are set out below to demonstrate the way in which the law has developed and the reasons given for this, to enable a full examination of the point.

i. The Canadian Cases

The *Bouianova* decision can be seen applied in its narrow original, and (it is suggested), correct understanding in a decision of McKeown J in the Federal Court of Canada in *Katkova v Canada (MCI)* (1997) 130 FTR 192. The question in the case was whether, given the religio-cultural antecedents of a Jewish citizen of Ukraine, Israel should be treated alongside Ukraine as a country of nationality by reason of its Law of Return allowing entry and settlement by persons of Jewish heritage: 5.34

> I agree with the analysis of Board member Kalvin ...
>
> In *Bouianova* and [*Desai v Canada (MCI)* (1994), 88 FTR 161 (TD)] the desire to live in the countries under consideration was not a condition precedent to obtaining nationality in those countries. I agree with the observations of Lorne Waldman in *Immigration Law and Practice* where he indicates that *Bouianova* and *Desai* stand for the proposition that a refugee claimant cannot choose to be stateless when application to the authorities of a particular country for citizenship would result in the confirmation of a *pre-existing* status. This situation may be contrasted with that of a claimant who has *potential* rather tha[n] *pre-existing* status as a national of a particular country.
>
> It is clear from the facts of the case [*Bouianova*] that this decision does not stand for the proposition that claimants are required to apply for citizenship and prove a well-founded fear of persecution from each potential country of nationality. The applicant in this case was a citizen of Russia by birth, and, as a result of the operation of Russian law and the application to the Russian consulate, was merely asking for recognition of a pre-existing status. Upon application, the Consulate would put a stamp in her passport and this stamp would merely be a declaration or confirmation of the applicant's actual nationality. This situation is clearly different from that of a person who does not have nationality at the time the application for refugee status is made, but who must make an application in order for citizenship to be conferred. The application in the latter case is a necessary step to the obtaining of citizenship and not merely an application for recognition of a pre-existing status. In such a circumstance, the applicant need not demonstrate a fear of persecution from this country of 'potential nationality'.
>
> ...
>
> The Board in the case before me concluded that the applicant has a connection with Israel but it appears to have ignored *Canada (Attorney-General) v Ward* (1993) 103 DLR (4th) 1 (SCC). It is important that potential nationality is not confused with actual nationality. In my view, the *Ward* decision does not deal with potential nationality and it will be helpful to review some of La Forest J's comments in *Ward*.

5.35 The primary engine for an expansion of the interpretation of 'the country of his nationality' in Canada has been a line of decisions in the Federal Court of Canada of which the following are examples. In *Desai v Canada (MCI)* (1994) 88 FTR 161 (TD), Muldoon J dismissed a refugee claimant's application for judicial review on the basis that Indian citizenship was a viable option for that claimant. He was born in Kuwait of Indian parents, but had never visited or lived in India, and was stateless. Indian citizenship laws, however, allow certain persons born outside India to acquire deemed Indian citizenship after first registering at an Indian embassy, high commission, or consulate. Thus, the Court held, Indian citizenship awaited the applicant upon application. The applicant need only present himself at an Indian diplomatic or consular office with evidence that his parents were born in India in order to have his Indian citizenship confirmed. In *Grygorian v Canada (MCI)* (1995) 33 Imm LR (2d) 52 (FCTD) the applicant was an Jewish citizen of Azerbaijan who sought refugee status. The decision-maker rejected her application on the basis that the applicant was entitled to Russian Federation citizenship by virtue of her birth, and to Israeli nationality under the provisions of Israel's Law of Return. The Court declined to intervene, stating that the basic principle of refugee law is to grant such status only to those requiring surrogate protection and not to those who have a ready and automatic right to another country's nationality. Two years later, in *De Rojas v Canada (MCI)* (1997) IMM-1460-96 Gibson J found that the applicant, a naturalised citizen of Venezuela who was accepted as possessing a well-founded fear of persecution as regards that country, could regain the nationality of the country of her birth, Colombia, so that Colombia fell to be treated as a second 'country of [her] nationality':

> The Tribunal determined the applicant to have a well-founded fear of persecution if she were required to return to Venezuela. The Tribunal went on to determine that the applicant lost her Colombian citizenship when she acquired Venezuelan citizenship but that she had the right to reacquire Colombian citizenship '... upon compliance with requirements that are mere formalities'. On the evidence that was before the Tribunal, I am satisfied that this conclusion was reasonably open to it. The Tribunal determined that the applicant faced no serious possibility of persecution should she be required to go to Colombia
>
> ...
>
> While the facts of *Bouianova* can be distinguished from those in this matter, the principles are identical. In this matter, by complying with a mere formality, the applicant could have formal Colombian nationality. By simply choosing not to comply with the mere formality, the applicant cannot claim that Colombia is not a country of nationality for her.

5.36 In *De Barros v Canada (MCI)* [2005] FC 283, [2005] FCJ No 361 (QL) the applicants were Brazilian nationals who had come from that country and related their fear of persecution to criminality there:

> [5] The applicants' claim for refugee protection was rejected on the basis that they had state protection available in Portugal. The Board found that because the applicant's father was a citizen of Portugal, the applicant was eligible to obtain Portuguese citizenship. This

> finding was based on information contained in a Response to Information Request (RIR) issued by the Board's Research Directorate. The RIR, dated June 1995, states that a person born of Portuguese parents who is under the age of 14 will be recognized as a citizen if he or she is registered with a consulate or embassy. A person who is 14 years or older can still be recognized as a citizen but the process is not immediate and their application must be processed in Portugal.

Kelen J rejected the application for review, treating *Bouianova* as grounding the proposition that 'Accordingly, a person who is able to obtain citizenship in another country by complying with mere formalities is not entitled to avail themselves of protection in Canada' and judging that 'The question in this case is whether there was sufficient evidence to support the Board's conclusion that the applicant was entitled to obtain Portuguese citizenship through compliance with mere formalities. I am satisfied there was'.

A very important subsequent decision embedding and in practice extending this wider interpretation of 'the country of his nationality' is that of the Canadian Federal Court of Appeal (Décary, Létourneau and Nadon JJA), in *Canada (MCI) v Williams* [2005] FCA 126, [2005] 3 FCR 429, 253 DLR (4th) 449. In *Williams* the respondent to an appeal by the Minister was a national of Rwanda. He had been born in Rwanda to a Rwandan national father and Ugandan national mother, and had lived alternately in the two countries. On reaching 18 he chose to retain Rwandan citizenship and ceased to be a Ugandan national by operation of (Ugandan) law. Notwithstanding this, he retained under the Ugandan Constitution an unconditional right to resumption of Ugandan nationality, upon renouncing his other (Rwandan) nationality. Counsel for the respondent accepted that 'country of nationality' should be read as including 'potential countries of nationality' where it was within the applicant's control to acquire such a nationality. The judgment of Décary JA, concurred in by other members of the panel, states that: 5.37

> [19] It is common ground between counsel that refugee protection will be denied where it is shown that an applicant, at the time of the hearing, is entitled to acquire by mere formalities the citizenship (or nationality, both words being used interchangeably in this context) of a particular country with respect to which he has no well-founded fear of persecution.
>
> [20] This principle flows from a long line of jurisprudence starting with the decisions of our Court in *Canada (Attorney General) v Ward*, [1990] 2 FC 667 (CA), and in *Canada (Minister of Employment and Immigration) v Akl* (1990), 140 NR 323 (FCA), where it was held that, if an applicant has citizenship in more than one country, he must demonstrate a well-founded fear of persecution in relation to each country of citizenship before he can seek asylum in a country of which he is not a national. Our ruling in *Ward* was confirmed by the Supreme Court of Canada (at paragraph 12 of these reasons) and the principle eventually made its way into the IRPA, section 96 referring to 'each of their countries of nationality'.
>
> [21] In another decision rendered before the Supreme Court of Canada rendered its own in *Ward, Bouianova v Canada (Minister of Employment and Immigration)* (1993),

67 FTR 74, Rothstein J (sitting then in the Trial Division of the Federal Court of Canada) broadened the holding of our Court in *Akl*. He held that if, at the time of the hearing, an applicant is entitled to acquire the citizenship of a particular country by reason of his place of birth, and if that acquisition could be completed by mere formalities, thereby leaving no room for the State in question to refuse status, then the applicant is expected to seek the protection of that State and will be denied refugee status in Canada unless he has demonstrated that he also has a well-founded fear of persecution in relation to that additional country of nationality.

[22] I fully endorse the reasons for judgment of Rothstein J, and in particular the following passage at paragraph 12:

> The condition of not having a country of nationality must be one that is beyond the power of the applicant to control.

The true test, in my view, is the following: if it is within the control of the applicant to acquire the citizenship of a country with respect to which he has no well-founded fear of persecution, the claim for refugee status will be denied. While words such as 'acquisition of citizenship in a non-discretionary manner' or 'by mere formalities' have been used, the test is better phrased in terms of 'power within the control of the applicant' for it encompasses all sorts of situations, it prevents the introduction of a practice of 'country shopping' which is incompatible with the 'surrogate' dimension of international refugee protection recognized in *Ward* and it is not restricted, contrary to what counsel for the respondent has suggested, to mere technicalities such as filing appropriate documents. This 'control' test also reflects the notion which is transparent in the definition of a refugee that the 'unwillingness' of an applicant to take steps required from him to gain state protection is fatal to his refugee claim unless that unwillingness results from the very fear of persecution itself.

...

[24] The principle has also been recognized in England (*Tecle v Secretary of State for the Home Department*, 2002 EWCA Civ 1358, England and Wales Court of Appeal (Civil Division), in Australia (see 'Refugee Status and Multiple Nationality in the Indonesian Archipelago: Is there a Timor Gap?', R Piotrowicz (1996), 8 *Int J Refugee L* 319) and in France (see Spivak, Conseil d'État, No 160832, April 2, 1997; Denis Alland and Catherine Teitgen-Colly, *Traité du droit de l'asile*, Paris: Presses Universitaires de France, 2002, page 446, where reference is made to *Bouianova*).

[25] It follows that Pinard J erred in finding that 'countries of nationality', in section 96 of the IRPA, did not include potential countries of nationality. It is true that the French text, '*tout pays dont elle a la nationalité*', as well as both the French and English texts of Article 1A(2) of the Refugee Convention, could support a restrictive interpretation, but such an interpretation, as appears from the case law, would be incompatible with the true purpose of international refugee protection.

Several aspects of the *Williams* decision in retrospect appear very unfortunate. The Court was not asked to revisit the true significance of the *Bouianova* decision or to consider the effect of VCLT69 interpretive standards. Considerable authority is cited for the narrower principle—that in the *Ward* case, by which an applicant must seek the protection of any (actual, present) country of nationality. At paragraph 21 *Bouianova* is treated as having extended this to cover situations in which nationality is not already extant, but could be sought. As already seen however it is not clear that this, rather than the narrower *Ward* principle, is what the *Bouianova* decision pointed to. The emphasis on the surrogacy principle (as expressed in the UNHCR *Handbook* and emphasised in *Ward*) as justification for the widened definition neglects the absence of evidence in CSR51 itself for a special meaning of 'nationality', the absence of holdings to this effect in any other jurisdiction, the presumed secondary effect of such a holding as creating the ability to qualify as a refugee under article 1A(2) by reference to a 'country of nationality' without possessing nationality, and the absence of parallel special meaning in any other area of international law in which nationality is significant—for instance it is plain that diplomatic protection cannot be extended to a non-national, subject to possible exceptions for resident refugees and stateless persons, even if that individual might have obtained nationality. At paragraph 23 the initial use of the past tense ('was obtained') suggests a narrow interpretation whereas the reference to obtaining nationality points to the wider one. And it does not appear that the citations cited at paragraph 24, going to related but different issues such as credibility or so-called 'effectiveness' of nationality, actually provide support for a wider interpretation of 'the country of his nationality' in article 1A(2) CSR51. Overall the somewhat diverse citations actually suggest a risk that in *Williams* citation of *Bouianova* on the narrow interpretation elsewhere was treated as support for it on the wider one. The Court rejected the narrow legal argument for the respondent that cases in which nationality had to be renounced for access to another nationality to be realised should be distinguished from the broader *Bouianova* principle.

Subsequent Canadian decisions have treated *Williams* as authority for the treatment of a State as being a 'country of nationality' if it is one to which 'within the control of the applicant to acquire the citizenship of a country with respect to which he has no well-founded fear of persecution'. This has created some uncertainty. Must the application, or also the result, be within the applicant's control? What does 'within the applicant's control' mean in terms of the degree of effort or time an individual is expected to apply to obtaining such a nationality? The cases illustrate the tensions inherent in the *Williams* test. In *Gil Roncagliolo v Canada (MCI)* [2005] FC 1024, Blanchard J dealt with an application for review by a Peruvian navy officer who had sought asylum in Canada. His wife and children held citizenship of France as well as of Peru. The Minister refused recognition on the basis that the applicant could seek naturalisation as a French citizen by reason of his marriage: **5.38**

> [22] In this case the applicant, by virtue of his marriage to a woman holding French citizenship, has the right to be a citizen of France. The fact that he needs to make an application which in the circumstances requires a few administrative formalities, does not open the door to the applicant's argument that the Board mistakenly assessed his refugee claim on the assumption that he had French citizenship.

5.39 That decision, postdating the decision of the Federal Court of Appeal in the *Williams* case, might be contrasted with another decided close to it in time. In *Fabiano v Canada (MCI)* [2005] FC 1260, Russell J set aside a decision of the Board that the reference country for an Argentine citizen whose parents had been Italian citizens was Italy, and directed reconsideration. The Board had adjudged that:

> application for citizenship in Italy is a mere formality, and that the Italian law of ascendancy would suggest that the authorities of Italy do not have the discretion to refuse the claimant's application which I find on a balance of probabilities can be made from within Italy, a country with which he is already familiar, and whose language he speaks. Those who are granted citizenship automatically by the operation of legal provisions are definitely nationals of that state.

Russell J characterised the conclusion of the Board as speculative and without evidentiary basis, because there was no evidence that the applicant was able either to travel to Italy to pursue citizenship procedures there or to remain in Canada whilst these were progressed. The Board had not assessed the risk to the applicant in Argentina because of its exclusive focus on Italy, but in the absence of ability to travel to Italy or remain in Canada, delays to any procedure for acquisition of Italian citizenship meant the risk of intervening return to Argentina. At [42] the Court concluded with the observation that 'In other words, given the evidence that was before the Board, the Board's findings of fact and conclusions on the central issue of country of reference were patently unreasonable'.

5.40 In *Canada (MCI) v Kaaib* [2006] FC 870, [2006] 297 FTR 69 the respondents were Lebanese citizens, but were recorded as having asserted birth in Syria, and one had previously travelled on a Syrian passport. Shore J held that the fact-finding Board had erred in failing to analyse the matter of whether the applicants were Syrian citizens or could have obtained that citizenship by mere formalities. The application for judicial review was allowed, and the decision remitted to a differently constituted panel for reconsideration. In *Alvarez v Canada (MCI)* [2007] FC 296, 156 ACWS (3d) 437 the principal applicant was a Colombian citizen married to a dual Colombian–Venezuelan citizen. She had been a lawyer in Colombia and was accepted as possessing a well-founded fear of persecution from FARC guerrillas. Applying *Williams* and citing *Bouianova*, Phelan J declined to intervene in the decision of the Board refusing the applicant's claim to refugee status, on the basis that she could acquire Venezuelan citizenship on the basis of her marriage. By contrast, the applicant's daughter and brother, who were found not to have a relevant entitlement to Venezuelan nationality, were recognised as refugees.

5.41 In a significant success for claimants, *Canada (MCI) v Hua Ma* [2009] FC 779, members of a nuclear family group of Chinese origin settled in the Solomon Islands. In 2006 their family business and residence was burned to the ground during anti-Chinese rioting. One respondent was outside the country. The others respondents were evacuated to China on emergency travel documents, the Government of China having stepped in to assist persons of Chinese descent by sending aircraft to evacuate them from the Solomon Islands. Some time later the respondents travelled to Canada and claimed asylum. The Immigration and Refugee Board concluded that both parents had acquired Solomon Islands nationality so that their nationality of the People's Republic of China had lapsed and their children, born in the Solomon Islands, would not be considered Chinese nationals. The Minister appears to have pressed to expand further the *Williams* extension to an ordinary language understanding of 'the country of his nationality', the submission made on his behalf being that where authorities of a third country (here the People's Republic of China) have a discretion to grant or restore nationality, an applicant was required to show evidence that that discretion would in practice not be exercised positively.

Russell J rejected the attempt to go beyond *Williams*: **5.42**

> [114] The Board also demonstrates its awareness of what is at issue by making a direct comparison between the situation in *Williams*—'Ugandan citizenship was there for him to acquire, if he had the will to acquire it'—and the situation of the Respondents in this present case:
>
>> This is not exactly the issue in the case at hand. The bars to re-obtaining Chinese nationality are not only contingent upon perfunctory renunciation of their Solomon Island status, as was the issue in *Williams*. The process with respect to China is not automatic, involved an application process, and required approval by government officials.
>
> [115] Consequently, the Board found that the Respondents 'met the tests set out in *Williams*': The Board says 'In accordance with *Williams*, it is not within his power to acquire it'.
>
> [116] What is more, in applying *Williams*, the Board provides full reasons as to why it is not within the Respondents power to acquire Chinese citizenship.
>
> [117] There was evidence before the Board to demonstrate that it was not within the control of the Respondents to acquire Chinese citizenship, which is the test dictated by *Williams*. The children alone would cause them all kinds of problems and [the mother of the family] gave evidence that she might also be subjected to forced sterilization.
>
> [118] The Applicant wants to push this issue further to say that the Respondents should have been required to demonstrate that it was more likely than not that, if they applied, they would not be granted Chinese citizenship. In fact, at the refugee hearing and as part of this application, the Applicant also argued that the Respondents were under an obligation to show that they had applied for, and had been refused, Chinese citizenship.
>
> [119] This argument was, in my view, correctly rejected by the Board as being contrary to *Williams*. But it does show where the Applicant wants to push this issue. In my view, to go beyond *Williams* in order to do what the Applicant wants to do would impose an intolerable burden upon people in the position of the Respondents.
>
> [120] It is certainly within the control of the Respondents to submit an application for Chinese citizenship but, on the evidence, it was not within the control of the Respondents

> to acquire Chinese citizenship, and the evidence suggested to the Board that they faced serious problems in doing so.

The application was dismissed.

5.43 In *Kim v Canada (MCI)* 2010 FC 720 [2010] FCJ No 870 (QL) the applicants were nationals of North Korea. The material question was whether South Korean nationality was relevantly available to them. It had been held that they were not entitled to protection because entitlement to South Korean nationality was 'automatic'. On the evidence Hughes J found 'on the best evidence, that it is by no means "automatic" or "within the control" of the Applicants that they will receive South Korean citizenship':

> [15] In a 'Responses to Information Requests' received by the Board on June 3, 2008, it was stated that perhaps on a strict reading of the south Korean constitution, North Koreans could obtain South Korean citizenship; however, North Koreans are not automatically accepted, a 'will and desire' to live in South Korea must be established and persons who have 'resided in a third country for an extended period of time' are not eligible (the Applicants have lived in China and Canada).

5.44 Hughes J found that the decision of the Board was not sustainable:

> [18] The Board member erred in assuming that the question was whether North Koreans could 'automatically' obtain South Korean citizenship and that she was required to give a yes or no answer to that question. The proper question is whether or not, on the evidence before the Board, there is sufficient doubt as to the law, practice, jurisprudence and politics of South Korea such that citizenship cannot be considered as automatic or fully within the control of these particular Applicants.
>
> [19] Here the evidence is that it is by no means clear that these particular Applicants will, in the circumstances of their case, automatically be given South Korean citizenship or that the acquisition of such citizenship is entirely within their control. There are considerations as to the 'will and desire' to live in South Korea that must be assessed by some official and perhaps the courts there as well as consideration given to the length of time that the Applicants have resided in China and Canada. There is no certainty as to the outcome.

The application was allowed and the case remitted for redetermination by the Board.

5.45 In two later cases applicants failed to overturn decisions that they possessed nationality of States other than the index State in relation to which they claimed a well-founded fear. In *Ashby v Canada (MCI)* [2011] FC 277, the applicant had been found by the Board to be a citizen both of St Vincent and the Grenadines and of Grenada. She sought asylum in Canada on the basis of abuse by her stepfather in St Vincent, and asserted that her Guyanese nationality had been lost by operation of Guyanese law when she affirmed citizenship in St Vincent, a decision not notified to the Guyanese authorities. Near J declined to set aside the decision challenged, because on examination the Constitution of Guyana suggested that loss of Guyanese nationality upon taking another nationality was not automatic—in such a case discretion to remove Guyanese nationality was placed in the President of Guyana, which in the instant case had never been exercised against the applicant. Accordingly the applicant remained a Guyanese national. In *Yah Abedalaziz v Canada (MCI)* [2011] FC 1066 [2011] FCJ 1271 (QL) the applicant for refugee status was born in Jordan and applied for a student visa stating himself to be a Jordanian citizen. He subsequently sought asylum stating that he was a stateless Palestinian from the West Bank, and that he had used a Jordanian temporary passport not proving citizenship in that country. Shore J held that the applicant had failed to refute the presumption of Jordanian citizenship created by his possession of a Jordanian passport.

Many Canadian cases in recent years have concerned Tibetans from diaspora communities outside Tibet. In *Buchung v Canada (MCI)* [2009] FC 381, Russell J overturned the decision of the fact-finder that the applicant, a Tibetan refugee in Nepal, had failed to show that he did not have Nepalese citizenship, where the Nepalese authorities had confirmed in writing that the applicant had been a resident Tibetan refugee but not a Nepalese national, and had no entitlement to apply for status as a Nepalese national. More recently several cases have reached entirely divergent conclusions on the position of Tibetan refugees in India. The Citizenship Act of India and decisions of senior Indian courts[21] have together established that Tibetans born in India between 26 January 1950 and 1 July 1987 are Indian citizens by nationality laws based in that period upon *ius soli*. However, there is strong evidence of resistance to implementation at and even above the administrative level.[22] In *Wanchuk v Canada (MCI)* 2014 FC 885 O'Reilly J held, having reviewed evidence, that: 5.46

> [10] In my view, this evidence shows a mere possibility that Mr Wanchuk could obtain Indian citizenship. It would require, at a minimum, that the [Indian Government's Central Tibetan Authority] exercise its discretion not to withhold its approval and that Indian authorities recognize *Dolkar* as binding precedent. In fact, Mr Wanchuk might well have to litigate the issue. I note that Ms Dolkar [the litigant in the leading Indian case] expended several years in administrative and legal battles in order to obtain Indian citizenship.
>
> [11] In these circumstances, I find the Board's conclusion that obtaining Indian citizenship was within Mr Wanchuk's control was unreasonable.

In *Dolker v Canada (MCI)* 2015 FC 124, the Board found that the applicant, who had an Indian passport, was a citizen of India, and in the alternative that even if 5.47

[21] *Namgyal Dolkar v Government of India, Ministry of External Affairs*, WP(C) 12179/2009 (India: Delhi High Court, 22 December 2010), available at: www.refworld.org/docid/52ca85264.html; *Tenzin Cheophag Ling Rinpoche v Government of India, Ministry of External Affairs*, WP(C) 15437/2013 (India: Karnataka High Court, 7 August 2013), available at www.refworld.org/docid/52ca86c24.html.

[22] Canada: Immigration and Refugee Board of Canada; India: Citizenship recognition for Indian-born children of Tibetan refugees in the context of the 22 December 2010 Delhi High Court Ruling; whether it has become procedural or if it requires legal action (2011–August 2013), 15 August 2013, IND104530.E, available at: www.refworld.org/docid/525e4e854.html.

she was not a citizen of India, she bore the onus of establishing that she had sought and been refused citizenship by the Indian authorities. Hughes J dismissed the challenge to the first finding but in *obiter* reasoning addressed the Board's alternative finding. He acknowledged that no Canadian authority required an applicant to first seek and be refused citizenship in a safe country before claiming refugee status in Canada, but expressing concern that the applicant in the course of peaceably living in India took no steps to acquire full Indian citizenship. In *Tretsetsang v Canada (MCI)* 2015 FC 455, Mosley J on similar material to that in *Wanchuk* declined to follow the earlier decision:

> [31] This is where I must, with respect, decline to follow *Wanchuk*. At para 10 of that decision, Justice O'Reilly expressed the view that obtaining Indian citizenship was a 'mere possibility' for a similarly situated applicant, since it might require litigation. That does not, in my view, amount to the level of the 'intolerable burden' that Justice Russell found to apply in *Hua Ma* in light of the one child policy and other considerations in China. Nor is it consistent with the teachings of *Williams*. Applicants are expected to take reasonable steps to acquire or enforce any citizenship rights which are available to them. A right which is enshrined in legislation and has been enforced by the courts amounts to more than a 'mere possibility'. There is nothing unreasonable about expecting the applicant to take legal action if his state of nationality attempts to deny his rights.

5.48 In *Paldenn v Canada (MCI)* 2015 FC 787, Locke J found sustainable a decision of the Board that India was a country of relevant nationality, relying upon the presumption raised by the applicant's past use of an apparently valid Indian passport. In another nearly contemporaneous decision, *Dolma v Canada (MCI)* 2015 FC 703 Tremblay-Lamer J set aside the decision of the Board:

> [39] Despite the overwhelming documentary evidence that the Indian authorities continued to treat Indian-born Tibetans as foreigners following the *Dolkar Decision*, the Board found that the *Dolkar Decision* clarified that there was no *legal* basis for the authorities to do so and that therefore the applicant had not established that Indian citizenship was not within her control:
>
>> [25] The panel finds that the recent decision has clarified that there is no legal basis for the Indian authorities to treat Indian-born Tibetans any differently from any other Indian-born citizens. Even if some Indian-born ethnic Tibetans are still experiencing difficulties in acquiring Indian passports or other benefits of citizenship, despite this decision, such cases do not serve to establish that Indian citizenship is not within their control, as per the applicable test in *Williams*.
>>
>> ...
>>
>> [26] As an individual born in India between January 26, 1959 and July 1, 1987 in India, the claimant is an Indian citizen by birth, irrespective of her declared nationality, and there is no need for her to apply to obtain Indian citizenship.
>>
>> [27] The panel is not persuaded by the evidence before it that the claimant is not a citizen of India, as she has alleged, or that her citizenship in India is not automatic or non-discretionary, as submitted by counsel [Emphasis added].

> [40] My concern with this approach is that it focuses solely on the legal entitlement to citizenship and not on the practical reality and need to have that citizenship recognized by the relevant authorities. As Hathaway & Foster state, nationality must be effective, rather than merely formal. Elements in the concept of 'effective nationality' include recognition of the nationality by the state of nationality and the absence of practical impediments to accessing the benefits of nationality (pp 56–57).
>
> [41] Since the requirement in the definition of a refugee reflects the principle that international refugee protection is surrogate protection and is only available to individuals who are not able to obtain protection in one of their countries of nationality, in my opinion the legal right to citizenship is not the only relevant factor. If the authorities do not recognize the legal right, it is doubtful that they will offer protection if and when needed. In other words, where citizenship in a country is purely formal rather than pragmatically effective, the country in question should not be considered as a country of reference. Given the humanitarian objects of the *Refugee Convention*, it could not have been intended that a person would be denied international protection by virtue of a formal but relevantly ineffective nationality (Hathaway & Foster at 57, citing *Jong Kim Koe* (Aus FFC, 1997) at 520–521).

The extension of this line of cases, without direct regard to the interpretation of CSR51 applying VCLT69 principles, is unfortunate. The first case in this line, *Bouianova*, is comprehensible in two senses as compatible with CSR51. First, as Waldman indicated near-contemporaneously, it was a case in which the evidence indicated possession of the nationality in question (that of the Russian Federation) at the time of status determination. The Russian Federation was for Ms Bouianova 'the country of [her] nationality': 5.49

> §8.351 It is clear from the facts of the case that this decision does not stand for the proposition that claimants are required to apply for citizenship and prove a well-founded fear of persecution from each potential country of nationality. The applicant in this case was a citizen of Russia by birth, and, as the result of the operation of Russian law, and the application to the Russian Consulate, was merely asking for recognition of a pre-existing status. Upon application, the Consulate would automatically put a stamp in her passport and this stamp would merely be a declaration or confirmation of the applicant's actual nationality.[23]

Second, the observation of Rothstein J that Ms Bouianova had taken a decision not to assist in ascertaining relevant facts when she could readily have done so was on the facts of the case obviously relevant. Such a finding could be held to impact proceedings as an aspect of Ms Bouianova's conduct relevant to the assessment of her credibility as a witness or good faith in other relevant respects, and more specifically as conduct going to whether Ms Bouianova should enjoy the benefit of the doubt in status determination, should this becomes determinative.[24]

---

[23] Waldman (n 13 above) §8.351.

[24] UNHCR, *Handbook and Guidelines on Procedures and Criteria for Determining Refugee Status* (n 3 above) para 203: 'After the applicant has made a genuine effort to substantiate his story there may

It represented a breach by the claimant of the shared duty relevant to establishment of the facts.[25]

5.50 However, *Bouianova* does not appear to have been authority that 'the country of his nationality' includes a country which precisely is *not* a country of nationality, but rather one to which application could be made for a grant of nationality. That proposition appears to have developed through a line of other decisions such as *Desai*, *Grygorian* and *De Rojas*, and then to have been uncontested in the *Williams* case, the only decision at the level of the Federal Court of Appeal. In inspiration these cases share common ground with the true *Bouianova* cases, like *Bouianova* itself, *Kaaib* and *Dolker*. At a level of decision in individual cases there has of course been justified concern to avoid rewarding behaviour by applicants seen as not in good faith or otherwise insufficient. At a level of interpretation it has been held that the 'last resort' status of international protection means that countries of potential nationality should be invoked as 'the country of his nationality' because the acquisition of refugee status should not be manipulated: in the words of Rothstein J in *Bouianova*, highlighted by Décary JA in *Williams*, 'The condition of not having a country of nationality must be one that is beyond the power of the applicant to control'. This does not appear to have involved either interpretation applying VCLT69 principles or close examination of the significance of nationality in article 1A(2) CSR51 itself. The considerable flaws in the position that for purposes of article 1A(2) CSR51, 'the country of his nationality' should be held to include a country whose nationality an applicant does not possess, are addressed in section B4.vi below.

5.51 Section 96(a) of the Canadian domestic statute, the Immigration and Refugee Protection Act, provided that 'A Convention refugee is a person who ... (*a*) is outside each of their countries of nationality and is unable or, by reason of that fear, unwilling to avail themself of the protection of each of those countries'. This seems to refer to and repeat the language of CSR51 rather than, as is possible in a State adopting a dualist approach to international law, imposing within domestic statute a special meaning extending or limiting the scope of the international obligation at the point of translation into domestic law. However, understandably

still be a lack of evidence for some of his statements. As explained above (paragraph 196), it is hardly possible for a refugee to "prove" every part of his case and, indeed, if this were a requirement the majority of refugees would not be recognized. It is therefore frequently necessary to give the applicant the benefit of the doubt'.

[25] UNHCR, *Handbook and Guidelines on Procedures and Criteria for Determining Refugee Status* (n 3 above) para 205(a) '(a): The *applicant* should: (i) Tell the truth and assist the examiner to the full in establishing the facts of his case. (ii) Make an effort to support his statements by any available evidence and give a satisfactory explanation for any lack of evidence. If necessary he must make an effort to procure additional evidence. (iii) Supply all pertinent information concerning himself and his past experience in as much detail as is necessary to enable the examiner to establish the relevant facts. He should be asked to give a coherent explanation of all the reasons invoked in support of his application for refugee status and he should answer any questions put to him'.

in light of the case law reviewed above, the expansion in Canada of the definition of 'country of his nationality' is now reflected in the Interpretation of the Refugee Definition in the Case Law document of the Immigration and Refuge Board of Canada. This states that:

> 2.1.3 Right to Citizenship
>
> The term 'countries of nationality', in section 96(*a*) of *IRPA*, includes potential countries of nationality. Where citizenship in another country is available, a claimant is expected to make attempts to acquire it and will be denied refugee status if it is shown that it is within his or her power to acquire that other citizenship. Consequently, a person who is able to obtain citizenship in another country by complying with mere formalities is not entitled to avail themself of protection in Canada.
>
> In view of its importance and complexity, normally notice should be given before the hearing if multiple nationality is an issue, so as to avoid taking claimants by surprise and allow them an opportunity to obtain evidence relating to that matter.[26]

However, that document shows further confusion over the distinction between current nationality and potential nationality. Under the same heading it states that:

> The Trial Division has also held, in non-successor state contexts, that a legal entitlement to citizenship by birth in a place (jus soli), through one's parents or by descent (jus sanguinis), through marriage, or even through ancestry may also confer effective nationality. One cannot 'choose' to be stateless in these circumstances.

As explained in chapter one (see para 1.43), citizenship by birth or descent are modes of original acquisition of nationality and operate automatically. An individual does not apply for the grant of nationality in those circumstances, but for acknowledgement or evidence of a pre-existing nationality. Marriage or ancestry may lead to nationality automatically. In any such case again an application may be for acknowledgement or evidence, but no application for nationality can be in prospect because the individual already is a national. Any of these cases are addressed satisfactorily by the narrow *Bouianova* principle that where an individual is the national of a State under its laws, that State is a reference country for purposes of article 1A(2) CSR51 because it is 'the country of his nationality'. No special meaning is necessary in such a case—an individual cannot 'choose to be stateless' in such circumstances because he or she is not. On a correct understanding an application for nationality itself is conceivable only where an individual is not already a national—as for instance by naturalisation through presence on the territory, or marriage or ancestry, if domestic laws of citizenship provide for derivative acquisition in these circumstances and application for the primary status is necessary.

---

[26] See: www.irb-cisr.gc.ca/Eng/BoaCom/references/LegJur/Pages/RefDef02.aspx#n21.

ii. New Zealand

5.52 The concept of an expanded definition of 'country of his nationality' has drifted to other jurisdictions, though reception has been distinctly uneven. The New Zealand Immigration and Protection Tribunal in *AB (Iraq)* [2011] NZIPT 800014 addressed the position of an Iraqi born in the 1940s to a woman of mixed French and Iraqi Arabic extraction. She appears to have been a French citizen until 1976 when she renounced that citizenship. The Tribunal set out the issues as including both actual nationality and potential nationality:

> [2] As against Iraq, the appellant's claim to refugee status must succeed. The question, however, is whether he is also a French national by descent. If so, he must also establish his claim against France in order to be recognised as a refugee or a protected person. The central issue is thus whether his mother's French nationality means that France, today, recognises the appellant as a French national or, alternatively, whether the steps necessary for him to acquire French nationality would be no more than a mere formality.

The appellant had himself never presented or been treated as a French citizen and the Tribunal having considered French nationality law found that the appellant was not a French citizen:

> [35] Notwithstanding those findings, it is necessary to address the third question raised by the Convention. This is because the underlying assumption in refugee law is that, where available, national protection takes precedence over international protection—see JC Hathaway, *The Law of Refugee Status* at p 57 and the UNHCR's *Handbook on Procedures and Criteria for Determining Refugee Status*, at para 106. If a refugee claimant possesses more than one nationality he or she must establish a well-founded fear of being persecuted in respect of each before the surrogate protection of the international community comes into play. Put simply, if the appellant is a French national and can thus avail himself of the protection of that country, New Zealand's surrogate protection obligation is not engaged.
>
> [36] By logical extension, the same outcome is reached if the acquisition of French nationality is a mere formality. See, for example, [*Refugee Appeal No 72635*, [2002] NZRSAA 344] (6 September 2002) at [138]–[141] and [*Refugee Appeal Nos 72558 & 72559*, [2002] NZRSAA 423] (19 November 2002) at [83], both citing *Tatiana Bouianova v Minister of Employment and Immigration* [1993] FCJ No 576; (1993) 67 FTR 74 (FC:TD). Those decisions considered the question of the attainment of nationality by persons who are otherwise stateless but the principle is the same.

The Tribunal held that 'it cannot be said that he has the effective protection of the French state as a national, or that recognition as such is a mere formality' and 'It follows that the appellant is not, today, to be regarded as a national of France and the question of any protection obligation which would arise from having the citizenship of that country does not arise'.

5.53 *AB (Iraq)* raises in acute form an important, and valid, question also touched on in some of the Canadian cases, namely how to deal with a possible second or further nationality which is long dormant. In *AB (Iraq)* it was found that there was no nationality because nationality was not acknowledged by the authorities of the State and was in this respect or in respect of protection ineffective. But nationality hangs upon the nationality law of the State, in this case France rather than by the presence of protection. Applied to *AB (Iraq)*, if the appellant in that matter was in fact a French citizen by descent as at the time of his birth in the 1940s, but in practice his status as such was not reasonably provable to the satisfaction of the French authorities, whether France remained a 'country of his nationality' should have depended upon the assessment of its nationality laws alone. This further point is separate from that of 'potential nationality', and illustrates an important question in relation to plural nationality, addressed in section B7 below.

iii. The United Kingdom

In the United Kingdom the decision in *Bouianova* has been less frequently referred to than in either Canada or New Zealand, and it is necessary to examine the cases with some care to determine the actual *ratio* in each, given the multiple contexts in which that case might be cited. In the Scottish case of *R v SSHD ex p Bradshaw* [1994] Imm AR 359, Lord MacLean, in the Outer House of the Court of Session, doubted the claim to statelessness of a former citizen of the USSR, not an asylum claimant, who had shown reluctance to make any enquiry to the Ukrainian or Russian Federation authorities to establish the truth of her claim about loss of nationality. His observation was not necessary to the resolution of the application before him, and so was *obiter*, but in any event is best understood as a reflection going to whether Ms Bradshaw was able to make out her case, and/or the effect upon any assessment of her credibility of failure to take an elementary step to assist enquiry. The case was decided in parallel with, rather than by reference to, the nearly contemporaneous *Bouianova* decision. Subsequently, the Court of Appeal in England and Wales held in *Tecle v SSHD* [2002] EWCA Civ 1358, that on the facts a subordinate tribunal had been entitled to treat as relevant to credibility the failure of the applicant, whose refugee claim was founded on persecution by Ethiopia, to ascertain by approaching the authorities her standing as a national or otherwise vis-a-vis Eritrea, the country of her birth. 5.54

The decisions in *Bouianova*, *Bradshaw* and *Tecle* were all cited subsequently by the Immigration Appeal Tribunal in *YL (Nationality, Statelessness, Eritrea, Ethiopia) Eritrea CG* [2003] UKIAT 00016. Like *Tecle* the case concerned an individual of Eritrean background who left Ethiopia on a national passport and subsequently sought asylum on the basis of denial of citizen status and of return by Ethiopia. She contested the assertion that she was an Eritrean national. The Tribunal observed that: 5.55

> Since it is common ground that the appellant is not as yet recognised as a national of Eritrea, it may be asked, why is it legitimate to even consider whether she is a national

> of Eritrea? Fortunately in order to answer this question we do not need to embark on an analysis of the complexities of nationality law. That is because, following *Bradshaw* [1994] Imm AR 359, we consider it settled law that when a person does not accept that the Secretary of State is correct about his nationality, it is incumbent on him to prove it, if need be by making an application for such nationality. That is all the more necessary in the case of someone claiming to be a refugee under the Refugee Convention. Under that Convention, establishing nationality (or statelessness) cannot be left as something that is optional for the claimant. The burden of proof is on the claimant to prove his nationality (or lack of it). To leave it as an optional matter would also make it possible for bogus claimants to benefit from international protection even though in law they had nationality of a country where they would not be at risk of persecution—simply by not applying for that nationality. Furthermore, leaving it as an optional matter would render unnecessary key provisions of the definition in Art 1A(2) which require a person to be outside the country of his nationality or outside the country of his former habitual residence and which place special conditions on persons who have more than one nationality. As was said by Rothstein J in the Canadian Federal Court case of *Tatiana Bouianova v Minister of Employment and Immigration* [1993] FCJ No 576, a case dealing with statelessness, '[t]he definition should not be interpreted in such a manner as to render some of its words unnecessary or redundant'.
>
> Bearing in mind that the burden of proof rests on the claimant, it is always relevant to enquire in such cases whether a person has taken steps to apply for the nationality of the country in question or, if they have taken steps, whether they have been successful or unsuccessful.
>
> We would accept that in asylum cases the *Bradshaw* principle has to be qualified to take account of whether there are valid reasons for a claimant not approaching his or her embassy or consulate—or the authorities of the country direct—about an application for citizenship or residence. In some cases such an approach could place the claimant or the claimant's family at risk, because for example it would alert the authorities to the fact that the claimant has escaped pursuit by fleeing the country. However, by no means can there be a blanket assumption that for all claimants such approaches would create or increase risk. It is a matter to be examined on the evidence in any particular case. The 1979 UNHCR Handbook does not require a different position to be taken: paragraph 93 clearly contemplates a case-by-case approach.

In the *YL* case the essential question was evidential, and based in assessment of actions or omissions by the claimant. Further, the Tribunal expressly asked not whether the claimant *was already* a national of Eritrea, but whether assuming she held such nationality (which she would have held from Eritrean independence years earlier) that State would recognise her as such. In such circumstances the primary question for the Tribunal, determining whether Eritrea was a country of reference, was whether the appellant was an Eritrean national. On the facts, it appeared that if the claimant held nationality she held it as from Eritrean independence so Eritrea was a 'country of [her] nationality' even if as yet her nationality was unacknowledged by that State. *YL* therefore does not appear to be authority for inclusion within the definition of 'the country of his nationality' of countries to which application could be made for derivative acquisition (see chapter one, section A4). Like the New Zealand decision in *AB (Iraq)* this English case points to an important separate issue concerning the treatment of plural nationality, considered in section B7 below.

The issue of access to Eritrean nationality by asylum claimants from Ethiopia was considered again by the Immigration Appeal Tribunal in *FA (Eritrea, nationality) Eritrea CG* [2005] UKIAT 00047: **5.56**

> 24. The third ground in its first limb highlighted a point which, as Mr Fripp conceded, has been raised by him in a number of previous cases. It encapsulates what might be termed the 'present nationality' approach. However, as Mr Fripp should well know, that approach has been consistently and emphatically rejected in leading cases before the Court of Appeal and the Tribunal. This proper approach to nationality determination has been set out in some detail by the Tribunal in the *YL* case as follows: [quotation of YL, [44]–[47] follows].

The Tribunal's reference to previous authority was evidently to some mixture of the decisions in *Bouianova*, *Bradshaw*, *Tecle* and *YL*. All of the decisions referred to were decisions concerning evidence, standard of proof, and/or credibility. The objection to an apparent conclusion that these provided authority for the interpretation of 'country of his nationality' as including a State of potential future nationality, is that all of those cases were, correctly understood, cases in which if nationality existed in the claimant, it was already extant by the time of status determination by birth and/or state succession.

Later the Court of Appeal of England and Wales in *MA (Ethiopia) v SSHD* [2009] EWCA Civ 289, [2010] INLR 1 reiterated the *Bradshaw* point, Elias LJ, with whom Mummery and Stanley Burnton LJJ concurred, holding that: **5.57**

> 50. In my judgment, where the essential issue before the AIT is whether someone will or will not be returned, the Tribunal should in the normal case require the applicant to act *bona fide* and take all reasonably practicable steps to seek to obtain the requisite documents to enable her to return. There may be cases where it would be unreasonable to require this, such as if disclosure of identity might put the applicant at risk, or perhaps third parties, such as relatives of the applicant who may be at risk in the home state if it is known that the applicant has claimed asylum. That is not this case, however.

MA (Ethiopia) arose from the same nexus as *Tecle* and *YL*, that is, the treatment by Ethiopia of persons of Eritrean or part-Eritrean background after the outbreak of war between the two countries in 1998, though in *MA (Ethiopia)* it was the Ethiopian authorities the Court judged had to be approached by the applicant with a satisfactory level of disclosure and frankness. The Court of Appeal appears not to have revisited this issue subsequently, though it has touched on the separate issue of 'effective nationality' addressed below. The occasion for that, in *SSHD v SP (North Korea) & Ors* [2012] EWCA Civ 114, was appeal by the Secretary of State to the Court from a leading decision of the Upper Tribunal in *KK and others (Nationality: North Korea) Korea CG* [2011] UKUT 92.

5.58 In *KK and others* the Upper Tribunal (Mr Ockelton VP, SIJ Gleeson) considered appeals which, like the near-contemporaneous Canadian proceedings in *Kim*, arose from asylum claims by citizens of North Korea resisted on the basis that they were also South Korean citizens under the law of that country, and possessed no relevant fear of persecution as regards South Korea. The Tribunal appears to have endorsed (at [37]) an opinion of Professor Guy Goodwin-Gill to the effect that:

> In my Opinion, the express words of the second paragraph of Article 1A(2) of the 1951 Convention do not permit an interpretation which would require the asylum seeker to take steps to obtain a possible second nationality. On the other hand, an asylum seeker who is recognised as possessing another nationality is obliged, in the absence of a well-founded fear of persecution in that other country, to take steps to avail himself or herself of its protection.

The Tribunal stated that 'We have no difficulty at all in accepting that conclusion' following this with the observation that 'in the case where an individual actually has (as distinct from able to obtain) more than one nationality, we see no basis for treating either or any one of his nationalities as subsidiary to the others for the purposes of refugee status determination'.

5.59 In the event the appellants all succeeded. The Tribunal held that the appellants had been South Korean citizens but that by South Korean practice they would be treated as having ceased to be South Korean nationals through a presumption of expatriation during absence from the Korean peninsula:

> 91. The appellants acquired South Korean citizenship at birth, but each of them has been outside Korea for more than ten years. They remain North Korean nationals, but on the evidence before us we are satisfied that South Korea would treat them as persons who had lost their South Korean nationality on the presumption of the acquisition of another nationality. For that reason they have no subsisting or demonstrable entitlement to South Korean nationality documents: they would have to apply to re-acquire South Korean nationality, and we see no reason to suppose that it would be granted to them as a matter of routine.
>
> 92. The appellants are therefore all persons with one nationality only, that of North Korea. It is common ground that in that case they are refugees. We allow their appeals.

5.60 Although it was not necessary to the reasoning in *KK and others*, and was therefore *obiter*, the Tribunal at the commencement of the determination identified three possible situations in relation to the phrase 'country of his nationality' at article 1A(2) CSR51:

> 4. The phrasing of the references to nationality in Article 1A(2) is in the present tense: 'has more than one nationality'; 'countries of which he is a national'. It may be necessary to draw clear distinctions between three possible situations. The first is where a person *has* nationality of more than one country: that is to say each of the countries in question recognises him as a national. The second is where a person *is entitled to* nationality of a second country: that is to say that recognition of his nationality will depend on an application by him, but on the facts his nationality is a matter of entitlement, not of discretion. The third is where a person *may be able to obtain* nationality of a second country: that is

to say, where it cannot be said that, on application, he would be recognised as a national, but that he might be granted nationality. The difference between the first and the second situation is of status, not of documentation. A person may be a national of a country that has not yet issued him with any documentation evidencing that nationality. Such a person exemplifies the first situation, not the second.

As to the mutually distinct character of each of the three situations it identified, the Tribunal is clearly correct. It will be noted that the Tribunal in relation to the second group—entitlement to nationality on a non-discretionary basis—either does not adopt the Canadian approach in *Williams* – of 'within the control of the applicant'– or adopts an extremely restrictive variant of it. The Tribunal does not indicate whether it believed it was following, or whether it was differing from, *Williams*, though the Tribunal was shown a copy of that decision.

The Tribunal in *KK and others* set out reasoning, which it recognised as *obiter*,[27] under the heading 'The right to acquire nationality'. It cited, *inter alia*, the decision of McKeown J in *Katkova* and decisions of Australian courts in other cases concerning the Israeli Law of Return: *NAGV v Minister for Immigration* [2005] HCA 6 and *MZXLT v Minister for Immigration* [2007] FMCA 799 (see 5.65-7 below).[28] It noted that: 5.61

80. [C]ourts have found (though not in every case, as discussion in *Katkova* makes clear) that a person who may be able to obtain nationality of Israel under the Law of Return is not to be regarded as being a national of Israel. Similarly, we can see no general basis for treating persons as nationals of a state of which they are not presently nationals, and of which they have presently no entitlement to nationality.

81. On the other hand, there may be cases where the acquisition of a nationality not yet obtained is a matter not of discretion but of entitlement and of mere formality. Russian nationality was capable of being acquired by right by the claimants in *Bouianova v MEI* (1993) 67 FTR 74 and *Zdanov v MEI* (1994) 81 FTR 246. These were Canadian cases where the claimants were individuals who claimed to be stateless but, as Rothstein J said in *Bouianova* at [76] (as cited by McKeown J in *Katkova*):

'In my view, the applicant, by simply making a request and submitting her passport to be stamped, becomes a citizen of Russia. On the evidence before me, there is no discretion by the Russian officials to refuse her Russian citizenship. I do not think the necessity of making an application, which in these circumstances is nothing more than a mere formality, means that a person does not have a country of nationality just because they choose not to make such an application'.

82. In summary, for the purposes of the Refugee Convention, where a person already has a nationality (even if he has no documents to that effect) that is the end of the matter: he

[27] *KK and others (Nationality: North Korea) Korea CG* [2011] UKUT 92, [79]: 'A person may have the nationality in question; or he may not have it but be entitled to have it; or he may be a potential beneficiary of a discretion to grant him the nationality in question. The appellants fall within the first category in relation to South Korea, and it is therefore not strictly necessary to consider the others. In the light of the submissions we heard, however, it is right to give our views briefly'.

[28] Ibid, [80].

is a national of the country concerned. If he is entitled to nationality, subject only to his making an application for it, he is also to be regarded as a national of the country concerned. But if he is not a national and may be refused nationality, he is not to be treated as being a national of the country concerned. Subject to questions as to the 'effectiveness' of nationality, the same principle applies to entitlement to a second nationality as to entitlement to a first.

We should say that we regard that summary as consistent with authority, including *Bradshaw* [1994] Imm AR 359, and *MA*. In both of those cases there is more than a suggestion (in *Bradshaw* it is stated as a rule) that in order to establish a claim not to have a particular nationality, a person ought to apply, using his or her best endeavours, to obtain nationality of a country with which he or she is associated. But it seems to us that that must be a matter of evidence rather than of legal principle. For example, if the evidence is that nationality will be acquired on application, a decision maker ought to be entitled without more to treat the person as a national of the country in question, for the purposes of the Refugee Convention. If, on the other hand, there is evidence that the grant of nationality is a matter of discretion, it is not easy to see why a refugee claimant should be regarded, to his disadvantage, as having a nationality that he does not possess and may never possess. There may be borderline cases, and we would with respect strongly endorse what was said by Stanley Burnton LJ in *MA* at [83], as set out above.

5.62 The Tribunal does state, in its brief *obiter* view at [82], that 'If he is entitled to nationality, subject only to his making an application for it, he is also to be regarded as a national of the country concerned'. No support in law for the statement is set out, though the passage opening the next paragraph suggests that the Tribunal believed *Bradshaw* and/or *MA (Ethiopia)* to provide support for it. As will be clear those cases in fact supported different points and both involved a nationality already either possessed or not, the issue being the reasonable consequences of failure to seek acknowledgement by the authorities of the States concerned or insufficient good faith in such enquiry. The Tribunal has not set out the submissions of the parties, and whilst it was aware of the Canadian decision in *Williams*,[29] the Tribunal does not examine that decision. Given that a number of significant legal points were dealt with briefly in *obiter* reasoning, on which it is not clear that any submission was ever made, it is unfortunate that the Tribunal has set out in its summary of the points established by the decision a 'general conclusion' on at least one such point, the content of 'the country of his nationality' in article 1A(2) CSR51. The Tribunal states that:

90. We summarise our general conclusions as follows.

(1) Law

(a) For the purposes of determining whether a person is 'of' or 'has' a nationality within the meaning of Article 1A(2) of the Refugee Convention, it is convenient to distinguish between cases where a person (i) is (already) of that nationality; (ii) is

---

[29] Ibid, [58].

not of that nationality but is entitled to acquire it; and (iii) is not of that nationality but may be able to acquire it.

(b) Cases within (i) and (ii) are cases where the person is 'of' or 'has' the nationality in question; cases within (iii) are not.

The appellants succeeded in *KK* on the basis that despite apparent nationality they did not have access to protection by South Korea. The success of the appellants in *KK* was challenged unsuccessfully on appeal by the Secretary of State in *SSHD v SP (North Korea) & Ors* [2012] EWCA Civ 114, but the interpretation of article 1A(2) CSR51 was not an issue raised on the appeal. **5.63**

KK has been followed by a further decision ratifying its factual conclusions, *GP and Ors (South Korean citizenship) North Korea CG* [2014] UKUT 391. Whilst the decision is of some importance in relation to the examination of so-called 'effective nationality' concepts, it is difficult to see it as a satisfactory authority for the acceptance in the United Kingdom of the wider Canadian approach to 'the country of his nationality'. In *R (otao GP (Democratic People's Republic of Korea) & Ors) v SSHD* [2015] EWCA Civ 1116 (29 January 2015) an application for permission to appeal to the Court of Appeal was rebuffed by the Court (Gloster and Briggs LJJ), Briggs LJ observing that: **5.64**

> It is common ground that as a matter of South Korean law, which is the relevant law for this purpose, all the appellants are also South Korean citizens because of their birth in the Korean Peninsula, which includes, of course, North Korea, and their North Korean parentage.

iv. Australia

There is senior Australian authority which might be taken as inconsistent with the extended definition of 'country of his nationality'. As in the Canadian decisions in *Grygorian v Canada (MCI)* (1995) 33 Imm LR (2d) 52 (FCTD) and *Katkova v Canada (MCI)* (1997) 130 FTR 192, the appeal before the High Court of Australia in *NAGV and NAGW of 2002 v MIMA* [2005] HCA 6, raised the issue of whether applicants could be required to go to Israel, which country was considered likely to admit them as Jews immigrating under its 1950 Law of Return, rather than engaging a 'protection obligation' in Australia. Previously the Full Federal Court had in *NAEN v MIMIA* [2004] FCAFC 6 held that there was no 'protection obligation' where removal to a safe third country was viable. **5.65**

In *NAGV and NAGW* the Court (Gleeson CJ and McHugh, Gummow, Kirby, Hayne, Callinan and Heydon JJ) unanimously rejected the argument of the State that the appellants were outside the scope of protection obligations. The Court in joint reasons concluded that the possibility of admission to Israel did not disapply article 1A(2) CSR51: **5.66**

> 42. Having regard to the subject, scope and purpose of the Reform Act, the adjectival phrase in s 26B(2) (repeated in s 36(2)) 'to whom Australia has protection obligations

under [the Convention]' describes no more than a person who is a refugee within the meaning of Art 1 of the Convention. That being so and the appellants answering that criterion, there was no superadded derogation from that criterion by reference to what was said to be the operation upon Australia's international obligations of Art 33(1) of the Convention.

5.67 Kirby J concurred in the joint reasons whilst seeking to delimit these 'on a narrower footing', concluding that the State's construction of the statute was a strained one which failed, read in the light of the Convention, and with regard to the purposes of both the statute and the Convention:

> 89. Because there is nothing in the Convention, either expressly or by implication, to remove from Australia its protection obligations with respect to the appellants, as accepted there, in circumstances where, although the Convention is engaged in the State to which the applicant has had recourse, the applicant might have obtained protection elsewhere, such obligations continue to exist. But should a negative implication be read into the Convention in a case such as the present? I think not.
>
> 90. The notion can be tested this way. It would suggest that no Contracting State ever has 'protection obligations' to a refugee who may (on whatever basis) be entitled by law to protection by another State. For example, the constitutions of numerous countries create rights to seek and obtain asylum. Specifically, until 1993, the *Grundgesetz* (The Basic Law for the Federal Republic of Germany) provided that '[p]olitically persecuted individuals enjoy the right of asylum'. This was an 'absolute right' and included the rights of entry and non-refoulement. The Minister argued that the issue in this appeal was whether s 36 of the Act 'conferred an entitlement to a protection visa upon persons who have a well-founded fear of being persecuted for a Convention reason in their country of nationality but who have the right to enter, and settle in, a third country in which they do not have a well-founded fear of persecution or of expulsion'. If the Minister's argument were accepted, and if the Minister's argument with respect to the Law of Return were applied to the German Constitution as it stood before 1993, it would seem to follow that Australia would never have owed protection obligations to any person. All such persons would have had a right to asylum in Germany. It would be an absurd result if the generosity of other States' refugee laws meant that Australia was thereby relieved of international obligations that it voluntarily accepted with other nations. Such a result should not be reached by implication. It could not have been what was intended by Parliament when it enacted s 36(2).
>
> 91. I agree with the submission for the appellants that such a principle would render the Convention self-destructive. It would deprive the Convention of the practical effect that it was intended to have in the case of vulnerable persons such as the appellants who can establish that the Convention criteria apply in their case in the State where they have arrived and in which they claim the benefit of such protections.
>
> 92. The notion of an implied exclusion of 'protection obligations' is one that would, if given effect as part of the Convention scheme, potentially send applicants for refugee status shuttling between multiple countries. Their entitlements under the Convention would be hostage to arrangements purportedly made affecting their nationality by countries with which they may have no real connection. It would shift obligations clearly imposed by international law to contingencies that, in some cases, may be imponderable.

It would introduce a serious instability and uncertainty of 'protection obligations' into the Convention's requirements. Without clear language in the Convention to support such a course, I would not introduce such relief from Convention 'protection obligations' by a process of implication inimical to the Convention's objectives, terms and practical operation.

93. I leave aside a case where a refugee applicant has a clearly established entitlement to protection which has been exercised and engaged before resort to Australia, as in a case of transit. Such were the factual circumstances in *Minister for Immigration and Multicultural Affairs v Thiyagarajah*. Those facts are quite different from the present case. Neither of the appellants in this case has ever been to Israel. Neither has any personal connection with that country. Neither has ever claimed or exercised a 'right of return' as provided by Israeli law. The notion that such a municipal law (which is not unique to Israel) could cut a swathe through the international obligations assumed under the Convention is not one that is easily reconciled either with the Convention's language or its purpose.

94. Least of all is it an attractive notion in the case of a refugee who is a Jew, claiming protection under the Convention including on the basis of his status as a Jew. Historically, the Convention was, in part, a response of the international community to the affront to the international conscience caused by the mass migrations that occurred in Europe before, during and immediately after the Second World War.

...

96. It would also be astonishing if the enactment by the State of Israel of the Law of Return, without more, meant that the Convention's 'protection obligations', accepted by other countries, were thereby withdrawn throughout the world, by implication and not express terms, from application to all persons who were, or might be, classified as Jewish. This is especially so, given the role of Jewish organisations in drafting the Convention, and given that the definition of 'refugee' was directly influenced by the Nazi persecution of Jews.

97. It would require the clearest language of the Convention to have such a discriminatory operation. Far from being clear, the Convention, in its terms, does not withdraw its protection from applicants, otherwise 'refugees', who happen to be of Jewish religion or ethnicity or any other religion or ethnicity that might somewhere fall within some other country's unilateral enactment of return rights. Jews, however defined, are protected by the Convention like everyone else. The enactment of the Law of Return by the State of Israel does not deprive them of that protection which derives from the international law expressed in the Convention. As far as I am concerned, any ambiguity that might exist in the Convention (or the Act) must be construed to prevent such an unjust operation.

v. Commentary

The interpretation of 'the country of his nationality' as including a country whose nationality is not possessed at the relevant time therefore remains primarily a **5.68**

Canadian innovation perpetuated by domestic precedent. As seen above, it has been cited in New Zealand and again in the United Kingdom, albeit *obiter* and without detailed consideration, in *AB (Iraq)*, *FA (Eritrea)* and *KK*. In the last-named case, as seen above, the approach appears to differ from that set out in *Williams*. But however elucidated, an interpretation of the phrase 'the country of his nationality' in article 1A(2) CSR51 as including a country of potential nationality runs against a substantial body of opinion and jurisprudence elsewhere. In *Kuhai v Immigration and Naturalization Service*, 199 F 3d 909, 913–14 (7th Cir 1999), the Seventh Circuit of the United States Court of Appeals (Cudahy, Easterbrook, Kanne CJs) treated the appeal by an Uzbek citizen said to be able to return to Ukraine, her place of birth, as depending upon actual possession of nationality, and alternatively upon whether deportation to Ukraine, treating it as a safe third country, was consistent with CSR51. In *Zayed v Gonzales*, 368 F.3d 902 (6th Cir. 2005) heard by the Seventh Circuit of that Court (Nelson and Cole CJs, Sargus, DJ) the appeal of a Palestinian from the West Bank facing removal to Jordan failed on the basis that he had been found to possess Jordanian citizenship and was not at risk there. The balance of judicial decision and commentary considers 'the country of his nationality' to mean just that (that is, the State of his nationality, or any such), and not more.

5.69 This view is supported by the early commentators Robinson[30] and Grahl-Madsen,[31] the *Handbook*,[32] and recent authoritative commentators such as Zimmermann[33] and Anker.[34] The USCIS training material does not cite the wider interpretation of article 1A(2) CSR51.[35] Symes and Jorro do not cite it as part of the law in the United Kingdom, or elsewhere.[36] Goodwin-Gill and McAdam cite *Williams* in a footnote reference without endorsing it, or the interpretation of 'country of his nationality' it reflects ('Strictly speaking, the refugee must also be without the protection of any other nationality which he or she may possess, or be able to "activate"') and also refer to the Australian decision in *NAGV v Minister for Immigration* [2005] HCA 6, addressed at paragraphs 5.65–67 above.[37] Hathaway and Foster in a section headed 'inchoate nationality' provide a careful account noting opinion of Germov and Motta as rejecting the proposition that a country of potential nationality may be

---

[30] N Robinson, *Convention relating to the Status of Refugees, its History, Contents, and Interpretation* (Institute of Jewish Affairs, 1953) 50.

[31] A Grahl-Madsen, *The Status of Refugees in International Law*, vol I (AW Sijthoff, 1966) 154–57, §70.

[32] UNHCR, *Handbook and Guidelines on Procedures and Criteria for Determining Refugee Status* (n 3 above) §87.

[33] Mahler and Zimmermann (n 2 above) 442, §583.

[34] D Anker, *The Law of Asylum in the United States* (7th edn, Thomson Reuters, 2014) 537–40, §5.85–86.

[35] USCIS Asylum Officer Basic Training Course (n 12 above) 8.

[36] M Symes and P Jorro, *Asylum Law and Practice* (2nd edn, Bloomsbury Professional, 2010) 207, §4.6, 312–14, §6.3–6.4.

[37] Goodwin-Gill and McAdam (n 5 above) 63, fn 65.

treated as 'the country of his nationality'.[38] They then refer to the existence of some of the decisions set out above, and set out the somewhat guarded opinion that:

> At least when a country's nationality is available for the asking and could be acquired by means of a non-discretionary formality, there is indeed a strong substantive logic to treating that state as a country of reference. Taking account of the object and purpose of the treaty, it can reasonably be said that a country with which an applicant has a 'genuine link' and that has made its citizenship available to an applicant is, in substance, a country of nationality for refugee law purposes.[39]

On examination it is clear that Hathaway and Foster do not accept the correctness of the treatment given to 'potential nationality' in many of the cases cited above, holding to a much more limited extension of nationality ('non-discretionary formality'), and they do not endorse the *Williams* approach as consistent with CSR51. Insofar as they accept 'inchoate nationality', they do so on a narrow, carefully circumscribed, basis, concluding that with 'inchoate nationality', **5.70**

> the citizenship actually exists in embryonic form and needs simply to be activated by means of a request that will clearly be acceded to. Where an individual possesses inchoate nationality, there is no principled basis to distinguish her circumstances from those of a person born with dual or multiple nationality, whose claim would of necessity be assessed by reference to each of her countries of citizenship. Assuming of course that there is a genuine link between the individual and the country of inchoate citizenship, and that the citizenship once activated will indeed be effective citizenship, a country of inchoate nationality is a country of reference for the assessment of refugee status.[40]

The limitation to already-extant if unacknowledged nationality is wholly consistent with a VCLT69 based interpretation of CSR51. However extension to contemplated rather than actual nationality is, it is suggested, problematic.

Hathaway and Foster go on to outline three strong concerns: first, that 'judicial reasoning has at times elided nondiscretionary access with contingent access to nationality', *Grygorian* being cited as an example; second, that some courts have gone beyond the permissible interpretation of 'inchoate nationality' (that acquisition is 'mere formality' and that a 'genuine link' exists), citing *Williams*; and third and finally, that courts had erred in refusing protection on the sole basis of failure to apply to the authorities of the relevant State—in this connection both *Williams* and *Tecle* are cited. Insofar as 'inchoate nationality' refers to extant but unrecognised or unacknowledged nationality, the conclusion by Hathaway and Foster is consistent with other commentators and with the position which is retained in a majority of jurisdictions as regards interpretation of CSR51. **5.71**

[38] R Germov and E Motta, *Refugee Law in Australia* (Singapore, OUP, 2003) 147: ('[w]here nationality remains "prospective" (that is, according to the law of that country the applicant does not, at the time of determination of the refugee claim, possess "in fact" that nationality) then the Convention does not require assessment of the applicant's claims against that state as a country of nationality)'.

[39] Hathaway and Foster (n 6 above) 57–64, 58.

[40] Ibid, 59.

vi. Discussion and Conclusion: 'Nationality' Means Current Nationality Only

5.72 The Canadian cases appear to have developed through domestic precedent and policy rather than starting from (or being supported by) interpretation of article 1A(2) CSR51 according to VCLT69. As seen in chapter three, the general rule at article 31(1) VCLT69 is that a treaty 'shall be interpreted in good faith in accordance with the ordinary meaning to be given to the terms of the treaty in their context and in the light of their object and purpose'.

5.73 The 'ordinary meaning' of the term 'the country of his nationality' in article 1A(2) CSR51 can only be a State. This is because the State is one of the basic units of the international legal order, with an established status at the core of international law, and only a State may create a bond of nationality—a 'historico-biological' nation may not (see chapter one, section A3). Were more needed, it can also be seen that the invocation in article 1A(2) CSR51 of 'the protection of that country' emphasises that 'the country of his nationality' must be a State, because the State is in international law the primary entity ordinarily expected to provide protection of relevant types, both generally and within article 1A(2) CSR51 itself (see in chapter one, section A6, and this chapter, section A3 above).

5.74 So 'the country of his nationality' means a State, the nationality of which is held by the subject of the article 1A(2) CSR51 examination. The raison d'être of article 1A(2) CSR51 is to delineate the protected class ('refugees') and it does so, *inter alia*, by reference to the existence of a well-founded fear of persecution for a relevant reason. It provides that should there be such a fear—which could exist only where the State is unwilling or unable to provide protection sufficient to remove the cause(s) of such fear—then the subject individual is in general entitled to receive surrogate protection from another non-national State. This is confirmed by much jurisprudence of which the decision of the Supreme Court of Canada in *Canada (Attorney General) v Ward* [1993] 2 SCR 689, (1993) 103 DLR (4th) 1 may be taken as emblematic. La Forest J delivered the judgment of the four judges who took part in the judgment (La Forest, L'Heureux-Dubé, Gonthier and Iacobucci JJ) at 12a-d:

> At the outset, it is useful to explore the rationale underlying the international refugee protection regime, for this permeates the interpretation of the various terms requiring examination. International refugee law was formulated to serve as a back-up to the protection one expects from the state of which an individual is a national. It was meant to come into play only in situations when that protection is unavailable, and then only in certain situations. The international community intended that persecuted individuals be required to approach their home state for protection before the responsibility of other states becomes engaged. For this reason, James Hathaway refers to the refugee scheme as 'surrogate or substitute protection', activated only upon failure of national protection; see *The Law of Refugee Status* (1991), at p 135. With this in mind, I shall now turn to the particular elements of the definition of 'Convention refugee' that we are called upon to interpret.

It is important to the interpretation of article 1A(2) CSR51 that 'protection' is owed by a country of nationality only. It is not owed by a country to which there is any connection short of actual nationality, even where that individual could apply for nationality. No duty of protection is owed by a potential country of future nationality, as opposed to a state of current nationality. In this context, and taking note of the object and purpose of CSR51 more widely, there is no justification to go beyond the 'ordinary meaning' of 'the country of his nationality', considered in context and in the light of the object and purpose of the instrument. The correct interpretation of 'the country of his nationality' is 'the State of (current) nationality'.

Some further observations might be made: 5.75

i. First, the drafters of article 1A(2) CSR51 deliberately adopted a concrete, hard-edged test by the use of a concept closely defined in international law: nationality. Albeit ascertaining nationality in some cases may involve a degree of legal and factual complexity, the possession or absence of nationality should properly be identified as a hard-edged or bright-line rule.
ii. Second, even a high level of connection—for instance through birth or extended lawful residence or service in a military or diplomatic role—does not make the State in question a 'country of nationality' for article 1A(2) purposes in the absence of nationality itself. Had the drafters contemplated this they could have achieved it by including a special meaning in the instrument itself, for instance, employing the words 'a country to which he has a strong connection' or (the language later adopted at article 12(4) International Covenant on Civil and Political Rights 1966 (ICCPR66)) 'his own country'. They did not do so.
iii. Third, if the phrase 'the country of his nationality' bore a special, implied, meaning, such as 'a country to which he has a strong connection', or indeed 'a country of nationality or a country to which he could apply for nationality which he would receive on a non-discretionary basis' (the formula implicitly summoned by the United Kingdom Upper Tribunal in *KK and others (Nationality: North Korea) Korea CG* [2011] UKUT 92 (see para 5.61 above)) or 'a country of nationality or a country to which he could apply for nationality, the application being within his control' (the formula in *Canada (MCI) v Williams* [2005] FCA 126, [2005] 3 FCR 429, 253 DLR (4th) 449 (see para 5.37 above)), then this would have to apply not only for purposes of invoking a non-persecutory State to which application for nationality might be made, thus undermining a potentially good entitlement, but also for purposes of qualification. An individual would be entitled to refugee status on the basis of relevant fear 'in the country of his nationality' (not as stateless, with a relevant fear in the country of former habitual residence) if there was a country to which he or she could relevantly apply for nationality, as regards which a well-founded fear of persecution for relevant reason arose. To the best of the author's knowledge no serious lawyer or commentator has ever suggested that this is the case.

iv. Fourth, CSR51 does expressly consider the possibility of seeking 'admission into another country'. However, it does not do so in article 1, the provision adumbrating conditions for qualification as a refugee, but at article 31(2), in a provision applicable only to refugees and therefore only engaged where article 1 is already accepted as satisfied.

v. Fifth, it is an important factor that the adoption of a meaning which invokes a state as a reference country whilst no duty of protection reflecting a tie of nationality actually exists, undermines the fundamental purpose of CSR51, which is protection from *refoulement* of those without current national protection, achieved through the combination of articles 1 and 33(1) CSR51. Surrogate protection is needed whilst national protection is unavailable. If an individual gains nationality of a State, then the protection of that State becomes relevant. It is in this context immediately understandable why the drafters of CSR51 associated protection with a current State of nationality (or any such State), because only in respect of such a State is any expectation of protection invoked. Until that time it is important that protection from *refoulement* not be removed. A serious obstacle to the wider interpretation of 'the country of nationality' implied by the more recent Canadian cases, is that this unwarranted interpretative addition seriously undermines the critical protection against *refoulement*, given that, for example, the Peruvian and Argentine claimants in the *Roncagliolo* or *Fabiano* cases, or the Tibetan claimant in *Tretsetsang*, were in effect deprived of protection under CSR51 against transmission to Peru, Argentina, or the People's Republic of China, in each case a country in relation to which well-founded fear was alleged, without having immediate entitlement to alternative protection from Italy or Portugal or India.

vi. Sixth, further doubts about the viability of a special interpretation of 'the country of his nationality' including a country of potential future nationality are supported by the evident failure to develop and apply cogently any hard-edged or bright-line rule applicable to such cases. As the Tibetan cases in Canada show, this has not been cured, and may have been exacerbated, by the 'control' test of Décary JA in *Canada (MCI) v Williams*. In practice a substantial risk arises that judgments stray into subjectivity, or that standards are so amorphous as to militate against consistent decision-making—as in the Israeli cases (*Grygorian* and *Katkova*) and more recently the Indian Tibetan cases (*Wanchuk*, *Tretsetsang* and *Dolma*). The serious reservations expressed by Hathaway and Foster (see para 5.71 above) provide potent reasons to reject the underlying interpretation of 'the country of his nationality.'

5.76 The response to this might be that the approach of treating 'the country of his nationality' as extending to a country of possible future nationality only applies to some countries of nationality, not to others. In particular it might be said not to apply to a 'primary nationality' but rather to other nationalities in cases of plural nationality. This proposition will be examined here. As a basic understanding it is plain that article 1A(2) CSR51 requires attention to each potential State of nationality. Again the decision of the Supreme Court of Canada in *Canada (Attorney General) v Ward* [1993] 2 SCR 689, (1993) 103 DLR (4th) 1 may be taken as emblematic. The decision of the four judges who took part in the judgment (La Forest, L'Heureux-Dubé, Gonthier and Iacobucci JJ) was given by La Forest J at 42e:

> In considering the claim of a refugee who enjoys nationality in more than one country, the Board must investigate whether the claimant is unable or unwilling to avail him- or herself of the protection of each and every country of nationality.
>
> ...
>
> As described above, the rationale underlying international refugee protection is to serve as 'surrogate' shelter coming into play only upon failure of national support. When available, home state protection is a claimant's sole option ... The assessment of Convention refugee status most consistent with this theme requires consideration of the availability of protection in all countries of citizenship.

The approach of the drafters to plural nationality may be seen in article 1A(2) 5.77
CSR51 itself. As the United Kingdom Upper Tribunal perceptively observed in *KK and others (Nationality: North Korea) Korea CG* [2011] UKUT 92: 'We would note, however, that in the case where an individual actually has (as distinct from able to obtain) more than one nationality, we see no basis for treating either or any one of his nationalities as subsidiary to the others for the purposes of refugee status determination'. Article 1A(2) CSR51 does not reflect any bifurcation in the treatment of different nationalities in a plural nationality case. This is plain from the drafting, whereby the second paragraph of article 1A(2) CSR51 makes each country of nationality interchangeably 'the country of nationality' for purposes of the first paragraph:

> In the case of a person who has more than one nationality, the term 'the country of his nationality' shall mean each of the countries of which he is a national, and a person shall not be deemed to be lacking the protection of the country of his nationality if, without any valid reason based on well-founded fear, he has not availed himself of the protection of one of the countries of which he is a national.

The interpretation of this provision, by which article 1A(2) CSR51 addresses plural nationality, is addressed more fully in section B7 below. But for present purposes its importance is that it makes it difficult to advance a credible submission that 'the country of his nationality' in article 1A(2) acquires a different, special meaning only in some cases (those of plural nationality), and only for some nationalities—what might be called secondary or further nationalities. It is difficult to see that at the level of initial interpretation article 1A(2) CSR51 admits any such differentiation.

The problem of the line of predominantly Canadian authority which has led 5.78
to local extension of the reading of 'the country of his nationality' beyond the

interpretation consistent with VCLT69 is that the departure from close interpretation is not actually justified or required by the understandable factors—the desire not to reward perceived bad faith or non-co-operation, and the importance of the surrogacy principle—cited in the decisions. Issues of bad faith or insufficient co-operation by applicants are in general capable of sanction within determination procedures, and/or resound on applicants through relevance to the assessment of reliability or good faith in respects such as credibility, benefit of the doubt, or failure to fulfil a specific duty of co-operation by applicants in status determination. The adoption of an interpretive stance which elides a protection as fundamental to the CSR51 regime as that against *refoulement* by broad judgements that refugee status 'should not be optional' possesses close parallels to situations where questions of refugee status depend on voluntary behaviour by applicants. This is not a primary subject of the instant work, but the way such cases have been dealt with, without distorting the interpretation of article 1A(2) CSR51, may be shown by a series of key cases in England and Wales. In *SSHD v Iftikhar Ahmed* [1999] EWCA Civ 3003, [2000] INLR 1, the claimant was an Ahmadi Muslim who, it was accepted, had been a vocal preacher of his faith despite risks of persecution, and who stated, credibly in the finding of the Tribunal, that by reason of a sense of personal vocation would resume preaching there if forcibly returned to Pakistan even though this could draw persecution. Simon Brown LJ in the main judgment referred to *Danian v SSHD* [1999] EWCA Civ 3000, [1999] INLR 533, in which the question was whether entitlement to protection attached to an individual who was considered to have taken part in political activities in the United Kingdom in a cynical attempt to create the basis for a claim to protection:

> Essentially what *Danian* decides is that in all asylum cases there is ultimately but a single question to be asked: is there a serious risk that on return the applicant would be persecuted for a Convention reason? If there is, then he is entitled to asylum. It matters not whether the risk arises from his own conduct in this country, however unreasonable. It does not even matter whether he has cynically sought to enhance his prospects of asylum by creating the very risk on which he then relies—cases sometimes characterised as involving bad faith. When I say that none of this matters, what I mean is that none of it forfeits the applicant's right to refugee status, provided only and always that he establishes a well-founded fear of persecution abroad. Any such conduct is, of course, highly relevant when it comes to evaluating the claim on its merits, ie to determining whether in truth the applicant is at risk of persecution abroad. An applicant who has behaved in this way may not readily be believed as to his future fears.
>
> True it is that *Danian* was a decision about the effect of conduct in this country on an applicant's claim to be a refugee by reason of events which happened after his arrival here, a question which Buxton LJ in paragraph 12 of his judgment describes as 'different and conceptually more difficult' than that considered by Balcombe LJ in [*Mendis v Immigration Appeal Tribunal and the Secretary of State for the Home Department* [1989] Imm AR 6]. It is the latter question which now directly arises on this appeal, namely the effect of 'a threat or inclination to speak out against the government of the applicant's

native country were he to be returned there' (using again the language of Buxton LJ). To my mind, however, the same principle must apply equally in both cases. Of course, as Mr McCullough rightly points out, the conduct in question in *Danian* (a) will already have occurred and (b) (a related point) will have occurred in this country. Whoever, therefore, is having to decide the asylum claim will be presented with a *fait accompli*, however cynically the applicant may have acted. Here, by contrast, the conduct in question by definition will not have occurred and indeed will not occur if asylum is granted. But I cannot see how this consideration avoids the need to address the critical question: if returned, would the asylum seeker in fact act in the way he says he would and thereby suffer persecution? If he would, then, however unreasonable he might be thought for refusing to accept the necessary restraint on his liberties, in my judgment he would be entitled to asylum.

Simon Brown LJ focused on credibility ('Any such conduct is, of course, highly relevant when it comes to evaluating the claim on its merits, ie to determining whether in truth the applicant is at risk of persecution abroad'), to which a failure of good faith might go. The decision is important, *inter alia*, because it respects a central, perhaps *the* most central, part of the CSR51 regime, which is that an individual meeting the refugee definition at article 1A in the absence of cessation or exclusion (articles 1C–1F) is protected from *refoulement* (article 33(1)) save in the special case of reasonable grounds of danger to national security or conviction of a 'particularly serious' crime and danger to the community in the country of refuge (article 33(2)). The imposition by strained interpretation of an implied exception to the terms of article 1A(2) for 'bad faith' or 'voluntary action' cases will undermine the fundamental non-*refoulement* protection CSR51 is intended to create.

Another, and serious, weakness in the reasoning underlying the treatment of 'the country of his nationality' as including countries of potential rather than actual nationality is that it is not justified by the need for avoidance of abuse of CSR51. Put shortly, this is because CSR51 is a refugee instrument, not an asylum treaty. The receiving State is bound not to *refoule* a refugee to a State of origin or of relevant risk, but not bound to allow the refugee to remain on its own territory—indeed, article 31(2) CSR51 implies the possibility of transfer, as has the UNHCR Executive Committee by ExCom Conclusion 15 (XXX), 'Refugees without an asylum country'.[41] The limited non-expulsion protection at article 32 CSR51 attaches only where the refugee is lawfully present, lawfulness being identified by reference to domestic law.[42] The other rights arising from CSR51 for the refugee—especially that of protection from *refoulement*—are vital, but include no general right of remaining in a particular country. Removal to a safe country of a refugee who is not protected by the non-expulsion protection at article 32 CSR51 does not contravene CSR51. This is directly affirmed, for example, by the American decisions 5.79

[41] UNHCR, ExCom Conclusion 15 (XXX), 'Refugees without an asylum country', 16 October 1979, available at: www.unhcr.org/3ae68c960.html.

[42] See for instance *R (otao ST (Eritrea)) v SSHD* [2012] UKSC 12, [2012] 2 AC 135.

in *Kuhai* and *Zayed* (see para 5.68 above), in which the nationality of a third country was found to be present. The principle also applies where the refugee is not a national of the safe country, as for instance in the decision of the Australian Full Federal Court in *NAEN* (para 5.65 above) and the case before the United Kingdom Supreme Court in *R (otao ST (Eritrea)) v SSHD* [2012] UKSC 12 [2012] 2 AC 135. Decisions justifying an artificial extension of the meaning of 'the country of his nationality' by reference to abuse arguments generally fail to acknowledge that the CSR51 scheme allows reliance upon recourse elsewhere without the need for a link of nationality to the third country.

5.80 The treatment of potential recourse elsewhere, in the absence of current nationality, has attracted substantial discussion as an aspect of 'protection elsewhere'. The Colloquium on Challenges in International Refugee Law held at the University of Michigan in November 2006 led to what are now known as the *Michigan Guidelines on Protection Elsewhere*.[43] The introductory text recognises that 'Refugees increasingly encounter laws and policies which provide that their protection needs will be considered or addressed somewhere other than in the territory of the state where they have sought, or intend to seek, protection':

> Such policies—including 'country of first arrival', 'safe third country', and extraterritorial processing rules and practices—raise both opportunities and challenges for international refugee law. They have the potential to respond to the Refugee Convention's concern 'that the grant of asylum may place unduly heavy burdens on certain countries' by more fairly allocating protection responsibilities among states. But insistence that protection be provided elsewhere may also result in the denial to refugees of their rights under the Refugee Convention and international law more generally. The challenge is to identify the ways in which the protection regime may be made more flexible without compromising the entitlements of refugees.

Under the heading 'When States May Implement Protection Elsewhere Policies' the *Guidelines* recognise that:

> 1. The 1951 Convention and 1967 Protocol relating to the Status of Refugees ('Convention') neither expressly authorize nor prohibit reliance on protection elsewhere policies. As such, protection elsewhere policies are compatible with the Convention so long as they ensure that refugees defined by Art 1 enjoy the rights set by Arts 2–34 of the Convention.
>
> 2. Because the Convention does not contemplate the devolution of protection responsibilities to a non-state entity, any sharing-out of protection responsibility must take place between and among states. While it is preferable that the state to which protection is

[43] University of Michigan Law School, *The Michigan Guidelines on Protection Elsewhere*, 3 January 2007, available at: www.refworld.org/docid/4ae9acd0d.html (also at (2007) 28 *Michigan Journal of International Law* 207; a related text is M Foster, 'Protection Elsewhere: The Legal Implications of Requiring Refugees to Seek Protection in Another State' (2007) 28 *Michigan Journal of International Law* 223.

assigned ('receiving state') be a party to the Convention, such status is not a requirement for implementation of a protection elsewhere policy which respects international law.

The *Guidelines* rightly, in the view of this work, emphasise the importance of examining whether there is a well-founded fear of persecution in any country of nationality—in contrast, for example, with the failure to do so in some cases when diverted from such scrutiny, as in the *Roncagliolo* case in which the Board shelved this question and treated the first enquiry as being whether the applicant possessed a well-founded fear of persecution in the country of his wife's second nationality (France).

In sum, the phrase 'the country of his nationality' in article 1A(2) CSR51, interpreted on VCLT69 principles, means current nationality. This follows the ordinary meaning and it is consistent with the object and purpose of the instrument. The concerns at potential abuse which have driven, in particular, the Canadian cases, are legitimate but misdirected, because status as a refugee provides a limited but extremely important range of rights, particularly protection from *refoulement*—but no right to remain independent of this. The cases illustrate the difficulty—it might reasonably be said the impossibility—of establishing a coherent bright-line rule separate from that identified by the ordinary language of the drafters—the possession of nationality itself. The cases also illuminate the degree to which this unwarranted interpretative addition undermines the critical protection of non-*refoulement*. It is suggested that the best response to a situation in which it is said that an individual may be able to access nationality of a third country is not to impose a distorted meaning upon the phrase 'the country of his nationality', but rather to consider whether 'protection elsewhere' applies, looking to standards such as those adumbrated following the Colloquium on Challenges in International Refugee Law in 2006 by the *Michigan Guidelines on Protection Elsewhere*.[44] 5.81

vii. Coda: Mixed Nationality Families

One interesting problem highlighted by the Canadian cases in particular is the question of mixed nationality families. It is reasonable to assume that these are increasing in number due to a number of factors including the gradual disappearance of most of the discriminatory laws which formerly removed the nationality of women upon marriage to a foreign national (and consequentially the passing of that nationality to children) and the disappearance of the hostility to multiple nationality formerly shown by States (see chapter one, section A7). In *Roncagliolo v Canada (MCI)* [2005] FC 1024 the claim involved a family group in which the father of the family held Peruvian citizenship only, whereas his wife and 5.82

[44] Ibid.

children also held French citizenship. In *De Barros v Canada (MCI)* [2005] FC 283, [2005] FCJ No 361 (QL) all members of the family held Brazilian nationality, and the father held plural Portuguese nationality. In *Alvarez v Canada (MCI)* [2007] FC 296, 156 ACWS (3d) 437 the mother of the family was a Colombian national only, but her husband and son held plural Venezuelan nationality.

5.83 In such cases it is entirely possible that some family members will be refugees under article 1A(2) CSR51 whereas others, by reason of their possession of a non-persecuting State of plural nationality, will not be. In essence, not all members of the family unit will require surrogate protection: as Zimmermann and Mahler have judged (reading 'country of origin' as 'country of nationality'):

> It is ... only when the respective country of origin does *de facto* provide protection from such persecution that the need for surrogate international protection by the community of contracting parties of [CSR51] does not arise.[45]

5.84 This is not a situation directly addressed in the main text of CSR51, perhaps understandably, as plural nationality was considerably rarer when the regime was created. If contemplated then, it would likely have seemed an issue to be left to States to resolve such questions as arose in a commonsense manner, though family unity more broadly attracted non-binding action by the signatory States in the Conference of Plenipotentiaries, whose Recommendation B ('Principle of unity of the family') emphasises the importance of measures for the protection of the refugee's family, in particular:

> (1) Ensuring that the unity of the refugee's family is maintained particularly in cases where the head of the family has fulfilled the necessary conditions for admission to a particular country.
> (2) The protection of refugees who are minors, in particular unaccompanied children and girls, with special reference to guardianship and adoption.

Family unity and the interests of children of a family are of course now emphasised in international human rights laws: the first at article 23 ICCPR66 and the second at article 24 ICCPR66 and articles 3, 9 and 22 of the Convention on the Rights of the Child 1989, to take the most important instances only.

5.85 In the light of this it seems logical that in due course principles might be agreed amongst States, whether at the international, regional, or bilateral level, or at the lowest domestic policies put in place, which enable consistent dealing with plural nationality family cases where one or more members of the family are refugees. Whether ultimately States judged it better to regard a non-persecuting country of nationality of some family members as the appropriate destination for the whole family (on which approach Canada might have transferred the Roncagliolo family to France, the De Barros family to Portugal and the Alvarez family to Venezuela),

[45] Mahler and Zimmermann (n 2 above) 445–46, §§596–600.

or by admitting the whole family group to the reception country with some members as dependants rather than refugees (in which case the family groups might have remained, assuming entitlement to protection under CSR51, in Canada), consistent treatment of cases of this type does seem a matter on which States could, in the interest both of humanitarian outcome and of smoother administration, seek to agree appropriate arrangements.

B5. Nationality Means Nationality Recognised on the International Plane

By article 1 of the Convention on Certain Questions Relating to the Conflict of Nationality Laws 1930 'It is for each State to determine under its own law who are its nationals'. The proposition this expresses is reinforced at article 2 of the 1930 Convention. However, it is matched in article 1 of the same Convention by an express statement of principle, widely considered as reflecting customary international law, by which the status of nationality determined by the State is not subject to any absolute duty of recognition on the part of other States. Indeed, the exclusivity of domestic laws in relation to the creation of nationality is matched by a duty of recognition expressly disapplied where the law in question is not 'consistent with international conventions, international custom, [or] the principles of law generally recognised with regard to nationality'. 5.86

Some instances in which the grant or withdrawal of a nationality status may attract non-recognition have been identified in chapter one, section A10. A range of circumstances may be envisioned in which questions of recognition fall to be examined. In some cases the question may be whether to treat as 'the country of his nationality' a country whose nationality has been imposed upon the subject in a manner not consistent with international law. In an appropriate case it may be appropriate to do this, prioritising the realisation of protection from *refoulement*: this would be consistent with guidance according to Lauterpacht's maxim *ex iniuria ius non oritur* and the *Namibia* Advisory Opinion.[46] Against such a course would be the reflection of Merrills, taking issue with Mann, that non-recognition should follow from the nature of the action whatever the consequence for the individual,[47] and the reservation of Lord Cross in *Oppenheimer v Cattermole*: 'But it surely cannot be right for the question whether the decree should be recognised or not to depend on the circumstances of the particular case'.[48] 5.87

---

[46] *Legal Consequences for States of the Continued Presence of South Africa in Namibia (South West Africa) notwithstanding Security Council Resolution 276 (1970)* (Advisory Opinion) [1971] ICJ Rep 16, 56 [125–26].

[47] See JG Merrills, 'One Nationality or Two? The Strange Case of *Oppenheimer v Cattermole*' (1974) 23 *International & Comparative Law Quarterly* 143, 152, 156.

[48] *Oppenheimer v Cattermole* [1976] AC 249, 278.

5.88 However, it seems likely that the most frequent circumstance in which recognition requires consideration will be denationalisation. That is because of the importance of identification of the 'country of his nationality' as the reference country at article 1A(2) CSR51, and the possibility that a State may cease to be the reference country through a direct effect of acts which may constitute or relate to persecution for one or more relevant reasons. Is an unlawful and arbitrary deprivation of nationality, based in discrimination on the basis of race or some other Convention reason, and effective under domestic law, to be recognised so that the denationalising State ceases to be the country of reference for purposes of article 1A(2) CSR51?

5.89 In many cases in which the applicant is stateless, the shift to a country of former habitual residence as the reference country does not make a difference, because the country which has denationalised the claimant is in any event the country of former habitual residence. Because of this, in the series of decisions in the United Kingdom concerning persons from Ethiopia in respect of whom it was found that that country had denationalised claimants,[49] the country of reference was unaffected by denationalisation. This also meant that the proceedings did not potentially depend upon whether the measures instituted by Ethiopia had been consistent with Ethiopia's domestic laws. If an arbitrary deprivation was invalid under domestic law (even if not identified as such by national authorities) then it would leave Ethiopia as the country of reference ('the country of his nationality'), whereas one which was lawful domestically even though arbitrary would not. This would have required a complex consideration of Ethiopian constitutional law by various authorities in the United Kingdom—in *EB (Ethiopia) v SSHD* [2007] EWCA Civ 809 [2009] QB 1 Pill LJ noted the existence in Ethiopia of a constitutional prohibition of unilateral deprivation of nationality by the State, though the Court understandably did not explore the effect of this upon the position in Ethiopian domestic law.[50] But in *EB (Ethiopia)* and the other cases, the Court was not required to give close consideration to the legal effectiveness of deprivation under Ethiopian domestic law: first, because a measure being consistent with domestic law does not prevent a conclusion on the international level that this (or the continued deprivation following it) constituted persecution for purposes of article 1A(2) CSR51 (or a breach of international human rights law, international humanitarian law, or customary law);[51] and second, because Ethiopia was the reference country whether as the country of nationality or (assuming an effective

---

[49] *EB (Ethiopia) v SSHD* [2007] EWCA Civ 809 [2009] QB 1; *MA (Ethiopia) v SSHD* [2009] EWCA Civ 289 [2010] INLR 1, and *ST (Ethnic Eritrean—nationality—return) Ethiopia CG* [2011] UKUT 252 (IAC).

[50] *EB (Ethiopia) v SSHD* [2007] EWCA Civ 809 [2009] QB 1, [17]. Article 33(1) of the 1995 Constitution of the Federal Democratic Republic of Ethiopia provides, *inter alia*, that 'No Ethiopian national shall be deprived of his or her Ethiopian nationality against his or her will'.

[51] Ultimately this reflects the *Alabama Claims* principle: see ch 1, para 1.36.

denationalisation recognised for purposes of CSR51) as the country of former habitual residence. In consequence the Court could focus immediately on whether the action taken (denationalisation and exclusion from the territory) was part of a factual nexus giving rise to a well-founded fear of persecution for relevant reason.

By contrast, in two relatively recent cases in senior courts the possible effect of denationalisation, as shifting the focus of article 1A(2) CSR51 to a second State as the country of former habitual residence, has troubled successively the Federal Administrative Court in Germany[52] and the High Court of Ireland,[53] in the latter case prompting reference to the Irish Supreme Court.[54] **5.90**

In Germany the Federal Administrative Court in *10 C 50.07* (BVerwG 26 February 2009) considered a case arising from claimed denationalisation raising issues including the meaning of the 'country of his nationality'. The complainants, a mother and son, were stated to be of mixed ethnic Armenian descent. The mother had been born and thereafter lived in Azerbaijan. After the collapse of the Soviet Union she was targeted for threats by reason of her descent. She left Azerbaijan in 1992 for Russia, where she resided irregularly and met another Armenian, the father of her son born in Russia in 1994. In September 1998, whilst the complainants remained in Russia, the nationality laws of Azerbaijan were amended to define as citizens only those persons who maintained Azerbaijani nationality by registered residence in Azerbaijan. Ultimately, motivated by the fact that their situation in Russia was irregular and difficult, the complainants travelled to Germany and claimed asylum there. **5.91**

Late in 2002 the German status authority rejected the complainants' applications, and in 2003 initial appeals were unsuccessful. In May 2007 the Higher Administrative Court modified the lower court's decision, directing that the complainants were qualified as refugees on the basis of findings that the complainants were stateless, and that examination of the risk of persecution should have focused on Azerbaijan as the country of their former habitual residence. **5.92**

That decision was in turn both appealed to the Federal Administrative Court by the status authority, and cross appealed by the complainants. The Federal Administrative Court therefore confronted a number of issues. Its decision reveals a strong affirmation of denationalisation, in appropriate circumstances, as founding valid claim to well-founded fear of persecution ('In its approach, the court below correctly assumed that a deprivation of citizenship for reasons relevant to asylum may represent persecution … and may thus result in recognition of **5.93**

---

[52] *10 C 50.07* (BVerwG 26 February 2009).

[53] *DT (No 2) v Refugee Appeals Tribunal and others* [2012] IEHC 562.

[54] The question referred to the Irish Supreme Court is set out in the description of the case at para 5.94 below. The appeal to that Court was outstanding as at the date of publication.

asylum status under Section 3(1) of the Asylum Procedure Act').[55] The Federal Administrative Court however found that the court below had failed in important respects including in its conclusion that statelessness following denationalisation by Azerbaijan changed the reference country to the Russian Federation, the country of former habitual residence:

> 17(a) The case law of the Federal Administrative Court has recognised that the withdrawal of citizenship may also constitute persecution relevant to asylum ... Here the focus must always be on the state whose nationality was held by the person affected by the withdrawal until the act of withdrawal. No other actor—such as a third state or a private adversary—comes into consideration for this specific act of exclusion.
>
> ...
>
> 25(c) [the Higher Administrative Court] incorrectly assumed that even in the case of a deprivation of citizenship by the Azerbaijani state, with relevance to asylum, the Complainants' claim to refugee status should be judged by the standards for stateless persons, and therefore it additionally examined whether the Complainants—now as stateless persons—also had their previous habitual residence in that country within the meaning of Section 3(1) of the Asylum Procedure Act. But this examination is not necessary in the case of a deprivation of citizenship that is relevant to asylum. If the persecution lies precisely in the creation, by the state of the individual's former nationality, of a condition of statelessness that is relevant to asylum, this must be viewed under asylum law as a (continuing) persecution specifically by that state of the person's (former) nationality.[56]

The case was remitted for reconsideration.

5.94 More recently, O'Keeffe J in the High Court of Ireland granted leave to appeal to the Supreme Court of Ireland in *DT (No 2) v Refugee Appeals Tribunal and others* [2012] IEHC 562. The applicant was an asylum claimant born in Bhutan belonging to the minority Nepali community. In support of his claim he stated, *inter alia*, that having been a Bhutanese national he had fled Bhutan for Nepal in 1990 after politically and/or ethnically motivated detention and torture by the Bhutanese authorities, and then was stripped of Bhutanese citizenship. He returned to Bhutan in 2010 after international pressure was placed on the Bhutanese authorities to enable this, but escaped that country after another episode of arrest, detention and torture, ultimately seeking refugee status in Ireland. The domestic status authority accepted that the applicant originated in Bhutan but determined his application on the basis that he was stateless and that his country of former habitual residence was Nepal. The Refugee Appeals Tribunal upheld this. Before O'Keeffe J the applicant submitted that the Irish authorities should have treated him either as a Bhutanese national or as a stateless person whose country of former habitual residence was Bhutan. The Court held conclusions

[55] *10 C 50.07* (BVerwG 26 February 2009) [16]–[24].
[56] Ibid, [25].

that the applicant was stateless and that Nepal was his country of former habitual residence were sustainable, but granted leave to appeal to the Supreme Court of Ireland on the following question:

> Where the executive agencies of a State arbitrarily deny a person his or her citizenship, is it correct to assess that person's claim to refugee status on the basis that that State is his or her 'country of nationality' … or is it correct to regard that person as 'stateless?'

The two cases above demonstrate the potential importance of the phrase 'the country of his nationality' in the context of refugee status determination following denationalisation, and also the dilemma which may appear to arise. On the one hand, the potential consequence of treating a denationalising State of origin as having ceased to be the reference State in favour of a non-national State of former habitual residence is additional prejudice to someone already the victim of a heinous form of state mistreatment—it adds a potential denial of international protection to the arbitrary removal of that individual's nationality and intuitively seems wrong. On the other hand, to treat an individual as still a national of his or her State after a domestically effective denationalisation seems inconsistent with the fact that the individual is no longer a national of that country under its domestic law, because the country has removed the previous nationality. **5.95**

There is learning which points to a legitimate practice of interpretation, or judicial practice, which ignores the effect of deprivation of nationality where this is connected to the reasons for asylum being sought. A feature significant in the work of Grahl-Madsen, an early commentator of considerable penetration, is express reference to articles 1 and 2 of the Convention on Certain Questions Relating to the Conflict of Nationality Laws 1930 in the context of interpretation of 'the country of his nationality'. **5.96**

Of articles 1 and 2 of the 1930 Convention, Grahl-Madsen in 1966 concluded both that 'These provisions may be considered a codification of generally accepted rules of international law' and that the same provisions 'are, in principle at least, applicable also when it comes to the determination of the national status of an applicant for recognition as a "refugee"'.[57] Grahl-Madsen then outlined and endorsed a view he attributed to Zink: **5.97**

> [A] person who loses his nationality by leaving his home country (or, in more general terms, by becoming a refugee), should be placed in the former, not in the latter category. If a person has lived in a country as a national of that country up to the time when he becomes a refugee, such country should be considered the country of his nationality—not only the country of his former habitual residence—for the purpose of Article 1A(2). There cannot be seen to be any reason why the same should not apply *mutandis mutandis* to persons who become refugees *sur place*. If the country where such persons fear persecution should decide to 'personalize' them by withdrawing their nationality the

[57] Grahl-Madsen (n 31 above) 155, §70.

> moment they declare themselves as refugees, it would hardly be warranted to let such withdrawal affect such persons' claims to refugeehood under [CSR51].[58]

Zink is cited by Grahl-Madsen as 'contend[ing] that the phrase "the country of his nationality" should be understood in the sense "the country whose nationality he possesses, or whose nationality he has lost in connexion with leaving the country"', an opinion of which Grahl-Madsen says, 'This view is not devoid of virtue. In fact, one is in good company if one refuses to give effect to measures of denationalization against persons still residing in their home country'.[59]

5.98 The Zink and Grahl-Madsen approach as regards identification of the reference State refers to international law principles regarding recognition, but pre-dates important later developments in IHRL and non-discrimination in international law (see chapter one, section A10 above). Whilst non-recognition might operate in other circumstances, a particular situation in which this arises is denationalisation on the basis of discrimination against an ethnic or other relevant group, which has come to be regarded as a serious breach of the principle of non-discrimination in international law, and of international human rights law.

5.99 In 1963 Brownlie had observed that in relation to nationality of another State arising as a consequence of acts inconsistent with international law, such as aggression or over-extensive nationality law, a State 'may refuse to give effect to change of nationality because it regards the origin of the change … to be contrary to international law'.[60] In relation to denationalisation, he rejected the claim that a general rule of illegality arose, but expressly observed that non-recognition was appropriate in some circumstances:

> At the two extremes of opinion one finds the view that denationalization is illegal *tout court* and the view that denationalization is within the discretion which States have in the matter of nationality and is therefore lawful. Much will depend on the context in which the issue arises and even those alleging a rule of illegality differ as to the reasons for the rule. However, principle and existing practice give some support to and, at the least, do not contradict certain positions. If the deprivation is part and parcel of a breach of an international duty then the act of deprivation will be illegal. If the deprivation is not a part of a delictual act but merely involves denationalization of groups of citizens domiciled within the frontiers of a State, who lack any other links, then there is no delict—as there would be, for example, if they were forced to try to gain admission illegally in neighbouring States—but the deprivation is not entitled to recognition by others because it disregards the doctrine of effective link and represents an attempt to avoid the responsibilities of territorial sovereignty and statehood.[61]

[58] Ibid, 158–59, §71. The reference is to K Zink, 'Das Asylrecht in der Bundesrepublik Deutschland nach dem Abkommen vom 28 Juli 1951 über die Rechtsstellung der Flüchtlinge' (Erlangen-Nürnberg, dissertation, 1963) 32ff.

[59] Ibid, 159, §71.

[60] I Brownlie, 'The Relations of Nationality in International Law' in *British Yearbook of International Law 1963* (OUP, 1965) 284, 326–27.

[61] Ibid, 339–40.

An important watershed thereafter is the decision of the House of Lords in *Oppenheimer v Cattermole* [1976] AC 249, in which Lord Cross, in a decision which responded to academic criticism of past decisions, and represented a strongly marked change of approach from previous decisions, concluded that: 5.100

> It may be said, perhaps, that though international law sets limits to the jurisdiction of sovereign states so far as concerns the granting of nationality it sets no limits whatever to their power to withdraw it. I am not prepared to accept that this is so. I think, for example, that Martin Wolff, Private International Law, 2nd ed, p 129, may well be right in saying that, if a state withdraws its citizenship from some class of its citizens living within its borders to which it has taken a dislike and of whom it would be glad to be rid, other states are not obliged to regard such people as 'stateless' ... But I think ... that it is part of the public policy of this country that our courts should give effect to clearly established rules of international law ... what we are concerned with here is legislation which takes away without compensation from a section of the citizen body singled out on racial grounds all their property on which the state passing the legislation can lay its hands and, in addition, deprives them of their citizenship. To my mind a law of this sort constitutes so grave an infringement of human rights that the courts of this country ought to refuse to recognise it as a law at all.[62]

By 1979, the development of international law had reached a stage at which Weis, an eminent expert cautious in his interpretation of the extent of international law, judged that following ICCPR66 and the Convention on the Reduction of Statelessness 1961 the prohibition of discriminatory denationalisation had become a rule of international law: 5.101

> Considering that the principle of non-discrimination may now be regarded as a rule of international law or as a general principle of law, prohibition of discriminatory denationalisation may be regarded as a rule of present-day international law. This certainly applies to discrimination on the ground of race which may be considered as contravening a peremptory norm of international law but also, in the present writer's view, to discrimination on the other grounds mentioned in the Charter of the United Nations, *ie* sex and religion.[63]

In 1988 Plender noted that developments in international human rights law, especially the coming into force of ICCPR66 had had a 'profound effect' on the development of international law, so that: 5.102

> The evidence suggests that in current international law a State cannot always release itself of its obligation to admit certain of its own nationals to its territory by promulgating a decree which deprives such persons of their nationality. A decree which discriminates on racial grounds, or is in any other sense 'arbitrary', need not be recognized by other States as effective to derive of their nationality those to whom it purports to apply.[64]

---

[62] *Oppenheimer v Cattermole* [1976] AC 249, 276H–278G. The principle in that case was endorsed and applied in *Kuwait Airways Corporation v Iraqi Airways Company & Anor* [2002] UKHL 19, [2002] 2 AC 883.

[63] Weis (n 7 above) 125.

[64] R Plender, *International Migration Law* (2nd edn, Martinus Nijhoff, 1988) 149.

5.103 The change of approach by the House of Lords in 1972, the approach to recognition outlined subsequently by the High Court of Australia in *Sykes v Cleary* [1992] HCA 60, (1992) 176 CLR 77, and the views of recent commentators such as Brownlie, Mann, Merrills, Weis and Plender, reflect a coming together between Lauterpacht's development of a principled doctrine of recognition, on the one hand, and the developments in international law which have been continuous since the Second World War, most particularly the gradual realisation of a body of international human rights law and the ascendancy of the principle of non-discrimination in international law, on the other. In a circumstance such as the assessment of a claim to refugee status under article 1A(2) CSR51 from a claimant who has been denationalised by reason of one or more relevant matters, established international law principles point to the appropriateness of non-recognition so that analysis will generally parallel the approach of the German Federal Administrative Court expressed in *10 C 50.07* (BVerwG 26 February 2009) by which, in examining a refugee claim based on denationalisation, 'the focus must always be on the state whose nationality was held by the person affected by the withdrawal until the act of withdrawal. No other actor—such as a third state or a private adversary—comes into consideration for this specific act of exclusion'. In a different context (such as whether that individual should be treated as an enemy alien, or a spouse lose the nationality of the State of sojourn), application of the maxim *ex iniuria ius non oritur* and the principle adumbrated in the *Namibia* Advisory Opinion[65] present no barrier to recognition for a particular purpose. Also, refusal to recognise deprivation as rendering a State immune from treatment as the reference State for purposes of article 1A(2) does not prevent assessment of any factually sensitive question on the basis of what has occurred, including what that State has or has not done and the nature of continuing actions or omissions by it. In particular, non-recognition for purposes of determining 'the country of his nationality' does not inhibit the proper examination of another question, that of whether the individual is outside his or her country owing to well-founded fear of persecution and owing to such fear unable or unwilling to avail himself or herself of its protection of that country. To treat an act of denationalisation as ineffective for certain purposes on the international plane is not to deny that it has occurred, or that individuals are materially affected by it.

5.104 In the current state of development of international law, therefore, the effect of non-recognition is that the interpretation of the term 'the country of his nationality' in article 1A(2) should in many cases in which denationalisation is potentially relevant to asylum include the State which has denationalised its former citizen in a manner contrary to established international law principles, because the community of States engaged in the CSR51 regime, and/or the individual

[65] *Legal Consequences for States of the Continued Presence of South Africa in Namibia (South West Africa) notwithstanding Security Council Resolution 276 (1970)* (Advisory Opinion) [1971] ICJ Rep 16, 56, [125–26].

State considering whether a claimant's situation engages that regime, will not give effect to that change for the purpose of identifying the reference State under article 1A(2) CSR51 and then determining whether a well-founded fear of persecution for a relevant reason exists in relation to that State. This is wholly consistent with the ordinary meaning of 'country of his nationality' in article 1A(2) CSR51 once account is given to the international law context, as encapsulated in article 1 of the Convention on Certain Questions Relating to the Conflict of Nationality Laws 1930 and subsequently explored by Lauterpacht, Chen, Brownlie, Mann, Merrills, Plender and others, in relation to questions regarding the recognition of the effects of Nazi policies (see chapter one, section A10 above). It reflects the taking into account 'together with the context', of 'relevant rules of international law applicable in the relations between the parties', in line with article 31(3)(c) VCLT69. Additionally, such an interpretation is favoured by examination of the 'object and purpose' of the CSR51 regime, in relation to which it might be noted that: (i) it would be, at the lowest, counter- intuitive to adopt an interpretation which placed outside the CSR51 regime cases in which a State brought about withdrawal of national protection through arbitrary denationalisation, because CSR51 was expressly formed to mitigate the humanitarian and international relations consequences of such action by the provision of surrogate protection including protection from *refoulement* in such a case; (ii) the 'country of his former habitual residence' may be a State with a much smaller relevance to the problems which force an individual to seek protection under CSR51 than a State which has denationalised that person, so that the function of identifying a need for surrogate protection strongly favours retaining focus on the latter; and (iii) retaining focus in an appropriate case upon the State responsible for an arbitrary denationalisation prevents that State from escaping identification as the State responsible for a refugee-creating problem displacing a burden of protection on to other States. It may be these or similar reasons which underlie the position set out by the German Federal Administrative Court in the *10 C 50.07* case (BVerwG 26 February 2009). Whether based directly on international law principles relating to recognition, or instead upon a parallel interpretive policy or practice, an interpretation of article 1A(2) CSR51which treats the term 'the country of his nationality' as including a State which has denationalised its former citizen in a manner contrary to international law appears to possess strong foundations in the context and object and purpose of the text, at least where an operative question is whether a claimant's situation discloses a well-founded fear of persecution for a relevant reason in relation to that State. This of course does not require facts such as denationalisation or exclusion to be overlooked in considering whether a well-founded fear of persecution for relevant reason arises as regards a particular State- ensuring that such facts are considered as part of status determination, rather than elided from the process by a change of reference State arising from a significant breach of international law, is an important consequence of this approach. Nor does this approach require a State which has denationalised an individual to be treated artificially as a source of alternative national protection where the affected individual is a plural national and possesses a relevant fear as regards another country of nationality (see section B7, and in particular para 5.143, below).

5.105 In relation to the interpretation indicated above, it may also be worth noting that had the drafters intended to exclude consideration of recognition, this would have been easy to accomplish. It was done shortly thereafter in a closely related instrument, namely the Convention relating to the Status of Stateless Persons 1954 (CSSP54). Article 1(1) CSSP54, which defines 'stateless person' as a person 'not considered as a national by any State under the operation of its law', appears engaged by a status determined expressly and exclusively by the operation of domestic law. This effectively excludes the question of whether, so far as the application of CSSP54 is concerned, there is a nationality in respect of which non-recognition might otherwise apply. The evident aim of the article 1(1) CSSP54 definition is direct and exclusive focus upon the position of the State whose nationality is relevant.[66]

5.106 The meaning of 'the country of his nationality' in the context of denationalisation was, as seen above, considered by Grahl-Madsen. It has received little scrutiny by more recent commentators, perhaps an indication of the drift away from examination of CSR51 in the close conjunction with nationality that it undoubtedly had at the time of inception. An exception is the view of Zimmermann and Mahler who state that 'Under international law, it is for each State to determine which persons are to be considered its nationals', and go on to state that even an unlawfully imposed or withdrawn nationality binds the assessment of refugee status:

> Yet, even in cases where the attachment of nationality (eg in the case of illegal annexation of territory) or where acts of denationalization (eg because of being based on discriminatory grounds) are illegal under international law, one has to note that such acts are not *opposable*. Accordingly, the country where the applicant is seeking refuge must disregard the illegality of such acts and must, therefore, consider the person as not having acquired, or lost respectively, the nationality of the country concerned.[67]

No authority is cited, and the large volume of adverse material over the 80 years since the 1930 Convention is not addressed. The conclusion of Zimmermann and Mahler is not consistent with the approach of the Federal Constitutional Court in *10 C 50.07* (BVerwG 26 February 2009) and seems to be mistaken on the larger issue of recognition, even if on a separate and limited examination restricted to opposability (as opposed to non-recognition, or the approach advanced by Zink and approved by Grahl-Madsen), it is well founded. Overall, the best approach seems to be that in certain circumstances the action of a

---

[66] This is explicable in context because the object of the enquiry is to ascertain the attitude of that State to the individual, specifically whether it recognises an individual as one in respect of which nationality creates a protective link.

[67] Mahler and Zimmermann (n 2 above) 443, §§584—85.

State as regards nationality does not command recognition by another State or international body in the application of article 1A(2) CSR51.

B6. Opposability in General Applicable in Bilateral Situations and Inapplicable in Relation to Article 1A(2) of the Convention Relating to the Status of Refugees 1951

Opposability has arisen in a different context, that of bilateral disputes in relation to international protection (see chapter one, section A11). Whilst the *Nottebohm* case may establish a principle as regards acquisition of nationality which is capable of expression in exceptional circumstances in the realm of recognition, that would move the context from opposability. In general opposability is not relevant to the meaning or content of 'the country of his nationality' in article 1A(2) CSR51. In this respect the conclusion of Mahler and Zimmermann, asserting nationality decisions as not opposable in any circumstance including arbitrary deprivation, is correct so long as a narrow focus on opposability, to the exclusion of recognition, is maintained.[68] 5.107

B7. Plural Nationality

i. Analysis

The term 'plural nationality' here denotes either possession by a human person of more than one nationality, the most common form of which will be dual nationality (possession of two nationalities) or one of the nationalities possessed by such person. In recent decades plural nationality has increasingly been accommodated by national laws, and has become more frequent. As already seen in chapter one, section A7, this reflects a marked change since the 1930 Convention on Certain Questions Relating to the Conflict of Nationality Laws, when plural nationality and statelessness were viewed by many as equal threats to the desirable international norm. 5.108

The social changes which have modified views of plural nationality do not themselves affect the interpretation of article 1A(2) CSR51. This obviously takes account of the existence of plural nationality and the potential for claims by persons possessing it, as is clear from the second paragraph of article 1A(2): 5.109

> In the case of a person who has more than one nationality, the term the 'country of his nationality' shall mean each of the countries of which he is a national, and a person shall not be deemed to be lacking the protection of the country of his nationality if, without

[68] Ibid, 443.

any valid reason based on well-founded fear, he has not availed himself of the protection of one of the countries of which he is a national.

5.110 Paragraph 106 of the UNHCR *Handbook and Guidelines on Procedures and Criteria for Determining Refugee Status*, which often provides persuasive guidance but does not constitute primary authority, states of the second paragraph of article 1A(2) that:

> 106. This clause, which is largely self-explanatory, is intended to exclude from refugee status all persons with dual or plural nationality who can avail themselves of the protection of at least one of the countries of which they are nationals. Wherever available national protection takes precedence over international protection.[69]

5.111 The combined effect of paragraphs 1 and 2 of article 1A(2) CSR51 indicates equal treatment of different nationalities, rather than identifying criteria to distinguish initially between so-called 'primary' and 'secondary' nationalities. This is consistent with the observation of the United Kingdom Upper Tribunal (Mr Ockelton VP, SIJ Gleeson) in *KK and others (Nationality: North Korea) Korea CG* [2011] UKUT 92, at [38], that:

> We would note, however, that in the case where an individual actually has (as distinct from able to obtain) more than one nationality, we see no basis for treating either or any one of his nationalities as subsidiary to the others for the purposes of refugee status determination.

5.112 Subject to questions of recognition, as addressed in chapter one, section A10 and in section B5 above, the degree of closeness of an individual's connection to a country of nationality is irrelevant to whether that country is considered as 'the country of his nationality'. As the USCIS Asylum Officer Basic Training Course states, 'The asylum officer must evaluate asylum eligibility with respect to any country of which the applicant is a citizen, even if the applicant never resided in, or established personal ties to, a country of citizenship'.[70] The desire of an individual not to rely upon the protection of a particular country of nationality is also *per se* irrelevant, as already set out in section B3 above. This does not mean that the reasons for that desire may not be relevant, if properly relatable to the objects of CSR51 as examined in this section.

5.113 According to the language and formation of article 1A(2) CSR51 and to the primacy given to national over international protection where the former is available, any country which falls within the definition of 'his country of nationality' is relevant at the initial stage of examination. Given the principles set out in chapter one and in this chapter (above), this means, in essence, any State of current nationality recognised for relevant purposes on the international plane. The first

[69] UNHCR, *Handbook and Guidelines on Procedures and Criteria for Determining Refugee Status* (n 3 above).

[70] USCIS Asylum Officer Basic Training Course (n 12 above) 11.

stage in assessing the claim is likely to be the assessment of what State or States count as 'the country of nationality'.

Once countries of nationality have been identified, the logical next enquiry focuses on the definitive question at article 1A(2), paragraph 1—whether, as regards one or more countries of nationality, the individual in question is outside that country and unable or unwilling to avail himself or herself of its protection by reason of a well-founded fear of persecution for a relevant reason (or reasons). If that question is answered positively as regards every 'country of his nationality', then the individual in question is a refugee under article 1A(2) CSR51. This is also the case in the opposite of a plural nationality situation—one in which the claimant is within the category of those 'not having a nationality'—and as regards the country of former habitual residence he or she is 'unable or, owing to such fear, is unwilling, to return to it'. 5.114

By contrast the individual in respect of whom there is no country of nationality (or the country of former habitual residence in an appropriate case) in relation to which the question is answered positively, is not a refugee under article 1A(2) CSR51. Axiomatically an individual who possesses no well-founded fear of persecution for relevant reason in any relevant country is not a refugee. 5.115

Neither of the situations contemplated above requires any further special examination. The reflections set out below address the residual category of case in which an individual outside his or her country of nationality is, *inter alia*, unable or unwilling to avail himself (or herself) of its protection by reason of well-founded fear of persecution for a relevant reason (or reasons), but there remains at least one other non-persecutory country of nationality. 5.116

It is important to consider how such cases should be dealt with, and it is plain that they cannot be treated, without more, as cases in which the article 1A(2) CSR51 definition is not satisfied. The reason for this is that if a person claiming asylum in a country of which she is an alien, and therefore without any general right of entry or stay, meets the requirements of article 1A(2) as regards one country of nationality (country A), and does not do so as regards another country (country B), she can ordinarily be expected to seek the protection of country B. This rational expectation however is frustrated if country B, for example, refuses to admit her, or indeed if there is a relevant risk that country B would admit her and then *refoule* her to country A. Such factors do not undermine the existence of nationality which renders country B a reference State. However they do reduce the degree to which that reference State can be taken as displacing any need for surrogate international protection. 5.117

The immediate question is how the existence of a non-persecutory State of nationality is related to a central purpose of the regime—the protection of refugees from *refoulement*. It has most often been identified as a question of 'effective nationality', perhaps the best known cases being two decisions of the Federal Court of Australia, first *Jong Kim Koe v MIMA* [1997] FCA 306, [1997] ALR 695, 5.118

(Black CJ, Foster and Lehane JJ) and second, *Lay Kon Tji v MIMA* [1998] FCA 1380, (1998) 158 ALR 681 (Finkelstein J). Both decisions concerned the question of whether claimants from East Timor were also Portuguese citizens under the law of that country[71] and if so, what incidents of protection by Portugal attached to this.

5.119 In the international law relating to diplomatic protection, 'effective nationality' is employed in two situations, concisely explained by Dörr in the *Max Planck Encyclopedia of Public International Law*:

> In cases of multiple nationality the right of diplomatic protection is traditionally subject to some restrictions which arise from the general principle of sovereign equality ... As between two States of nationality of a person, the traditional rule of equality was set out in Art 4 Convention on Certain Questions relating to the Conflict of Nationality Laws, according to which a State may not afford diplomatic protection to one of its nationals against a State whose nationality such a person also possesses. In the *Reparation for Injuries Suffered in the Service of the United Nations* Advisory Opinion the ICJ described this concept as the 'ordinary practice' of States ([1949] ICJ Rep 174 at 186). In relation to a third State, it was the traditional view that only one of the States of nationality shall be entitled to exercise diplomatic protection and that is the State of the effective or dominant nationality.[72]

5.120 Article 1A(2) CSR51 follows a different approach—instead of isolating a single country of nationality it expressly requires consideration of every such country. The term 'effective nationality' was taken from paragraph 107 of the UNHCR *Handbook*:

> 107. There will be cases where the applicant has the nationality of a country in regard to which he alleges no fear, but such nationality may be deemed to be ineffective as it does not entail the protection normally granted to nationals. In such circumstances, the possession of the second nationality would not be inconsistent with refugee status.

The brevity of that entry is understandable, but it will be noted that it leaves undefined 'the protection normally granted to nationals', essentially deferring the critical enquiry.

5.121 In the *Lay Kon Tji* decision Finkelstein J concluded that:

> In my view, conformably with the views expressed in the United Nations Handbook and conformably with the purpose and object of the Refugees Convention, 'effective nationality' is a nationality that provides all of the protection and rights to which a national is entitled to receive under customary or conventional international law.

---

[71] The occupation of East Timor by Indonesia, despite its being inconsistent with international law, had been recognised by Australia, and no question was raised in the Australian courts as regards recognition of Indonesian nationality - had this occurred then these might well have been cases in which recognition was appropriate for the limited purpose of avoiding prejudice to the applicants in refugee status determination by reason of the illegal occupation of their home territory by Indonesia: see section B5 above.

[72] O Dörr, 'Nationality' in *Max Planck Encyclopedia of Public International Law* (online edn, OUP, 2015) [55]. See also Weis (n 7 above) 170–76.

The earlier decision in the *Jong Kim Koe* case was criticised by Sidhom as expressing the ambit of 'effective nationality' wrongly because it was reached 'without reference to the object and purpose of asylum obligations'.[73] The second decision, in *Lay Kon Tji*, was censured by Piotrowicz as going beyond the sanction of CSR51: 'para 107 of the Handbook in referring to the protection "ordinarily granted to nationals" cannot be read as imposing a requirement of complete equivalence in the situation of nationals within a State'.[74] The range of views—and absence of cohesive definition subsequently—illustrate the insufficiency of the phrase 'effective nationality' even read with the *Handbook*. The phrase is unsatisfactory without substantial further definition, as outlined in chapter one, section A9, and may be opaque or misleading whenever used without such definition.

The term 'effective nationality' is also misleading in that the core of the enquiry concerns not nationality itself (although the enquiry is reached as a consequence of a non-persecuting nationality arising) but protection. Central to the examination at this point is a realistic acknowledgement that not every non-persecuting nationality represents a source of protection, or of protection adequate to the object and purpose of CSR51. In *KK and others (Nationality: North Korea) Korea CG* [2011] UKUT 92, the Upper Tribunal (Mr Ockelton VP, SIJ Gleeson) examined the 'full and informative treatment of the issue in *Jong Kim Koe*', and identified the core issue as protection: **5.122**

> 67. Secondly, it is clear that the issue is the availability of protection. If an individual has protection available to him from a country of which he is a national, the Refugee Convention is not engaged. That is not the same as saying that a person of dual nationality is not a refugee. Such ought to be obvious. What is less obvious, but clear from *Jong Kim Koe*, is that a country of nationality which is not itself a country of persecution may nevertheless be a country in which the applicant has a 'valid reason based on well-founded fear' for not availing himself of its protection.[75]

The interpretation of the term 'protection' in article 1A(2) CSR51 has been considered in section A3 above. In context, 'protection' at article 1A(2) CSR51 means protection from persecution or from well-founded fear of being persecuted. Such a fear, as regards a country of nationality (or of former habitual residence in the absence of a nationality) is a requirement of article 1A(2) CSR51. However, the same test cannot be straightforwardly applied to states of plural nationality. If it did a claim would succeed only if a well-founded fear of persecution was shown as regards every country of nationality. On any adequate account of the content, object and purpose of CSR51 such an interpretation of article 1A(2) cannot be **5.123**

[73] M Sidhom, 'Jong Kim Koe v Minister for Immigration and Multicultural Affairs: Federal Court Loses Sight of the Purpose of the Refugee Convention' (1998) 20(2) *Sydney Law Review* 315.

[74] R Piotrowicz, '*Lay Kon Tji and Minister for Immigration & Ethnic Affairs*: The Function and Meaning of Effective Nationality in the Assessment of Applications for Asylum' (1999) 11(3) *International Journal of Refugee Law* 544.

[75] Paras [62]–[67].

acceptable, because it would have the following consequences which are, it is suggested, incompatible with the basic form and purpose of the CSR51 scheme:

i. The requirement for well-founded fear of persecution for a relevant reason in *every* country of nationality would result in a claimant being unsuccessful if there was a non-persecuting state of plural nationality even if that State would *refoule* the claimant to the State which is the *locus* of the well-founded fear or persecution.
ii. The claimant would also be unsuccessful if the non-persecuting State would refuse to admit the claimant, so that, having failed to satisfy the article 1A(2) definition by reason of the existence of a plural nationality, the claimant is left without legal protection from *refoulement.*
iii. Finally, a broad range of factual circumstances, difficult to categorise closely, arise in which, without direct *refoulement* or refusal of admission by the non-persecuting State, conditions in a non-persecuting plural nationality State may be so adverse as to generate very significant pressure either to *refoulement* by others (the State or non-state agents) or to self-*refoulement*. For instance the non-persecuting State may be subject to foreign occupation or international armed conflict, or there may be severe civil conflict or famine or epidemic disease. The non-persecuting State might also be subject to some form of wide-ranging ecological collapse, such as the loss of its territory to vulcanism or rising sea level. In such circumstances it seems wholly justified to interpret article 1A(2) as not displacing the entitlement to protection by reason of the existence of a non-persecutory State of nationality.

5.124 Could it reasonably be suggested that in any of the circumstances above an individual is notwithstanding the problems attached to the non-persecutory State of nationality disbarred from refugee status, and therefore unprotected from direct *refoulement* to the persecuting State?

5.125 No serious commentator has suggested that the answer to the last question is 'yes'. There appears to be a consensus the other way—that in certain circumstances an individual will be a refugee notwithstanding that there is a non-persecuting country of nationality to which he or she could go. For instance, the UNHCR *Handbook* states that:

> 107. In examining the case of an applicant with dual or plural nationality, it is necessary, however, to distinguish between the possession of a nationality in the legal sense and the availability of protection by the country concerned. There will be cases where the applicant has the nationality of a country in regard to which he alleges no fear, but such nationality may be deemed to be ineffective as it does not entail the protection normally granted to nationals. In such circumstances, the possession of the second nationality would not be inconsistent with refugee status. As a rule, there should have been a request for, and a refusal of, protection before it can be established that a given nationality is ineffective. If there is no explicit refusal of protection, absence of a reply within reasonable time may be considered a refusal.

The problems attaching to the phrase 'effective nationality' have already been identified. The *Handbook* does not assist in reaching any reasonably firm conclusion as to when a non-persecuting country of nationality vitiates the potential for satisfaction of the requirement of article 1A(2) CSR51 for, *inter alia*, a well-founded fear of persecution for a relevant reason. 5.126

In fact a principled approach may be developed, adding fibre to the vague and unsatisfactory formulation of effective nationality offered by the *Handbook* and focusing upon protection from direct or indirect *refoulement*. A useful start is a short survey of relevant learning. 5.127

Amongst early commentators Robinson provided a relatively full account in relation to this issue: 5.128

> The second subparagraph of [article 1A(2)] treats of persecutes who possess dual or triple nationality. Since only those persons with a nationality are deemed to be refugees who do not enjoy the protection of a government, the circumstance that a person is unable or unwilling to avail himself of the protection of one country is not sufficient if there is another country willing to extend to him protection and there exists no valid reason for him to refuse such protection. Again, since the unwillingness to avail himself of the protection must be based on well-founded fear of persecution, the valid reasons for refusing such protection must be based on this fear. Obviously, no valid reason based on fear of persecution is required if the country of nationality refuses to grant protection, for instance, if the laws of the country consider [an act] tantamount to renunciation of the former citizenship.[76]

In 1991 Hathaway, describing the requirement of alienage from the State of nationality, stated that an exception arose to the principle that any State of nationality could be expected to provide protection: 5.129

> The major caveat to the principle of deferring to protection by a state of citizenship is the need to ensure *effective*, rather than merely formal, nationality. It is not enough for example, that the claimant carries a second passport from a non-persecutory state if that state is not *in fact* willing to afford protection against return to the country of persecution. While it is appropriate to presume a willingness on the part of a country of nationality to protect in the absence of evidence to the contrary, facts that call into question the existence of basic protection against return must be carefully assessed (original emphasis).[77]

He went on, observing that the *de jure* entitlement to nationality was not to be equated with realistic access to protection, to emphasise the importance of an inquiry into 'effective nationality': 5.130

> The dilemma here is a logical extension of concern to ensure *effective* nationality before assessing the adequacy of a refugee claim: only the degree of risk in those states that are

76 Robinson (n 30 above) 54.

77 J Hathaway, *The Law of Refugee Status* (Butterworths Canada, 1991) 59. This and the following citations are reiterated in Hathaway and Foster (n 6 above) 55–57.

known to be *obliged* to allow the re-entry of the claimant is relevant, as it is to one of those states that the putative refugee would in most cases be sent back if not admitted to the country of refuge (original emphasis).[78]

5.131 The view of Professor Hathaway referred to principles then recently adumbrated by the Canadian Federal Court of Appeal in *Canada (Attorney-General) v Ward* [1990] 2 FCR 667, 67 DLR (4th) 1, in which the Court considered a proceedings concerning the refugee claim of a national of the Republic of Ireland and the United Kingdom who had deserted from a sectarian paramilitary group in Northern Ireland. The Immigration Appeal Board considered that the applicant was credible and possessed a well-founded fear as regards the Republic of Ireland, but did not examine whether he could avail himself of protection from the authorities of the United Kingdom. The Court was of the view that the Board had erred in failing to consider whether Ward could avail himself of the protection of the United Kingdom. Its decision was upheld on further appeal in the Canadian Supreme Court, in *Canada (Attorney General) v Ward* [1993] 2 SCR 689, (1993) 103 DLR (4th) 1. As already seen, the judgment of the Court given by La Forest J noted the requirement to consider whether any country of nationality was able to afford protection. But, in a passage less often noted, it also acknowledged that consequential questions arose including that of whether an individual would be admitted to the non-persecuting country of nationality:

> The assessment of Convention refugee status most consistent with this theme requires consideration of the availability of protection in all countries of citizenship.
>
> ...
>
> Clearly, the inability of a second state of nationality to protect can be established where the claimant has actually approached the state and been denied protection. Where, as in the case of Ward, the second state has not actually been approached by the claimant, the principles delineated above regarding the home state should apply. In other words, Great Britain should be presumed capable of protecting its nationals.
>
> An underlying premise of this presumption, however, is that citizenship carries with it certain basic consequences. One of these, as noted by MacGuigan JA, at p 699, is the right to gain entry to the country at any time. The appellant presented evidence, albeit not by way of expert opinion, of the existence of the *Prevention of Terrorism (Temporary Provisions) Act 1984*. The current version of this Act (*Prevention of Terrorism (Temporary Provisions) Act 1989*, 1989 (UK), c 4), which replaced the *Prevention of Terrorism (Temporary Provisions) Act 1984*, seems to enable the British Government to prohibit a national from being in, or entering, Great Britain, if the national has been 'concerned in the commission, preparation or instigation of acts of terrorism' connected with the affairs of Northern Ireland; see ss 4 and 5 of the Act. Such evidence might serve to rebut the presumption by demonstrating a lack of protection afforded by Great Britain. Denial

[78] Ibid, 59.

> of admittance to the home territory is offered by the UNHCR in its Handbook, at paragraph 99, as a possible example of what might amount to a refusal of protection. The applicability of the presumption and its rebuttal are matters that depend upon the particular circumstances of this case and which must be determined by the Board.

The Supreme Court of Canada accepted therefore that *inability to protect* might be established where a State was not inclined to grant entry to its territory.

The Canadian courts appear to have maintained a practice of examining plural nationalities and considering whether they are 'effective'. In many cases this may represent a form of balancing, alleviating the effect of the expansive—from the international perspective over-expansive—Canadian approach by which 'the country of his nationality' is said to include States of potential future nationality. As at 2010, the guidance of the Immigration and Refugee Board of Canada referred to *Ward* and then stated that, **5.132**

> after citing *Ward* and James C Hathaway's *The Law of Refugee Statius* in [*Martinez v MCI (FCTD no IMM-462-96)*], the Federal Court—Trial Division [Gibson J] appeared to accept that there is a need to ensure that a state of citizenship accords effective, rather than merely formal nationality, as well as to assess any evidence impeaching that state's protection against return to the country of persecution.[79]

This approach, or some parallel, can be seen in a number of cases already referred to—for instance in *Katkova v Canada (MCI)*, McKeown J decided the case on the absence of current Israeli nationality, but went on to refer to *Ward*, a decision he identified as not dealing with potential nationality but with protection from an actual state of nationality in the context of plural nationality, concluding after reference, *inter alia*, to the *Nottebohm* decision of the ICJ that a 'genuine connection and physical link' was necessary in such a case. In *Fabiano v Canada (MCI)* [2005] FC 1260 (a 'potential future nationality' case) Russell J concluded that Italy was not shown to be an appropriate country of reference by the evidence, because acquisition of Italian citizenship was accessible in safety only after a process lasting a substantial time and the claimant's safety from his country of immediate origin could be guaranteed only by permission to stay in Canada, or go to and remain in Italy, during the process.

Another jurisdiction in which the question of protection in plural nationality cases fell to be examined around the same time as the earliest decisions in Canada is Australia. The immediate context was a flow of refugee claimants from East Timor, then subject to unlawful occupation by Indonesia. Many East Timorese appeared, on the face of Portuguese law, to possess the nationality of Portugal, the mandatory power in East Timor prior to occupation of the territory by Indonesia in 1975. In *Jong Kim Koe v MIMA* [1997] FCA 306, [1997] ALR 695, **5.133**

[79] Immigration and Refugee Board of Canada Refugee Protection Division, *Interpretation of the Convention Refugee Definition in the Case Law*, ch 2, para 2.1.4.

the Federal Court of Australia (Black CJ, Foster and Lehane JJ) addressed such a case. It referred to paragraph 107 of the *Handbook* and to Hathaway's writings:

> The passage we have just quoted reveals a clear view that the inquiry does not necessarily end, in the case of a person with dual nationality, once it is concluded that the person has a second nationality and has no fear of persecution for a convention reason in the country of the second nationality. In such a case there remains the question whether the nationality is 'effective', which in turn may lead to an inquiry as to the 'availability' of protection.
>
> Professor Hathaway supports this view.
>
> ...
>
> We should note too that counsel for the respondent accepted that Article 1A(2) refers to persons who are 'able to avail themselves of protection from a country of nationality'.
>
> What is involved here is the proper construction of Article 1A(2) of the Refugees Convention. To interpret 'nationality' for the purposes of Article 1A(2) as something of a 'merely formal' character (to use the language of Professor Hathaway), instead of something effective from the viewpoint of a putative refugee, would be liable to frustrate rather than advance the humanitarian objects of the Refugees Convention. Nor would such a construction advance, in any practical way, another object of the Refugees Convention, namely the precedence of national protection over international protection. That precedence has no obvious relevance where national protection is not effective; as the *UNHCR Handbook* puts it (paragraph 107), in circumstances where a second nationality may be deemed to be ineffective because it does not entail the protection normally granted to nationals, 'the possession of the second nationality would be not inconsistent with refugee status'.
>
> Given the objects of the Convention, it can hardly have been intended that a person who seeks international protection to which, but for a second nationality he or she would clearly be entitled, would, as a consequence of a formal but relevantly ineffective nationality, be denied international protection and, not being a 'refugee', could be sent back to the country in which he or she feared, and had a real chance of, being persecuted.
>
> In these circumstances, to construe 'nationality' where it first appears in the second paragraph of Article 1A(2) of the Refugees Convention as referring to nationality that is effective as a source of protection and which is not merely formal is, in our view, to interpret Article 1A(2) in the manner required by the Vienna Convention as explained in the High Court in [*Applicant A v Minister for Immigration and Ethnic Affairs* (1997) 142 ALR 331], that is to say, in accordance with the ordinary meaning of the text but considering also the context and the object and purpose of the Refugees Convention.
>
> Effective nationality for this purpose is of course something that must be assessed in the light of all the circumstances of a particular case. The inquiry will thus extend to a range of practical questions, parallel to those posed by the expression 'unable' in the first paragraph of Article 1A(2).

> It follows from the construction we consider to be correct that findings that a person has dual nationalities but lacks a well-founded fear of persecution in one of the countries of nationality will not necessarily preclude a finding that the person is a refugee ...
>
> It is true that the alternative approach just outlined is contrary to an observation of La Forest J in *Canada (Attorney General) v Ward* (1993) 103 DLR 4th 1 at 42, that an applicant for recognition as a refugee bears a burden which 'includes a showing of well-founded fear of persecution in all countries of which the claimant is a national'. But, as his Lordship's judgment proceeds to recognise, there is an exception, at least in the case where the second country of nationality does not offer protection to the applicant. Once that is recognised, it seems to us, with respect, that there may be a degree of artificiality in approaching the matter on a basis which requires first a consideration of whether effective protection is offered and, only if that test is passed, a separate consideration of whether the applicant can avail himself of that protection.
>
> However that may be, the Tribunal in our view fell into error because it proceeded on the basis that once Portuguese nationality was established Mr Jong was not a refugee unless it could be shown (as it could not) that he had a well-founded fear of persecution in Portugal.

The decision represented authority for the proposition, following *Ward*, that there was a requirement to consider not only whether an individual possessed a well-founded fear for relevant reason in every country of nationality, but also, exceptionally, whether given possession of such a fear as regards one or more countries of nationality, any other country 'does not offer protection to the applicant'. Following *Ward* again, this necessarily means more than 'protection from fear of persecution for a Convention reason', but what 'protection' consisted in was left without any close definition.[80]

The task of defining what protection was required for a country of nationality to be treated as affording protection through 'effective' nationality was completed a short time later in *Lay Kon Tji v Minister for Immigration & Multicultural Affairs* [1998] FCA 1380, (1998) 158 ALR 681 (Finkelstein J) in the Federal Court of Australia. The case was another East Timor/Portugal claim, effectively different from that in *Jong Kim Koe* only in the intervening development of the evidence concerning Portuguese nationality and protection. Finkelstein J noted, *inter alia*, that articles 1C(3) and IE CSR51 provided for cessation where a refugee 'acquired a new nationality, and enjoys the protection of the country of his new nationality' and non-application 'to a person who is recognized by the competent authorities of the country in which he has taken residence as having the rights and obligations which are attached to the possession of the nationality of that country', treating these standards as guidance in ascertaining the content of 'effective nationality': **5.134**

> It would seem to be a curious result to say the least if a person who would otherwise be a refugee would cease to hold that status if he acquires a new nationality, or a new

[80] For a representative criticism, see Sidhom (n 73 above).

de facto nationality, that confers all of the rights of nationality, but, in a case where a person has dual nationality, refugee status would be denied if the country of second nationality provided only some of the protections conferred by that state on its other nationals. Moreover, it must be remembered that by the Refugees Convention those countries which do grant refugee status to an individual are also required to accord to the refugee freedom of religion (Article 4), to allow the refugee freedom of association (Article 15), to permit the refugee to have free access to local courts (Article 16). If the country of second nationality would not confer those rights on the putative refugee, being rights which by international law must be afforded to a national, it could hardly be supposed that it was intended that the putative refugee must seek the protection of that state. The reason a putative refugee need not seek the protection of that state is because the nationality that the state offers cannot be regarded as a truly effective nationality.

In my view, conformably with the views expressed in the United Nations Handbook and conformably with the purpose and object of the Refugees Convention, 'effective nationality' is a nationality that provides all of the protection and rights to which a national is entitled to receive under customary or conventional international law.

5.135 The decision in each case has been subject to powerful criticism: *Jong Kim Koe* for absence of clarity and *Lay Kon Tji* as setting a standard in effect too generous to claimants. Piotrowicz has forcefully pointed out that the rubric suggested by Finkelstein J in *Lay Kon Tji* is unsupported by the object or purpose of CSR51, that nothing in CSR51 suggests that it is designed to ensure complete protection of all internationally recognised rights ('[CSR51] does not say that an asylum seeker should only be required to go somewhere else if guaranteed freedom of assembly, the right to vote and complete freedom of speech') and that paragraph 107 of the *Handbook* in referring to the protection 'ordinarily granted to nationals' cannot be read as imposing a requirement of complete equivalence in the situation of nationals within a State.[81] His criticisms of the *Lay Kon Tji* decision individually and collectively possess considerable strength, and the conclusion that *Lay Kon Tji* is, if read literally, overly extensive in the requirements it prescribes for a plural nationality to be 'effective', appears well founded. If *Lay Kon Tji* is overgenerous however there remains the question of how the standard for discounting a country of plural nationality from reference in article 1A(2) CSR51 can in practice be delineated.

5.136 Subsequent statutory change appears to have reduced the scope for refinement of the point in Australia. In *Mire v Minister for Immigration & Multicultural Affairs* [2000] FCA 1149, a case concerning protection, though not invoking plural nationality, Marshall J found that the mere absence of a valid up to date travel document for South Africa on the part of a Somali applicant who had previously been granted refugee status by South Africa, and had destroyed his South African identity document, did not indicate absence of 'effective protection' by South Africa. But Australian law was amended by the Border Protection Legislation

[81] R Piotrowicz, '*Lay Kon Tji and Minister for Immigration & Ethnic Affairs*: The Function and Meaning of Effective Nationality in the Assessment of Applications for Asylum' (1999) 11(3) *International Journal of Refugee Law* 544.

Amendment Act 1999 to reduce access to adjudication of entitlement to protection in Australia. Under sections 91P and 91Q of the Migration Act 1958, inserted by the 1999 Act, a person to whom Subdivision AK applies, may not make a valid application for a protection visa while he or she remains in the Australian migration zone, unless the Minister has first made a non-compellable personal determination permitting such an application to be made within seven working days. Section 91N(1) applies these provisions to 'a non-citizen at a particular time if, at that time, the non-citizen is a national of 2 or more countries': *Szouy & Ors v Minister for Immigration & Anor* [2011] FMCA 347.

Thereafter the earlier Australian cases have been referred to on a number of occasions in the United Kingdom, where overall there is a marked absence of consistency on this point—despite, or perhaps because, of the relatively small number of decisions. The principle of effective protection was endorsed in the High Court, Administrative Court, by Harrison J in *R v SSHD ex p Milisavljevic* [2001] EWHC Admin 203 [2001] Imm AR 580, [2001] All ER(D) 165 (March), having been accepted as common ground by counsel for the Secretary of State. The judgment refers to Hathaway's writings and paragraph 107 of the *Handbook* as persuasive, no previous decision being specifically cited. **5.137**

Subsequently the decision of the Australian Federal Court in *Jong Kim Koe* was expressly adopted by the Immigration Appeal Tribunal (Mr Latter VP, Mr Aujla) in *MA (Ethiopia—Eritrea—mixed ethnicity—dual nationality) Eritrea* [2004] UKIAT 00324, at [46]: **5.138**

> 46. The Tribunal accepts that the protection offered by a state of second nationality must be 'effective' as envisaged in the UNHCR Handbook [paras 106–7] and in [*Jong Kim Koe v MIMA*] which endorsed a comment from Professor Hathaway's book that there is a need to ensure effective rather than formal nationality and that it is not enough that the claimant carries a second passport from a non-persecutory state if that state is not in fact willing to afford protection.

That determination was subsequently set aside, but not on grounds affecting its holding on this point.

In *FA (Eritrea, nationality) Eritrea CG* [2005] UKIAT 00047, [27], the Immigration Appeal Tribunal (Ouseley J, Dr Storey VP, HHJ Risius) distinguished *Jong Kim Koe* from the case before it—which concerned the question of whether the claimant possessed Eritrean nationality—on the basis that the Australian case was concerned with a plural nationality. In *KA (statelessness: meaning and relevance) Stateless* [2008] UKAIT 00042, an interim decision by a differently composed panel of the Tribunal (Mr Ockelton VP, IJ Hall), the Tribunal without reference to previous decisions expressed reservations concerning any use at all of an 'effectiveness' criterion: **5.139**

> 7. If a person is at risk of persecution in one of his countries of nationality the possession (or the possibility of acquiring) nationality of another country will only prevent him from being a refugee if he is not at risk of persecution there or at risk of being returned to the first country from there.

The case in question was one in which the primary country of reference appeared to be Ethiopia. That State had on his case denationalised and expelled the appellant by reason of Eritrean background. Eritrea was then cited by the Secretary of State for the Home Department as a potential State of plural nationality. The preliminary judgment of the Tribunal was not tested subsequently, because proceedings were broken off when the appellant was recognised as a refugee and permitted to remain.

5.140 Most recently in *KK and others (Nationality: North Korea) Korea CG* [2011] UKUT 92, the Upper Tribunal (Mr Ockelton VP, SIJ Gleeson) considered the position of North Koreans. The Tribunal noted having received submissions on effective nationality and a 'full and informative treatment of the issue in *Jong Kim Koe*'.[82] In closing its reflections on the issue it sets out certain matters:

> 67. Consideration of this issue is likely to require us to go further than was merited by the submissions before us. We would make three observations. The first is that, in principle, an Australian court might properly decide that it was persuaded that the applicant had Portuguese nationality, and might allow him to be removed there, knowing that if Portugal did not accept him as a national Portugal could not return him to a country of nationality in which he feared persecution for a Convention reason. Those considerations might be different if the country of return was not a party to the Refugee Convention or some other convention of equivalent nature. Secondly, it is clear that the issue is the availability of protection. If an individual has protection available to him from a country of which he is a national, the Refugee Convention is not engaged. That is not the same as saying that a person of dual nationality is not a refugee. Such ought to be obvious. What is less obvious, but clear from *Jong Kim Koe*, is that a country of nationality which is not itself a country of persecution may nevertheless be a country in which the applicant has a 'valid reason based on well-founded fear' for not availing himself of its protection. If the result of his availing himself of the protection of that country is that he will find himself (for one reason or another) returned to the country in which he fears persecution, that would appear to be such a reason. Thirdly, the individual occasions when a country will not accept the return of its own nationals must be very rare and, as *Jong Kim Koe* also makes clear, the prospect of such treatment is a matter to be established on the individual facts of the case.

This decision shares an author with *KA (statelessness: meaning and relevance)*, and the different view expressed in the later decision, showing a strong acknowledgement of the importance attached by CSR51 to avoidance of indirect *refoulement* and to protection considerations, would appear to reflect an evolution in views.

ii. Discussion and Conclusion: Protection by a State of Plural Nationality (the 'National Protection Alternative')

5.141 The survey set out immediately above demonstrates that there has been uncertainty and disagreement as to what standards apply in judging whether

[82] Paras [62]–[67].

otherwise established status as a refugee must be denied by reason of the existence of a non-persecuting State of plural nationality. Ultimately, whether the language preferred is that of 'effective nationality' employed in *Jong Kim Koe*, *Lay Kon Tji*, and other cases, or that of 'protection' (preferred in the United Kingdom decision in *KK and others*) the absence of clarity and consensus in the authorities points to the existence of a present need to establish what the applicable standards are, with proper regard to the interpretation of article 1A(2) CSR51 on VCLT69 principles.

A starting point is the treatment of every country of nationality as 'the country of nationality' for purposes of article 1A(2), paragraph 1, established by the first part of article 1A(2) CSR51, paragraph 2 ('In the case of a person who has more than one nationality, the term "the country of his nationality" shall mean each of the countries of which he is a national'). If this were read in isolation it might lead to an interpretation by which a claimant would have to demonstrate well-founded fear of persecution for relevant reason in every country of nationality. However, this is offset by the second part of article 1A(2), paragraph 2 ('and a person shall not be deemed to be lacking the protection of the country of his nationality if, without any valid reason based on well-founded fear, he has not availed himself of the protection of one of the countries of which he is a national') which, interpreted by ordinary meaning in the light of context, would indicate that a person shall be deemed to be lacking the protection of the country of his nationality if he or she has valid reason based on well-founded fear, for failure to avail himself of the protection of a State or States of plural nationality. On this reading there must be sufficiently serious reason for failure to rely upon the protection of a plural nationality, and that reason must be based upon well-founded fear. The 'well-founded fear' in question might be understood as reference to exclusively fear of some relevant matter in connection with the State of plural nationality. But another, interpretation, which in the view of the author should be preferred, is that this may also include well-founded fear of persecution for a Convention reason in the persecutory or index State, and the well-founded fear in relation to a State of plural nationality is well-founded fear based upon the absence of safety from relevant risk of some form of *refoulement* to the index State. On the second interpretation, which appears more consistent with the object and purpose of prevention of *refoulement* to persecution, the avoidance of relevant risk of *refoulement* provides the overarching standard. **5.142**

It follows from this interpretation that a person shall be deemed to be lacking the protection of the country of his nationality if he or she has valid reason based on well-founded fear for failure to avail himself of the protection of a State or States of plural nationality (having already established a well-founded fear of persecution for a Convention reason as regards the index country). The logic of protection from *refoulement* points to the conclusion that valid reason for failure to avail himself of the protection of a State or States of plural nationality is shown in any of the following circumstances: **5.143**

i. If there is a relevant risk that the non-persecuting State or non-state agents on its territory would directly or indirectly *refoule* the claimant to a State which is the *locus* of the well-founded fear or persecution for Convention reason ('the index State');

ii. If there is a relevant risk that the non-persecuting State would refuse to admit the claimant, so perpetuating the risk of *refoulement* to an index State. A State does not afford an 'effective nationality' (if the terminology is retained) if it will not admit that individual to its territory (including where it will not admit the individual by reason of resistance to the claim of nationality itself). This seems abundantly supported by authority including *Ward*. In *Refugee Appeal No 72635*, [2002] NZRSAA 344 the New Zealand Refugee Status Appeals Authority made this explicit:

> [37] The protection must not be illusory, however. Neither notional, nor merely asserted, nationality will suffice. What must be established is effective protection, because protection in name only is, of course, no protection at all. The starting point for establishing effective protection must thus be the recognition of nationality by the state in question. This was the view reached in *Lay Kon Tji v Minister for Immigration and Ethnic Affairs* (1998) 158 ALR 681, at pp 693–696, where it was held by Finkelstein J that an essential element in the concept of an 'effective nationality' is the recognition of the existence of that nationality by the state in question.

iii. If relevant risk arises based upon factual circumstances in a non-persecuting State so adverse as to generate relevant pressure either to *refoulement* by others (the State or non-state agents) or to self-*refoulement*. In this situation the expectation of reliance upon a country becomes objectively unreasonable. Relevant factual circumstances might include, *inter alia*, foreign occupation, international armed conflict, severe civil conflict, famine, epidemic, or ecological collapse. Whilst not extending to the whole range of internationally protected human rights as suggested by Finkelstein J in *Lay Kon Tji*, the situations enumerated above as examples are linked by the potential for serious breaches of fundamental rights and/or for equivalent challenge to human dignity.

5.144 If the formulation above is accepted, then it still leaves one further question to be addressed. What is the standard to be applied in the assessment of the potentially diverse factual circumstances which may be relevant?

5.145 Because the question is one of importance deserving reflection in the light of concrete cases, some reticence is appropriate. On the other hand, a provisional answer does seem possible given reflection on the cases set out above and on a parallel issue which has been extensively considered judicially and by commentators, namely that of internal protection/relocation/flight alternative. Each issue concerns the position which is contemplated as arising when an individual who possesses a well-founded fear of persecution for relevant reason(s) in at least part of one State of which he is a citizen, seeks refuge in another place, within the territory of the index State (internal relocation) or by reference to a plural nationality State. A practical advantage of this starting point is that, despite the absence of complete concordance amongst the leading courts of different jurisdictions, or amongst commentators, a considerable body of learning has been brought into being by collective decision-making and collaborative study. But the similarity of the concepts is a consequence of their similar function in the operation of article 1A(2) CSR51. So for instance the First Colloquium on Challenges in International Refugee Law convened by the University of Michigan Law School in April 1999 led to publication of the *Michigan Guidelines on the Internal Protection Alternative*[83] which set out the 'analytical framework' as being that:

> 1. The essence of the refugee definition set out in Art 1(A)(2) of the 1951 Convention relating to the Status of Refugees ('Refugee Convention') is the identification of persons who are entitled to claim protection in a contracting state against the risk of persecution in their own country. This duty of state parties to provide surrogate protection arises only in relation to persons who are either unable to benefit from the protection of their own state, or who are unwilling to accept that state's protection because of a well-founded fear of persecution.
>
> 2. It therefore follows that to the extent meaningful protection against the risk of persecution is genuinely available to an asylum-seeker, Convention refugee status need not be recognized.

The subsequent Summary Conclusions of the expert roundtable organised by the UNHCR at San Remo in September 2001 state: **5.146**

> 1. IPA/IRA/IFA can sometimes be a relevant consideration in the analysis of whether an asylum seeker's claim to refugee status is valid, in line with the object and purpose of the Refugee Convention. The relevance of considering IPA/IRA/IFA will depend on the particular factual circumstances of an individual case.
>
> 2. …
>
> 3. The individual whose claim to refugee status is under consideration must be able—practically, safely, and legally—to access the proposed IPA/IRA/IFA. This requires consideration of physical and other barriers to access, such as risks that may accrue in the process of travel or entry; and any legal barriers to travel, enter, or remain in the proposed IPA/IRA/IFA.
>
> 4. If the asylum seeker would be exposed to a well-founded fear of being persecuted, including being persecuted inside the proposed IPA/IRA/IFA or being forced back to and persecuted in another part of the country, an IPA/IRA/IFA does not exist.
>
> 5. The mere absence of a well-founded fear of being persecuted is not sufficient in itself to establish that an IPA/IRA/IFA exists. Factors that may be relevant to an assessment of the availability of an IPA/IRA/IFA include the level of respect for human rights in the proposed IPA/IRA/IFA, the asylum seeker's personal circumstances, and/or conditions in the country at large (including risks to life, limb, or freedom).

[83] *The Michigan Guidelines on Protection Elsewhere* (n 43 above).

6. Given its complexity, the examination of IPA/IRA/IFA is not appropriate in accelerated procedures, or in deciding on an individual's admissibility to a full status determination procedure.

7. More generally, basic rules of procedural fairness must be respected, including giving the asylum seeker clear and adequate notice that an IPA/IRA/IFA is under consideration.

8. Caution is desirable to ensure that return of an individual to an IPA/IRA/IFA does not arbitrarily create, or exacerbate, situations of internal displacement.

5.147 These standards may, in a manner wholly consistent with the ordinary meaning to be given to the terms of CSR51 in their context and in the light of its object and purpose, be applied to potential situations of external relocation, of the type grappled with in the 'effective nationality' cases, with little immediate change beyond the substitution of 'national relocation alternative' for 'internal relocation alternative'. The name 'national protection alternative' has the merit of identifying the root of the category—the presence of nationality and the consequent question of whether demurral of international responsibility on the basis of the existence of a non-persecuting State of nationality is (to copy language employed in the context of internal relocation) unduly harsh or unreasonable. A further merit is that it better reflects the relevant question, which is not whether nationality arises but whether the nationality is one which vitiates well-founded fear of persecution in another State of nationality. The standards above seem to align with those already expressly acknowledged or inferred in the balance of authority and comment in relation to internal relocation– for example the need for practical, safe and legal access to the proposed place of relocation. As Baroness Hale indicated in *SSHD v AH (Sudan) & Ors* [2007] UKHL 49, [2008] 1 AC 678, elucidating the standards applicable to internal relocation of Darfurians to Khartoum:

> 20. We are all agreed that the correct approach to the question of internal relocation under the Refugee Convention is that set out so clearly by my noble and learned friend, Lord Bingham of Cornhill, in *Januzi and others v Secretary of State for the Home Department* [2006] UKHL 5, [2006] 2 AC 426, at para 21:
>
> > 'The decision-maker, taking account of all relevant circumstances pertaining to the claimant and his country of origin, must decide whether it is reasonable to expect the claimant to relocate or whether it would be unduly harsh to expect him to do so'.
>
> As the UNHCR put it in their very helpful intervention in this case,
>
> > 'the correct approach when considering the reasonableness of IRA [internal relocation alternative] is to assess all the circumstances of the individual's case holistically and with specific reference to the individual's personal circumstances (including past persecution or fear thereof, psychological and health condition, family and social situation, and survival capacities). This assessment is to be made in the context of the conditions in the place of relocation (including basic human rights, security conditions, socio-economic conditions, accommodation, access to health care facilities), in order to determine the impact on that individual of settling in the proposed place of relocation and whether the individual could live a relatively normal life without undue hardship'.

> I do not understand there to be any difference between this approach and that commended by Lord Bingham in paragraph 5 of his opinion. Very little, apart from the conditions in the country to which the claimant has fled, is ruled out.
>
> 21. We are also all agreed that the test for internal relocation under the Refugee Convention is not to be equated either with a 'well-founded fear of persecution' under the Convention or with a 'real risk of ill-treatment' contrary to article 3 of the European Convention on Human Rights. By definition, if the claimant had a well-founded fear of persecution, not only in the place from which he has fled, but also in the place to which he might be returned, there can be no question of internal relocation. The question pre-supposes that there is some place within his country of origin to which he could be returned without fear of persecution. It asks whether, in all the circumstances, it would be unduly harsh to expect him to go there. If it is reasonable to expect him to go there, then he can no longer claim to be outside his country of origin because of his well-founded fear of persecution. Mercifully, the test accepts that if it is not reasonable to expect him to go there, then his continued absence from his country of origin remains due to his well-founded fear of persecution.

Accordingly an appropriate starting point in the identification of standards for reliance upon a State of plural nationality (a 'national protection alternative') may be to look tentatively for parallels within the established concept, that of internal relocation alternative, whilst remaining sensitive to the potential for functional divergence between national protection alternative and internal relocation alternative. **5.148**

C. 'Not Having a Nationality'

The approach to determining possession of nationality for purposes of 'the country of his nationality' has been set out above. A claimant 'not having a nationality' is one to whom no nationality can be attributed applying those principles. **5.149**

There may be a category of case in which the class of individuals 'not having a nationality' for purposes of article 1A(2), is more limited than the otherwise contiguous group of those who are stateless persons as defined at article 1(1) CSSP54. As outlined in chapter one, the latter for its own purposes gives a definition of 'stateless person' which potentially extends beyond the source of nationality law under the Convention on Certain Questions Relating to the Conflict of Nationality Laws 1930 (article 1: 'It is for each State to determine under its own law who are its nationals'; article 2: 'Any question as to whether a person possesses the nationality of a particular State shall be determined in accordance with the law of the State') to include also absence of nationality according to 'the operation of' its laws by the State. **5.150**

6

Persecution by Denial of Nationality

Interpretation of the term 'persecution' is guided by reference to relevant provisions of international human rights law and the international principle of non-discrimination. In turn the interpretation of open-ended provisions of human rights law may be assisted by indirect reference to other areas of international law dealing with particular subject matter, including where relevant the international law concerning nationality and statelessness. Whilst adjudication involves the assessment of facts as well as the application of legal standards, a considerable body of international jurisprudence supports the proposition that the requirement for 'persecution' will in most circumstances be met where there is deprivation of nationality accompanied by exclusion or expulsion, and the action taken has continuing effect, is arbitrary in international law terms, is by reason of a Convention reason or reasons, and renders the subject stateless or effectively so. Other cases will be less clear and fall to be evaluated by reference to international human rights standards as above, with indirect reference to other areas of international law where justified.

Contents

A. Introduction

A1. Text of Article 1A(2) of the Convention Relating to the Status of Refugees 1951

6.1 As already seen, article 1A(2) of the Convention relating to the Status of Refugees 1951 (CSR51), as modified by the 1967 Protocol relating to the Status of Refugees, defines a refugee as a person who:

> 1A(2) [O]wing to well-founded fear of being persecuted for reasons of race, religion, nationality, membership of a particular social group or political opinion, is outside the country of his nationality and is unable or, owing to such fear, is unwilling to avail himself of the protection of that country; or who, not having a nationality and being outside the country of his former habitual residence as a result of such events, is unable or, owing to such fear, is unwilling to return to it.

The second paragraph may be set aside for present purposes.

A2. Significance of the Term 'Persecution' in Article 1A(2) of the Convention Relating to the Status of Refugees 1951

6.2 The term 'persecution' represents a critical element in the passage within article 1A(2) CSR51, by which a refugee is defined. This has sometimes been described as raising as a 'single composite question'. In *R v IAT & Anor ex p Rajendrakumar; Sandralingham & Anor v SSHD* [1995] EWCA Civ 16, [1996] Imm AR 97 Simon Brown LJ held that:

> the issue whether a person or group of people have a 'well-founded fear … of being persecuted for [Convention] reasons' … raises a single composite question. It is, as it seems to me, unhelpful and potentially misleading to try to reach separate conclusions as to whether certain conduct amounts to persecution, and as to what reasons underlie it. Rather the question whether someone is at risk of persecution for a Convention reason should be looked at in the round and all the relevant circumstances brought into account. I know of no authority inconsistent with such an approach and, to my mind, it clearly accords both with paragraph 51 of the UNHCR Handbook and with the spirit of the Convention.

6.3 The treatment of the core definition as raising a single composite question does not obviate the need for interpretation of its terms. In *Sepet v SSHD* [2003] UKHL 15, [2003] 1 WLR 856, Lord Bingham observed that analysis required consideration of particular terms, and identified the term 'persecution' as central to this:

> 7. Although it is no doubt true, as stated by Simon Brown LJ at *Sandralingham v SSHD* that the Convention definition raises a single composite question, analysis requires consideration of the constituent elements of the definition. At the heart of the definition lies the concept of persecution. It is when a person, suffering or fearing persecution in

country A, flees to country B that it becomes the duty of country B to afford him (by the grant of asylum) the protection denied him by or under the laws of country A. History provides many examples of racial, religious, national, social and political minorities (sometimes even majorities) which have without doubt suffered persecution. But it is a strong word. Its dictionary definitions (save in their emphasis on religious persecution) accord with popular usage: 'the infliction of death, torture, or penalties for adherence to a religious belief or an opinion as such, with a view to the repression or extirpation of it'; 'A particular course or period of systematic infliction of punishment directed against the professors of a (religious) belief': *Oxford English Dictionary*, 2nd ed, (1989). Valuable guidance is given by Professor Hathaway (*The Law of Refugee Status* (1991), p 112) in a passage relied on by Lord Hope of Craighead in *Horvath v SSHD* [2001] 1 AC 489, 495:

> 'In sum, persecution is most appropriately defined as the sustained or systemic failure of state protection in relation to one of the core entitlements which has been recognized by the international community'.

In this passage Professor Hathaway draws attention to a second requirement, no less important than that of showing persecution: the requirement to show, as a condition of entitlement to recognition as a refugee, that the persecution feared will (in reasonable likelihood) be for one or more of the five Convention reasons. As Dawson J pointed out in the High Court of Australia in *Applicant A v Minister for Immigration and Ethnic Affairs* (1997) 190 CLR 225, 247–48:

> By including in its operative provisions the requirement that a refugee fear persecution, the Convention limits its humanitarian scope and does not afford universal protection to asylum seekers. No matter how devastating may be epidemic, natural disaster or famine, a person fleeing them is not a refugee within the terms of the Convention. And by incorporating the five Convention reasons the Convention plainly contemplates that there will even be persons fearing persecution who will not be able to gain asylum as refugees.

Article 1A(2) CSR51 has been held authoritatively to require a well-founded fear of persecution (by reason of relevant matter(s)) as a condition for qualification as a refugee. Statelessness alone (or statelessness plus inability or unwillingness to return) does not without more give rise to refugee status. The jurisprudence has consistently found that a stateless claimant must, to meet the article 1A(2) CSR51 definition, show a well-founded fear of persecution for relevant reason.[1] 6.4

The preceding chapters examined the use of the term 'nationality' in article 1A(2) CSR51 both in the context of the list of 'Convention reasons' (chapter four) and then within interconnected references first to 'the country of his nationality' then to being 'unable or unwilling to avail himself of the protection of that country', and finally to the position of a person 'not having a nationality' (chapter five). 6.5

---

[1] *Revenko v SSHD* [2000] EWCA Civ 500, [2001] QB 601; *Diatlov v MIMA* (1999) 167 ALR 313, 321 [29]; *MIMA v Savvin* [2000] FCA 478, (2000) 98 FCR 168, affirmed *in QAAE of 2002 v MIMIA* [2003] FCAFC 46; *Fedosseeva v Gonzales*, 492 F 3d 840, 845 (7th Cir 2007); *Arafa v MEI* (1993) 70 FTR 178 (Gibson J); and *Maarouf v Canada (MEI)* [1994] 1 FCR 723, 4–5; *SHM v Minister for Justice, Equality and Law Reform* (Unreported, Irish High Court, Clark J, 12 March 2009).

This chapter examines the degree to which acts or omissions related to national status fall within or without the scope of 'persecution'. It does not attempt a broader or more exhaustive examination of acts which may come within the meaning of the term. But some attention is needed to issues of wider significance in the interpretation of the term.

6.6 Assessments as to whether particular facts show persecution in article 1A(2) CSR51 terms raise questions of combined fact and law. In *MA (Ethiopia) v SSHD* [2009] EWCA Civ 289 [2010] INLR 1, Stanley Burnton LJ, with whom Mummery and Elias LJJ concurred, summarised the nature of the relationship:

> 62. What is the meaning of persecution in Article 1(A)(2) is a question of law. It has been the subject of helpful exegesis, as by Laws LJ in *Amare* [2005] EWCA Civ 1600, in a judgment with which the other members of the Court agreed. Thus what ill treatment is capable of being persecutory is a question of law. But whether ill treatment in a particular case constitutes persecution is a mixed question of fact and law: it is the application of the denotation of persecution to the particular facts.

6.7 This was emphasised in *MI (Pakistan) v SSHD* [2014] EWCA Civ 826 by Gloster LJ (with whom Gross LJ and Sir Stanley Burnton agreed) at [24]:

> 24. Moreover, as the Supreme Court pointed out [*per* Lord Neuberger in *Re B (a Child) (FC)* [2013] UKSC 33, [2013] 1 WLR 1911] whether a particular statutory threshold has been crossed (in that case whether a child was 'likely to suffer significant harm' under section 31(2) of the Children Act 1989) usually requires the judge to take at least three steps: (i) he has to determine the factual issues on the evidence before him; (ii) he has to identify the nature of the threshold, which involves the construction of the relevant section; and (iii) he has to decide, whether on the primary facts he has found, and the assessments which he has made, the relevant threshold has been crossed; see eg per Lord Neuberger at paragraphs 49 to 50.

B. Approach to Interpretation

B1. Ordinary Meaning

6.8 The term 'persecution', is defined by the *Oxford English Dictionary* as 'The action of persecuting or pursuing with enmity and malignity; especially the infliction of death, torture, or penalties for adherence to a religious belief or an opinion as such, with a view to the repression or extirpation of it'. The verb 'persecute' is given three relevant meanings including 'To pursue, chase, hunt, drive (with missiles, or with attempts to catch, kill, or injure', 'to pursue with malignancy or enmity and injurious action; esp to oppress with pains and penalties for the holding of a belief held to be injurious or heretical' and 'to harass, trouble, vex, worry; to importune'.[2]

---

[2] *Oxford English Dictionary*, vol XI (2nd edn, Clarendon, 1989) 591–92.

It is also attributed a Latin origin in the word '*persequi*', the accepted meaning of which has been 'to follow with hostile intent'.[3]

This is a useful starting point to interpretation, introducing themes first of hostility or ill-treatment, and second, of differential treatment for a particular reason. But the language is in practice permissive of a wide span of possible interpretations and a narrowly text-based interpretation is inadequate without substantial reference to other factors cited in article 31(1) of the Vienna Convention on the Law of Treaties 1969 (VCLT69), namely context, object and purpose. 6.9

B2. Historical Context

Some assistance may be provided by a short history of the term 'persecution' as employed in relevant contexts, and of the means by which it came to form part of article 1A(2) CSR51. The term had no significant use in the interwar regimes. However, by the time CSR51 was drafted, it had a place in ordinary language and in the particular language used contemporaneously in relation to human rights. In the course of the Second World War the term 'persecution' came to denote the targeted infliction upon particular persons or groups of persons of serious violations of human rights, as for instance in the 1942 United Nations Declaration on the Persecution of the Jews.[4] Use of the term in this sense is significant as part of the background to CSR51 and as part of the prehistory to development after the Second World War of a separate concept of persecutions in international criminal law.[5] 6.10

By the time of the December 1946 Constitution of the International Refugee Organisation (IRO), the concept of persecution as part of a refugee definition had additional currency. Following the precedent of earlier instruments, the IRO Constitution identified persons as refugees by specific categories, such as 'victims of the Nazi or fascist regimes or of the quisling or similar regimes which assisted them against the United Nations', and persons considered to be refugees 'before the outbreak of the second world war, for reasons of race, religion, nationality, or political opinion'.[6] The IRO Constitution introduced a wider supplementary test for entitlement which in hindsight represents a watershed ('the term "refugee" also 6.11

---

[3] *Oxford English Dictionary* (n 2 above) 591; C Mahler and A Zimmermann, 'Article 1A para 1 1951 Convention' in A Zimmerman (ed), *The 1951 Convention Relating to the Status of Refugees and its 1967 Protocol: A Commentary* (OUP, 2011) §220.

[4] For instance see 'Persecution of the Jews: Allies' Declaration', HL Deb 17 December 1942, vol 125, cols 607–12.

[5] eg, in Case IT-95-14-A *Prosecutor v Timomir Blaskic* (29 July 2004) the Appeals Chamber of the International Criminal Tribunal for the Former Yugoslavia defined persecutions as including crimes against humanity in the form of acts or omissions of a type which 'discriminates in fact and which denies or infringes upon a fundamental right laid down in international customary or treaty law (the *actus reus*); and ... was carried out deliberately with the intention to discriminate on one of the listed grounds, specifically race, religion or politics (the *mens rea*)'.

[6] Constitution of the International Refugee Organisation 1946, Annexe 1, part 1, section A, paras 1–2 and 4.

applies to persons who, having resided in Germany or Austria, and being of Jewish origin or foreigners or stateless persons, were victims of Nazi persecution and were detained in, or were obliged to flee from, and were subsequently returned to, one of those countries as a result of enemy action, or of war circumstances, and have not yet been firmly resettled therein').[7] Further, the IRO Constitution cited 'persecution, or fear, based on reasonable grounds of persecution because of race, religion, nationality or political opinions, provided these opinions are not in conflict with the principles of the United Nations, as laid down in the Preamble of the Charter of the United Nations' as a valid reason for a refugee objecting to repatriation.[8]

6.12 Contemporaneously, the term 'persecution' was employed frequently by the United Nations Relief and Rehabilitation Administration and by the military authorities in occupied Europe: as Grahl-Madsen noted, the term in this period could be said to have been 'in the air'.[9] And in 1948, article 14 of the Universal Declaration of Human Rights (UDHR48) enjoined that 'Everyone has the right to seek and to enjoy in other countries asylum from persecution', not defining the latter term.

6.13 The immediate route by which the term 'persecution' came to be incorporated into what is now article 1A(2) CSR51 was by a series of decisions taken by the Ad Hoc Committee on Statelessness and Related Problems set up under Resolution 248 (IX) of the United Nations Economic and Social Council of 8 August 1949.[10] A memorandum of the UN Secretary-General to the Ad Hoc Committee of 3 January 1950 invited the former to consider how entitlement to protection as a refugee could be delineated, referring as alternative potential approaches first to the historical practice of identification through membership in a particular category of persons without national protection, and second to the preferred if relatively unprecedented option of a general definition delineating entitlement to international refugee status without regard to more specific requirements such as a particular place of origin. The Committee opted for the second route. It further took the decision not to include in the definition all persons lacking the protection of their State of origin or of any State, but rather to protect as refugees only a subclass of that group it perceived as warranting more immediate protection, employing at what became article 1A(2) CSR51 the term 'persecution', without further definition, as a part of the rubric for qualification.[11] At the Conference of Plenipotentiaries, Mr Robinson of Israel, who had been a member of the working group appointed by the Ad Hoc Committee to advance

---

[7] Ibid, section A, para 3.

[8] Ibid.

[9] A Grahl-Madsen, *The Status of Refugees in International Law*, vol I (AW Sijthoff, 1966) 189, §80.

[10] UN Ad Hoc Committee on Refugees and Stateless Persons, *Ad Hoc Committee on Statelessness and Related Problems, Elimination of Statelessness—Memorandum Prepared by the Secretary-General*, 17 January 1950, E/AC.32/4, available at: www.refworld.org/docid/3ae68c250.html.

[11] T Einarson, 'Drafting History of the 1951 Convention and the 1967 Protocol' in A Zimmermann (ed), *The 1951 Convention Relating to the Status of Refugees and its 1967 Protocol: A Commentary* (OUP, 2011) 54–57, §33–38.

the drafting of the refugee definition, noted that: 'Of the three factors governing the definition of the term "refugee", practically no attention had been paid to the substantive requirements for qualification as a refugee'.[12]

Accordingly, whilst as Steinbock later noted, 'the Convention's inclusion of persecution for reasons of race, religion, and nationality speaks most directly to [the Nazi persecutions of 1933–45]',[13] and to kindred inflictions of harm by Fascists and Falangists, the exact scope of the protective definition appears not to have been consciously developed at the time of negotiation. The early commentators add little. Robinson (Nehemiah, brother of the Israeli representative at the Conference, Jacob Robinson)[14] stated in the first instance that 'Par A(2) contains a number of terms requiring elucidation', somewhat mysteriously failing to address the definition of 'persecution' as one of these.[15] Weis, who had been Legal Adviser to the IRO and then became Legal Adviser to the newly established Office of the United Nations High Commissioner for Refugees (UNHCR), stated in 1960 that 'the term "persecution" has nowhere been defined and this was probably deliberate'.[16] A few years later Grahl-Madsen agreed, noting that 6.14

> as pointed out by [Weis], it seems as if the drafters have wanted to introduce a flexible concept which might be applied to circumstances as they might arise; or in other words, that they capitulated before the inventiveness of humanity to think up new ways of persecuting fellow men.[17]

B3. International Human Rights Law and the Principle of Non-Discrimination as a Primary Interpretive Tool

The first paragraph of the Preamble to CSR51 points to the 1945 United Nations Charter and to UDHR48 as affirming that: 6.15

> THE HIGH CONTRACTING PARTIES
>
> Considering that the Charter of the United Nations and the Universal Declaration of Human Rights approved on 10 December 1948 by the General Assembly have affirmed the principle that human beings shall enjoy fundamental rights and freedoms without discrimination.

---

[12] UN Conference of Plenipotentiaries on the Status of Refugees and Stateless Persons, *Summary Record of the Twenty-second Meeting*, 26 November 1951, A/CONF.2/SR.22, available at: www.unhcr.org/refworld/docid/3ae68cde10.html.

[13] D Steinbock, 'The Refugee Definition as Law: Issues of Interpretation' in F Nicholson and P Twomey (eds), *Refugee Rights and Realities: Evolving International Concepts and Regimes* (CUP, 1999) 18, citing J Garvey, 'Towards a Reformulation of International Refugee Law' (1985) 26 *Harvard Journal of International Law* 483.

[14] Einarson (n 11 above) 54, §32.

[15] N Robinson, *Convention relating to the Status of Refugees, its History, Contents, and Interpretation* (Institute of Jewish Affairs, 1953) 45–54.

[16] P Weis, 'The Concept of Refugee in International Law' (1961) (UN Doc HCR/INF/49) 22.

[17] Grahl-Madsen (n 9 above) 193, §82.

6.16 Whilst the delineation of fundamental human rights in binding international instruments was relatively slow to follow, the Preamble provides strong evidence for international human rights law (IHRL) and non-discrimination as basic sources from which the content of 'persecution' under article 1A(2) CSR51 should be delineated. Jacques Vernant, in his 1953 survey of refugee problems, requested by the then United Nations High Commissioner for Refugees, Gerrit Jan van Heuven Goedhart, noted that:

> If no exact definition can be found for the term persecution as used in Article 14 [UDHR48] and consequently for the term refugee, it seems desirable that there should be some kind of international arbiter as free as possible of the shackles of national pressures and ideological bias.[18]

Vernant pointed to the failure so far to finalise an International Covenant on Human Rights, ultimately made good later by the International Covenant on Civil and Political Rights 1966 (ICCPR66) and the International Covenant on Economic, Social and Cultural Rights 1966 (ICESCR66), so as to widen the enforceability of the rights called for by UDHR48, the weakness of which, in the absence of a binding Covenant he recognised, describing UDHR48 as 'nothing more than an international code of honour couched in very general terms [which] lays a purely moral obligation upon States'.[19] Notwithstanding this, Vernant identified UDHR48 as a general starting point for definition of 'persecution':

> Some lack of precision, therefore, is apparently inevitable for the time being in the definition of a refugee as anyone who can prove that his person or property is either threatened, or as good as threatened, with severe measures and sanctions of an arbitrary nature, incompatible with the principles set forth in [UDHR48].[20]

His approach to the definition of persecution was relatively general, consistently with the generality of the standards to which persecution could then be related. However, it shows an appreciation of the significance of IHRL to questions of entitlement under CSR51 and anticipates the further interpretative developments enabled some years later by ICCPR66 and ICESCR66.

6.17 Fortunately for those who perceived this need, the enactment and development over time of the principles advanced in UDHR48 by ICCPR66 and ICESCR66 had now begun to provide a basis on which to advance the work of definition which had not been available to Vernant and was untested when Grahl-Madsen wrote his compendious work.

6.18 Following the coming into force in 1976 of ICCPR66 and ICESCR66, the interpretation of CSR51 was able to look to the development of a fuller body of IHRL extending the principles earlier advanced by UDHR48. Goodwin-Gill in 1983 identified basic human rights as providing a framework for the definition

---

[18] J Vernant, *The Refugee in the Post-War World* (George Allen & Unwin, 1953) 8.

[19] Ibid, 8.

[20] Ibid, 7–8.

of persecution, focusing particularly upon those rights identified by the International Court of Justice (ICJ) in the *Barcelona Traction* case as obligations *erga omnes* ('against all'):

> Such obligations derive, for example, in contemporary international law, from the outlawing of acts of aggression, and of genocide, as also from the principles and rules concerning the basic rights of the human person, including protection from slavery and racial discrimination. Some of the corresponding rights of protection have entered into the body of general international law ... others are conferred by international instruments of a universal or quasi-universal character.[21]

Goodwin-Gill focused this analysis by reference to those rights identified as non-derogable in ICCPR66.[22]

In 1991 the effort to achieve a framework definition based primarily upon the developing body of IHRL was expanded by Hathaway. He concluded that: **6.19**

> A well-founded fear of persecution exists when one reasonably anticipates ... a form of serious harm which the government cannot or will not prevent, including either specific hostile acts or ... an accumulation of adverse circumstances such as discrimination existing in an atmosphere of insecurity and fear.[23]

Hathaway's approach as expressed at that time (and maintained subsequently, with development over time) followed from identification of basic rights which states 'are bound to respect as a minimum condition of legitimacy', those rights being expressed in UDHR48, ICCPR66 and ICESCR66,[24] so that for Hathaway, 'In sum, persecution is most appropriately defined as the sustained or systemic failure of state protection in relation to one of the core entitlements which has been recognized by the international community'.[25] Despite the use of the term 'sustained or systemic', it is clear from Hathaway's unreserved inclusion of arbitrary deprivation of life *contra* article 6 ICCPR66 and torture or cruel, inhuman, or degrading treatment *contra* article 7 ICCPR66, that the ambit of protection for Hathaway also extended to other serious violations which might be understood as (in a literal sense) neither sustained nor systemic: such as, for example, the risk of arbitrary execution for a relevant reason.[26] Hathaway delineated four categories of rights starting with those most firmly protected by the international community, including (i) first, UDHR48 provisions translated into ICCPR66

---

[21] *Barcelona Traction (Belgium v Spain) (Second Phase)* [1970] ICJ Rep 3 [33].

[22] G Goodwin-Gill, *The Refugee in International Law* (Clarendon Press, 1983) 38–46.

[23] J Hathaway, *The Law of Refugee Status* (Butterworths Canada, 1991) 105, referring to, inter alia, G Goodwin-Gill, 'Entry and Exclusion of Refugees: The Obligations of States and the Protection Function of the Office of the UNHCR' (1980) *Michigan Yearbook of International Legal Studies* 291; S Young, 'Who is a Refugee? A Theory of Persecution' (1982) 5 *In Defence of the Alien* 38; D Anker and M Posner, 'The Forty Years' Crisis: A Legislative History of the Refugee Act of 1980' (1981) 82 *San Diego Law Review* 1, 67.

[24] Hathaway (n 23 above) 106–08.

[25] Ibid, 112.

[26] Ibid, 109.

and made non-derogable even in times of pressing national emergency, breach of which will constitute persecution in any circumstances; (ii) second, ICCPR66 rights which are derogable during an officially recognised and sufficiently serious public emergency, such as, *inter alia*, the right to be free from arbitrary arrest and detention and the right of freedom to expression, where the State cannot demonstrate any valid justification for temporary curtailment, violation of which will generally constitute persecution; (iii) third, category ICESCR66 rights where discriminatory discrimination or extreme deprivation amounts to persecution; and finally (iv) fourth, some UDHR48 rights not codified in ICCPR66 or ICESCR66, violation of which would not ordinarily constitute persecution.[27]

6.20 The interpretation of article 1A(2) CSR51 based upon IHRL, anticipated by Vernant and delineated later, in the light of an increasingly developed IHRL, by Goodwin-Gill and Hathaway, is now effectively established. The elucidation of that approach by Hathaway has been endorsed by the Supreme Court of Canada,[28] in England and Wales by the House of Lords,[29] and by the New Zealand Refugee Status Appeals Authority.[30] It appears now to be broadly accepted that IHRL represents the primary medium for interpretation of the content of persecution. Hathaway wrote that 'the dominant view … is that refugee law ought to concern itself with actions which deny human dignity in any key way', linking this to the delineation of rights in IHRL.[31] Goodwin-Gill has written more recently that 'Persecution results where the measures in question harm [fundamental, protected interests] and the integrity and inherent dignity of the human being to a degree considered unacceptable under prevailing international standards', identifying the need for analysis in terms of 'reasons, interests, and measures' supported by analogous approaches in IHRL.[32] And Hathaway, writing with Foster, has in the second edition of his text again advocated an IHRL-based approach, expressed somewhat differently but not inconsistently with his earlier writings: 'Drawing on these express limitations and authorized forms of flexibility [within IHRL], international human rights law positions refugee decision-makers to take a non-absolutist yet principled approach to the identification of serious harm'.[33]

6.21 In *Appellant S395/2002 v MIMA* (2003) 216 CLR 473, McHugh and Kirby JJ said:

> 40. Persecution covers many forms of harm ranging from physical harm to the loss of intangibles, from death and torture to state sponsored or condoned discrimination in social life and employment. Whatever form the harm takes, it will constitute persecution

---

[27] Ibid, 108–12.

[28] *Canada (Attorney General) v Ward* [1993] 2 SCR 689.

[29] *Horvath v SSHD* [2000] UKHL 37, [2001] 1 AC 489, 495 (Lord Hope of Craighead); *Sepet v SSHD* [2003] UKHL 15, [2003] 1 WLR 856, 862 [7] (Lord Bingham); and *R (Ullah) v Special Adjudicator* [2004] UKHL 26, [2004] 2 AC 323 [32] (Lord Steyn).

[30] Refugee Status Appeals Authority (RSAA), *Refugee Appeal No 71427/99* [2000] NZAR 545.

[31] Hathaway (n 23 above) 108.

[32] G Goodwin-Gill and J McAdam, *The Refugee in International Law* (3rd edn, OUP, 2007) 131–32.

[33] J Hathaway and M Foster, *The Law of Refugee Status* (2nd edn, CUP, 2014) 205.

only if, by reason of its intensity or duration, the person persecuted cannot reasonably be expected to tolerate it.

That observation was adopted by Lord Hope in *HJ (Iran) and HT (Cameroon) v SSHD* [2010] UKSC 31, [2011] 1 AC 596. Having quoted it, and the observations of Lord Bingham in *Sepet* (cited above), he went on: 6.22

12. The Convention does not define 'persecution'. But it has been recognised that it is a strong word: *Sepet and Bulbul v SSHD* [2003] UKHL 15, [2003] 1 WLR 856, para 7, per Lord Bingham … Article 9(1)(a) of the EC Council Directive 2004/83/EC on minimum standards for the qualification and status of third country nationals or stateless persons as refugees ('the Qualification Directive') states that acts of persecution must '(a) be sufficiently serious by their nature or repetition as to constitute a severe violation of basic human rights … or (b) be an accumulation of various measures, including violations of human rights which is sufficiently severe as to affect an individual in a similar manner as mentioned in (a)'.

13. To constitute persecution for the purposes of the Convention the harm must be state sponsored or state condoned. Family or social disapproval in which the state has no part lies outside its protection. As Professor JC Hathaway in *The Law of Refugee Status* (1991), p 112 has explained, 'persecution is most appropriately defined as the sustained or systemic failure of state protection in relation to one of the core entitlements which has been recognised by the international community'. The Convention provides surrogate protection, which is activated only upon the failure of state protection. The failure of state protection is central to the whole system: *Horvath v SSHD* [2001] 1 AC 489, 495. The question is whether the home state is unable or unwilling to discharge its duty to establish and operate a system for the protection against persecution of its own nationals.

14. The reference in the preamble to the Universal Declaration of Human Rights of 1948 shows that counteracting discrimination was a fundamental purpose of the Convention. Article 2 states:

> 'Everyone is entitled to all the rights and freedoms set forth in this Declaration, without distinction of any kind, such as race, colour, sex, language, religion, political or other opinion, national or social origin, property, birth or other status'.

15. The guarantees in the Universal Declaration are fundamental to a proper understanding of the Convention. But the Convention itself has, as the references in para 12 show, a more limited purpose. It is not enough that members of a particular social group are being discriminated against. The contracting states did not undertake to protect them against discrimination judged according to the standards in their own countries. Persecution apart, the Convention was not directed to reforming the level of rights prevailing in the country of origin. Its purpose is to provide the protection that is not available in the country of nationality where there is a well-founded fear of persecution, not to guarantee to asylum-seekers when they are returned all the freedoms that are available in the country where they seek refuge. It does not guarantee universal human rights. So the conditions that prevail in the country in which asylum is sought have no part to play, as matter of legal obligation binding on all states parties to the Convention, in deciding whether the applicant is entitled to seek asylum in that country: *Januzi v SSHD* [2006]

UKHL 5, [2006] 2 AC 426, paras 16, 46. As Laws LJ said in *Amare v SSHD* [2005] EWCA Civ 1600, [2006] Imm AR 217 para 31:

> 'The Convention is not there to safeguard or protect potentially affected persons from having to live in regimes where pluralist liberal values are less respected, even much less respected, than they are here. It is there to secure international protection to the extent agreed by the contracting states'.

6.23 The development of IHRL since ICCPR66 and ICESCR66, and the body of decision-making which has developed around them, have increasingly enabled the elaboration through IHRL of key standards relevant to the modern interpretation of article 1A(2) CSR51. In tandem with these instruments there has developed a body of others expressing IHRL standards in particular contexts, such as: the International Convention on the Elimination of All Forms of Racial Discrimination 1966 (ICERD66); the Convention on the Elimination of All Forms of Discrimination against Women 1979 (CEDAW79); the Convention against Torture and other Cruel, Inhuman or Degrading Treatment or Punishment 1984 (CAT84); the Convention on the Rights of the Child 1989 (CRC89); and more recent extensions such as: the Convention on the Protection of the Rights of All Migrant Workers and Members of Their Families 1990; the Convention on the Rights of Persons with Disabilities 2006 (CRPD06); and the Convention for the Protection of All Persons from Enforced Disappearance 2006 (CPED06).

6.24 The adoption of an approach to the interpretation of the term 'persecution' based upon IHRL is subject to at least two caveats. First, such an approach should be treated as a guide, not a rigid calculus. Second, even treating IHRL as a guide, it will remain necessary to keep an open mind—as Edwards has said, 'it would be unwise to limit its application to serious human rights abuses. It is possible that all forms of persecution have not yet been identified or codified in international human rights law'.[34]

B4. Relevance of Other International Instruments as *Lex Specialis*

6.25 If IHRL and the principle of non-discrimination (which is a part of customary international law, as well as being incorporated into human rights treaties) provide the primary source of interpretive content for 'persecution' in article 1A(2), what is the position as regards standards established elsewhere in international law? The question is highly relevant in this context because substantial parts of the international law of nationality (including that relating to the status of stateless persons and reduction of statelessness) do not fall directly within IHRL.[35]

---

[34] A Edwards, 'Age and Gender Dimensions in International Refugee Law' in E Feller, V Türk and F Nicholson (eds), *Refugee Protection in International Law* (CUP, 2003) 50.

[35] The definition of international human rights law (IHRL) applied here is that of J Crawford, *Brownlie's Principles of Public International Law* (8th edn, OUP, 2012) 638–44, which includes

Nor do other provisions which may be relevant in the context of decisions concerned with nationality or of the key incidents thereto, such as the prohibition in international humanitarian law (the law related to conduct in armed conflict) on transfer of civilians from occupied territories. Article 49 of the Convention (IV) relative to the Protection of Civilian Persons in Time of War, Geneva, 12 August 1949 (the Fourth Geneva Convention) for instance provides, *inter alia*, that, 'Individual or mass forcible transfers, as well as deportations of protected persons from occupied territory to the territory of the Occupying Power or to that of any other country, occupied or not, are prohibited, regardless of their motive' and also that, 'The Occupying Power shall not deport or transfer parts of its own civilian population into the territory it occupies'.

As Meindersma and others have shown convincingly, these provisions of international humanitarian law, together with core protections under IHRL, represent a fundamental obstacle to forced transfers or exchanges of the sort entered into after each World War.[36] Would the fact of breach of article 49 of the Fourth Geneva Convention be relevant to whether an individual facing such transfer feared 'persecution'? In principle a breach might be relevant, albeit indirectly through influence upon the understanding of specific IHRL norms. **6.26**

Looking to recent developments in international law, including important decisions of the ICJ, it can now be seen that the organic development of IHRL has involved express acknowledgment of the potential relevance of international law regimes as *lex specialis*, in the specific sense of providing norms which, whilst separate from IHRL, may inform assessment of open-ended IHRL standards. The term *lex specialis*, which is employed in many contexts in international law, in the present context identifies this relationship by which other legal norms may have indirect effect upon the content ascribed to open-ended IHRL norms. In 2006 the Report of the Study Group of the International Law Commission (ILC) on Fragmentation of International Public Law, chaired by Martii Koskenniemi, sought to delineate the core application of the term: **6.27**

> The maxim *lex specialis derogat legi generali* is a generally accepted technique of interpretation and conflict resolution in international law. It suggests that whenever two or more norms deal with the same subject matter, priority should be given to the norm that is more specific. The principle may be applicable in several contexts: between provisions

(i) multilateral conventions which 'fall into four general categories: first, the two comprehensive International Covenants adopted in 1966; secondly, regional conventions; thirdly, conventions dealing with specific wrongs: for example, genocide, racial discrimination, torture, and disappearances; and fourthly, conventions related to the protection of particular categories of people: for example, refugees, women, children, migrant workers, and people with disabilities', and (ii) customary international law (including the prohibition of genocide or racial discrimination).

[36] C Meindersma, 'Population Exchanges: International Law and State Practice—Part 1' (1997) 9(3) *International Journal of Refugee Law* 335; C Meindersma, 'Population Exchanges: International Law and State Practice—Part 2' (1997) 9(4) *International Journal of Refugee Law* 613.

within a single treaty, between provisions within two or more treaties, between a treaty and a non-treaty standard, as well as between two non-treaty standards.[37]

6.28 In the Advisory Opinion of the ICJ in the *Nuclear Weapons* case of 8 July 1996 the majority found that international humanitarian law did not have to be looked to independently where IHRL opened the way to its relevance as *lex specialis*:

> 25. The test of what is an arbitrary deprivation of life, however, then falls to be determined by the applicable *lex specialis*, namely, the law applicable in armed conflict which is designed to regulate the conduct of hostilities. Thus whether a particular loss of life, through the use of a certain weapon in warfare, is to be considered an arbitrary deprivation of life contrary to Article 6 of the Covenant can only be decided by reference to the law applicable in armed conflict and not deduced from the terms of the Covenant itself.[38]

6.29 In its *Construction of a Wall in the Occupied Palestinian Territory* decisions, of July 2004, the same Court cited its earlier Advisory Opinion in the *Nuclear Weapons* case and developed the theme of complementarity referring to international humanitarian law as a *lex specialis* in the sense of a *lex* potentially applicable in parallel with IHRL, rather than one indirectly relevant as informing IHRL norms: but this reflects the particular facts of the Palestinian situation by which international humanitarian law norms are directly applicable as well as IHRL standards.

6.30 The Study Group of the ILC on Fragmentation of International Public Law identified international humanitarian law as having a legitimate role as a *lex specialis* in relation to international standards concerning peacetime norms on the same subjects, referring to the *Nuclear Weapons* case:

> 103. It is often stated that the laws of war are *lex specialis* in relation to rules laying out the peace-time norms relating to the same subjects. In the *Legality of the Threat or Use of Nuclear Weapons* case, the ICJ discussed the relationship between the International Covenant on Civil and Political Rights and the laws applicable in armed conflict. Article 6 (1) of the Covenant established the right not arbitrarily to be deprived of one's life. This right, the Court pointed out, applies also in hostilities. However:
>
>> The test of what is an arbitrary deprivation of life, however, then falls to be determined by the applicable *lex specialis*, namely, the law applicable in armed conflict which is designed to regulate the conduct of hostilities.
>
> 104. To regard this as a situation of *lex specialis* draws attention to an important aspect of the operation of the principle. Even as it works so as to justify recourse to an exception, what is being set aside does not vanish altogether. The Court was careful to point out that human rights law continued to apply within armed conflict. The exception—humanitarian law—only affected one (albeit important) aspect of it, namely the relative assessment of 'arbitrariness'. Humanitarian law as *lex specialis* did not suggest that human

---

[37] ILC, Report of the Study Group, 'Fragmentation of international law: difficulties arising from the diversification and expansion of international law', Fifty-eighth Session (13 April 2006) (UN Doc A/CN.4/L.682) [14(5)].

[38] *Legality of the Threat or Use of* Nuclear Weapons (Advisory Opinion) of 8 July 1996, [1996] ICJ Reports 226, 240, [25].

> rights were abolished in war. It did not function in a formal or absolute way but as an aspect of the pragmatics of the Court's reasoning.[39]

The interrelationship of international humanitarian law and IHRL, with IHRL the source of direct interpretive assistance in the present context, illustrates the wider relationship between directly applicable norms- IHRL and non-discrimination- and other norms potentially capable of indirect influence upon the interpretation of 'persecution' in article 1A(2) CSR51. In practice, where a question as to the limits of 'persecution' arises, reference is to a limited range of norms identified in the Preamble to CSR51. But those norms are often open-textured, and the delineation of 'persecution' is likely to depend first upon whether IHRL applies and with what effect, and second and indirectly, whether IHRL is or is not informed by the content of a *lex specialis*. This is in practice not conceptually unique or even particularly complex: it is a process not very different from the way in which the content of open-ended standards in more general instruments such as ICCPR66 may in appropriate circumstances be informed by more detailed and specific IHRL norms in, for instance, ICERD66. **6.31**

C. Standards Informing Content of 'Persecution'

A survey of relevant standards is below, considering first customary international law and then international human rights law. **6.32**

C1. Non-Discrimination in Customary International Law

As already seen, by the time the second edition of his book was published in 1979, Weis had changed the view he had taken in 1956 and held that discriminatory deprivation of nationality represented a breach of customary international law: **6.33**

> Considering that the principle of non-discrimination may now be regarded as a rule of international law or as a general principle of law, prohibition of discriminatory denationalisation may be regarded as a rule of present-day international law. This certainly applies to discrimination on the ground of race which may be considered as contravening a peremptory norm of international law but also, in the present writer's view, to discrimination on the other grounds mentioned in the Charter of the United Nations, *ie* sex and religion.[40]

In 1988 Plender concluded that developments in IHRL, especially the coming into force of ICCPR66, had had a 'profound effect' on the development of international **6.34**

[39] ILC, Report of the Study Group, 'Fragmentation of international law' (n 37 above) [103]–[04].
[40] P Weis, *Nationality and Statelessness* (2nd edn, Brill, 1979) 125.

law, so that discriminatory deprivation of nationality was inconsistent with international law:

> The evidence suggests that in current international law a State cannot always release itself of its obligation to admit certain of its own nationals to its territory by promulgating a decree which deprives such persons of their nationality. A decree which discriminates on racial grounds, or is in any other sense 'arbitrary', need not be recognized by other States as effective to derive of their nationality those to whom it purports to apply.[41]

6.35 In 2012 Crawford observed in Brownlie's *Principles of Public International Law* that:

> Existing practice and jurisprudence do not support a general rule that deprivation of nationality is unlawful. On the other hand, Article 15(2) [UDHR48] stipulates that persons may not be 'arbitrarily deprived' of their nationality, and although this has no equivalent in [ICCPR66] there is some basis for holding it to be a rule of customary international law.[42]

He refers to the *Partial Award: Civilians Claims—Eritrea's Claims 15, 16, 23 and 27–32* of the Eritrea–Ethiopia Claims Commission, which found that in certain circumstances denationalisation by Ethiopia of persons of Eritrean national background had been contrary to international law.[43]

6.36 The views of Weis, Plender and Crawford already quoted are consistent with that of Hofmann in the *Max Planck Encyclopaedia of Public International Law*, last updated in 2013:

> 17. The above analysis shows that it is difficult to argue that there is a universal customary law right to a nationality. This implies that it is equally difficult to argue that there exists a right not to be arbitrarily deprived of one's nationality under current universal customary international law. Therefore, it seems as if the only limit imposed by customary international law on States' powers to withdraw nationality is the one banning measures of denaturalization based solely on racial or religious reasons since such acts would infringe the customary law rule on non-discrimination on grounds of race and religion.[44]

The precise extent of the non-discrimination rule, expressed in the *Barcelona Traction* decision by reference to race, by Weis as broader but including as examples sex and religion, and by Hofmann by reference to race and religion, may be regarded as not fully settled. This question however may well be academic in the present context given that, as will be seen below, international human rights conventions now bar discrimination on a substantial variety of relevant bases.

---

[41] R Plender, *International Migration Law* (2nd edn, Martinus Nijhoff, 1988) 149.

[42] Crawford (n 35 above) 522. In the case of a child ICCPR66 does provide nationality right by article 24(3) ICCPR66. In a footnote Crawford observes that, 'A discriminatory denationalization would infringe Art 26 [ICCPR66]'.

[43] *Eritrea Ethiopia Claims Commission, Partial Award: Civilians Claims—Eritrea's Claims 15, 16, 23 & 27–32*, Permanent Court of Arbitration, The Hague, 17 December 2004, esp §72, §75, available at: www.pca-cpa.org/ER%20Partial%20Award%20Dec%20048515.pdf?fil_id=148.

[44] R Hofmann, 'Denaturalization and Forced Exile' in *Max Planck Encyclopedia of Public International Law* (online edn, OUP, 2015); O Dörr, 'Nationality' in Max Planck Encyclopedia of Public International Law (online edn, OUP, 2015) [17].

There has in recent years been a considerable focus by United Nations human rights organs upon arbitrary denationalisation and other nationality-related acts or omissions of States. In December 2009 the UN Human Rights Council in a report prepared on behalf of the United Nations Secretary-General, *Human rights and arbitrary deprivation of nationality: Report of the Secretary-General* said that: **6.37**

> 23. While the question of arbitrary deprivation of nationality does not comprise the loss of nationality voluntarily requested by the individual, it covers all other forms of loss of nationality, including those that arbitrarily preclude a person from obtaining or retaining a nationality, particularly on discriminatory grounds, as well as those that automatically deprive a person of a nationality by operation of the law, and those acts taken by administrative authorities that result in a person being arbitrarily deprived of a nationality.
>
> 24. Concerning the notion of arbitrary deprivation, it should be recalled that the Human Rights Committee has shed light on the meaning of the concept of 'arbitrary' in the context of the International Covenant on Civil and Political Rights. In its general comment No16, the Committee stated that the expression 'arbitrary interference' was relevant to the protection of the right provided for in article 17. In the Committee's view, the expression 'arbitrary interference' could also extend to interference provided for under the law. The introduction of the concept of arbitrariness was intended to guarantee that even interference provided for by law should be in accordance with the provisions, aims and objectives of the Covenant and should, in any event, be reasonable in the particular circumstances. In its general comment No 27, the Committee further indicated that the reference to the concept of arbitrariness in this context was intended to emphasize that it applied to all State action, legislative, administrative and judicial, and guaranteed that even interference provided for by law should be in accordance with the provisions, aims and objectives of the Covenant and should, in any event, be reasonable in the particular circumstances.
>
> 25. Thus, while international law allows for the deprivation of nationality in certain circumstances, it must be in conformity with domestic law and comply with specific procedural and substantive standards, in particular the principle of proportionality. Measures leading to the deprivation of nationality must serve a legitimate purpose that is consistent with international law and, in particular, the objectives of international human rights law. Such measures must be the least intrusive instrument of those that might achieve the desired result, and they must be proportional to the interest to be protected. In this respect, the notion of arbitrariness applies to all State action, legislative, administrative and judicial. The notion of arbitrariness could be interpreted to include not only acts that are against the law but, more broadly, elements of inappropriateness, injustice and lack of predictability also.
>
> 26. The prohibition of arbitrary deprivation of nationality, which aims at protecting the right to retain a nationality, is implicit in provisions of human rights treaties that proscribe specific forms of discrimination.
>
> …
>
> 27. In the report of the Secretary-General on arbitrary deprivation of nationality (A/HRC/10/34), the United Nations High Commissioner for Refugees (UNHCR)

indicated that deprivation of nationality resulting in statelessness would generally be arbitrary unless it served a legitimate purpose and complied with the principle of proportionality.[45]

6.38 In a later report, *Human rights and arbitrary deprivation of nationality: Report of the Secretary-General*, it was reiterated that loss or deprivation of nationality 'must meet certain conditions in order to comply with international law, in particular the prohibition of arbitrary deprivation of nationality', and the avoidance of statelessness was identified as a factor tending to indicate arbitrariness:

> 4. Any interference with the enjoyment of nationality has a significant impact on the enjoyment of rights. Therefore, loss or deprivation of nationality must meet certain conditions in order to comply with international law, in particular the prohibition of arbitrary deprivation of nationality. These conditions include serving a legitimate purpose, being the least intrusive instrument to achieve the desired result and being proportional to the interest to be protected. Where loss or deprivation of nationality leads to statelessness, the impact on the individual is particularly severe. International law therefore strictly limits the circumstances in which loss or deprivation of nationality leading to statelessness can be recognized as serving a legitimate purpose.[46]

6.39 The treatment of arbitrary deprivation of nationality as impinging on international law is repeated in the resolutions of the United Nations Human Rights Council concerning human rights, arbitrary deprivation of nationality and related subjects. Its Resolution of 23 June 2014, *Human rights and arbitrary deprivation of nationality*, states, *inter alia*, that:

> *Guided also* by article 15 of the Universal Declaration of Human Rights, according to which everyone has the right to a nationality and no one shall be arbitrarily deprived of his or her nationality,
>
> *Reaffirming* Human Rights Council resolutions 7/10 of 27 March 2008, 10/13 of 26 March 2009, 13/2 of 24 March 2010, 20/4 of 5 July 2012 and 20/5 of 16 July 2012, as well as all previous resolutions adopted by the Commission on Human Rights, on the issue of human rights and the arbitrary deprivation of nationality,
>
> *Reaffirming also* Human Rights Council resolution 19/9 of 22 March 2012, in which the Council took into consideration the fact that persons without birth registration may be vulnerable to statelessness and associated lack of protection,
>
> [the Council]
>
> *Reaffirms* that the right to a nationality of every human person is a fundamental human right enshrined in, *inter alia*, the Universal Declaration of Human Rights;

---

45 UN Human Rights Council, *Human rights and arbitrary deprivation of nationality: Report of the Secretary-General*, 14 December 2009 (UN Doc A/HRC/13/34), available at: www.refworld.org/docid/4b83a9cb2.html.

46 UN Human Rights Council, *Human rights and arbitrary deprivation of nationality: Report of the Secretary-General*, 19 December 2013 (UN Doc A/HRC/25/28) para 4, available at: www.refworld.org/docid/52f8d19a4.html.

Reiterates that arbitrary deprivation of nationality, especially on discriminatory grounds such as race, colour, sex, language, religion, political or other opinion, national or social origin, property, birth or other status is a violation of human rights and fundamental freedoms;

Also reiterates that the prevention and reduction of statelessness are primarily the responsibility of States, in appropriate cooperation with the international community;

Calls upon all States to refrain from taking discriminatory measures and from enacting or maintaining legislation that would arbitrarily deprive persons of their nationality on grounds of race, colour, sex, language, religion, political or other opinion, national or social origin, property, birth or other status, especially if such measures and legislation render a person stateless;

Urges all States to adopt and implement nationality legislation with a view to avoiding statelessness, consistent with the principles of international law, in particular by preventing arbitrary deprivation of nationality and statelessness as a result of State succession;

Notes that the full enjoyment of all human rights and fundamental freedoms of an individual might be impeded as a result of arbitrary deprivation of nationality, and that such individuals are placed in a situation of increased vulnerability to human rights violations.[47]

There is accordingly considerable evidence in the views of commentators and elsewhere that arbitrary deprivation of nationality based on relevant discrimination represents a breach of customary international law. This provides an important point of engagement between deprivation of nationality and the CSR51 regime, to which victimisation or discriminatory treatment on the basis of an improper reason is central. As expressed in the speech of Lord Hoffmann in *Islam v SSHD and Another; R v SSHD ex p Shah* [1999] UKHL 20, [1999] 2 AC 629, 650–51: **6.40**

In my opinion, the concept of discrimination in matters affecting fundamental rights and freedoms is central to an understanding of the Convention. It is concerned not with all cases of persecution, even if they involve denials of human rights, but with persecution which is based on discrimination. And in the context of a human rights instrument, discrimination means making distinctions which principles of fundamental human rights regard as inconsistent with the right of every human being to equal treatment and respect.

C2. International Human Rights Instruments

i. Universal Declaration of Human Rights 1948

The Universal Declaration of Human Rights 1948 (UDHR48), was promulgated as a resolution of the United Nations General Assembly (UNGA Resolution 217A) **6.41**

[47] UN Human Rights Council, *Human rights and arbitrary deprivation of nationality* (UN Doc A/HRC/26/L.25) (23 June 2014).

passed on 10 December 1948. Although UDHR48 rights are not directly enforceable, UDHR48 represents an important milestone in the development of IHRL. *Inter alia*, it cites fundamental human rights notably including rights to 'life, liberty and security of person' (article 3), prohibition of 'torture or cruel, inhuman or degrading treatment or punishment' (article 5), 'discriminatory denial of equal protection' (article 7), 'arbitrary arrest, detention or exile' (article 9), and 'arbitrary interference with privacy, family, home or correspondence' against which 'Everyone has the right to the protection of the law' (article 12). An important aspect of almost every human rights regime is a prohibition of discrimination on enumerated grounds. Article 2 UDHR48 provides that:

> Everyone is entitled to all the rights and freedoms set forth in this Declaration, without distinction of any kind, such as race, colour, sex, language, religion, political or other opinion, national or social origin, property, birth or other status. Furthermore, no distinction shall be made on the basis of the political, jurisdictional or international status of the country or territory to which a person belongs, whether it be independent, trust, non-self-governing or under any other limitation of sovereignty.

6.42 Articles 13 and 15 respectively provide that:

> Article 13
>
> (1) Everyone has the right to freedom of movement and residence within the borders of each State.
> (2) Everyone has the right to leave any country, including his own, and to return to his country.
>
> Article 15
>
> (1) Everyone has the right to a nationality.
> (2) No one shall be arbitrarily deprived of his nationality nor denied the right to change his nationality.

These provisions reflected the then recent historical phenomenon of large-scale deprivation of nationality and expulsion or exclusion by the Soviet Union and by Nazi Germany. Although UDHR48 is not a binding instrument, articles 13(2) and 15 are historically important for the specific affirmation that the right of entry by a person to 'his own country', or the right to hold nationality, could be the subject of protection under IHRL. As Schram has stated of article 15 UDHR48:

> Until then [the human rights aspect of nationality] had never received this degree of recognition. Article 15 thus constitutes a remarkable development in international human rights law, providing a foundation upon which an elaborate legal structure has since been built.[48]

6.43 The right to a nationality attested in article 15 UDHR48 and in later instruments has been interpreted as meaning that in principle no one should be without a

[48] G Schram in A Eide, G Alfredsson et al (eds), *The Universal Declaration of Human Rights: A Commentary* (Scandinavian University Press, 1992) 229.

nationality, reflecting the importance of nationality given that, notwithstanding other protections for human rights, 'an individual's legal bond to a particular state through citizenship remains in practice an essential prerequisite to the enjoyment and protection of the full range of human rights'.[49] It does not however have the effect that any particular State is identified as subject to the duty to provide its nationality to a particular individual.[50]

UDHR48 contains two limiting clauses of general application, at articles 29 and 30. Article 29, *inter alia*, provides that: 'Everyone has duties to the community in which alone the free and full development of his personality is possible' (article 29(1)); that 'In the exercise of his rights and freedoms, everyone shall be subject only to such limitations as are determined by law solely for the purpose of securing due recognition and respect for the rights and freedoms of others and of meeting the just requirements of morality, public order and the general welfare in a democratic society' (article 29(2)); and that rights and freedoms may not be exercised 'contrary to the purposes and principles of the United Nations' (article 29(3)). Article 30 states that: 'Nothing in this Declaration may be interpreted as implying for any State, group or person any right to engage in any activity or to perform any act aimed at the destruction of any of the rights and freedoms set forth herein'. **6.44**

ii. International Covenant on Civil and Political Rights 1966

It was anticipated that UDHR48 would be followed both by regional instruments and by a binding international instrument. The first regional instrument was the European Convention on Human Rights and Fundamental Freedoms 1950 (ECHR50). The realisation of a single international Covenant on Human Rights was ultimately frustrated by political disagreement, but the purpose accomplished in 1966 by ICCPR66 and ICESCR66, the United Nations having decided to produce two instruments, whilst incorporating a lower level of impetus ('progressive accomplishment') as regards goals identified in the latter. These instruments eventually entered into force in 1976. ICCPR66 now has 177 States Parties. **6.45**

ICCPR66 is a significant pillar of IHRL. By article 2 ICCPR66 the ICCPR66 rights apply generally to all persons present in the territory or otherwise subject to the State's jurisdiction. Save where the contrary is specified, they apply regardless of nationality, citizenship, or legality of presence based upon presence in territory. Whilst the right to nationality at article 15 UDHR48 has not been reiterated in ICCPR66, the latter instrument provides for protection of life at article 6 ICCPR66, **6.46**

[49] M Adjami and J Harrington, 'The Scope and Content of Article 15 of the Universal Declaration of Human Rights' (2008) 27(3) *Refugee Survey Quarterly* 94.

[50] See for instance R Plender, 'The Right to a Nationality as Reflected in International Human Rights Law and the Sovereignty of States in Nationality Matters' (1995) 49 *Austrian Journal of Public International Law* 43, 43–44.

prohibits torture or cruel inhuman or degrading treatment by article 7 ICCPR66 and, in the context of entry and remaining on the territory, provides a key provision at article 12(4) ICCPR66 prohibiting arbitrary deprivation of the right to enter one's 'own country':

> Article 12
>
> 1. Everyone lawfully within the territory of a State shall, within that territory, have the right to liberty of movement and freedom to choose his residence.
>
> 2. Everyone shall be free to leave any country, including his own.
>
> 3. The above-mentioned rights shall not be subject to any restrictions except those which are provided by law, are necessary to protect national security, public order (ordre public), public health or morals or the rights and freedoms of others, and are consistent with the other rights recognized in the present Covenant.
>
> 4. No one shall be arbitrarily deprived of the right to enter his own country.

6.47 The United Nations Human Rights Committee (UNHRC) has found in a number of cases that refusal of a national passport breached article 12 ICCPR66. In *Sophie Vidal Martins v Uruguay*, Communication No R.13/57, UN Doc Supp No 40 (A/37/40) at 157 (1982) a journalist of Uruguayan nationality resident outside that country was denied a passport by Uruguayan authorities without explanation, which she inferred as conduct to punish her for past journalistic activity or to prevent further such activity in Uruguay. The UNHRC held that article 12(2) applied whether or not the individual was in the territory of the State Party. In *Oló Bahamonde v Equatorial Guinea*, Communication No 468/1991, UN Doc CCPR/C/49/D/468/1991 (1993), the UNHRC found the rights at article 12(1) and (2) breached by arbitrary confiscation of the petitioner's national passport, allegedly on the orders of the President of Equatorial Guinea, and refusal of exit from his country of nationality.

6.48 The right of entry to his or her 'own country' under article 12(4) necessarily implies the right to remain. The UNHRC has concluded that exile from one's 'own country' is barred by ICCPR66,[51] and in *Simalae Toala v New Zealand*, Communication No 675/1995, UN Doc CCPR/C/70/D/675/1995 (2000) treated deprivation of nationality as potentially within its remit because of the consequential loss of the right to enter.

6.49 In the context of article 12(4) ICCPR66, the term 'his own country' contemplates the possibility of a relevant link not dependent upon the possession of nationality or citizenship. Hannum, writing in 1987 before the UNHRC had begun to develop any substantial body of decisions, considered the best interpretation, on VCLT69 interpretation, to be that it encompassed 'nationals, citizens, and

[51] UNHRC, 'Concluding Observations on the Dominican Republic' (UN Doc CCPR/C/790/Add 18) (1993) para 6.

permanent residents'.[52] The extent of article 12(4) has been interpreted somewhat more restrictively by the UNHRC, which in particular has not included permanent residents, *per se*, within the protection of article 12(4) CSR51. The Committee has issued valuable guidance both in Concluding Observations on reports by States[53] and in its General Comment 27, *Freedom of Movement (Article 12)*, which states that:

> 19. The right of a person to enter his or her own country recognizes the special relationship of a person to that country. The right has various facets. It implies the right to remain in one's own country. It includes not only the right to return after having left one's own country; it may also entitle a person to come to the country for the first time if he or she was born outside the country (for example, if that country is the person's State of nationality). The right to return is of the utmost importance for refugees seeking voluntary repatriation. It also implies prohibition of enforced population transfers or mass expulsions to other countries.
>
> 20. The wording of article 12, paragraph 4, does not distinguish between nationals and aliens ('no one'). Thus, the persons entitled to exercise this right can be identified only by interpreting the meaning of the phrase 'his own country'. The scope of 'his own country' is broader than the concept 'country of his nationality'. It is not limited to nationality in a formal sense, that is, nationality acquired at birth or by conferral; it embraces, at the very least, an individual who, because of his or her special ties to or claims in relation to a given country, cannot be considered to be a mere alien. This would be the case, for example, of nationals of a country who have there been stripped of their nationality in violation of international law, and of individuals whose country of nationality has been incorporated in or transferred to another national entity, whose nationality is being denied them. The language of article 12, paragraph 4, moreover, permits a broader interpretation that might embrace other categories of long-term residents, including but not limited to stateless persons arbitrarily deprived of the right to acquire the nationality of the country of such residence. Since other factors may in certain circumstances result in the establishment of close and enduring connections between a person and a country, States parties should include in their reports information on the rights of permanent residents to return to their country of residence.
>
> 21. In no case may a person be arbitrarily deprived of the right to enter his or her own country. The reference to the concept of arbitrariness in this context is intended to emphasize that it applies to all State action, legislative, administrative and judicial; it guarantees that even interference provided for by law should be in accordance with the provisions, aims and objectives of the Covenant and should be, in any event, reasonable in the particular circumstances. The Committee considers that there are few, if any, circumstances in which deprivation of the right to enter one's own country could be reasonable. A State party must not, by stripping a person of nationality or by expelling an individual to a third country, arbitrarily prevent this person from returning to his or her own country.[54]

---

[52] H Hannum, *The Right to Leave and Return in International Law and Practice* (Martinus Nijhoff, 1987) 59.

[53] Ibid.

[54] UNHRC, General Comment 27, *Freedom of Movement (Art 12)*, UN Doc CCPR/C/21/Rev.1/Add.9 (1999) paras 20–21.

6.50 Article 12(4) ICCPR66 is, therefore, potentially relevant to a denial of the right of entry including a denial of entry which follows from an arbitrary deprivation of nationality. It appears likely that in most cases the possession of a State's nationality would make that State an individual's 'own country', but this will not always be the case.

6.51 Article 12(4) ICCPR66 invokes the concept of arbitrariness, common to other provisions in ICCPR66 and elsewhere in international law, for example, prohibitions on arbitrary arrest or detention (at article 9 ICCPR66) and arbitrary interference in private or family life (at article 17 ICCPR66). Arbitrariness may denote a deprivation which defies national law or one which is in accordance with such law but is objectionable for some other reason, such as discrimination for some prohibited reason or absence of due process. In the General Comment regarding article 9 ICCPR66, the Committee stated that:

> An arrest or detention may be authorized by domestic law and nonetheless be arbitrary. The notion of 'arbitrariness' is not to be equated with 'against the law', but must be interpreted more broadly to include elements of inappropriateness, injustice, lack of predictability and due process of law,[55] as well as elements of reasonableness, necessity and proportionality.[56]

6.52 In the *Elettronica Sicula SpA (ELSI) (United States of America v Italy)* case, the mayor of Palermo had issued an order under Italian law requisitioning the plant and assets of an enterprise owned by United States enterprises. This was said by the United States to be, *inter alia*, unreasonable or unfair because it was arbitrary. The ICJ rejected this. In doing so it said of arbitrariness that:

> Arbitrariness is not so much something opposed to a rule of law, as something opposed to the rule of law. This idea was expressed by the Court in the Asylum case, when it spoke of 'arbitrary action' being 'substituted for the rule of law'. It is a wilful disregard of due process of law, an act which shocks, or at least surprises, a sense of juridical propriety.[57]

6.53 A key circumstance in which an action will be considered arbitrary for the purposes of international law is where it is coloured by prohibited discrimination. Article 2 ICCPR66 provides that other rights under that instrument are to be respected and ensured 'without distinction of any kind, such as race, colour, sex, language, religion, political or other opinion, national or social origin, property, birth or other status'. More specific protection against discrimination is provided for particular groups, such as members of racial minorities, women, children and the disabled, at article 26 ICCPR66, and by other instruments, variously in ICERD66, CEDAW79, CRC89 and CRPD06, as examined below.

---

[55] 1134/2002, *Gorji-Dinka v Cameroon*, para 5.1; 305/1988, *Van Alphen v Netherlands*, para 5.8.

[56] UNHRC, General Comment 35, *Article 9 (Liberty and security of person)*, UN Doc CCPR/C/GC/35 (2014) para 12.

[57] *Elettronica Sicula SpA (ELSI)* (*United States of America v Italy*) [1989] ICJ Rep 15, 76.

Exceptions to the application of article 12(4) in such circumstances might arise, for example, where an act is held not arbitrary or a State terminating nationality is held not to be an individual's 'own country' because the possession of nationality has been of a fleeting or purely technical nature. In *Simalae Toala v New Zealand*, the UNHRC found that the cancelation of a hitherto unrealised entitlement to nationality by operation of law, in the absence of other significant connection to the territory of the State of nationality, did not give rise to an arbitrary denial of the right to return to an individual's 'own country': 6.54

> 11.4 The Committee's general comment on article 12 observes that 'A State party must not by stripping a person of nationality or by expelling an individual to a third country, arbitrarily prevent that person from returning to his or her own country'. In this case, the Committee considers that the circumstances in which the authors gained and then lost New Zealand citizenship need to be examined in the context of the issues which arise under article 12(4).
>
> 11.5 The Committee notes that in 1982 the authors had no connection with New Zealand by reason of birth, descent from any New Zealander, ties with New Zealand or residence in New Zealand. They were unaware of any claim to New Zealand citizenship at the time of [the decision in *Falema'i Lesa v The Attorney General (New Zealand)* [1982] UKPC 30 [1983] 2 AC 20] and had acquired New Zealand citizenship involuntarily. It also appears that, with the exception of Mr Toala, none of the authors had ever been in New Zealand. All these circumstances make it arguable that New Zealand did not become their 'own country' by virtue of the *Lesa* decision. But in any event, the Committee does not consider that the removal of their New Zealand citizenship was arbitrary. In addition to the circumstances already mentioned, none of the authors had been in New Zealand between the date of the *Lesa* decision and the passage of the 1982 Act. They had never applied for a New Zealand passport or claimed to exercise any rights as New Zealand citizens. The Committee is therefore of the view that article 12(4) was not violated in the authors' case.

The UNHRC in responses to petitions has generally followed a restrictive path as to the question of at what stage settled immigrants or those unlawfully present for a substantial time may treat the country of residence as their 'own'. In *Charles E Stewart v Canada*, Communication No 538/1993, UN Doc CCPR/C/58/D/538/1993 (1996) 12.5–12.9; *Giosue Canepa v Canada* (UNHRC, 558/93, 3 April 1997, UN Doc CCPR/C/59/D/558/1993); and *Francesco Madafferi and Anna Maria Immacolata Madafferi v Australia*, UN Doc CCPR/C/81/D/1011/2001 (26 August 2004) 9.6 the UNHRC held that a person who enters as an immigrant cannot normally regard the state of residence as his or her 'own country' when that person has not acquired its nationality and continues to retain the nationality of a country of origin, though an exception might arise in limited circumstances, such as those created by arbitrary or unreasonable impediments on the acquisition of nationality. More recently there have been two decisions of the UNHRC in deportation cases, published together in 2011, which appear to show a more expansive approach to the concept of 'own country'. These are *Nystrom v Australia* (1557/2007, 6.55

1 September 2011, UN Doc CCPR/C/102/D/1557/2007) and *Warsame v Canada* (1959/2010, 1 September 2011, UN Doc CCPR/C/102/D/1959/2010).

6.56 In *Nystrom v Australia* a majority of the UNHRC, at paragraphs 7.4–7.6 found that Australia was the 'own country' of the petitioner, a Swedish national aged 30 who had arrived in Australia as a migrant aged 27 days: and that his deportation in 2006 had been arbitrary. Five members recorded dissenting views, primarily because of their perception that the decision was disloyal to the majority decision in *Stewart v Canada*, including the importance to be given to absence of naturalisation where a system of naturalisation without unreasonable impediments existed, and/or because they viewed the decision as misconstruing the effect of General Comment 27 through failure to recognise the latter as focusing protection upon circumstances involving the deprivation or arbitrary denial of nationality, whereas there was no doubt that, however reduced his connection to Sweden, the petitioner was not an Australian national and he remained a Swedish national.

6.57 The scope of the *Nystrom v Australia* decision might have been said to turn on the fact that the petitioner had been in the care of the State as a minor without attention being given to his nationality position. But, as was stated in the dissents, this position is undermined by the decision of the UNHRC in *Warsame v Canada*. The petitioner in that case was an adult born in Saudi Arabia of Somali descent. He never obtained Saudi Arabian citizenship and came to Canada aged four as a dependant of his mother, without being accorded refugee status. Subsequently he was convicted aged 20 of robbery, for which he was sentenced to nine months' imprisonment, and two years later he was convicted of possession of a scheduled substance for the purpose of trafficking, in respect of which he was sentenced to two years' imprisonment. Faced with deportation he was unable to appeal, appeal against deportation being denied by Canadian law in cases where a custodial sentence of two years or more had been given. On a pre-removal risk assessment by the State it was found in early 2007 that removal to Somalia posed a risk to life and a risk of cruel and unusual treatment or punishment. The case was referred to a Minister's Delegate who concluded that the petitioner did not face relevant personal risk if removed to Somalia and that he represented a danger to the Canadian public, outweighing humanitarian and compassionate hardships. The petitioner failed to challenge this having been refused legal aid. A majority of the UNHRC's members, at paragraph 8.5, found that the petitioner's connections to Canada rendered it 'his own country':

> 8.5 In the present case, the author arrived in Canada when he was four years old, his nuclear family lives in Canada, he has no ties to Somalia and has never lived there and has difficulties speaking the language The Committee observes that it is not disputed that the author has lived almost all his conscious life in Canada, that he received his entire education in Canada and that before coming to Canada he lived in Saudi Arabia and not in Somalia.

As in *Nystrom v Australia* there was forceful dissent.

The UNHRC has found that it is incumbent upon an individual alleging a breach of article 12(4) ICCPR66 to prove that the State in question is 'his own country', though as for instance in *JM v Jamaica*, Communication No 165/1984, UN Doc CCPR/C/OP/2 (1984) at 17, the State may be expected to demonstrate that it has discharged any burden upon it to make enquiries in response to a claim of relevant linkage. **6.58**

Articles 17 and 23(1) ICCPR66

In expulsion cases two mutually reinforcing provisions relating to family and/or private life—articles 17 and 23(1) ICCPR66—are repeatedly cited. **6.59**

> Article 17
>
> 1. No one shall be subjected to arbitrary or unlawful interference with his privacy, family, or correspondence, nor to unlawful attacks on his honour and reputation.
>
> 2. Everyone has the right to the protection of the law against such interference or attacks.
>
> Article 23
>
> 1. The family is the natural and fundamental group unit of society and is entitled to protection by society and the State.

The UNHRC in General Comment 17, article 17 ('The right to respect of privacy, family, home, correspondence, and protection of honour and reputation') has said that: **6.60**

> 3. The term 'unlawful' means that no interference can take place except in cases envisaged by the law. Interference authorized by States can only take place on the basis of law, which itself must comply with the provisions, aims and objectives of the Covenant.
>
> 4. The expression 'arbitrary interference' is also relevant to the protection of the right provided for in article 17. In the Committee's view the expression 'arbitrary interference' can also extend to interference provided for under the law. The introduction of the concept of arbitrariness is intended to guarantee that even interference provided for by law should be in accordance with the provisions, aims and objectives of the Covenant and should be, in any event, reasonable in the particular circumstances.[58]

As to the term 'family' the UNHRC said in the same General Comment that: **6.61**

> 5. Regarding the term 'family', the objectives of the Covenant require that for purposes of article 17 this term be given a broad interpretation to include all those comprising the family as understood in the society of the State party concerned. The term 'home' in English, 'manzel' in Arabic, 'zhùzhái' in Chinese, 'domicile' in French, 'zhilische' in Russian and 'domicilio' in Spanish, as used in article 17 of the Covenant, is to be understood to indicate the place where a person resides or carries out his usual occupation.

[58] UNHRC, General Comment 17, *Article 17 (The right to respect of privacy, family, home, correspondence, and protection of honour and reputation)*, HRI/GEN/1/Rev.9 (Vol I) 191 (1988) paras 3–4.

> In this connection, the Committee invites States to indicate in their reports the meaning given in their society to the terms 'family' and 'home'.

This reference to the need to consider the local concept of 'family' is also reflected in General Comment 19.[59] The UNHRC has made clear that a State cannot frustrate the application of ICCPR66 by imposing for this purpose a definition of 'family' or 'home' narrower than that which it would otherwise apply: *Hopu and Bessert v France* (549/93, 29 July 1997, UN Doc CCPR/C/60/D/549/1993/Rev.1). It expressly rejected, in an individual petition relating to the Netherlands, the proposition that 'family' for purposes of article 23, paragraph 1, ICCPR66, referred only to a family unit during marriage, not extending to relationships between a divorced parent and the child of that marriage residing with the former spouse: *Hendriks v Netherlands* (201/85, 27 July 1988, UN Doc CCPR/C/33/D/201/1985). Unequal treatment of immigrants or their spouses according to gender is an important area in which relevant standards have been found to have been breached: *Aumeeruddy-Cziffra and 19 Other Mauritian Women v Mauritius* (35/78, 9 April 1981, UN Doc CCPR/C/12/D/35/1978).

Article 24 ICCPR66

6.62 Whilst ICCPR66 does not echo the universal right to nationality at Article 15 UDHR48, it does assert important rights for children, in particular the right to immediate birth registration and to *acquisition of* nationality. The last named goes further than UDHR48:

> Article 24
>
> ...
>
> 1. Every child shall be registered immediately after birth and shall have a name.
>
> 2. Every child has the right to acquire a nationality.

6.63 Article 24(3) ICCPR66 does not compel a State to provide its nationality to a child on its territory, though in many cases, if not all cases, it may have that effect where a child does not acquire a nationality by birth or descent and so would otherwise be stateless. The UNHRC in its General Comment 17 stated that:

> 8. While the purpose of this provision is to prevent a child from being afforded less protection by society and the State because he is stateless, it does not necessarily make it an obligation for States to give their nationality to every child born in their territory. However, States are required to adopt every appropriate measure, both internally and in cooperation with other States, to ensure that every child has a nationality when he is born. In this connection, no discrimination with regard to the acquisition of nationality should be admissible under internal law as between legitimate children and children

---

[59] UNHRC, General Comment 19, *Article 23 (Protection of the family, the right to marriage, and equality of the spouses)*, HRI/GEN/1/Rev.9 (Vol I) 198, para 2.

born out of wedlock or of stateless parents or based on the nationality status of one or both of the parents.[60]

Article 24(3) is interpreted as requiring a State Party to confer its nationality on stateless children born or found within their territory, though Nowak, an authoritative commentator, has argued that the obligation upon a State Party in whose territory a stateless minor is sojourning is secondary to the obligation which may attach to another State Party to which there is an arguably stronger binding tie, for example, through parental nationality.[61] The UNHRC has related the article 24(3) ICCPR66 obligation, *inter alia*, to discriminatory practices impeding birth registration of children of undocumented refugees in Ecuador (which would support their identification as citizens by birth on the territory),[62] failure by Colombia to confer its nationality on children born stateless on its territory,[63] and Zimbabwean laws denying its citizenship to the children of Zimbabwean parents born abroad.[64] Article 24(3) does not prevent denationalisation in every circumstance: in *Rajan v New Zealand* (820/1998, 7 August 2003, UN Doc CCPR/C/78/D/820/1998), the parents of the child were Fijian nationals who had been admitted to New Zealand with their infant son on showing Australian residence permits whilst failing to disclose an ongoing investigation in Australia into whether those permits had been fraudulently obtained. One of the parents was subsequently granted New Zealand citizenship, still on the basis of omission to disclose relevant facts, and her Fijian citizenship was automatically annulled as a result. Their son was also granted New Zealand citizenship. Several months later, the authorities having ascertained the true facts took steps to revoke both grants of citizenship and to deport the family. Whilst the appeal was in progress a daughter was born and acquired New Zealand citizenship by birth in the territory. The UNHRC found their claims of breaches of articles 17, 23(1) and 24(1) to be unsubstantiated, observing that on the evidence the parent deprived of New Zealand citizenship was held by the Fijian authorities thereafter to have a present status as a Fijian citizen and the son deprived of his New Zealand nationality retained Australian citizenship by birth and had not been rendered stateless. 6.64

Article 26 ICCPR66

Article 26 ICCPR66 sets out a broad requirement for equal protection of the law including mandatory action by the State for prohibition of discrimination and 'equal and effective' protection from discrimination on any of the enumerated 6.65

60 UNHRC, General Comment 17 (n 58 above).
61 M Nowak, *UN Covenant on Civil and Political Rights: CCPR Commentary* (K Engel, 1993) 424–25.
62 (1998) UN Doc CCPR/C/79/Add 92.
63 (1997) UN Doc CCPR/C/79/Add 75.
64 (1998) UN Doc CCPR/C/79/Add 89, para 19.

forms of status. In the absence from ICCPR66 of a right to nationality extending beyond the article 24 ICCPR66 right limited to children, article 26 is significant as a legal norm relevant to arbitrary deprivation of nationality on a relevantly discriminatory basis, even without article 12(4) ICCPR66 being engaged by expulsion or exclusion:

> Article 26
>
> All persons are equal before the law and are entitled without any discrimination to the equal protection of the law. In this respect, the law shall prohibit any discrimination and guarantee to all persons equal and effective protection against discrimination on any ground such as race, colour, sex, language, religion, political or other opinion, national or social origin, property, birth or other status.

6.66 Article 26 ICCPR66 has been held to apply to discrimination on the basis of absence of national status. In *Mümtaz Karakurt v Austria*, Communication No 965/2000, UN Doc CCPR/C/74/D/965/2000 (2002) 8.4, the UNHRC held that the exclusion of a worker from a 'works council' after his election to it, because although a permanent resident he was not a national of Austria or another European Economic Area State, constituted prohibited discrimination:

> [I]t is necessary to judge every case on its own facts. With regard to the case at hand, the Committee has to take into account the function of a member of a work council, ie, to promote staff interests and to supervise compliance with work conditions. In view of this, it is not reasonable to base a distinction between aliens concerning their capacity to stand for election for a work council solely on their different nationality.

In numerous cases against the Czech Republic the UNHRC has held that Czech law limiting restitution for confiscation during the Communist period to present holders of Czech nationality breaches article 26: see for instance *Karel Des Fours Walderode v Czech Republic*, Communication No 747/1997, UN Doc CCPR/C/73/D/747/1997 (21 November 1996) and much later *Victor Drda v Czech Republic*, Communication No 1581/2007, UN Doc CCPR/C/100/D/1581/2007 (29 October 2010).

6.67 The UNHRC has also considered that article 26 ICCPR66 applied in principle to decisions withholding nationality from long-term residents. Indeed, it is a notable feature of the Committee's decisions that even in the absence of any international law entitlement to acquire nationality by derivative means, and faced with tightly drawn domestic legislation, it has not treated nationality decisions as falling within a reserved sphere of state activity. In *Vjatšeslav Borzov v Estonia*, Communication No 1136/2002, UN Doc CCPR/C/81/D/1136/2002 (26 July 2004) 7.4, the Committee found that the withholding of Estonian nationality from former members of the armed forces of the USSR was justified:

> [T]he State party concluded that a grant of citizenship to the author would raise national security issues generally on account of the duration and level of the author's military training, his rank and background in the armed forces of the then USSR.

In a later proceeding, that of *Gennady Sipin v Estonia*, Communication No 1432/2005 UN Doc CCPR/C/93/D/1423/2005 (9 July 2008), the Committee indicated that 'reasonable and objective' justification was required:

> 7.3 In this particular case, article 26 requires no more than reasonable and objective justification and a legitimate aim for the operation of distinctions. The Committee observes that the enactment of the Citizenship Act 1995 and, in particular, a blanket prohibition to grant Estonian citizenship to anyone who 'served as a professional member of the armed forces of a foreign state or who has been assigned to the reserve forces thereof or has retired therefrom' cannot be examined outside its factual context. While the above-mentioned blanket prohibition does amount to differential treatment, in the circumstances of the present case, the reasonableness of such differential treatment depends on how the State party justifies its national security arguments.
>
> 7.4 In the present case, the State party has concluded that granting citizenship to the author would raise national security issues on account of his former service in the armed forces of another country, including a country that had previously occupied Estonia, and that the denial of any discretionary power to administrative authority in the application of the Citizenship Act was not disproportionate. The Committee notes that neither the Covenant nor international law in general spell out specific criteria for the granting of citizenship by naturalization, and that the author indeed was able to have the denial of his citizenship application reviewed by the State party's courts.
>
> 7.5 The Committee also notes that the category of individuals excluded by the State party's legislation from the benefit of Estonian citizenship is closely linked to considerations of national security. Furthermore, where such justification for differential treatment is persuasive, it is unnecessary that the application of the legislation be additionally justified in the circumstances of an individual case. The decision in *Borzov* is consistent with the view that distinctions made in the legislation itself, where justifiable on reasonable and objective grounds, do not require additional justification on these grounds in their application to an individual. Consequently, the Committee does not, in the circumstances of the present case, conclude that there was a violation of article 26 of the Covenant.

C3. Post International Covenant on Civil and Political Rights 1966 Instruments

Since ICCPR66 there has been a string of instruments directed more specifically at human rights questions of particular types or affecting particular groups, for example: ICERD66, the International Convention on the Suppression and Punishment of the Crime of Apartheid 1974 (ICSPCA74); CEDAW79; CAT84; CRC89; CRPD06; and CPED06. **6.68**

In general a feature of these regimes is a substantial level of support by States underpinning the broad reach of IHRL. As at 1 January 2016, the respective numbers of States Parties were as follows: ICERD66, 177; ICSPCA74, 109; CEDAW79, 189; CAT84, 158; CRC89, 196; CRPD06, 160; CPED06, 51. **6.69**

These instruments are examined below, in turn. **6.70**

i. International Convention on the Elimination of All Forms of Racial Discrimination 1966

6.71 ICERD66 is an instrument formulated to combat racial discrimination because this is inconsistent with the dignity and equality of all human beings. Racial discrimination is defined at article 1(1) ICERD66:

> Article 1
>
> 1. In this Convention, the term 'racial discrimination' shall mean any distinction, exclusion, restriction or preference based on race, colour, descent, or national or ethnic origin which has the purpose or effect of nullifying or impairing the recognition, enjoyment or exercise, on an equal footing, of human rights and fundamental freedoms in the political, economic, social, cultural or any other field of public life.

6.72 Article 1(2) ICERD66 disapplies the Convention's protections from situations in which distinction is drawn 'between citizens and non-citizens'. Article 1(3) ICERD66 expressly protects from intrusion most domestic laws of nationality and citizenship, something which might be compared negatively with the greater readiness to address these areas in more recent treaties. Finally, by article 1(4) ICERD66 special measures seeking to promote equality:

> shall not be deemed racial discrimination, provided, however, that such measures do not, as a consequence, lead to the maintenance of separate rights for different racial groups and that they shall not be continued after the objectives for which they were taken have been achieved.

6.73 Article 5 ICERD66 provides, *inter alia*, for protection of individuals from discrimination in relation to certain nationality rights:

> Article 5
>
> In compliance with the fundamental obligations laid down in article 2 of this Convention, States Parties undertake to prohibit and to eliminate racial discrimination in all its forms and to guarantee the right of everyone, without distinction as to race, colour, or national or ethnic origin, to equality before the law, notably in the enjoyment of the following rights:
>
> ...
>
> (d) Other civil rights, in particular:
>
> (ii) the right to leave any country, including one's own, and to return to one's country;
> (iii) the right to nationality.

ii. International Convention on the Suppression and Punishment of the Crime of Apartheid 1974

6.74 ICSPCA74 may be relevant to treatment of persons by a State as regards nationality by reason of the linkage between deprivation of nationality, or the imposition of differential status, and policies within the definition of *apartheid*. By article I of ICSPCG48 the States Parties declare that:

> *apartheid* is a crime against humanity and that inhuman acts resulting from the policies and practices of apartheid and similar policies and practices of racial segregation and discrimination, as defined in article II of the Convention, are crimes violating the principles of international law, in particular the purposes and principles of the Charter of the United Nations, and constituting a serious threat to international peace and security.

Apartheid is defined and examples described in article II: **6.75**

> Article II
>
> For the purpose of the present Convention, the term 'the crime of apartheid', which shall include similar policies and practices of racial segregation and discrimination as practised in southern Africa, shall apply to the following inhuman acts committed for the purpose of establishing and maintaining domination by one racial group of persons over any other racial group of persons and systematically oppressing them:
>
> ...
>
> (c) Any legislative measures and other measures calculated to prevent a racial group or groups from participation in the political, social, economic and cultural life of the country and the deliberate creation of conditions preventing the full development of such a group or groups, in particular by denying to members of a racial group or groups basic human rights and freedoms, including ... the right to a nationality, the right to freedom of movement and residence;
>
> (d) Any measures including legislative measures, designed to divide the population along racial lines by the creation of separate reserves and ghettos for the members of a racial group or groups, the prohibition of mixed marriages among members of various racial groups, the expropriation of landed property belonging to a racial group or groups or to members thereof;
>
> ...
>
> (f) Persecution of organizations and persons, by depriving them of fundamental rights and freedoms, because they oppose apartheid.

iii. Convention on the Elimination of All Forms of Discrimination Against Women 1979

By article 1 CEDAW79, 'discrimination against women' means: **6.76**

> any distinction, exclusion or restriction made on the basis of sex which has the effect or purpose of impairing or nullifying the recognition, enjoyment or exercise by women, irrespective of their marital status, on a basis of equality of men and women, of human rights and fundamental freedoms in the political, economic, social, cultural, civil or any other field.

6.77 Article 3 CEDAW79 provides that States Parties shall take all appropriate measures in all fields to ensure the full development and advancement of women so as to guarantee the 'exercise and enjoyment of human rights and fundamental freedoms on a basis of equality with men'. Article 4 provides for positive discrimination without breach of the prohibition on discrimination, in certain circumstances.

6.78 There is a specific protection as regards equal rights to nationality, at article 9 CEDAW79:

> Article 9
>
> 1. States Parties shall grant women equal rights with men to acquire, change or retain their nationality. They shall ensure in particular that neither marriage to an alien nor change of nationality by the husband during marriage shall automatically change the nationality of the wife, render her stateless or force upon her the nationality of the husband.
>
> 2. States Parties shall grant women equal rights with men with respect to the nationality of their children.

iv. Convention Against Torture and Other Cruel, Inhuman or Degrading Treatment or Punishment 1984

6.79 CAT84 has been signed and ratified by the United Kingdom. It has a limited bearing on questions of nationality but the high general importance of CAT84 means that even a limited relevance should be acknowledged where present. It seems likely that the primary relevance of CAT84 to an enquiry as to whether state treatment of an individual touching on nationality constitutes persecution for purposes of article 1A(2) CSR51 will be where: (i) acts constituting torture under CAT84 are used or threatened in conjunction with such treatment; or (ii) conversely where actions concerning nationality (for example, the threat of denationalisation or other change of status) are an adjunct to conduct within the scope of CAT84; (iii) where nationality related conduct by a State of origin has had the effect of *refoulement* to torture elsewhere—as where a State denationalises an individual and in the course of expulsion transmits her to another state where such treatment is suffered.

6.80 Article 1(1) CAT84 defines torture for purposes of the instrument as

> any act by which severe pain or suffering, whether physical or mental, is intentionally inflicted on a person for such purposes as obtaining from him or a third person information or a confession, punishing him for an act he or a third person has committed or is suspected of having committed, or intimidating or coercing him or a third person, or for any reason based on discrimination of any kind, when such pain or suffering is inflicted by or at the instigation of or with the consent or acquiescence of a public official or other person acting in an official capacity. It does not include pain or suffering arising only from, inherent in or incidental to lawful sanctions.

Article 2 CAT84 stresses the absolute nature of the prohibition of torture: **6.81**

> 1. Each State Party shall take effective legislative, administrative, judicial or other measures to prevent acts of torture in any territory under its jurisdiction.
>
> 2. No exceptional circumstances whatsoever, whether a state of war or a threat of war, internal political instability or any other public emergency, may be invoked as a justification of torture.
>
> 3. An order from a superior officer or a public authority may not be invoked as a justification of torture.

In relation to *refoulement*, article 3 CAT84 is particularly important: **6.82**

> 1. No State Party shall expel, return *(refouler)* or extradite a person to another State where there are substantial grounds for believing that he would be in danger of being subjected to torture.
>
> 2. For the purpose of determining whether there are such grounds, the competent authorities shall take into account all relevant considerations including, where applicable, the existence in the State concerned of a consistent pattern of gross, flagrant or mass violations of human rights.

The principle of non-*refoulement* codifies a widening of the scope of non-*refoulement* to prevent return to torture or other relevant treatment, so that

> a State violates the absolute prohibition of torture not only if its own authorities subject a person to torture, but also if its authorities send a person to another state where there are substantial grounds for believing that the person would be in danger of being subjected to torture.[65]

Non-*refoulement* similarly arises in relation to the prohibition on cruel, inhuman and degrading treatment or punishment and torture, under both article 7 ICCPR66 and provisions in regional instruments such as Article 3 ECHR50. In contrast to those treaties, the scope of non-*refoulement* under article 3 CAT84 is a narrow one: it applies *only* to acts of torture, as defined under article 1 CAT84, which expressly requires 'infliction by or with the acquiescence of a public official or other person acting in an official capacity'. The Committee against Torture has adopted a relatively broad and non-literal interpretation of that formulation, however, expressly finding in *Elmi v Australia*, Communication No 120/1998, UN Doc CAT/C/22/D/120/1998 (1999) that proposed return to Somalia, where centralised authority had collapsed, might still breach CAT84 because of the existence of *de facto* rule by local armed factions. The Committee however revisited the same question three years later, in *HMHI v Australia*, Communication No 177/2001, UN Doc CAT/C/28/D/177/2001 (2002). By that time Somalia had a Transitional National Government. Whilst that administration was highly insecure, the Committee concluded that by reason of its existence cases where the risk of torture arose from other entities, as in *Elmi*, no longer fell within CAT84.

[65] M Nowak et al, *The United Nations Convention against Torture: A Commentary* (OUP, 2008) 127.

Article 3 CAT84 does *not* apply to all acts that constitute cruel, inhuman or degrading treatment or punishment, a formula which encompasses a wider range of activity.[66]

6.83 The fact the State to be returned to displays a consistent pattern of gross, flagrant or mass violations of human rights, lends support to a finding that there are substantial grounds to believe the applicant would be tortured on return, as seen in *Mutombo v Switzerland*, Communication No13/1993, UN Doc A/49/44 at 45 (1994). It is not however a prerequisite, and in one particular case—*VNIM v Canada*, Communication No 119/1998, UN Doc CAT/C/29/D/119/1998 (2002)—where there was no finding of a personal risk, the Committee did not even deem it necessary to consider the human rights situation in the country where the applicant was to be returned. Equally, such a finding does not make removal of an individual contrary to article 3 CAT84 where there is an absence of personal risk. Indeed, in *HMHI v Australia*, the Committee concluded that a consistent pattern of gross, flagrant or mass violations of human rights were to be found in Somalia, but that the applicant's removal there was not contrary to article 3 CAT84 because there were no substantial grounds for believing he personally would be at risk of torture.

6.84 Whether or not an individual has been tortured in the past is also relevant to the determination of future risk For example, in *CT and KM v Sweden*, Communication No 279/2005, UN Doc CAT/C/37/D/279/2005 (2007), the Committee's finding that the first applicant was at risk of torture on return to Rwanda relied heavily on the fact she had been repeatedly raped whilst in detention there, prior to fleeing to Sweden. Whilst her account of being at risk of return was not deemed credible by the Swedish authorities, there was no dispute that she was a victim of torture; indeed, the rapes were evidenced by the birth of a child, shortly after the applicant arrived in Sweden.

v. Convention on the Rights of the Child 1989

6.85 The United Kingdom has signed and ratified CRC89, which contains provisions relevant to the protection of children's rights. Articles 7 and 8 CRC89 contain provisions relevant to the acquisition and retention of birth registration and nationality by children:

> Article 7
>
> 1. The child shall be registered immediately after birth and shall have the right from birth to a name, the right to acquire a nationality and as far as possible, the right to know and be cared for by his or her parents.

---

[66] CAT84 does however prohibit cruel, inhuman and degrading treatment or punishment separately from non-*refoulement*, by article 16 CAT84.

2. States Parties shall ensure the implementation of these rights in accordance with their national law and their obligations under the relevant international instruments in this field, in particular where the child would otherwise be stateless.

Article 8

1. States Parties undertake to respect the right of the child to preserve his or her identity, including nationality, name and family relations as recognized by law without unlawful interference.

2. Where a child is illegally deprived of some or all of the elements of his or her identity, States Parties shall provide appropriate assistance and protection, with a view to re-establishing speedily his or her identity.

The rights of the child to acquire and preserve nationality generally overlap with the protection of ICCPR66 where a State has ratified both instruments.

Article 9 CRC 89 sets out standards regarding family unity: **6.86**

Article 9

1. States Parties shall ensure that a child shall not be separated from his or her parents against their will, except when competent authorities subject to judicial review determine, in accordance with applicable law and procedures, that such separation is necessary for the best interests of the child.

vi. Convention on the Rights of Persons with Disabilities 2006

The United Kingdom has signed and ratified CRPD06, the purpose of which is identified at article 1 CRPD06, as being to 'promote, protect and ensure' the full and equal enjoyment of all human rights and fundamental freedoms by all persons with disabilities, and to promote respect for their inherent dignity. The subjects of the Convention, 'persons with disabilities' are given a non-exclusive definition in the second paragraph of article 1 CRPD06: **6.87**

Persons with disabilities include those who have long-term physical, mental, intellectual or sensory impairments which in interaction with various barriers may hinder their full and effective participation in society on an equal basis with others.

Article 18 CRPD06 sets out specific protection regarding nationality, documentation of national status, and incidents thereof including the right to leave or enter, as regards persons affected by disability: **6.88**

Article 18—Liberty of movement and nationality

1. States Parties shall recognize the rights of persons with disabilities to liberty of movement, to freedom to choose their residence and to a nationality, on an equal basis with others, including by ensuring that persons with disabilities:
   a. Have the right to acquire and change a nationality and are not deprived of their nationality arbitrarily or on the basis of disability;

   b. Are not deprived, on the basis of disability, of their ability to obtain, possess and utilize documentation of their nationality or other documentation of identification, or to utilize relevant processes such as immigration proceedings, that may be needed to facilitate exercise of the right to liberty of movement;
   c. Are free to leave any country, including their own;
   d. Are not deprived, arbitrarily or on the basis of disability, of the right to enter their own country.
2. Children with disabilities shall be registered immediately after birth and shall have the right from birth to a name, the right to acquire a nationality and, as far as possible, the right to know and be cared for by their parents.

vii. Convention for the Protection of All Persons from Enforced Disappearance 2006

6.89 CPED06 entered into force in 2010, but has not yet been signed or ratified by the United Kingdom and presently has only 51 States Parties. In the United Kingdom Parliament the responsible Minister indicated in 2007 that the government 'need[s] to conduct a detailed analysis of the provisions of the treaty and their implications for implementation in order to determine the UK's position towards ratification, including whether we would need to make any reservations'.[67] Belgium, France, Germany and Italy are amongst the State Parties, whilst Australia, Canada, New Zealand, the United Kingdom and the United States, are not. The Republic of Ireland has signed the treaty but not yet ratified it. CPED06 possesses limited application to questions of nationality as with CAT84 but the importance of the subject matter of CPED06 means that even a limited relevance should be acknowledged. The primary relevance of CAT84 to an enquiry as to whether State treatment of an individual touching on nationality constitutes persecution will likely be where: (i) acts breaching CPED06 are used or threatened in conjunction with such treatment; or (ii) conversely where actions concerning nationality (for example, the threat of denationalisation or other change of status) are an adjunct to conduct within the scope of CPED06; (iii) where nationality related conduct by a State has the prospective or actual effect of *refoulement* to enforced disappearance.

6.90 Article 16 CPED06 provides that:

1. No State Party shall expel, return *('refouler')*, surrender or extradite a person to another State where there are substantial grounds for believing that he or she would be in danger of being subjected to enforced disappearance.
2. For the purpose of determining whether there are such grounds, the competent authorities shall take into account all relevant considerations including, where applicable, the existence in the State concerned of a consistent pattern of gross, flagrant or mass violations of human rights.

---

[67] HL Deb 26 June 2007, col WA130.

C4. Regional Human Rights Instruments

i. European Convention on Human Rights and Fundamental Freedoms 1950

ECHR50 is notable for its lacunae in relation to nationality, notwithstanding the express protections which UDHR48 had elucidated shortly before in evident reaction to the abuses committed in Europe by Nazi Germany and other States since the First World War. Even if not admitted contemporaneously, this appears to have been deliberate, reflecting, *inter alia*, reluctance to expose to scrutiny under ECHR50 the effects of the post-war population transfers—in essence the expulsion of ethnic Germans, Hungarians and others from certain States in Central and Eastern Europe which had been approved by the main Allied Powers under the Potsdam Protocol of August 1945. The effect of this significant weakness in ECHR50 is exacerbated by the limitation of the anti-discrimination provision at Article 14 ECHR50 to non-discrimination in the enjoyment 'of the rights and freedoms set forth in this Convention'. ECHR50 is thus an instrument with significant overlapping weaknesses in relation both to protection of civil status and to discrimination. All members of the Council of Europe are required to be parties to the ECHR: there are presently 47 States Parties. As will be seen below, some attempt has been made to address the weakness of ECHR as regards nationality by the Fourth Protocol to ECHR50, done in September 1963, but that instrument is not one which is mandatory for a State wishing to join or remain in the Council of Europe. **6.91**

Article 3 ECHR50 provides that: **6.92**

> Article 3 Prohibition of Torture
>
> No one shall be subjected to torture or to inhuman or degrading treatment or punishment.

A perhaps unpredictable consequence of the absence of direct nationality-related protections in ECHR50 is that one of the most significant decisions taken under it, that of the European Commission of Human Rights in *East African Asians v UK* No 4403/70, [1973] ECHR 2, (1981) 3 EHRR 76 [207] and [212], was taken by reference to the prohibition on degrading treatment within Article 3 ECHR50. The Commission accepted that it had jurisdiction over claims by British passport holders from East Africa, of Asian origin, whose right of entry and stay in the United Kingdom, at a time when they faced expulsion from East African countries under policies of 'Africanisation', had been restricted by statute. The Commission found that the denial to its nationals of entry to and stay within its territory on discriminatory grounds, namely their colour or race, was so humiliating that it violated Article 3 ECHR50, though no violation of Article 3 was found regarding applicants who were not British nationals but only British protected persons. Subsequently, in *SH v UK* No 19956/06, [2010] ECHR 2254, (2012) 54 EHRR 4 [70], the Court held that where there were 'acts motivated by racial discrimination', **6.93** this would be an 'aggravating factor' in deciding whether treatment reached the threshold under Article 3 ECHR50.

6.94 Article 8 ECHR50 provides that:

> Article 8 Right to respect for private and family life
>
> 1. Everyone has the right to respect for his private and family life, his home and his correspondence.
> 2. There shall be no interference by a public authority with the exercise of this right except such as is in accordance with the law and is necessary in a democratic society in the interests of national security, public safety or the economic wellbeing of the country, for the prevention of disorder or crime, for the protection of health or morals, or for the protection of the rights and freedoms of others.

6.95 Whilst Article 8 ECHR50 does not guarantee a right to acquire a particular nationality or citizenship, an arbitrary denial of nationality will potentially engage Article 8 ECHR50: *Karassev v Finland* No 31414/96 (admissibility decision, 12 January 1999); *Slivenko v Latvia* [GC] No 48321/99, [2003] ECHR 498, (2004) 39 EHRR 24 [77]. Erasure from a residents' register leaving the applicant with no right of residence also constitutes an interference with Article 8 ECHR50: *Slivenko* at [96]; *Kurić and others v Slovenia* [GC] No 26828/06, [2012] ECHR 1083, (2013) 56 EHRR 20 [339]. Further, the confiscation of identity documents may constitute an interference with Article 8 where lack of documentation leads to various 'everyday inconveniences', including denial of access to employment and medical care: *Smirnova v Russia* No 46133/99; 48183/99, [2003] ECHR 397, (2004) 39 EHRR 22 [97].

6.96 A number of cases concerning alleged denial or deprivation of nationality have arisen where the applicants were denied the right of residence by reason of the absence of nationality. In *Sisojeva v Latvia* [GC] No 60654/00, [2007] ECHR 16, (2007) 45 EHRR 33, the applicants had in the late 1960s moved to Latvia as Soviet nationals. Upon Latvia reasserting independence in 1991, they became stateless and in 1996 their residence permits were revoked and their names taken off the residents' register. The European Court of Human Rights (ECtHR) recognised that the removal of their names from the register of residents had resulted in insecurity and legal uncertainty interfering with Article 8 ECHR50 rights, but Latvia's ultimate proposal to regularise their stay by granting them residence permits, even if temporary, was held 'adequate and sufficient to remedy their complaint', leading to the case being struck out (at [98]–[99]; [102]).

6.97 The Grand Chamber of the Court reviewed the issue of deprivation of nationality in the context of statelessness and lack of a right to residence in *Kurić and others v Slovenia*. The applicants had been nationals of the Former Republic of Yugoslavia (FRY) and other constituent republics who had acquired permanent residence in Slovenia prior to its independence. Later they failed to apply, or were unsuccessful in applications, for Slovenian citizenship, and their names were automatically deleted from the register of permanent residents in 1992. The Court at [339] confirmed that the erasure from the register and its impact on the applicants' lives interfered with their private and family life and found this continuing interference not to have been in accordance with the law; although this was not strictly necessary, the ECtHR continued to examine the proportionality of the measure. The ECtHR at [353] confirmed the legitimate aim of national security, but at [359]–[60] denied proportionality on the basis that a restriction of access to Slovenian citizenship could be justified but not the denial of permanent residence. The ECtHR further found a violation of Article 14 ECHR50 on the basis that non-nationals who were not nationals of the FRY had been able to retain permanent residence under Slovenian law, but nationals of the FRY had not (at [390]–[92]).

6.98 The denial of citizenship was found to fall within Article 8 ECHR50 in *Genovese v Malta*, No 53124/09, [2011] ECHR 1590, (2014) 58 EHRR 25 arising from proceedings concerning an applicant who had been born out of wedlock to a British mother and a Maltese father. Despite judicial determination of paternity, the applicant's father had refused to acknowledge his son on the birth certificate, leading to the Maltese authorities' refusal to grant the applicant Maltese citizenship. The applicant claimed that he had been discriminated against contrary to Article 14 taken with Article 8 ECHR50. The ECtHR rejected the applicant's claim that the denial of citizenship had interfered with his family life with his father resident in Malta given the father's lack of interest in a relationship with his son. It found, however, an interference with the applicant's private life based on the denial of citizenship ruling that 'its impact on the applicant's social identity was such as to bring it within' Article 8 ECHR50 (at [33]). The applicant had been treated differently on the basis that he had been born out of wedlock and the ECtHR held that no reasonable or objective grounds had been adduced for this (at [45]–[49]).[68]

ii. Fourth Protocol to the European Convention on Human Rights and Fundamental Freedoms 1950

6.99 Protocol 4 to ECHR50 entered into force on 2 May 1968. Whilst becoming a State Party is not mandatory for Council of Europe Member States, it had 43 States Parties as at 1 January 2016 including every Member State of the Council of Europe save Greece, Switzerland, Turkey and the United Kingdom (Turkey and the United Kingdom have signed but not ratified it). Article 3 of the Protocol provides as follows:

> Article 3: Prohibition of expulsion of nationals
>
> 1. No one shall be expelled, by means either of an individual or of a collective measure, from the territory of the State of which he is a national.

[68] This was cited by Ouseley J in *AHK and others v SSHD* [2013] EWHC 1426 (Admin), who found an element of arbitrariness or discrimination necessary for Article 8 to be engaged (see ch 11); for differential treatment based on the number of years someone had been a national, see also *Biao v Denmark* No 38590/10 (25 March 2014, not yet final).

2. No one shall be deprived of the right to enter the territory of the state of which he is a national.

6.100 Article 3 of Protocol 4 provides an absolute prohibition on the expulsion of nationals. The question of whether an applicant is a national is 'determined, in principle, by reference to national law': *Slivenko v Latvia* [GC] No 48321/99 (admissibility decision, 23 January 2002) [77]. Whilst the ECtHR has held that an arbitrary denial of nationality may amount to an interference with Article 8 ECHR50, it has not yet decided whether Article 3 of Protocol 4 prohibits the arbitrary withdrawal or revocation of nationality. The Court has however held that prohibition upon expulsion of nationals implies the right to return to a country of nationality: *L v Federal Republic of Germany*, No 10564/83 (Commission decision, 10 December 1984); *M and S v Italy and UK*, No 2584/11 (admissibility decision, 13 March 2012) [73].

iii. American Convention on Human Rights 1969

6.101 Under the American Convention on Human Rights 1969 (ACHR69), States Parties by article 1 undertake 'to respect the rights and freedoms recognized herein' and also 'to ensure to all persons subject to their jurisdiction the free and full exercise of those rights and freedoms, without any discrimination for reasons of race, color, sex, language, religion, political or other opinion, national or social origin, economic status, birth, or any other social condition'. The particular position of children is protected by article 19, by which every minor child 'has the right to the measures of protection required by his condition as a minor on the part of his family, society, and the state'.

6.102 In strong contrast to ECHR50, ACHR69 incorporates strong protections as regards nationality and its incidents, most particularly at articles 20 and 22:

Article 20: Right to Nationality

1. Every person has the right to a nationality.
2. Every person has the right to the nationality of the state in whose territory he was born if he does not have the right to any other nationality.
3. No one shall be arbitrarily deprived of his nationality or of the right to change it.

Article 22: Freedom of Movement and Residence

1. Every person lawfully in the territory of a State Party has the right to move about in it, and to reside in it subject to the provisions of the law.
2. Every person has the right to leave any country freely, including his own.
3. The exercise of the foregoing rights may be restricted only pursuant to a law to the extent necessary in a democratic society to prevent crime or to protect national security, public safety, public order, public morals, public health, or the rights or freedoms of others.

4. The exercise of the rights recognized in paragraph 1 may also be restricted by law in designated zones for reasons of public interest.
5. No one can be expelled from the territory of the state of which he is a national or be deprived of the right to enter it.

6.103 The Inter-American Court of Human Rights (IACHR) has been a leading forum for the adjudication of nationality-related rights. In its Advisory Opinion OC-4/84 of 19 January 1984, *Proposed Amendments to the Naturalization Provision of the Constitution of Costa Rica*, the IACHR examined proposed amendments to the Constitution of the referring State by reference to article 20 ACHR69 and other relevant provisions. The Court stated nationality to be 'an inherent right' of human beings:

> 32. It is generally accepted today that nationality is an inherent right of all human beings. Not only is nationality the basic requirement for the exercise of political rights, it also has an important bearing on the individual's legal capacity.
>
> Thus, despite the fact that it is traditionally accepted that the conferral and regulation of nationality are matters for each state to decide, contemporary developments indicate that international law does impose certain limits on the broad powers enjoyed by the states in that area, and that the manners in which states regulate matters bearing on nationality cannot today be deemed within their sole jurisdiction; those powers of the state are also circumscribed by their obligations to ensure the full protection of human rights.
>
> 33. The classic doctrinal position, which viewed nationality as an attribute granted by the state to its subjects, has gradually evolved to the point that nationality is today perceived as involving the jurisdiction of the state as well as human rights issues. This has been recognized in a regional instrument, the American Declaration of the Rights and Duties of Man of May 2, 1948 (hereinafter 'the American Declaration'), whose Article 19 reads as follows:
>
>> 'Every person has the right to the nationality to which he is entitled by law and to change it, if he so wishes, for the nationality of any other country that is willing to grant it to him'.
>
> Another instrument, the Universal Declaration of Human Rights (hereinafter 'the Universal Declaration'), approved by the United Nations on December 10, 1948, provides the following in its Article 15:
>
>> '1. Everyone has the right to a nationality.
>>
>> 2. No one shall be arbitrarily deprived of his nationality nor denied the right to change his nationality'.
>
> 34. The right of every human being to a nationality has been recognized as such by international law. Two aspects of this right are reflected in Article 20 of the Convention: first, the right to a nationality established therein provides the individual with a minimal measure of legal protection in international relations through the link his nationality establishes between him and the state in question; and, second, the protection therein accorded the individual against the arbitrary deprivation of his nationality, without which he would be deprived for all practical purposes of all of his political rights as well as of those civil rights that are tied to the nationality of the individual.

6.104 The IACHR held, *inter alia*, that preferential treatment for Central Americans, Ibero-Americans and Spaniards over other aliens in the acquisition of Costa Rican nationality through naturalisation did not constitute discrimination contrary to ACHR69:

> 60. Given the above considerations, one example of a non-discriminatory differentiation would be the establishment of less stringent residency requirements for Central Americans, Ibero-Americans and Spaniards than for other foreigners seeking to acquire Costa Rican nationality. It would not appear to be inconsistent with the nature and purpose of the grant of nationality to expedite the naturalization procedures for those who, viewed objectively, share much closer historical, cultural and spiritual bonds with the people of Costa Rica. The existence of these bonds permits the assumption that these individuals will be more easily and more rapidly assimilated within the national community and identify more readily with the traditional beliefs, values and institutions of Costa Rica, which the state has the right and duty to preserve.

However, as regards a proposal within the amendments that any foreign woman who became stateless by reason of marriage to a Costa Rican national should have to pass at least two years of marriage, whilst residing in Costa Rica, before becoming eligible for naturalisation, the IACHR unanimously concluded that the proposed amendment was incompatible with article 17(4) (equality of rights in marriage) and article 24 (equal protection of the law) ACHR69.

6.105 In another Advisory Opinion of 30 January 1987 the IACHR emphasised that the right to nationality under article 20 ACHR69 cannot be suspended, even in circumstances of national emergency: *Habeas Corpus in Emergency Situations (arts 27(2), 25(1) and 7(6) American Convention on Human Rights)* OC-8/87, Series A No 8, paragraph 23.

6.106 In the *Case of Ivcher Bronstein v Peru*, Merits, reparations and costs, IACHR Series C No 74, IHRL 1457, 6 February 2001, the applicant was the director of a television station in Peru who was identified by the President as insufficiently supportive. As a result the Peruvian administration in 1997 purported to rescind his nationality and took steps to confiscate his television interests. The IACHR found a breach of article 20 ACHR69:

> 95. From the foregoing, it is evident that Mr Ivcher did not expressly renounce his nationality, which is the only way of losing it, according to the Peruvian Constitution, but was deprived of it when his nationality title, without which he was unable to exercise his rights as a Peruvian national, was annulled. Moreover, the procedure used to annul the nationality title did not comply with the provisions of domestic legislation, because, according to Article 110 of Peru's Law on General Norms of Administrative Procedures, a nationality title may only be annulled within the six months following the date on which it was acquired (infra para 109). Since this certificate was annulled in July 1997, 13 years after it had been granted, the State failed to comply with the provisions of its domestic legislation and arbitrarily deprived Mr Ivcher of his nationality, violating Article 20(3) of the Convention.
>
> 96. Furthermore, the authorities who annulled Mr Ivcher's nationality title did not have competence. As it has been established (supra para 76.a), Mr Ivcher Bronstein acquired

Peruvian nationality through a 'supreme resolution' of the President, and his nationality title was signed by the Minister for Foreign Affairs; however, he lost his nationality as the result of a "'directorial resolution' of the Migration and Naturalization Directorate', which is undoubtedly of a lower rank than the authority that granted the corresponding right (supra para 76.q), and, consequently, could not deprive the act of a superior of its effects. Once again, this demonstrates the arbitrary character of the revocation of Mr Ivcher's nationality, in violation of Article 20(3) de the American Convention.

97. In view of the foregoing, the Court concludes that the State violated the right to nationality embodied in Article 20(1) and 20(3) of the American Convention, with regard to Baruch Ivcher Bronstein.

The IACHR has repeatedly and forcefully emphasised the strength of non-discrimination as a binding norm of international law. In an Advisory Opinion concerning the situation of unlawful migrants in Mexico, *Juridical Condition and Rights of the Undocumented Migrants*, OC-18, Inter-American Court of Human Rights (Series A) No 18 (17 September 2003), the Court stated that: 6.107

100. In particular, when referring to the obligation to respect and ensure human rights, regardless of which of those rights are recognized by each State in domestic or international norms, the Court considers it clear that all States, as members of the international community, must comply with these obligations without any discrimination; this is intrinsically related to the right to equal protection before the law, which, in turn, derives 'directly from the oneness of the human family and is linked to the essential dignity of the individual'. The principle of equality before the law and non-discrimination permeates every act of the powers of the State, in all their manifestations, related to respecting and ensuring human rights. Indeed, this principle may be considered peremptory under general international law, inasmuch as it applies to all States, whether or not they are party to a specific international treaty, and gives rise to effects with regard to third parties, including individuals This implies that the State, both internationally and in its domestic legal system, and by means of the acts of any of its powers or of third parties who act under its tolerance, acquiescence or negligence, cannot behave in a way that is contrary to the principle of equality and non-discrimination, to the detriment of a determined group of persons.

101. Accordingly, this Court considers that the principle of equality before the law, equal protection before the law and non-discrimination belongs to *jus cogens*, because the whole legal structure of national and international public order rests on it and it is a fundamental principle that permeates all laws. Nowadays, no legal act that is in conflict with this fundamental principle is acceptable, and discriminatory treatment of any person, owing to gender, race, color, language, religion or belief, political or other opinion, national, ethnic or social origin, nationality, age, economic situation, property, civil status, birth or any other status is unacceptable. This principle (equality and non-discrimination) forms part of general international law. At the existing stage of the development of international law, the fundamental principle of equality and non-discrimination has entered the realm of *jus cogens*.

The parallel emphases of the IACHR, upon nationality-related rights and upon non-discrimination, have latterly come together in two important decisions 6.108

on petitions directed against the Dominican Republic. In *Yean and Bosico v Dominican Republic* [2005] Inter-American Court of Human Rights (Series C) No 130 (8 September 2005), the IACHR considered a situation in which it was found that children of Haitian parents were prevented from acquiring citizenship in the Dominican Republic, the country of their birth, by deprivation of birth registration. The Court unanimously found a violation by the Dominican Republic of (amongst others) rights to nationality under article XIX of the American Declaration of the Rights and Duties of Man (which provides, *inter alia*, that 'every person has the right to the nationality to which he is entitled by law and to change it')[69] and to equal protection of the law. In the judgment of the Court it observed that:

> [137] The importance of nationality is that, as the political and legal bond that connects a person to a specific State, it allows the individual to acquire and exercise rights and obligations inherent in membership in a political community. As such, nationality is a requirement for the exercise of specific rights.
>
> [138] The Court has established that: It is generally accepted today that nationality is an inherent right of all human beings. Not only is nationality the basic requirement for the exercise of political rights, it also has an important bearing on the individual's legal capacity. Thus, despite the fact that it is traditionally accepted that the conferral and regulation of nationality are matters for each state to decide, contemporary developments indicate that international law does impose certain limits on the broad powers enjoyed by the states in that area, and that the manners in which states regulate matters bearing on nationality cannot today be deemed within their sole jurisdiction; those powers of the state are also circumscribed by their obligations to ensure the full protection of human rights ... The classic doctrinal position, which viewed nationality as an attribute granted by the State to its subjects, has gradually evolved to a conception of nationality [in] which, in addition to being the competence of the State, [this] is a human right.

6.109 In *Yean and Bosico* the IACHR found (at [166]) that the Dominican Republic 'by applying to the children requirements that differed from those requisite for children under 13 years of age in order to obtain nationality' in the absence of 'reasonable and objective criteria' had acted arbitrarily. This had resulted in an inability for the children to make effective their rights to nationality which 'placed [the children] outside the State's juridical system and kept them stateless, which placed them in a situation of extreme vulnerability, as regards the exercise and enjoyment of their rights'. The Court concluded (at [174]) that discrimination by Dominican Republic officials on the basis of Haitian descent constituted an arbitrary deprivation of the children's nationality in breach of article 20 ACHR69.

6.110 Almost a decade later, in the light of continued intransigence by the state authorities in the treatment of persons of Haitian background in the Dominican Republic, the IACHR revisited the issue in the *Case of Expelled Dominicans and Haitians v*

[69] American Declaration of the Rights and Duties of Man, OAS Res XXX, adopted by the Ninth International Conference of American States (1948), *reprinted in* Basic Documents Pertaining to Human Rights in the Inter-American System, OEA/Ser.L.V/II.82 doc.6 rev.1, 17 (1992) XIX.

Dominican Republic [2014] Inter-American Court of Human Rights (Series C) No 282 (28 August 2014). The background was that families were targeted by government officials on the basis of Haitian descent, taken from their homes or off the street, detained and expelled to Haiti. The authorities refused to allow some victims to present their identification documents in order to avoid expulsion, and they confiscated and destroyed the identification documents of other victims. Further, some of the child victims had no identification documents as a result of ongoing discriminatory practices denying Dominican children of Haitian descent access to identification documents. The IACHR found that actions of the Dominican Republic authorities in expelling persons of Haitian origin and either destroying documents adduced to prove nationality and identity or ignoring these, *inter alia* breached article 20 (paras 272–76). Addressing arguments relating to persons who had not been able to show documents, the IACHR found:

> 294. In this regard, the Court finds it desirable to indicate that, irrespective of the legal terms of State laws and regulations, or their interpretation by the competent State organs, as indicated by this Court in the *Case of the Yean and Bosico Girls v Dominican Republic*, basic standards of reasonableness must be followed in matters relating to the rights and obligations established in the American Convention. Thus, as the Inter-American Court indicated in that case, 'to consider a person as a transient or in transit, irrespective of the classification used, the State must respect a reasonable time frame, and be coherent with the fact that an alien who develops ties in a State cannot be compared to a transient or to a person in transit'.

In relation to those persons also, the IACHR found that there had, *inter alia*, been a breach of article 20 ACHR69 rights.

iv. African Charter on Human and Peoples' Rights 1981

The African Charter on Human and Peoples' Rights 1981 (ACHPR81) contains no provision creating expressly nationality-related rights. At article 3 ACHPR81 it is provided that every individual 'shall be equal before the law' (article 3(1)) and 'shall be entitled to equal protection of the law' (article 3(2)). By article 5, ACHPR81 provides rights to dignity and respect for legal status: **6.111**

> Every individual shall have the right to the respect of the dignity inherent in a human being and to the recognition of his legal status. All forms of exploitation and degradation of man, particularly slavery, slave trade, torture, cruel, inhuman or degrading punishment and treatment shall be prohibited.

At article 12 ACHPR81 restraints are placed upon expulsion of non-nationals and mass expulsion of non-nationals ('Mass expulsion shall be that which is aimed at national, racial, ethnic or religious groups') is prohibited.

Although ACHPR81 does not expressly cite nationality-related rights, the African Commission on Human and Peoples' Rights as supervisory body for ACHPR81 **6.112** has consistently found these to be capable of engagement through other provisions including articles 3(2) and 5 ACHPR81. The Commission has also attached great importance to protection against discriminatory expulsion of non-nationals, implying willingness to take an even stronger approach to such expulsions when linked to deprivation of nationality. In *Union Inter-Africaine des Droits de l'Homme, Federation Internationale des Ligues des Droits de l'Homme and Others v Angola, African Commission on Human and Peoples' Rights*, Communication No 159/96 (1997), (2008) 15 IHRR 832 the Commission held mass expulsion of non-nationals to constitute a 'special violation' of rights:

> 16. The Commission concedes that African States in general and the Republic of Angola in particular are faced with many challenges, mainly economic. In the face of such difficulties, States often resort to radical measures aimed at protecting their nationals and their economies from non-nationals. Whatever the circumstances may be, however, such measures should not be taken at the detriment of the enjoyment of human rights. Mass expulsions of any category of persons, whether on the basis of nationality, religion, ethnic, racial or other considerations 'constitute a special violation of human rights'.

6.113 In *Malawi African Association and Others v Mauritania, African Commission on Human and Peoples' Rights*, Communication Nos 54/91, 61/91, 98/93, 164/97 and 196/97 and 210/98 (2000), (2001) 8 IHRR 268, the Commission held in the wake of large-scale expulsions of foreign nationals by Mauretania (at [126]) that 'Evicting Black Mauritanians from their houses and depriving them of their Mauritanian citizenship constitutes a violation of [the right of freedom of movement and residence at] article 12.1'. In *Modise v Botswana, Decision on Merits*, Communication No 97/93, (2002) 9 IHRR 209, the Commission (at [88]) found serious breaches of ACHPR81 standards in the sustained refusal by Botswana to acknowledge the citizenship of a political oppositionist, as a consequence of which he underwent repeated expulsion and/or exclusion (at [91]: 'the Complainant was deported four times to South Africa, and on all these occasions, he was rejected. He was forced to live for eight years in the "homeland" of Bophuthatswana, and then for another seven years in "No Man's Land", a border strip between the former South African Homeland of Bophuthatswana, and Botswana'). In *Interights (on behalf of Pan African Movement and Citizens for Peace in Eritrea) v Ethiopia*, African Commission on Human and Peoples' Rights, Communication No 233/99 (2003), the Commission adjourned consideration of communications relating to acts by both Ethiopia and Eritrea during the armed conflict between them from 1998 to 2000 in order to await the resolution of related issues by the Eritrea–Ethiopia Claims Commission, noting (at [3]) that 'It is also alleged that between June 1998 and July 1999, more than sixty one thousand people of Eritrean ethnic descent who are legal residents or citizens of Ethiopia were deported from Ethiopia. Most of these are urban deportees' and (at [59]), anticipating future resolution, that 'It is probable that the African Commission will reach a decision finding the Respondent States in violation of the rights of the individuals on whose behalf Interights is acting'.

v. African Charter on the Rights and Welfare of the Child 1990

6.114 The African Charter on the Rights and Welfare of the Child 1990 (ACRWC90) provides that:

Article 3: Non-Discrimination

Every child shall be entitled to the enjoyment of the rights and freedoms recognized and guaranteed in this Charter irrespective of the child's or his/her parents' or legal guardians' race, ethnic group, colour, sex, language, religion, political or other opinion, national and social origin, fortune, birth or other status.

Article 4: Best Interests of the Child

1. In all actions concerning the child undertaken by any person or authority the best interests of the child shall be the primary consideration.

2. In all judicial or administrative proceedings affecting a child who is capable of communicating his/her own views, and opportunity shall be provided for the views of the child to be heard either directly or through an impartial representative as a party to the proceedings and those views shall be taken into consideration by the relevant authority in accordance with the provisions of appropriate law.

Article 6: Name and Nationality

1. Every child shall have the right from his birth to a name.

2. Every child shall be registered immediately after birth.

3. Every child has the right to acquire a nationality.

4. States Parties to the present Charter shall undertake to ensure that their Constitutional legislation recognize the principles according to which a child shall acquire the nationality of the State in the territory of which he has been born if, at the time of the child's birth he is not granted nationality by any other State in accordance with its laws.

6.115 The first decision of the African Committee of Experts on the Rights and Welfare of the Child (ACERWC), which supervises the ACRWC90 regime, concerned children within the Nubian community in Kenya, descended from soldiers recruited in Sudan by the British colonial authorities and then settled in Kenya. Members of the community had not become citizens under Kenyan law and were prejudiced in the provision of documents of birth and identity in that country. The evidence demonstrated that children often faced difficulties in securing birth registration or documentation, and thereafter continuing uncertainty and insecurity of status, even though they were by law eligible for registration as Kenyan citizens at 18. In its decision in *Institute for Human Rights and Development in Africa and the Open Society Justice Initiative (on behalf of Children of Nubian Descent in Kenya) v Government of Kenya*, ACERWC, Communication No 002/Com/002/2009 (22 March 2011) the Committee observed of birth registration (at [38]) that 'It is rightly said that birth registration is the State's first official acknowledgment of a child's existence, and a child who is not registered at birth is in danger of being shut out of society—denied the right to an official identity, a recognized name and a nationality'. It held (at [42]) that:

> 42. The seemingly routine practice (which is applied more of as rule than in highly exceptional instances) of the State Party that leaves children of Nubian descent without acquiring a nationality for a very long period of 18 years is neither in line with the spirit and purpose of Article 6, nor promotes children's best interests, and therefore constitutes a violation of the African Children's Charter.

The Committee, *inter alia*, held (at [55]–[57]), that there was a breach of article 3 ACRWC90 in that children of Nubian descent in Kenya were treated differently from other children in Kenya, for which there is no legitimate justification, amounting to unlawful discrimination and a violation of Article 3 of the Charter that imposition in relation to children of Nubian descent of a lengthy and arduous process of vetting (including requiring them to demonstrate the nationality of their grandparents, as well as the need to seek and gain the approval of Nubian elders and governmental officials, etc) was discriminatory.

vi. Arab Charter on Human Rights 2004

6.116 The Arab Charter on Human Rights 2004 (ACHR04) affirms principles found in the United Nations Charter, UDHR48, and the Cairo Declaration on Human Rights in Islam 1990 (which contained no nationality-related protections). The new instrument came into force in 2008 upon the seventh ratification. As at August 2015 the Charter had been signed by 17 States and ratified by 13. At article 29 the ACHR04 provides that:

> Article 29
>
> 1. Everyone has the right to nationality. No one shall be arbitrarily or unlawfully deprived of his nationality.
>
> 2. States parties shall take such measures as they deem appropriate, in accordance with their domestic laws on nationality, to allow a child to acquire the mother's nationality, having due regard, in all cases, to the best interests of the child.
>
> 3. No one shall be denied the right to acquire another nationality, having due regard for the domestic legal procedures in his country.

6.117 As Govil and Edwards have observed, this in substance duplicates the rights at article 15 UDHR48 whilst on the point of passage of nationality through a child's mother article 29(2) diverges from the equal rights in acquisition, change, and retention of nationality at article 9 CEDAW79.[70] Article 43 ACHR04 however provides that 'nothing in [ACHR04] may be construed or interpreted as impairing the rights and

[70] R Govil and A Edwards, 'Women, Nationality, and Statelessness' in A Edwards and L van Waas, *Nationality and Statelessness Under International Law* (CUP, 2014) 185.

freedoms … set forth in the international and regional human rights instruments which the states parties have adopted or ratified, including the rights of women, the rights of children and the rights of minorities', which addresses what could otherwise be a source of inconsistency or of reduction of rights attributable to other sources:

> Article 43
>
> Nothing in this Charter may be construed or interpreted as impairing the rights and freedoms protected by the domestic laws of the States parties or those set forth in the international and regional human rights instruments which the states parties have adopted or ratified, including the rights of women, the rights of children and the rights of minorities.[71]

Although ACHR04 has been criticised by Arab civil society and others as falling short of international human rights standards in many key ways, it does by article 45 establish an independent Arab Human Rights Committee charged with reviewing reports (submitted every three years) from ratifying states. **6.118**

C5. Some Other Conventions of Potential Relevance (Indirect Reference)

i. Convention on the Nationality of Married Women 1957

The Convention on the Nationality of Married Women 1957 was concluded to eliminate or allay prejudice to women derived from provisions concerning the loss or acquisition of nationality by women as a result of marriage, divorce, or change of nationality by a husband. It seeks gender equality in relation to nationality of women upon or after marriage. As at December 2015 it had 71 parties. Its key provisions are as follows: **6.119**

> Article 1
>
> Each Contracting State agrees that neither the celebration nor the dissolution of a marriage between one of its nationals and an alien, nor the change of nationality by the husband during marriage, shall automatically affect the nationality of the wife.
>
> Article 2
>
> Each Contracting State agrees that neither the voluntary acquisition of the nationality of another State nor the renunciation of its nationality by one of its nationals shall prevent the retention of its nationality by the wife of such national.
>
> Article 3
>
> 1. Each Contracting State agrees that the alien wife of one of its nationals may, at her request, acquire the nationality of her husband through specially privileged naturalization

[71] M Mattar, 'Article 43 of the Arab Charter on Human Rights: Reconciling National, Regional, and International Standards' (2013) 26 *Harvard Human Rights Journal* 91.

procedures; the grant of such nationality may be subject to such limitations as may be imposed in the interests of national security or public policy.

2. Each Contracting State agrees that the present Convention shall not be construed as affecting any legislation or judicial practice by which the alien wife of one of its nationals may, at her request, acquire her husband's nationality as a matter of right.

ii. Convention on the Reduction of Statelessness 1961

6.120 The Convention on the Reduction of Statelessness 1961 (CRS61) attempts to reduce the scope for creation and perpetuation of statelessness. There are presently 65 States Parties including Australia, Belgium, Canada, Germany, the United Kingdom and New Zealand. France is a signatory but not a State Party, having not yet ratified CRS61. The United States is not a signatory. Article 1 CRS61 requires a State Party to grant its nationality to a person born in its territory who would otherwise be stateless in specified circumstances. Article 2 CRS61 provides that 'A foundling found in the territory of a Contracting State shall, in the absence of proof to the contrary, be considered to have been born within that territory of parents possessing the nationality of that State' and this is extended to births on ships or aircraft by article 3 CRS61. By article 4 CRS61, the grant of nationality to someone 'not born in the territory of a Contracting State, who would otherwise be stateless, if the nationality of one of his parents at the time of the person's birth was that of that State' is required. Article 5 CRS61 provides that where domestic law entails loss of nationality as a consequence of any change in the personal status of a person, such as marriage, termination of marriage, legitimation, recognition or adoption, this will only occur if the individual is not thereby rendered stateless. Article 6 provides that any consequential loss of nationality by a spouse or child of a principal losing or being deprived of nationality should be conditional upon their possession or acquisition of another nationality:

Article 6

If the law of a Contracting State provides for loss of its nationality by a person's spouse or children as a consequence of that person losing or being deprived of that nationality, such loss shall be conditional upon their possession or acquisition of another nationality.

Article 7 provides standards restraining renunciation or deprivation of nationality of potential or actual statelessness save in specified circumstances:

Article 7

1. (a) If the law of a Contracting State permits renunciation of nationality, such renunciation shall not result in loss of nationality unless the person concerned possesses or acquires another nationality.

(b) The provisions of subparagraph (*a*) of this paragraph shall not apply where their application would be inconsistent with the principles stated in articles 13 and 14 of the

Universal Declaration of Human Rights approved on 10 December 1948 by the General Assembly of the United Nations.

2. A national of a Contracting State who seeks naturalization in a foreign country shall not lose his nationality unless he acquires or has been accorded assurance of acquiring the nationality of that foreign country.

3. Subject to the provisions of paragraphs 4 and 5 of this article, a national of a Contracting State shall not lose his nationality, so as to become stateless, on the ground of departure, residence abroad, failure to register or on any similar ground.

4. A naturalized person may lose his nationality on account of residence abroad for a period, not less than seven consecutive years, specified by the law of the Contracting State concerned if he fails to declare to the appropriate authority his intention to retain his nationality.

5. In the case of a national of a Contracting State, born outside its territory, the law of that State may make the retention of its nationality after the expiry of one year from his attaining his majority conditional upon residence at that time in the territory of the State or registration with the appropriate authority.

6. Except in the circumstances mentioned in this article, a person shall not lose the nationality of a Contracting State, if such loss would render him stateless, notwithstanding that such loss is not expressly prohibited by any other provision of this Convention.

Article 8 CRS61 prohibits a State Party from depriving an individual of its nationality if statelessness would result, save that this is permitted under certain carefully delimited exceptions: **6.121**

Article 8

1. A Contracting State shall not deprive a person of its nationality if such deprivation would render him stateless.

2. Notwithstanding the provisions of paragraph 1 of this Article, a person may be deprived of the nationality of a Contracting State:

(a) in the circumstances in which, under paragraphs 4 and 5 of Article 7, it is permissible that a person should lose his nationality;
(b) where the nationality has been obtained by misrepresentation or fraud.

3. Notwithstanding the provisions of paragraph 1 of this Article, a Contracting State may retain the right to deprive a person of his nationality, if at the time of signature, ratification or accession it specifies its retention of such right on one or more of the following grounds, being grounds existing in its national law at that time:

(a) that, inconsistently with his duty of loyalty to the Contracting State, the person
   (i) has, in disregard of an express prohibition by the Contracting State rendered or continued to render services to, or received or continued to receive emoluments from, another State, or
   (ii) has conducted himself in a manner seriously prejudicial to the vital interests of the State;

(b) that the person has taken an oath, or made a formal declaration, of allegiance to another State, or given definite evidence of his determination to repudiate his allegiance to the Contracting State.

4. A Contracting State shall not exercise a power of deprivation permitted by paragraphs 2 or 3 of this Article except in accordance with law, which shall provide for the person concerned the right to a fair hearing by a court or other independent body.

6.122 Article 9 CRS61 prohibits a State Party from depriving an individual of its nationality, whether or not statelessness would result, on the basis of discrimination for one of the four enumerated reasons:

Article 9

A Contracting State may not deprive any person or group of persons of their nationality on racial, ethnic, religious or political grounds.

6.123 Article 10 CRS61 seeks to prevent statelessness arising from transfer of territories between States:

Article 10

1. Every treaty between Contracting States providing for the transfer of territory shall include provisions designed to secure that no person shall become stateless as a result of the transfer. A Contracting State shall use its best endeavours to secure that any such treaty made by it with a State which is not a party to this Convention includes such provisions.

2. In the absence of such provisions a Contracting State to which territory is transferred or which otherwise acquires territory shall confer its nationality on such persons as would otherwise become stateless as a result of the transfer or acquisition.

iii. European Convention on Nationality 1997

6.124 The European Convention on Nationality 1997 (ECN97), a Council of Europe instrument, expresses a number principles and rules extending to all aspects of nationality. ECN97 is designed to make acquisition of a new nationality and recovery of a former one easier, to ensure that nationality is lost only for good reason, preventing arbitrary withdrawal, to guarantee that the procedures governing applications for nationality are just, fair and open to appeal, and to regulate the situation of persons in danger of being left stateless as a result of state succession. ECN97 also covers multiple nationality, military obligations and co-operation between States Parties.

6.125 The text represents a synthesis of recent thinking on this question in national and international law and is the first international text to do so. It reflects the demographic and democratic changes (in particular migration and state succession which have occurred in Central and Eastern Europe since 1989). A number of States have applied ECN97 in the amendment of their nationality laws. As of January 2016 there were 20 States Parties including Denmark, Germany and the Netherlands. France had signed but not yet ratified the treaty. Belgium, the Republic of Ireland, Turkey and the United Kingdom were amongst the States which had neither signed nor ratified ECN97.

In chapter II ('General principles relating to nationality') at article 3, ECN97 mirrors article 1 of the Convention on Certain Questions Relating to the Conflict of Nationality Laws 1930, balancing domestic exclusivity in the realm of nationality against conditions for external recognition ('acceptance'): **6.126**

> Article 3: Competence of the State
>
> 1. Each State shall determine under its own law who are its nationals.
>
> 2. This law shall be accepted by other States in so far as it is consistent with applicable international conventions, customary international law and the principles of law generally recognised with regard to nationality.

Chapter II also contains two articles which incorporate into ECN97 important principles of international law in the realm of nationality. These provisions demonstrate three interrelated themes of current public international law: non-discrimination, prohibition of arbitrary denationalisation, and restriction on statelessness. The article 4 expression of a right to a nationality follows UDHR48 and other instruments and does not imply a duty upon a particular State to bestow nationality. The apparent prohibition of statelessness goes beyond other instruments including CRS61, which whilst aiming at the reduction of statelessness do contemplate the existence of extreme circumstances in which statelessness may be created. Article 5(1) illustrates that whilst non-discrimination is an important developing principal of international law, the scope of it differs from instrument to instrument: the article 5(1) list might be taken as a reasonable account of the core bases of discrimination disapproved in international law, but is not exhaustive of international legal protections: for instance see the article 18 CRPD06 provisions engaging discrimination based on disability: **6.127**

> Article 4: Principles
>
> The rules on nationality of each State Party shall be based on the following principles:
>
> a. everyone has the right to a nationality;
> b. statelessness shall be avoided;
> c. no one shall be arbitrarily deprived of his or her nationality;
> d. neither marriage nor the dissolution of a marriage between a national of a State Party and an alien, nor the change of nationality by one of the spouses during marriage, shall automatically affect the nationality of the other spouse.
>
> Article 5: Non-discrimination
>
> 1. The rules of a State Party on nationality shall not contain distinctions or include any practice which amount to discrimination on the grounds of sex, religion, race, colour or national or ethnic origin.

2. Each State Party shall be guided by the principle of non-discrimination between its nationals, whether they are nationals by birth or have acquired its nationality subsequently.

6.128 Chapter III ('Rules relating to nationality') sets out restraints upon domestic rules in the area of nationality:

Article 6: Acquisition of nationality

1. Each State Party shall provide in its internal law for its nationality to be acquired *ex lege* by the following persons:

a. spouses of its nationals;
b. children of one of its nationals, falling under the exception of Article 6, paragraph 1, subparagraph a;
c. children one of whose parents acquires or has acquired its nationality;
d. children adopted by one of its nationals;
e. persons who were born on its territory and reside there lawfully and habitually;
f. persons who are lawfully and habitually resident on its territory for a period of time beginning before the age of 18, that period to be determined by the internal law of the State Party concerned;
g. stateless persons and recognised refugees lawfully and habitually resident on its territory.

Article 7: Loss of nationality *ex lege* or at the initiative of a State Party

1. A State Party may not provide in its internal law for the loss of its nationality *ex lege* or at the initiative of the State Party except in the following cases:

a. voluntary acquisition of another nationality;
b. acquisition of the nationality of the State Party by means of fraudulent conduct, false information or concealment of any relevant fact attributable to the applicant;
c. voluntary service in a foreign military force;
d. conduct seriously prejudicial to the vital interests of the State Party;
e. lack of a genuine link between the State Party and a national habitually residing abroad;
f. where it is established during the minority of a child that the preconditions laid down by internal law which led to the *ex lege* acquisition of the nationality of the State Party are no longer fulfilled;
g. adoption of a child if the child acquires or possesses the foreign nationality of one or both of the adopting parents.

2. A State Party may provide for the loss of its nationality by children whose parents lose that nationality except in cases covered by sub-paragraphs c and d of paragraph 1. However, children shall not lose that nationality if one of their parents retains it.

3. A State Party may not provide in its internal law for the loss of its nationality under paragraphs 1 and 2 of this article if the person concerned would thereby become stateless, with the exception of the cases mentioned in paragraph 1, sub-paragraph b, of this article.

Article 8: Loss of nationality at the initiative of the individual

1. Each State Party shall permit the renunciation of its nationality provided the persons concerned do not thereby become stateless.

2. However, a State Party may provide in its internal law that renunciation may be effected only by nationals who are habitually resident abroad.

Article 9: Recovery of nationality

Each State Party shall facilitate, in the cases and under the conditions provided for by its internal law, the recovery of its nationality by former nationals who are lawfully and habitually resident on its territory.

iv. Council of Europe Convention on the Avoidance of Statelessness in Relation to State Succession 2006

The replacement of one State by another in the responsibility for the international relations of a particular territory, or 'state succession', has been a significant source of statelessness, as seen following the reassertion of national sovereignty by the Baltic states against the Union of Soviet Socialist Republics and the partition of the former Yugoslavia. The ILC had in 1999 published 'Draft Articles on Nationality of Natural Persons in Relation to the Succession of States'. The Council of Europe Convention on the Avoidance of Statelessness in relation to State Succession 2006 (CASSS06) represents one of the first attempts to establish, by treaty, minimum standards applicable to the continuation of nationality in cases of succession. It seeks to build upon Chapter VI ECN97 by developing more detailed rules to be applied by States in the context of state succession with a view to preventing, or at least as far as possible reducing, cases of statelessness. As at January 2016 there were six States Parties to CASSS06: Austria, Hungary, Moldova, Montenegro, the Netherlands and Norway. Germany and Ukraine have signed but not yet ratified the treaty. **6.129**

Article 1 of CASSS06 provides that: **6.130**

Article 1—Definitions

For the purposes of this Convention:

a. 'State succession' means the replacement of one State by another in the responsibility for the international relations of territory;
b. 'State concerned' means the predecessor State or the successor State, as the case may be;
c. 'Statelessness' means the situation where a person is not considered as a national by any State under the operation of its internal law;
d. 'Habitual residence' means a stable factual residence;
e. 'Person concerned' means every individual who, at the time of the State succession, had the nationality of the predecessor State and who has or would become stateless as a result of the State succession.

It will be noteworthy that CASSS06 at article 1(c) provides a differently worded definition of 'statelessness' from that in the Convention relating to the Status of Stateless Persons 1954 (CSSP54), and examined in chapter one, section C. There may be some difference in practice between the two. By article 1c '"Statelessness" means the situation where a person is not considered as a national by any State under the operation of its internal law', the term 'internal law' having been defined previously at article 1d ECN97 ('"internal law" means all types of provisions of the national legal system, including the constitution, legislation, regulations, decrees, case-law, customary rules and practice as well as rules deriving from binding international instruments'). The operative standards in CASSS06 are as follows:

Article 2: Right to a nationality

Everyone who, at the time of the State succession, had the nationality of the predecessor State and who has or would become stateless as a result of the State succession has the right to the nationality of a State concerned, in accordance with the following articles.

Article 3: Prevention of statelessness

The State concerned shall take all appropriate measures to prevent persons who, at the time of the State succession, had the nationality of the predecessor State, from becoming stateless as a result of the succession.

Article 4: Non-discrimination

When applying this Convention, States concerned shall not discriminate against any person concerned on any ground such as sex, race, colour, language, religion, political or other opinion, national or social origin, association with a national minority, property, birth or other status.

Article 5: Responsibility of the successor State

1. A successor State shall grant its nationality to persons who, at the time of the State succession, had the nationality of the predecessor State, and who have or would become stateless as a result of the State succession if at that time:

a. they were habitually resident in the territory which has become territory of the successor State, or
b. they were not habitually resident in any State concerned but had an appropriate connection with the successor State.

2. For the purpose of paragraph 1, sub-paragraph b, an appropriate connection includes *inter alia:*

a. a legal bond to a territorial unit of a predecessor State which has become territory of the successor State;
b. birth on the territory which has become territory of the successor State;
c. last habitual residence on the territory of the predecessor State which has become territory of the successor State.

Article 6: Responsibility of the predecessor State

A predecessor State shall not withdraw its nationality from its nationals who have not acquired the nationality of a successor State and who would otherwise become stateless as a result of the State succession.

Article 7: Respect for the expressed will of the person concerned

A successor State shall not refuse to grant its nationality under Article 5 paragraph 1, sub-paragraph b, where such nationality reflects the expressed will of the person concerned, on the grounds that such a person can acquire the nationality of another State concerned on the basis of an appropriate connection with that State.

v. European Convention on the Adoption of Children 1967 and European Convention on the Adoption of Children (Revised) 2008

Two Council of Europe instruments address nationality in the context of the adoption of children. Article 11(2) of the European Convention on the Adoption of Children 1967 and article 12(2) of the European Convention on the Adoption of Children (revised) 2008 both provide that 'Loss of nationality which could result from an adoption shall be conditional upon possession or acquisition of another nationality'. The first of these has 16 current States Parties including Germany, the Republic of Ireland and the United Kingdom. The second has 10 States Parties including Belgium, Germany and all of the Scandinavian members of the Council except Iceland. **6.131**

C6. Summary of International Law Material

An account has been set out above of international standards within a number of different classes. First, IHRL and the prohibition of discrimination under customary international law make up the basic material upon which interpretation of the protective extent of CSR51, embedded in the term 'persecution', may be ascertained. Next, regional human rights standards are potentially important as demonstrating the further elaboration or extension of international standards. Finally, there exists a large and diverse body of international law standards which may be engaged indirectly through open-ended provisions of IHRL, such as, for example, the prohibition on 'inhuman or degrading treatment or punishment' at article 7 ICCPR66, or the concept of arbitrariness in deprivation of the right of return to one's 'own country' at article 12(4) ICCPR66. The potential role of standards in the final category is as part of a *lex specialis* informing the content of IHRL norms. In the context of enquiry as to whether a nationality-related action or omission by a State is within a correct interpretation of 'persecution', international laws concerning nationality are particularly likely to be important as *lex specialis* **6.132** to IHRL, but still other regimes, for example, international humanitarian law (see paras 6.26–6.27 above), may also be relevant as *lex specialis* to IHRL in particular contexts. Whilst such norms may be valuable in determining whether international human rights standards are relevantly breached, it will be evident that not every inconsistency with such norms indicates such a breach, or the existence of persecution for purposes of article 1A(2) CSR51.

D. Jurisprudence

6.133 There is now a substantial jurisprudence addressing denaturalisation and related phenomena in the context of defining the term 'persecution' in article 1A2 CSR51. An account of significant decisions is set out below.

D1. Australia

6.134 In *Tesfamichael v MIMA* [1999] FCA 1661, (1999) 60 ALD 223, Mansfield J in the Federal Court of Australia addressed the refusal of a protection visa to an Eritrean-born Ethiopian who had been in Australia at the outbreak of war between Ethiopia and Eritrea in 1998. The case was addressed on the basis that the applicant was an Ethiopian national facing expulsion on the basis of Eritrean racial or national background:[72]

> 53. In my judgment, the Tribunal has failed to determine whether the applicant has a subjective fear of being expelled to Eritrea were he to return to Ethiopia. That is a central issue which it was required to address in the light of the applicant's claim.
>
> 54. In my judgment, the expulsion of an Ethiopian national from the country of origin to Eritrea would itself constitute persecution: see the discussion of what constitutes persecution in Chan per McHugh J at 429–431; and of the Full Court in *Guo* at 570. It is not a term which is defined in the Convention or in the Act. To expel a national from that person's country of nationality, perhaps leaving behind family and property, would fall within the category of harm sufficient to constitute persecution. That conclusion is also consistent with the views of Goodwill-Gill 'The Refugee in International Law' (Clarendon Press, Oxford, 1983 at 38–41) and the United Nations Handbook on Procedures and Criteria for Determining Refugee Status (pars 51–53).

---

[72] Many subsequent cases were dealt with on the basis that there had been denationalisation by Ethiopia In this case the claim was filed on 7 August 1998, when the denationalisation issue (as opposed to the occurrence of mass expulsion) was considerably less well defined: on the chronology of events see generally *The Horn Of Africa War: Mass Expulsions and the Nationality Issue (June 1998—April 2002)* (Human Rights Watch Africa Division, January 2003), available at: www.hrw.org/sites/default/files/reports/ethioerit0103.pdf.

The *Tesfamichael* decision was applied later in *V03/16458* [2004] RRTA 592, wherein the RRT (Ms K Magnussen) addressed a claim essentially based on *de facto* or *de jure* withdrawal of Ethiopian nationality/citizenship as well as denial of entry. The RRT found that the applicant remained an Ethiopian national (and was not an Eritrean national): **6.135**

> The applicant claims that he has been refused a renewal of his passport, with the effect that he has been deprived of his nationality, or effectively refused the international or diplomatic protection of his country. Alternatively, he claims that if he were permitted to re-enter Ethiopia, he would then be expelled from the territory of Ethiopia, or held in a border camp.
>
> There is no clear judicial authority that deprivation of citizenship is of itself persecution. Hathaway characterises persecution as a sustained or systematic violation of basic human rights. Other commentators have argued that denationalisation resulting in statelessness would be arbitrary, and any deprivation would be incompatible with international human rights norms, as the right to nationality is regarded as a fundamental right … In *Tesfamichael v MIMA* [1999] FCA 1661; (1999) 60 ALD 223, which involved similar facts to those which I accept in the present case, Mansfield J proceeded upon the assumption that expulsion from one's country of nationality in itself would amount to persecution.
>
> I consider and find that the withholding of the rights accorded to other citizens, including the repudiation of citizenship itself (including the right to enter and not be expelled from one's own country, to not be arrested or detained arbitrarily, and the full range of economic and social rights including the right to work and to subsist) is capable of constituting Convention persecution and serious harm in the terms of s 91R of the Migration Act.

The RRT directed that the applicant was entitled to refugee status.

The decision of Mansfield J in *Tesfamichael* was considered by the RRT (Ms J Wood) in *V00/11398* [2001] RRTA 419 in relation to claim to refugee status by a stateless Palestinian from Gaza, based on anticipated refusal of readmission to Gaza. The RRTA held that denial of entry to Gaza could, depending upon the reason, constitute persecution: **6.136**

> If the Applicant was denied entry then this could constitute persecution. It is a fundamental right recognised under both the Universal Declaration of Human Rights and the International Covenant on Civil and Political Rights (ICCPR) that a person has a right to re-enter their own country. While a State is entitled to take measures derogating their obligations at times of public emergency, it cannot do this on discriminatory grounds (see Article 4, ICCPR). In this case, the reason to refuse or seriously hinder re-entry, either to Israel or to Gaza in particular, would be solely on the grounds of the Applicant's Palestinian identity.
>
> It is an arguable point as to whether the identity of Palestinian is a political, racial or national identity. The Tribunal is satisfied that, while in the past it referred to a nationality, in common usage it now overlaps with all three of these and so satisfies the requirement for a Convention ground to be made out.

On the facts the RRT was not satisfied that the applicant was at risk of persecution in the form of exclusion attributable to the Palestinian Authority, but found that the applicant was a refugee because he faced persecution at the hands of the paramilitary/political Hamas movement, and a relevant risk of discrimination amounting to persecution by Israel as a Palestinian: 'there is a real chance that he would be denied or hindered in re-entering his place of habitual residence … his fear of persecution is well-founded'.

D2. Canada

6.137 In 1994 Cullen J in *Maarouf v Canada (MEI)* [1994] 1 FCR 723, [1993] FCJ No 1329 (QL), considering an application for judicial review of the status decision of a stateless Palestinian concluded that 'the claimant does not have to be legally able to return to a country of former habitual residence as denial of a right of return may in itself constitute an act of persecution by the state'.

6.138 Shortly thereafter in *Altawil v Canada (MCI)* (1996) FCJ No 986 (QL), [1996] 114 FTR 241 (FCTD), the applicant was a stateless Palestinian born in Gaza under Egyptian occupation who later lived in Qatar, but moved to Afghanistan to study. Conflict in Afghanistan prevented his compliance with the Qatar requirement that permanent residents of Qatar residing outside the country should report to authorities in Qatar every six months; the applicant was excluded from return to Qatar. Simpson J, observing that the reporting requirement applied generally to non-citizen residents of Qatar, concluded that its application to the applicant did not constitute persecution:

> While it is clear that a denial [of] a right to return may, in itself, constitute an act of persecution by a state, it seems to me that there must be something in the real circumstances which suggests persecutorial intent or conduct.

6.139 In *Thabet v Canada (MCI)* [1998] 4 FC 21 the Court of Appeal (Linden and McDonald JJA and Henry J) a stateless Palestinian born and formerly living in Kuwait, faced the refusal of that country to allow his return from Canada after university study. Whilst complex issues arose concerning identification of the country of former habitual residence, on the question of persecution the Court approved *Maarouf* and *Altawil*, observing that:

> To ensure that a claimant properly qualifies for Convention refugee status, the Board is compelled to ask itself why the applicant is being denied entry to a country of former habitual residence because the reason for the denial may, in certain circumstances, constitute an act of persecution by the state. The issue, therefore, is whether the Board asked itself this question.

On the facts however it was held that the Board had sufficiently enquired into the reasons for inability to return to Kuwait on the part of the appellant:

> It appears from these passages that the Board did address the question as to why the appellant was unable to return to Kuwait: he lacked a valid residency permit. This satisfies the requirement that the Board inquire into the reasons for denial of entry into one's country of former habitual residence.

There have been a number of other cases. One, which might be selected for illustration purposes, is *Daghmash v Canada (MCI)* [1998] 149 FTR 280, which concerned another stateless Palestinian, born and formerly living in Saudi Arabia. Lutfy J looked at evidence phrased as reflecting not a denial of rights to Palestinians in that country, but a withdrawal of special 'privileges' granted to Palestinians as against other non-Saudi nationals, concluding that the decision challenged on judicial review was sustainable because the claimant's inability to return to Saudi Arabia resulted from 'the expiry of the claimant's sponsorship, and not the general treatment of Palestinians in Saudi Arabia'. **6.140**

D3. United Kingdom

A number of significant cases have addressed questions of denationalisation or exclusion of nationals. In *Lazarevic v SSHD; Nooh v SSHD; Radivojevic v SSHD* [1997] EWCA Civ 1007, [1997] 1 WLR 1107, the relevant question was whether Yugoslav draft evaders, who were outside their country of nationality and whose country was unwilling to accept their return were, for that reason, refugees. It was held both that there was no Convention reason behind their fear of persecution and that they had not fled for a Convention reason. Hutchison LJ, with whom Simon Brown and Thorpe LJJ concurred, indicated that: **6.141**

> If a State arbitrarily excludes one of its citizens, thereby cutting him off from enjoyment of all those benefits and rights enjoyed by citizens and duties owed by a State to its citizens, there is in my view no difficulty in accepting that such conduct *can* amount to persecution. Such a person may properly say both that he *is being* persecuted and that he *fears* [continued] persecution in the future. I see no reason, given the scope and objects of the Convention, not to accept Professor Hathaway's formulation; and I am encouraged to do so by the fact that Simon Brown LJ cited it in terms which at least implied approval in [*R v Immigration Appeal Tribunal & Anor ex p Rajendrakumar; Ravichandran & Anor v SSHD* [1995] EWCA Civ 16, [1996] Imm AR 97] at 107. However, even accepting that refusal to permit return can constitute persecution for a Convention reason, I would not myself accept that that would be so in the case of those who, like these appellants, are anxious at all costs not to return: how can they be said to be harmed by such a refusal?

The appeal could not succeed on the back of this proposition because exclusion on the basis of draft evasion had been held, in the particular circumstances of the cases, not to be arbitrary.

Subsequently the Court of Appeal in *EB (Ethiopia) v SSHD* [2007] EWCA Civ 809, [2009] QB 1 decisively confirmed that arbitrary deprivation of key incidents of nationality resulting in inability to enter or reside in the country or otherwise obtain its protection, would in appropriate circumstances amount to persecution. The appeal concerned the position of a former resident of Ethiopia of Eritrean background deprived of Ethiopian nationality, or of the key incidents attaching thereto. The Asylum and Immigration Tribunal in the decision below had dismissed the appeal concluding that deprivation of nationality and exclusion was **6.142** not in itself sufficient to found a good claim under CSR51. The Court of Appeal found that the Tribunal's conclusion was unsustainable.

6.143 The Court was not required to consider whether the actions of the State were effective to terminate nationality under domestic law, because Ethiopia was in any the event the reference country for article 1A(2) CSR51 purposes. In *EB (Ethiopia)* Pill LJ setting out the background noted the decision of the Eritrea–Ethiopia Claims Commission identifying denationalisation of persons of Eritrean background as having been, in certain categories of case, contrary to international law, and referred to article 15 UDHR48, article 12(4) ICCPR66 and article 8 CRS61, also citing a note of guidance by the UNHCR and writings by commentators including Grahl-Madsen, Hathaway and Goodwin-Gill. He noted as applicable Council Directive 2004/83/EC of 29 April 2004 (the EU Qualification Directive) in particular at article 9(2)(b): 'Legal, administrative, police and/or judicial measures which are in themselves discriminatory or which are implemented in a discriminatory manner'.

6.144 Pill LJ then referred to the decision of the US Supreme Court in *Trop v Dulles, Secretary of State*, 356 US 86 (1957), an appeal challenging penal denationalisation by the United States for desertion in wartime, and quoted first Warren CJ in the majority judgment (at 101):

> There may be involved [in denationalisation] no physical mistreatment, no primitive torture. There is instead a total destruction of the individual's status in organised society … the punishment strips a citizen of his status in the national and international political community. His very existence is at the sufferance of the country in which he happens to find himself. In short the expatriate has lost the right to have rights.

Pill LJ further cited Brennan J, concurring in *Trop v Dulles* (at 110), and dicta from the Canadian decisions in *Maarouf* and *Altawil*.

6.145 The decision sets out a summary of the submission for the appellant:

> 44. Mr Blake accepts that, if effective nationality were to be restored, the appellant would cease to be a refugee. Until that happens, she is entitled to refugee status. The fact finding Tribunal should ask itself why the appellant is outside Ethiopia. The correct answer is that she was persecuted in Ethiopia, and feared even more serious persecution. She was arbitrarily deprived of those rights for ethnic reasons. Inability to enjoy the ordinary civil rights of an Ethiopian national persists. There is no justification in the evidence, it is submitted, for the removal of those documents necessary to assert civil rights. While the appellant had a *de jure* constitutional right to Ethiopian nationality, she was treated as a non-Ethiopian and that was why she left. She was 'an outcast in (her) own land' (*Trop*). The right not to be deprived of nationality on racial or ethnic grounds is well-established. A right to state protection and to basic civil rights must be available to a national and to deprive a person of them may amount to persecution which can consist of or include discriminatory administrative measures.

6.146 Pill LJ concluded that the decision of the tribunal below could not be upheld:

> 51. [T]he Tribunal have insufficiently considered the principle that, in addition to physical violence, deportation and threatened deportation, persecution may take the form

of administrative and other measures which are discriminatory or are implemented in a discriminatory manner (paragraph 34 above). Measures which deprive a national of the opportunity to conduct a business, follow employment and retain the documentation on which the conduct of ordinary life often depends was an aspect of EB's case not specifically or sufficiently considered by the Tribunal. They concluded that, when EB left Ethiopia, she was not 'at risk of ill- treatment'. This was a partial approach to the case presented by EB which relied also on the loss of ordinary civil rights.

...

53. The Tribunal in [*MA (Ethiopia) and another v SSHD; SSHD v RG (Ethiopia-Eritrea-Mixed ethnicity-dual nationality)* [2004] UKIAT 00324], cited by the present Tribunal, stated, at paragraph 31:

> 'However the Tribunal accepts that the reality of the situation for an individual claimant is that he or she is effectively deprived of citizenship which leads to treatment which can be categorised as persecution then, subject to other requirements of the Convention, there is a right to claim refugee status'.

The Tribunal in *MA* there accepted the possible consequences of an effective deprivation of citizenship. When the present Tribunal stated that 'there must be other treatment [in addition to loss of nationality] which would lead to persecution', they appear to have failed to have regard to the consequences of effective loss of citizenship which may amount to persecution. I accept that those consequences may be such as amount to persecution within the meaning of article 1A(2) of the Convention.

54. It is necessary to consider the circumstances in which the statelessness has occurred. I am not prepared to hold that a deprivation of nationality, whether *de facto* or *de jure*, in itself necessarily gives rise to refugee status. Neither does a voluntary departure, unconnected with persecution, followed by refusal to allow re-entry necessarily give rise to refugee status, though it may be a breach of international law. An analysis is required of the circumstances including the loss of rights involved in the particular case and the causes and consequences of them. I am not pre-judging possible future findings of fact in the present case but where persecution of the type now alleged has led to the departure from the state of habitual residence, which then either refuses to permit re-entry, or permits it only in circumstances where the former conditions will continue, it is possible for refugee status to be established. On the first premise, the persecution is in the loss and continued loss of civil rights and, on the second, the fear of such continued treatment on return.

Whilst Pill LJ concluded that the decision should be remitted for reconsideration, the majority (Longmore and Jacob LJJ) found that the decision below fell to be set aside and the appeal allowed outright. Longmore LJ set out the primary judgment for the majority: **6.147**

66. I have already recorded the Secretary of State's apparent acceptance that if EB had, in fact, been deprived of her citizenship by the arbitrary action of state employees, that would have *prima facie* been persecution within the terms of the Refugee Convention. That is certainly my own view, but it is worth pausing for a moment to understand why this must be the position.

67. The reason is that, if a State by executive action deprives a citizen of her citizenship, that does away with that citizen's individual rights which attach to her citizenship. One of those most basic rights is to be able freely to leave and freely to re-enter one's country. (There may well be others such as the right to vote.) Different considerations might arise if citizens were deprived of their nationality by duly constituted legislation or proper judicial decision but a deprivation by executive action will almost always be arbitrary and, if EB had in fact been deprived of her citizenship by the removal of her identity documents by state agents, it would certainly have been arbitrary.

68. These propositions are virtually self-evident but are buttressed by Article 15 of the Universal Declaration of Human Rights stating both that 'Everyone has the right to a nationality' and that 'No one shall be arbitrarily deprived of his nationality'. Similarly and more particularly Article 12 of the International Covenant on Civil and Political Rights 1966 states:

> 'No one shall be arbitrarily deprived of the right to enter his own country'.

69. [Citation of the opinions of Warren CJ and Brennan J in *Trop v Dulles*] … It is considerations such as these that have persuaded me that, if EB had been deprived of her citizenship by reason of her father's Eritrean origins, she would be entitled to the status of a refugee.

70. The question, therefore, is whether the fact that EB had her identity documents taken from her in Ethiopia with the aim of making it difficult for her in future to prove her nationality and the fact that she has now indeed lost her nationality *prima facie* entitles her to refugee status on the basis that the taking of identity documents constituted persecution when it happened and constitutes persecution for as long as that deprivation lasts. It seems to me that there can be no difference between such circumstances and an actual deprivation of citizenship. The precariousness is the same; the 'loss of the right to have rights' is the same; the 'uncertainty and the consequent psychological hurt' is the same. In these circumstances the taking of EB's identity documents was indeed persecution for a Convention reason when it happened and the AIT in MA were, in my view, wrong to conclude that some further (presumably physical) ill treatment was required. It is the arbitrary nature of the state employees' action that, in my view, distinguishes this case from *Revenko v SSHD* … where, as my Lord says, the arguments were, in any event, very different. On this aspect of the case I therefore consider that the AIT in the present case erred in law although only for the understandable reason that it was following its previous decision in MA.

71. That does not, of course, conclude the question since the hypothetical question whether EB would suffer persecution (or would have a well-founded fear of such persecution) on her return is the critical question which has to be addressed. The question is hypothetical because Ethiopia will not currently allow EB to be returned but the question must be answered now, not as at some date in the unknowable future when Ethiopia might change its mind and decide to re-admit EB for some reason which cannot be currently predicted. Once it is clear that EB was persecuted for a Convention reason while in Ethiopia, there is no basis on which it can be said that that state of affairs has now changed. I would therefore conclude that EB has a well-founded fear of persecution for a Convention reason and that she is now entitled to the status of a refugee.

Jacob LJ added a short judgment concurring with Longmore LJ.

Subsequently, in *MA (Ethiopia)* [2009] EWCA Civ 289 [2010] INLR 1 the Court of Appeal examined a case in which the claimant had on the findings of the tribunal below left Ethiopia with a valid passport, and had made what was judged to be insufficient effort to ascertain her position through the Ethiopian diplomatic authorities in the United Kingdom. In *MA (Ethiopia)* the Court broadly reiterated the effect of the decision in *EB (Ethiopia)*, whilst noting that persecution in an individual case remained a question of fact. At [60] Elias LJ, with whom Mummery and Stanley Burnton LJJ agreed, observed that: **6.148**

> 60. In my judgment, however, the correctness or otherwise of EB does not arise directly in this case since if the appellant were able to establish that she has been arbitrarily refused the right to return to Ethiopia for a Convention reason, that would in my view amount to persecution. It would negate one of the most fundamental rights attached to nationality, namely the right to live in the home country and all that goes with that. Denial of that right of abode would necessarily prevent the applicant from exercising a wide range of other rights—if not all—typically attached to nationality, as well as almost inevitably involving an interference with private and/or family life in breach of Article 8 of the ECHR.

The Court identified as mistaken the approach of the Tribunal in the decision appealed, which had been to assess risk on the basis of contemplated presence in Ethiopia, eliding consideration of whether there arose a bar to return precisely by reason of a persecutory deprivation of rights related to nationality. Elias LJ at paragraph 43 observed that: **6.149**

> 43. I also accept, as Ms Giovannetti concedes, that the Tribunal should have dealt with the question of Ethiopia's attitude to return as part of its assessment whether there was a real risk of persecution. It is true that the Tribunal will not generally be concerned about the process of removal; it must determine asylum status without regard to that issue, which is a matter for the Secretary of State. So the fact that it may, for example, prove to be impossible in practice to return someone seeking asylum has no relevance to the determination of their refugee status. But where the applicant contends that the denial of the right to return is part of the persecution itself, the Tribunal must engage with that question.

Finally, the Court in *MA (Ethiopia)* emphasised, addressing the apparent reservation of Hutchinson LJ on the point in the earlier *Lazarevic* case, that refusal of readmission does not cease to be persecutory because the affected individual does not wish to return. Elias LJ, with whom Mummery and Stanley Burnton LJJ agreed, observed at [58] that: **6.150**

> 58. There are two further matters which deserve mention. The first is that it may be said with some force that what the appellant wishes is to be refused authorisation to return to Ethiopia, and it is therefore fanciful to suggest that denial of re-entry constitutes any persecution at all. How can it be persecution if a state denies you the right to do what you do not want to do? This is a deceptively attractive argument, but I think it is wrong. The question is whether objectively there is a real risk of persecution on return. If there is not, then of course her unwillingness to return is not founded on any fear of persecution

> and she falls outside Article 1(A)(2) of the Convention. If there is, and she is unable to return, she falls within the terms of the Article even if she would prefer not to return even if there were no such risk. There must be numerous cases where someone genuinely fears persecution in his own country but is not unhappy that that should be so if it means that he can sustain a better standard of living for himself and his family in England.

The appeal was dismissed, but the appellant subsequently filed evidence with the Secretary of State for the Home Department of further enquiries to the Ethiopian authorities, and then was recognised as a refugee under CSR51.

6.151 The decisions of the Court of Appeal in the Ethiopian–Eritrean cases, *EB (Ethiopia)* and *MA (Ethiopia)* represent the basis of the current law in the United Kingdom. A valuable analysis of the principles established by the cases, applied to a considerable body of expert and other evidence, is contained in the decision of the Upper Tribunal (SIJs P Lane and Ward) in *ST (Ethnic Eritrean—nationality—return) Ethiopia CG* [2011] UKUT 252 (IAC) [69]–[90], which remains in force as country guidance in relation to Ethiopian–Eritrean cases.

6.152 As regards denial as opposed to deprivation of nationality, in *BA and others (Bedoon—statelessness—risk of persecution) Kuwait CG* [2004] UKIAT 00256 the Immigration Appeal Tribunal (Dr Storey, Mr AR Mackey, Ms Gleeson) had found that the ongoing denial of nationality to stateless Kuwaiti Bedoon appellants, with the consequences thereof, constituted persecution in respect of Bedoon denied civil identification documents:

> 64. However, we do agree with Mr Bartram that as a matter of fact denial of nationality is a decisive factor in this case. That is because in Kuwait the authorities, having acted to exclude most Bedoon from Kuwaiti nationality and from lawful residence status, have then confined access to basic civil, political, social, economic and cultural rights to those having either Kuwaiti nationality or (as lawful residents) foreign nationality.
>
> 65. What it seems to us the Adjudicators overlooked is that the objective evidence relating to the position of the Bedoon in general is in particularly strong terms. The Human Rights Watch Report for 2000 identifies 'widespread and systematic discrimination [resulting] in violations of civil and political rights protected by the [International Covenant on Civil and Political Rights]'. The UN Human Rights Committee in its Concluding Observation of 26–27 July expressed particular concern about the denial to the Bedoon of a significant number of civil and political rights guaranteed by the International Covenant on Civil and Political Rights (ICCPR), in particular Kuwaiti refusal to grant many Bedoon living in Kuwait any type of nationality.
>
> 66. The detailed documentation of the problems facing many Bedoon in relation to their civil and political and economic, social and cultural rights, as set out in the Human Rights Watch Report and other materials submitted, has also to be considered in historical perspective. The steps taken by the Kuwaiti authorities to marginalize the Bedoon have been part of a deliberate state policy to drive large numbers of the Bedoon out of the country. The dramatic fall in the number of Bedoon in Kuwait over the past two decades—some 120,000 persons having left in circumstances often tantamount to forced

deportation—speaks for itself: We bear in mind that at international law the prohibition of forced deportation is widely considered to have the status of *ius cogens.*

That decision has with minor variation been followed by others and so expresses the continuing position in the United Kingdom*: NM (documented or undocumented Bidoon: risk) Kuwait CG* [2013] UKUT 356 (IAC).

The United Kingdom jurisprudence has been distinctly less encouraging as regards refusal of return to a place of former residence by stateless persons, something which has arisen most frequently in Palestinian-related cases. In *AK v SSHD* [2006] EWCA Civ 1117 [2007] INLR 195, a decision of the Court of Appeal, Richards LJ observed, on an *obiter* basis, that: **6.153**

> 47. That line of argument is beset with difficulties. I am far from satisfied that there is a true analogy between a state's denial of entry to one of its own citizens and denial of entry to a stateless person (who, unlike a citizen, has no right of entry into the country), or that denial of entry to a stateless person can be said to constitute a denial of his third category rights of sufficient severity to amount to persecution (especially given the possibility of his exercising those rights elsewhere).

In *MA (Palestinian Territories) v SSHD* [2008] EWCA Civ 304 [2008] Imm AR 617, [2009] INLR 163, Maurice Kay LJ, with whom Lawrence Collins LJ and Sir William Aldous agreed, noted (at para 23) that the Canadian and New Zealand decisions referred to in submissions 'at their highest go no further than acceptance that, in some circumstances, to deny a stateless person re-entry may amount to persecution', concluding that: **6.154**

> 26. It is now necessary to confront the question whether, in principle, it is persecutory without more, to deny a stateless person re-entry to 'the country of his former habitual residence'. In my judgment, it is not. The denial does not interfere with a stateless person's rights in the way that it does with the rights of a national. There is a fundamental distinction between nationals and stateless persons in that respect. It is one thing to protect a stateless person from persecutory return to the country of his former habitual residence (as the Refugee Convention does), but it would be quite another thing to characterise a denial of re-entry as persecutory. The lot of a stateless person is an unhappy one, but to deny him a right that he has never enjoyed is not, in itself, persecution.

This has been followed by further decisions of the same Court to like effect in *MT (Palestinian Territories) v SSHD* [2008] EWCA Civ 1149 and *SH (Palestinian Territories) v SSHD* [2008] EWCA Civ 1150, [2009] Imm AR 306.

A matter which may get acquire increased relevance is that, whilst the United Kingdom until recent years had no substantial jurisprudence concerning the weight to be given to retention of nationality in circumstances in which deprivation of nationality of the United Kingdom was proposed, or had been carried out, this has begun to change. In *Pham v SSHD* [2015] UKSC 19 [2015] 3 All ER 1015 the United Kingdom Supreme Court considered the effect of article 1(1) CSSP54, as transposed into a domestic law protection against deprivation of British nationality creating statelessness. The case concerned a naturalised British citizen of **6.155**

Vietnamese origin deprived of British nationality, whose possession of its nationality was not accepted by Vietnam. One question raised on the appeal, but not resolved, was whether European Union law required application, in respect of deprivation of British nationality, of a test of proportionality as suggested by Case C-135/08 *Rottmann v Freistaat Bayern* [2010] ECR I-1449 [2010] QB 761, a proposition earlier rejected *G1 (Sudan) v SSHD* [2012] EWCA Civ 867 [2013] QB 1008 (see chapter one, para 1.198). Lord Mance (with whom Lord Neuberger, Lady Hale and Lord Wilson agreed) observed of the domestic law power of deprivation that given its nature, a strict standard of review was necessary in any event:

> 98. Removal of British citizenship under the power provided by section 40(2) of the British Nationality Act 1981 is, on any view, a radical step, particularly if the person affected has little real attachment to the country of any other nationality that he possesses and is unlikely to be able to return there. A correspondingly strict standard of judicial review must apply to any exercise of the power contained in section 40(2), and the tool of proportionality is one which would, in my view and for the reasons explained in *Kennedy v Charity Commission*, be both available and valuable for the purposes of such a review. If and so far as a withdrawal of nationality by the United Kingdom would at the same time mean loss of European citizenship, that is an additional detriment which a United Kingdom court could also take into account, when considering whether the withdrawal was under United Kingdom law proportionate. It is therefore improbable that the nature, strictness or outcome of such a review would differ according to whether it was conducted under domestic principles or whether it was also required to be conducted by reference to a principle of proportionality derived from Union law. On these points, I agree with what Lord Carnwath says in paras 59–60 of his judgment, as well as with what Lord Sumption says in paras 108–109 of his judgment.

The adherence of four judges, a majority within a Court panel of seven, provides considerable support for that proposition, albeit it was not directly material to the outcome of the appeal in *Pham*. It seems likely that the issue of the standard applicable deprivation of nationality under domestic law will be revisited by the United Kingdom Supreme Court before substantial time has passed.

D4. Germany

6.156 In Germany the Bundesverwaltungsgericht, or Federal Administrative Court, in its decision *9 C 3.95* (BVerwG 24 October 1995) has acknowledged that deprivation of nationality for a Convention reason may constitute persecution under CSR51. In *9 B 474.99* (BVerwG 7 December 1999) the Court found that a complainant of Cuban origin, barred from return to Cuba having stayed outside that country beyond the time allowed by the Cuban authorities, was not a refugee because the provision which rendered her *de facto* stateless was of general application and no Convention reason was shown.

6.157 In *10 C 50.07* (BVerwG 26 February 2009) the Court considered appeal from a judicial decision below. The first complainant was an ethnic Armenian formerly resident in Baku, now in Azerbaijan, and the second was her son born in Russia after her departure from Baku. The alleged fear was of persecution by Azerbaijan by reason of loss or non-possession of nationality and resulting absence of protected status there. The Court overturned a decision below in the complainants' favour:

> 16. In its approach, the court below correctly assumed that a deprivation of citizenship for reasons relevant to asylum may represent persecution within the meaning of Section 60 (1) of the Residence Act in conjunction with Article 9 of Directive 2004/83/EC, and may thus result in recognition of asylum status under Section 3(1) of the Asylum Procedure Act.
>
> 17. (a) The case law of the Federal Administrative Court has recognised that the withdrawal of citizenship may also constitute persecution relevant to asylum (see decision of 24 October 1995—Federal Administrative Court 9 C 3.95—Buchholz 402.25 Section 1 Asylum Procedure Act No180). Here the focus must always be on the state whose nationality was held by the person affected by the withdrawal until the act of withdrawal. No other actor—such as a third state or a private adversary—comes into consideration for this specific act of exclusion.
>
> 18. A state measure of persecution need not consist solely of interference with life, limb and liberty. Violations of other rights to protection and freedom may also qualify as characterising elements of persecution, depending on the circumstances of the case. In terms of the intensity of interference, persecution must also fundamentally be seen in a state's withdrawing the material rights of citizenship from a citizen, thus excluding him from the general system of peace within the national unit (see decision of 24 October 1995, op cit, p 62). This also applies taking account of Article 9(1)a of Directive 2004/83/EC of 29 April 2004 (known as the 'Qualification Directive') ... Accordingly, persecution relevant to asylum includes acts which are sufficiently serious by their nature or repetition as to constitute a severe violation of basic human rights, in particular the rights from which derogation cannot be made under Article 15(2) [ECHR]. While it is true that deprivation of citizenship does not violate a right that persists even in public emergencies within the meaning of the ECHR, this is also not necessary, since Article 9(1)a of the Directive mentions it only as a non-limiting example. But it does violate Article 15 [UDHR].
>
> 19. In the view of this Court, the critical factor in regard to the severity of the violation of rights caused by deprivation of citizenship, within the meaning of Article 9(1)a of the Directive, is that the state deprives the individual in question of his or her fundamental status as a citizen, and thus necessarily denies residency protection, thereby rendering the person stateless and unprotected—in other words: It excludes him or her from the state's system of protection and peace. The case law of other European states likewise views deprivation of citizenship, when linked with characteristics relevant to asylum, as an act of persecution ([see *EB (Ethiopia) v SSHD* esp paras] 54 and 75).
>
> 20. We may leave open the question as to whether a severe violation within the meaning of Article 9(1)a of the Directive also exists if the individual who has been deprived of citizenship still has a second nationality. However, Article 15(1) [UDHR] argues against such a position, granting the right only to 'a' nationality.
>
> 21. In assessing the severity of the violation of rights caused by deprivation of citizenship, under Article 4(3)c of the Directive, attention must also be given to the individual

position and personal circumstances of the person concerned. This means that the individual must also be personally severely affected by the deprivation of citizenship. In assessing the severity of the violation of rights in an individual case, it may also be significant whether and to what extent the individual has endeavoured to reverse the deprivation of citizenship, and to recover the nationality that had been withdrawn, and if applicable, what reasons prevented him or her from doing so.

22. The effects of a deprivation of citizenship that are relevant to asylum do not cease with the act of deprivation itself. Rather, the 9th Division of the Federal Administrative Court, in its decision of 24 October 1995 (op cit, p 62), has already emphasised that such an act of exclusion causes ongoing, significant harm to the individual concerned. The present Court, the 10th Division, concurs with that case law.

23. *De facto* deprivations of citizenship may be relevant to asylum when the state leaves the individual with the formal legal position, but *de facto* denies him or her the resulting rights of citizenship, and in particular does not grant him or her the protection of the state. The assessment of exclusion measures in asylum law depends on the actual *de facto* consequences that are thus produced.

6.158 The Court went on to emphasise the need for relevant causation, in a denationalisation case said to engage the law of refugee status, noting that in other decisions the Court had found denationalisation not supportive of a claim to asylum. But it acknowledged (at [25]) that where relevant causation was present, denationalisation was a continuing act of persecution:

> If the persecution lies precisely in the creation, by the state of the individual's former nationality, of a condition of statelessness that is relevant to asylum, this must be viewed under asylum law as a (continuing) persecution specifically by that state of the person's (former) nationality. Equivalent considerations apply to the case, which the court below deemed possible, that the Complainants were only stateless *de facto*, but *de jure* might still have Azerbaijani nationality.

6.159 The Court noted (at [39]), before remitting the case, that if it were concluded that the complainant had omitted to make reasonable efforts to reassert Azerbaijani nationality and attached rights, 'the necessary severity of violation of rights under Article 9(1a) of the Directive may well be absent'.

D5. New Zealand

6.160 In *Refugee Appeal No 72635/01* (6 September 2002) the RSAA (Mr R Haines, chair) addressed the case of a Kuwaiti Bedoon, whose claim was based upon discriminatory exclusion from citizenship and from the territory of Kuwait. The RSAA provided a detailed review of international law relating to statelessness and nationality concluding that there was no duty upon States to confer nationality upon residents or others and that in general statelessness 'is considered to be the result of the operation and conflict of nationality laws, not the result of persecution' (paras 69–90). The law of New Zealand considers that a well-founded fear cannot be shown where return is impossible (contrast the UK and German position above and the US decisions below) so that the appellant could not succeed:

> [159] Applying the principles to the appellant's claim *vis-à-vis* Kuwait, we have earlier found that Bedoons for whom Kuwait is a country of former habitual residence and who are similarly placed to the appellant are denied re-entry and are refused re-admission. As a matter of fact the appellant will not be allowed or permitted by the Kuwaiti authorities to return to Kuwait. It follows that his fear of being persecuted in Kuwait is not a well-founded fear. The predicament he faces is the predicament of a stateless person, not of a Convention refugee.

It was held that in the alternative he would still fail for absence of a Convention reason: **6.161**

> 189. It is simply not possible to argue that because the nationality laws of a country do not confer nationality on all those born in the state, and because such persons are expelled and prevented from returning, such persons are refugees. Otherwise it would mean all stateless persons who are expelled and prevented from returning are refugees. This is precisely what the drafting history and all the jurisprudence says is *not* the position.
>
> 190. The statement that the nationality ground of persecution includes statelessness anticipates a situation in which the risk of serious harm or the failure of state protection is 'for reason of' the person's statelessness. An analogy can be drawn with the [example of discrimination in Nazi Germany against a hypothetical] Jewish shopkeeper postulated by Lord Hoffmann in *R v Immigration Appeal Tribunal; Ex parte Shah* [1999] 2 AC 629, 654A (HL).
>
> 191. But the facts of the appellant's case are very different. He is stateless because Kuwait applies the jus sanguinis principle and there is no Convention element to this circumstance. His expulsion and inability to return are simply consequences of his condition. Any other conclusion would mean that the expulsion of a stateless person for reason of his or her lack of nationality of the expelling state is persecution for a Convention reason. For the reasons already given, this is an untenable claim.

In a later decision *Refugee Appeal No 74467* (1 September 2004, Ms VJ Shaw) the RSAA considered another Kuwaiti Bedoon case, exploring the background to the situation at greater length (paras 41–72) and concluding that the evidence showed the underlying reason for alienation of the nomadic tribes from which the Bedoon descended as being the desire to separate them from entitlement to a share in the oil wealth by enacting a nationality law under which only 'settled' persons were eligible for citizenship. At paragraphs 61–65 the RSAA noted the content of a detailed Human Rights Watch report concluding that the discrimination faced by the Bedoon in Kuwait lay in calculated marginalisation by those controlling the State so that the nationality laws were in fact a manifestation of pre-existing antipathy towards *Bedoon*. The NZAA held in contrast to *Refugee Appeal No 72635/01* that nexus to a Convention reason did arise. In *Refugee Appeal No 74880* (29 September 2005, Mr CM Treadwell) the RSAA addressing another Kuwaiti Bedoon case finding (para 83) that 'The analysis of the country information and the finding of a nexus to a Convention reason in the historical **6.162** disenfranchisement of *bedoon* is persuasive' and that the appellant had shown he could not regularise his status, so that following a putatively irregular entry to Kuwait 'At worst, he risks being detained and/or deported' (para 84). This was followed and applied more recently in *Refugee Appeal No 76506* (29 July 2010, Mr AR Mackey).

D6. United States

6.163 Separately from the refugee context, the United States Supreme Court has delivered substantial decisions characterising denationalisation as breaching the prohibition upon cruel and unusual punishment in the Eighth Amendment to the United States Constitution. In *Trop v Dulles, Secretary of State* (1957) 356 US 86, at 101–03, on an appeal challenging deprivation of United States' citizenship for desertion in wartime, the effect of denationalisation was described in strong terms by Warren CJ, delivering the majority judgment of the Court:

> We believe, as did Chief Judge Clark in the court below, that use of denationalization as a punishment is barred by the Eighth Amendment. There may be involved no physical mistreatment, no primitive torture. There is, instead, the total destruction of the individual's status in organized society. It is a form of punishment more primitive than torture, for it destroys for the individual the political existence that was centuries in the development. The punishment strips the citizen of his status in the national and international political community. His very existence is at the sufferance of the country in which he happens to find himself. While any one country may accord him some rights and, presumably, as long as he remained in this country, he would enjoy the limited rights of an alien, no country need do so, because he is stateless. Furthermore, his enjoyment of even the limited rights of an alien might be subject to termination at any time by reason of deportation. In short, the expatriate has lost the right to have rights.
>
> This punishment is offensive to cardinal principles for which the Constitution stands. It subjects the individual to a fate of ever-increasing fear and distress. He knows not what discriminations may be established against him, what proscriptions may be directed against him, and when and for what cause his existence in his native land may be terminated. He may be subject to banishment, a fate universally decried by civilized people. He is stateless, a condition deplored in the international community of democracies. It is no answer to suggest that all the disastrous consequences of this fate may not be brought to bear on a stateless person. The threat makes the punishment obnoxious.
>
> The civilized nations of the world are in virtual unanimity that statelessness is not to be imposed as punishment for crime. It is true that several countries prescribe expatriation in the event that their nationals engage in conduct in derogation of native allegiance. Even statutes of this sort are generally applicable primarily to naturalized citizens. But use of denationalization as punishment for crime is an entirely different matter. The United Nations' survey of the nationality laws of 84 nations of the world reveals that only two countries, the Philippines and Turkey, impose denationalization as a penalty for desertion. In this country, the Eighth Amendment forbids this to be done.

The majority judgment conspicuously adopted language employed by Hannah Arendt in *The Origins of Totalitarianism*: 'the punishment strips a citizen of his status in the national and international political community. His very existence is at the sufferance of the country in which he happens to find himself ... In short the expatriate has lost the right to have rights'.[73] Frankfurter J dissented from the majority judgment, pointing (at 127) to the need for sensitivity to particular consequences of denationalisation:

> Nor has Congress fallen afoul of that prohibition on cruel and unusual punishment because a person's post-denationalization status has elements of unpredictability. Presumably a denationalized person becomes an alien *vis-à-vis* the United States. The very substantial rights and privileges that the alien in this country enjoys under the federal and state constitutions puts him in a very different condition from that of an outlaw in fifteenth-century England. He need not be in constant fear lest some dire and unforeseen fate be imposed on him by arbitrary governmental action—certainly not 'while this Court sits' (Holmes, J, dissenting in *Panhandle Oil Co v Mississippi ex rel Knor*, 277 U S 218, 223). The multitudinous decisions of this Court protective of the rights of aliens bear weighty testimony. And the assumption that brutal treatment is the inevitable lot of denationalized persons found in other countries is a slender basis on which to strike down an Act of Congress otherwise amply sustainable.

Whilst the Court in *Perez v Brownell* 356 US 44 (1958), decided at the same time as *Trop v Dulles*, declined to find unconstitutional denaturalisation by reason of expatriation and the demonstration of allegiance to another State, it reversed this decision later, in *Afroyim v Rusk*, 387 US 253 (1967). **6.164**

None of the United States Supreme Court cases concerned the definition of persecution for purposes of CSR51. The latter issue has however been considered in recent years in several significant decisions of the United States Federal Court of Appeals. **6.165**

In *Haile v Gonzales*, 421 F 3d 493 (7th Cir 2005) the US Federal Court of Appeals for the Seventh Circuit (Coffey, Manion, Rovner CJs) dealt with petitions for review from Ethiopians of Eritrean descent who asserted well-founded fear from Ethiopia including the withdrawal of recognition as citizens (and hence nationals). The Court referred to earlier decisions holding that denial of citizenship is not persecution ('The decision to bestow or deny citizenship is deeply-rooted in national sovereignty and must be left to the individual nation's discretion'), but observed that in earlier cases there had not been a deprivation of extant nationality based upon ethnic or national background and no case referred to 'nor any other case of which we are aware—suggests that a government has the sovereign right to strip citizenship from a class of persons based on their ethnicity': **6.166**

> It is arguable that such a program of denationalization and deportation is in fact a particularly acute form of persecution. We have suggested, for example, that 'a campaign of

[73] H Arendt, *The Origins of Totalitarianism* (2nd edn, Houghton Mifflin Harcourt, 1973) 295–96.

expulsions' based on ethnicity, even where not orchestrated by the government, would constitute persecution, see *Bucur, 109 F 3d at 403 (7th Cir 1997)*, and a leading authority on asylum law has asserted that '[e]xpulsion of citizens or nationals almost invariably constitutes persecution', see Deborah E Anker, Law of Asylum in the United States (3d ed 1999) at 246. Historically, denationalization has been a precursor to even worse things; it was one of the first steps taken by the Nazi regime against the Jews, see, eg, Lucy S Dawidowicz, The War Against the Jews, 1933–1945 (1975) at 67–69 (discussing the Reich Citizenship Law of 1935, which stripped German Jews of their citizenship); see also *Guchshenkov v Ashcroft*, [2004] USCA7 202; 366 F 3d 554, 559 (7th Cir 2004) ('The Nuremberg Laws, which subjected the Jews in Nazi Germany to persecution, were laws, but that doesn't mean that Jews were not persecuted'.) One human-rights group has expressed concern about the increasing use of denationalization as a political weapon, particularly in Africa, see Open Society Justice Initiative, 'Statelessness, Discrimination and Denationalization: Emerging Problems Requiring Action', Statement to the African Commission on Human and Peoples' Rights (April 29, 2005) … ([which expresses] concern that '[t]he victims of this form of persecution are unable to challenge it as it occurs under the guise of states' sovereign rights').

6.167 The Court further observed that:

> Whether denationalization as such amounts to persecution, and whether it is persecution in these cases, we are not yet able to say. The meaning of 'persecution' in immigration law remains ill-defined, see Sahi v Gonzales, [2005] USCA7 402; 416 F 3d 587, 2005 WL 1713417 at *2 (7th Cir July 25, 2005), and primary responsibility for determining that meaning lies with the Board of Immigration Appeals, see id, which to our knowledge has not addressed this question.

The cases were remitted.

6.168 In *Haile v Holder*, 591 F 3d 572, 574 (7th Cir 2010) the *Haile* case came back to a different panel of the same Circuit (Posner, Kanne, Rovner CJs), following a further decision of the Board dismissing the claim on the basis that denationalisation 'would not amount to persecution because a country has a right to determine who is or is not a citizen' which the Court found 'problematic' as failing to 'acknowledge the fundamental distinction between denying someone citizenship and *divesting* someone of citizenship'.

6.169 The Court reiterated and re-emphasised its earlier observation that 'It is arguable that such a program of denationalization and deportation is in fact a particularly acute form of persecution'. It differentiated situations referred to below of state succession in which new nationalities had been framed:

> From such observations the Board leapt to the conclusion that even if a person loses his citizenship because of a 'protected ground'—which is to say a ground on which US law permits a person to seek asylum, such as religion—such a loss of citizenship does not, without more, amount to persecution. We asked the Board's lawyer at argument whether this meant that had the United States after the 9/11 terrorist attacks stripped all Muslim citizens of the United States of their US citizenship, but allowed them to remain in the United States, this would not have been persecution—they would have to show additional harm. She said yes. By the same token, the mere fact of Nazi Germany's having

denationalized its Jewish citizens in 1941 would not have been persecution, though their subsequent further mistreatment would have been.

> We find it hard to believe that that is actually the Board's position. But in any event the Board's conclusion that the petitioner in this case had to prove 'denationalization plus' doesn't follow from its premise, and unlike a jury an administrative agency has to provide a reasoned justification for its rulings ... From the correct premise that a change of citizenship incident to a change in national boundaries is not persecution per se, it does not follow that taking away a person's citizenship because of his religion or ethnicity is not persecution. If Ethiopia denationalized the petitioner because of his Eritrean ethnicity, it did so because of hostility to Eritreans; and the analogy to the Nazi treatment of Jews is close enough to suggest that his denationalization was persecution and created a presumption that he has a well-founded fear of being persecuted should he be returned to Ethiopia ... Indeed, if to be made stateless is persecution, as we believe, at least in the absence of any reason for disbelief offered by the Board of Immigration Appeals, see *Giday v Gonzales*, 434 F 3d 543, 555–56 (7th Cir 2006); *Mengstu v Holder*, 560 F 3d 1055, 1059 (9th Cir 2009), then to be deported to the country that made you stateless and continues to consider you stateless is to be subjected to persecution even if the country will allow you to remain and will not bother you as long as you behave yourself.

In *Stserba v Holder*, 646 F 3d 964, 978 (6th Cir 2011) the US Federal Court of Appeals for the Sixth Circuit (Moore and White CJJ, Varlan DJ) remitted another appeal, which related to a claimant who was a former citizen of the USSR. She had not been granted the nationality of Estonia, where she resided, when this asserted its independence. The Court considered that there was a need, not met in the decision challenged or in adjudication below, to consider whether the nature of Estonia's nationality law and practice was discriminatory on a relevant basis: **6.170**

> Neither the IJ nor the BIA considered whether Estonia's citizenship law amounted to ethnically targeted denationalization, but there is reason to suspect that it did. By limiting citizenship to pre-1940 citizens and their descendants, Estonia manipulated its citizenship rules to exclude ethnic Russians who immigrated during the Soviet occupation. This limit even applied to residents such as Stserba who were born in Estonia. Although Estonia's policy of rolling back citizenship to 1940 did not mention ethnicity, the citizenship policy contained 'an irreducible ethnic element' because it 'base[d] citizenship for those who had become resident[s] during the Soviet era on language ability or knowledge of history—stratagems that effectively denationalized most Russians: Waters, The Blessing of Departure, supra, at 31; A.R348 (Open Society Institute Report).

E. Commentators

Whilst not all experts have addressed denationalisation and kindred acts in detail, amongst those who have there is a substantial consensus that denationalisation and/or the immediate consequences thereof may constitute persecution. Grahl-Madsen, an expert of considerable stature and the earliest commentator to examine **6.171** the definition of persecution in any detail,[74] concluded that 'As de-nationalisation (deprivation of citizenship) for political, ethnic, or similar reasons incurs loss of civil rights, that too may be classified as persecution'.[75]

6.172 Amongst the recent commentators, Zimmermann and Mahler provide a relatively succinct note that the Bundesverwaltungsgericht in *10 C 50.07* (BVerwG 26 February 2009) considered reduction of status as potentially constituting persecution:

> In particular, the court stated that also the violations of rights which are not included in the above-mentioned list may nevertheless lead to refugee status provided the violation is deemed severe, which might also be the case if a State deprives a citizen of constituting an equal part of society.[76]

Goodwin-Gill and McAdam in their general account acknowledge the difficulty in attaining a complete account of the content of persecution ('little purpose is served by attempting to list all its known measures'), but it appears that they accept denationalisation for relevant reason as likely to be persecution, at least where this is accompanied by expulsion or exclusion from the territory with continuing effect:

> Certain measures, such as the forcible expulsion of an ethnic minority, or of an individual, will clearly show the severance of the normal relationship between citizen and State, but the relationship of cause and effect may be less clear in other cases [as where there is only indirect motivation to depart].[77]

6.173 Anker sets out a particularly clear elucidation of linkage between nationality-related decisions or omissions by States and persecution in article 1A(2) terms, albeit one restricted to US authority. Citing, *inter alia*, the domestic authorities in *Haile v Gonzales*, *Haile v Holder* and *Stserba v Holder*, she concludes that:

> Expulsion of citizens or nationals almost invariably constitutes persecution, and expulsion of a noncitizen or non-national, under certain circumstances, also can amount to persecution. The definition of refugee includes persons who are citizens or nationals of a persecuting country as well as noncitizens and non-nationals of such a state.[78] Under international law, although states possess the right to expel noncitizens and non-nationals from their territor, that right is not unfettered.
>
> While mere status as a stateless person or inability to obtain citizenship generally does not amount to persecution, denationalisation, or a revocation of citizenship that leaves a person stateless, does amount to persecution.[79]

Anker provides a notably crisp, cogent, and realistic account well supported by references to jurisprudence and other relevant material.

---

[74] Neither Robinson nor Vernant did so.
[75] Grahl-Madsen (n 9 above) 215, §187.
[76] Mahler and Zimmermann (n 3 above) 353, §244.
[77] Goodwin-Gill and McAdam (n 32 above) 93–94.
[78] D Anker, *The Law of Asylum in the United States* (7th edn, Thomson Reuters, 2014) 323, §4.36.
[79] Ibid, 324–25, §4.36.

Some commentators seem to begin with the examination not of actions or omissions regarding stateless themselves, but from the effect thereof upon freedom of movement, and in particular the right to return. Symes and Jorro do this, though also referring specifically to denial of citizenship as a part of their analysis: 6.174

> The rights of an individual to depart from, and return to, their country of origin, possess a clear foundation in human rights law. [In *Lazarevic v SSHD*; *Nooh v SSHD*; *Radivojevic v SSHD* [1997] EWCA Civ 1007, [1997] 1 WLR 1107] Hutchinson LJ recognised that denial of the whole basket of rights accruing to citizenship could amount to persecution, ruling that this principle did not extend to persons who were anxious not to return at [for other reasons]. This is not to say that denial of citizenship alone will constitute persecution, albeit that it may constitute evidence of the same. Whether denial of citizenship is of requisite severity is a question of fact; arbitrary actions of a state are more likely to qualify. Denial of re-entry to the stateless is not the same as ... denying the same to citizens, but where some additional factor is present beyond bare denial, such as racial motivation, the requisite threshold may be met [subject to satisfaction of the persecution threshold].[80]

Hathaway and Foster also treat denationalisation initially by reference freedom of movement and the right to return: 6.175

> In contrast to persons who are outside their own country because they face the forward-looking rejection of re-entry, a person who has been denationalized- purely past persecution, and incapable of being repeated—will not necessarily be able to establish a forward-looking risk of serious harm. Unless able to show that the denationalization poses a real chance of denial of re-entry, a refugee claim by a denationalized person may be recognised only if she is able to distinct forward-looking risk of harm.[81]

This might appear to be a rejection of denationalisation as giving rise to a forward-looking risk of relevant harm. But in context it is clear that this is not what is suggested. The authors distinguish cases where denationalisation gives rise to a continued exclusion from 'the state's system of protection and peace', citing *10 C 50.07* (BVerwG 26 February 2009) and *Haile v Holder*, 591 F 3d 572 (7th Cir 2010), which as noted above referred to the Nazi denationalisations as a parallel, so that in the event of denationalisation by reason of ethnic or national discrimination 'the analogy to the Nazi treatment of Jews is close enough to suggest that his denationalization was persecution'. Hathaway and Foster plainly in the quoted passage and elsewhere acknowledge that a denationalisation with continuing consequences of sufficient seriousness, including exclusion from the territory, will give rise to a forward-looking risk of serious harm.

Overall Hathaway and Foster conclude that: 6.176

> In line with these decisions, despite the insufficiency of past denationalization *per se* to ground a claim of forward-looking serious harm, it is surely right to recognize the

---

[80] M Symes and P Jorro, *Asylum Law and Practice* (2nd edn, Bloomsbury Professional, 2010) 207, §4.6, 198–99, §3.50.

[81] Hathaway and Foster (n 33 above) 251.

> existence of serious harm at least in those cases where the denationalized person would, once in the country, face forms of consequential human rights abuse—including because of exclusion from the state's protective apparatus- that rise to the level of serious harm.
>
> In sum, the risk of denial of the right to internal freedom of movement and choice of residence will ordinarily amount to serious harm for refugee law purposes, unless that denial conforms to the strict requirements for valid limitation of that right at international law. Denial of the right to enter one's own country—a right not subject to limitations, and inhering in both citizens and in non-citizens who have a long-term attachment to the country—is also a clear breach of the internationally guaranteed right to freedom of movement, the risk of which will thus properly be understood to be serious harm for refugee law purposes.[82]

The view of Hathaway and Foster is a particularly important one, as they provide a relatively detailed analysis of the term 'persecution' in article 1A(2) CSR51, based upon international human rights laws. They do not state any belief that denationalisation in particular circumstances does not constitute persecution. Their analysis however stresses the need for a finding of a current forward-looking fear of persecution, and consequently for a forward-looking analysis of the consequences of denationalisation. They do not suggest that this analysis will not encompass the wider context including the origin, motivation and nature of particular measures, and their analysis conjecturally encompasses both persons able to return, but facing consequences of denationalisation, and those barred from return.

6.177 The treatment of denationalisation by some authors under the heading of freedom of movement might be thought not ideal, because it suggests an initial focus primarily on a single, albeit very important, area in which denationalisation may affect the individual, rather than upon the continuing deprivation of a status (national, citizen) connoting membership. But the reference by Hathaway and Foster to *10 C 50.07* implicitly acknowledges the broader context. And the treatment of freedom of movement as a starting point also possesses a potentially compensating merit, that of enabling Hathaway and Foster to deal together with exile or denationalisation of citizens, on the one hand, and on the other, exclusion from the 'own country' of a non-national, emphasising the extension of relevant protection to the latter class under the human rights standards examined earlier, most particularly if not exclusively article 12(4) ICCPR66.

6.178 In a recent article Lambert goes further than other commentators arguing that there are only limited circumstances in which deprivation of nationality will not amount to persecution in CSR51 terms:

> This article argues that short of engineering one's deprivation of nationality for personal convenience, all deprivation of nationality should amount to persecution (and inhuman or degrading treatment) because nationality is and continues to be the gateway for the exercise of most human rights. Where deprivation of nationality is found to be arbitrary

[82] Ibid, 251–52.

(eg discriminatory), this should lead to a finding of persecution for a Convention ground because race, nationality, and particular social group are deeply rooted in the prohibition against discrimination. The task is a simple one, even in the field of economic, social and cultural rights, because as argued by Roth, the 'nature of the violation, violator and remedy is clearest when it is possible to identify arbitrary or discriminatory governmental conduct that causes or substantially contributes to an economic, social, and cultural rights violation', as opposed to a problem of distributive justice.[83]

Even if much is treated as hanging on how arbitrariness is interpreted, this is a very expansive account. It has a significant merit in treating deprivation of nationality itself as the starting point of the enquiry, rather than deprivation of rights or incidents generally attached to that nationality and lost as a result of denationalisation. It also possesses certain weaknesses. First, as Hathaway and Foster have pointed out, article 1A(2) CSR51 requires a focus on current but forward-looking fear of persecution, rather than past persecution, and even though deprivation and denial of nationality may be seen as a continuing process, Lambert's analysis might be thought to assume this with too little scope for examination of individual cases. By contrast, the Hathaway and Foster analysis identifies the importance of looking closely at what continuing effects of denationalisation there are and whether these create a situation engaging article 1A(2) CSR51. Second, Lambert's analysis posits a conclusion with relatively little reference to the specific context, including the facts and what human rights apply in a given case or how these are informed by other standards. So, for example, an act of arbitrary denationalisation which removes a nationality given a short time earlier for equally arbitrary reasons (for instance a nationality given as a personal favour by a dictator, which a subsequent regime removes) is classed as persecution without more. Third, whilst international standards regarding statelessness may inform an assessment of arbitrariness (see for instance paras 6.37–6.38 and 6.51–6.54 above) the conclusion that arbitrary deprivation without more amounts to persecution, implicitly regardless of the subject's possession of any other nationality, neglects a feature of the jurisprudence which is that in every significant case in which denationalisation has been held to constitute persecution for article 1A(2) CSR51 purposes, the act resulted in either formal or *de facto* statelessness on the part of the affected individual.

F. Discussion and Conclusion

There is now a formidable body of jurisprudence and comment covering at least some forms of nationality related act or omission by States in the context of article 1A(2) CSR51. Review of the cases shows the extent to which development and application of international human rights laws have in turn enabled a relatively **6.179**

[83] H Lambert, 'Comparative Perspectives on Arbitrary Deprivation of Nationality and Refugee Status' (2015) 64 *International & Comparative Law Quarterly* 1, 36.

consistent assessment of some state behaviour in relation to nationality, and highlighted certain patterns. Albeit questions both of fact and law have to be considered in any given case, as Gloster LJ reiterated in *MI (Pakistan) v SSHD* [2014] EWCA Civ 826, citing observations of Lord Neuberger in the United Kingdom Supreme Court, these patterns provide a constructive framework for reflection.

F1. Cases Involving *De Jure* or Effective Deprivation of Nationality and Core Rights/Incidents Thereto

6.180 First, it is clear that formal (or *de jure*) denationalisation or effective deprivation of nationality, combined with the deprivation of substantial incidents generally attached to that status, has now been found to constitute persecution, or to be capable of doing so, in a substantial number of cases. There appears strong ground, looking to the decisions in *Tesfamichael* (para 6.134 above); *Lazarevic* (para 6.141 above); *EB (Ethiopia)* (paras 6.142–6.147 above); *MA (Ethiopia)* (paras 6.148–6.150 above); *ST (Ethiopia)* (para 6.151 above); *9 C 3.95* (para 6.156 above); *10 C 50.07* (paras 6.157–6.159 above); *Haile v Gonzales* (paras 6.166–6.167 above); *Haile v Holder* (paras 6.168–6.169 above); and *Stserba v Holder* (para 6.170 above), read in the light of relevant IHRL protections and the commentary of leading experts such as Grahl-Madsen, Zimmermann and Mahler, Goodwin-Gill and McAdam, Anker, Symes and Jorro, and Hathaway and Foster, to suggest the development of a consensus that persecution will in general be identified readily so long as certain requirements are met:

i. The affected individual is outside the reference country;
ii. He or she has substantial connections to that country, as for instance by birth and past residence there;
iii. The individual is subject to a continuing deprivation, or effective deprivation, of nationality by the reference country;
iv. The deprivation, or effective deprivation, has continuing consequences involving the denial of important rights or incidents of nationality, such as the right to enter and remain in his or her own country per article 12(4) ICCPR66;
v. The deprivation and/or effective deprivation of nationality and/or ongoing conduct of the State is within the definition of arbitrariness in international law terms;
vi. The subject possesses a well-founded fear of the ongoing deprivation, or effective deprivation and/or its ongoing consequences by reason of race, religion, nationality, membership of a particular social group, or political opinion.

Certain of the ACHPR81 decisions, such as *Malawi African Association and Others v Mauritania, African Commission on Human and Peoples' Rights* and *Modise v Botswana* (para 6.113 above) might be thought to provide particularly substantial parallels under human rights law.

The points identified above reflect the primary features shared by all or a significant majority of the paradigm cases in the jurisprudence already referred to. The formula is intended to include cases of imposed exile such as *Tesfamichael* even if there is no express denial of nationality. In such cases there is an effective denial which is implied by the imposition of exile, prohibited under article 12(4) ICCPR66 (para 6.148 above). There are certain other factors which may have considerable weight within the rubric above. In particular, the creation of actual or effective statelessness may go to one or more of the points identified above including whether there is a denial of important rights or incidents of nationality (point iv) and whether there is arbitrariness (point v). Another such factor might be whether there is a breach of the particular human rights standards intended to protect children. **6.181**

The list of points above is intended to identify matters seen consistently in the leading cases. It would be a serious mistake to conclude that it is intended to, or does, constitute a fixed rubric which must be met as the minimum standard of 'persecution' in article 1A(2) CSR51. The list does not do so. It identifies characteristics found in a substantial number of decisions across different jurisdictions in which article 1A(2) CSR51 has been found to be engaged. But this does not mean that cases may not succeed in other circumstances. For instance it is possible to construct conjectural circumstances in which a claim might succeed, as for example where an individual has a weaker connection to the reference country than in the main cases identified above but is faced with statelessness and exclusion as a result of arbitrary withdrawal of nationality and has no other country willing to permit entry or residence. Cases of detrimental reduction in status—such as reduction to a despised junior class of citizenship by reason of race or religion—might well also succeed. **6.182**

In the light of the treatment of deprivation of nationality in the paradigm cases, an interesting question is raised by the decisions of human rights monitoring bodies which show a significant category of case not mirrored in the refugee law jurisprudence. In *Yean and Bosico v Dominican Republic* and *Case of Expelled Dominicans and Haitians v Dominican Republic* (paras 6.108–6.110 above), and *Institute for Human Rights and Development in Africa and the Open Society Justice Initiative (on behalf of Children of Nubian Descent in Kenya) v Government of Kenya* (para 6.115 above), particular groups who were by law nationals or entitled to register as such were prevented from doing so by *de facto* obstacles, most particularly (though not exclusively) denial of birth registration. Given that the jurisprudence already attaches significant weight to other forms of effective deprivation of nationality, this may be a category requiring further reflection in the future. **6.183**

F2. Cases Concerning Denial or Withholding of Nationality

In his survey, referred to by the New Zealand Refuge Status Appeals Authority in *Refuge Appeal No 72635/01* (para 6.160 above) and elsewhere, Plender **6.184** concluded that the right to a nationality did not in general give rise to any right to naturalisation.[84] It follows that the adoption of a restrictive policy regarding naturalisation is not *per se* arbitrary, and that exposure to such a policy is not persecution without more. However, in *BA and others* the discriminatory withholding of citizenship and attached civil rights from a group with a very strong, longstanding connection to the territory was held to be 'a decisive factor', taken together with a finding that the State was attempting to marginalise the group and drive its members from the country (para 6.152 above), and *Refugee Appeal No 74467* is a kindred case. These might usefully be measured in conjunction with the 'own country' decisions of the UNHRC in relation to article 12(4) ICCPR66.

6.185 Overall, cases of denial or withholding of naturalisation appear to face significantly greater obstacles than denationalisation cases, though as the jurisprudence and commentary cited above shows, a number of cases have succeeded on the basis of particular facts which appear to include substantial denial of civil rights and discrimination notwithstanding strong ties to the territory.

6.186 What has yet to be seen is any substantial pattern of success in claims based on exclusion of migrants from gaining nationality in a host society—even in the instance of long-term stateless migrants such as Palestinians, present for a generation in States such as Saudi Arabia or Egypt. Here there is, as elsewhere, a need for close examination of relevant human rights standards, perhaps starting with articles 12(4), 24(3) and 26 ICCPR66. As noted above, there is development in these standards, and the 2011 decisions in *Nystrom v Australia* and *Warsame v Canada* (paras 6.55–6.57 above) may presage a loosening in the treatment of the 'own country' aspect of the test in article 12(4) ICCPR66.

F3. Arbitrary Exclusion of Non-Nationals

6.187 In Palestinian cases the possibility of exclusion grounding a claim to refugee status has been recognised, for example, in *Maarouf*, *Altawil*, and *Thabet* (paras 6.137–6.139 above), but the Court of Appeal in England and Wales in *MA (Palestinian Territories)* and subsequent decisions (para 6.154 above) treated these and other authorities as 'at the highest [going] no further than acceptance that, in some circumstances, to deny a stateless person re-entry may amount to persecution'. The protection from arbitrary expulsion is not restricted to stateless persons, but applies very acutely in their case because stateless persons may not have any route of admission to another State or territory. It is strongly arguable that a State may breach the protected human rights of an individual who is subjected to expulsion or exclusion even if no duty to grant citizenship arises. Anker notes a number

[84] Plender (n 50 above).

of American cases decided after the First Gulf War, and government legal advice clarifying applicable standards in the view of the responsible authorities:

> The question—whether expulsion can constitute persecution—arose in cases involving Palestinians during the Persian Gulf War, which began in 1990. Palestinians were forcibly expelled and then denied re-entry to, and had property confiscated by, various Middle Eastern countries (eg Kuwait, Saudi Arabia, Qatar, and the United Arab Emirates) because of the Palestinian Liberation Organization's ... public display of support for Iraq during that war. The legacy INS General Counsel's 1995 memorandum elaborates that expulsion or denial of re-entry qualifies a person as a refugee eligible for asylum if the expulsion violates basic human rights and therefore amounts to persecution and if such expulsion is on account of a protected ground.[85]

The legacy memorandum delineates a sensible approach by which non-nationals may demonstrate entitlement to status under CSR51 by reference to arbitrary exclusion. As seen previously—perhaps most clearly, if not uniquely, in the ACHPR81 decisions (para 6.113 above) and in decisions relating to ICCPR66 (section C2 ii above), strong IHRL standards exist, and arbitrary exclusion of habitually resident stateless persons appears an area to which international refugee law may have greater relevance than has been acknowledged hitherto. It might well prove to be an aspect of international refugee law particularly deserving of further examination in the future.

[85] Anker (n 78 above) 324, §4.36.

7

Cessation

The cessation provisions at article 1C of the Convention Relating to the Status of Refugees 1951 (CSR51) look to article 1A(2) and employ terms first used there in the context of the refugee definition. Interpretation of the cessation provisions requires reference to the meaning of those terms in relation to article 1A(2) CSR51.

Contents

A. Introduction

A1. Text of Article 1C of the Convention Relating to the Status of Refugees 1951

Article 1C of the Convention relating to the Status of Refugees (CSR51) provides that status under article 1A CSR51 will cease in six circumstances: 7.1

> C. This Convention shall cease to apply to any person falling under the terms of section A if:
>
> (1) He has voluntarily re-availed himself of the protection of the country of his nationality; or
> (2) Having lost his nationality, he has voluntarily re-acquired it; or
> (3) He has acquired a new nationality, and enjoys the protection of the country of his new nationality; or
> (4) He has voluntarily re-established himself in the country which he left or outside which he remained owing to fear of persecution; or
> (5) He can no longer, because the circumstances in connexion with which he has been recognized as a refugee have ceased to exist, continue to refuse to avail himself of the protection of the country of his nationality.
>
> Provided that this paragraph shall not apply to a refugee falling under section A(1) of this article who is able to invoke compelling reasons arising out of previous persecution for refusing to avail himself of the protection of the country of nationality.
>
> (6) Being a person who has no nationality he is, because of the circumstances in connexion with which he has been recognized as a refugee have ceased to exist, able to return to the country of his former habitual residence.
>
> Provided that this paragraph shall not apply to a refugee falling under section A(1) of this article who is able to invoke compelling reasons arising out of previous persecution for refusing to return to the country of his former habitual residence.

A2. Context

Cessation is not part of the analysis of inclusion within the refugee definition at article 1A(2) CSR51, which is conducted under article 1A(2) CSR51, but rather a separate, subsequent exercise. In the context of article 1C, Lord Brown *in Re B; Hoxha & Anor v Secretary of State for the Home Department* [2005] UKHL 19 [2005] 1WLR 1063 [60], said: 7.2

> The whole scheme of the Convention points irresistibly towards a two-stage rather than a composite approach to 1A(2) and 1C(5). Stage 1, the formal determination of an asylum-seeker's refugee status, dictates whether a 1A(2) applicant (who may, indeed be someone previously held not to qualify as a statutory refugee by the International Refugee Organisation—see the second paragraph of 1A(1)), is to be recognised as a refugee. 1C(5), a cessation clause, simply has no application at that stage, indeed no application at

any stage unless and until it is invoked by the state *against* the refugee in order to deprive him of the refugee status previously accorded to him.

A3. Scope of Interpretation

7.3 No attempt is made below to conduct an exhaustive analysis covering every facet of article 1C CSR51. However, it is appropriate to offer an account of the interpretation of important terms used in common with article 1A(2) CSR51 in one or more sub-articles of article 1C CSR51 which in many instances determine the meaning of provisions in article 1C. As with article 1A(2) these invoke international law concepts examined in chapters one and five ('nationality', 'the country', 'the country of his nationality'). They also invoke a concept which has numerous meanings and is used in different contexts in international law, in respect of which it is believed that a special meaning is created at article 1A(2) ('protection', 'the protection of that country'). It is also appropriate to identify points at which these shape the meaning of particular provisions in article 1C CSR51.

7.4 The use of terms emanating from international law ('nationality'/'country of nationality') or having a distinct meaning in CSR51 best understood after assessment of wider international law ('protection') recurs frequently at article 1C:

i. The term 'protection' employed only in the phrase 'the protection of the country of his nationality' or in its alternative 'the protection of the country of his new nationality' occurs four times—at 1C(1), 1C(3) and twice at 1C(5).
ii. The term 'country', used in the phrase 'the country of his nationality' or alternatively 'the country of his new nationality' occurs four times—at 1C(1), 1C(3), 1C(4) and twice at 1C(5).
iii. The term 'nationality', on its own or within the phrases 'the country of his nationality' or 'not having a nationality', occurs six times—at 1C(1), 1C(2), 1C(3), twice at 1C(5) and at 1C(6).

7.5 Such terms shape the meaning to be attached to particular provisions within article 1C CSR51, which too often are considered in isolation both from the wider international law context, and from article 1A(2) CSR51. The interpretation of provisions within article 1C CSR51 which employ relevant terms is therefore examined below.

B. Individual Provisions

B1. Article 1C(1): Voluntary Re-Availment of Nationality

7.6 The provision reads:

> 1C(1) He has voluntarily re-availed himself of the protection of the country of his nationality.

It has already been established in relation to article 1A(2) CSR51 that 'the country of his nationality' necessarily means a State and that 'nationality' in this context is, in Weis' formulation, 'a politico-legal term denoting membership of a State'.[1] Neither of these terms requires in article 1C(1) CSR51 a definition different from the definition given in article 1A(2) CSR51. In each case the continuation at article 1C(1) of the meaning at article 1A(2) CSR51 is consistent with ordinary meaning (in context) and with the object and purpose of the treaty. Continuation is strongly supported by the relationship of function between articles 1A(2) and 1C CSR51 in the light of which the latter, in the absence of supervening cause, might best be expected to reproduce the earlier usage. As to 'protection', as already set out (see chapter five, section A3) this means, in summary, internal protection from persecution sufficient that there is no well-founded fear of persecution for any relevant reason. In the words of Zimmermann and Mahler, 'It is ... only when the respective country of origin does *de facto* provide protection from such persecution that the need for surrogate international protection by the community of contracting parties of [CSR51] does not arise'.[2] This is consistent with the *Handbook*[3] and with the treatment of the issue both by Goodwin-Gill and McAdam,[4] and by Hathaway and Foster.[5] It is also consistent with ordinary meaning (in context) and with the object and purpose of the treaty.

A considerable degree of attention has gone over time to the question of whether a refugee engages article 1C(1) by obtaining national identity documents from her State of origin. This is understandable, given that the UNHCR *Handbook* elides in this respect the initial issue of the interpretation of 'protection'– chapter II section B(5) of the *Handbook* (paras 97–100) considers the interpretation of the phrase 'and is unable or, owing to such fear, is unwilling to avail himself of the protection of that country', but without addressing the particular meaning of the core term, 'protection'. Thereafter a single use of the term 'international protection' in the *Handbook* at paragraph 100 is unfortunate because it suggests 'diplomatic protection' rather than what is suggested as the better understanding, interpreting the treaty itself. This meaning is 'protection from persecution'. In article 1A(2) CSR51, 'protection' does not mean 'diplomatic protection', but 'protection from persecution'. This strongly suggests, barring textual indications to the contrary, that the 7.7

[1] P Weis, *Nationality and Statelessness* (2nd edn, 1979, Brill) 1.

[2] C Mahler and A Zimmermann 'Article 1A para 1 1951 Convention' in A Zimmerman (ed), *The 1951 Convention Relating to the Status of Refugees and its 1967 Protocol: A Commentary* (OUP, 2011) 445–46, §596–600.

[3] UNHCR, *Handbook and Guidelines on Procedures and Criteria for Determining Refugee Status under the 1951 Convention and the 1967 Protocol relating to the Status of Refugees*, Reissued, Geneva, December 2011, §90.

[4] G Goodwin-Gill and J McAdam, *The Refugee in International Law* (3rd edn, OUP, 2007) section 2.6.

[5] J Hathaway and M Foster, *The Law of Refugee Status* (2nd edn, CUP, 2014) ch 4, esp sections 4.1–4.2.

meaning in article 1C(1) CSR51 corresponds with the meaning of the term in the earlier, dominant provision:

> 119. This cessation clause implies three requirements:
>
> (a) voluntariness: the refugee must act voluntarily;
> (b) intention: the refugee must intend by his action to re-avail himself of the protection of the country of his nationality;
> (c) re-availment: the refugee must actually obtain such protection.[6]

7.8 The weakness in the guidance provided by the *Handbook* as to the interpretation of 'protection' continues at chapter III section B(1), where guidance regarding article 1C(1) is provided, again absent close analysis in relation to article 1C(1) of the 'protection' which provides the essential context to the content of 're-availment of protection':

> 122. A refugee requesting protection from the authorities of the country of his nationality has only 're-availed' himself of that protection when his request has actually been granted. The most frequent case of 're-availment of protection' will be where the refugee wishes to return to his country of nationality. He will not cease to be a refugee merely by applying for repatriation. On the other hand, obtaining an entry permit or a national passport for the purposes of returning will, in the absence of proof to the contrary, be considered as terminating refugee status. This does not, however, preclude assistance being given to the repatriant—also by UNHCR—in order to facilitate his return.
>
> 123. A refugee may have voluntarily obtained a national passport, intending either to avail himself of the protection of his country of origin while staying outside that country, or to return to that country. As stated above, with the receipt of such a document he normally ceases to be a refugee. If he subsequently renounces either intention, his refugee status will need to be determined afresh. He will need to explain why he changed his mind, and to show that there has been no basic change in the conditions that originally made him a refugee.

Here the emphasis on documentation rather than the identification of the underlying meaning is unfortunate, because whilst ambiguous overall a part of it again seems to suggest 'diplomatic protection'. But given 'protection from persecution' as a key element in the overall regime, and the absence of any textual evidence for a special meaning, this appears the correct sense in which 'protection' in 're-availed himself of the protection of the country of his nationality' should be understood.

7.9 The *Handbook* states in paragraph 122 that 'the most frequent case' of re-availment is where a refugee wishes to return to her country of nationality. This may be the case, although the statement appears to reflect an assumption rather than anything firmer; and even were this verifiably a deduction from concrete facts, those facts would have to be placed in relevant context. Paragraph 123 states that 'with the receipt of such a document he normally ceases to be a refugee'. The statement in

---

[6] UNHCR, *Handbook and Guidelines on Procedures and Criteria for Determining Refugee Status* (n 3 above) [205].

paragraph 122 may be correct. The statement in paragraph 123 is not, and should be recognised as another weak point in the *Handbook*. The tense used is not the conditional future but the past. But how can it be said that simply by reason of receiving a passport there has been a re-availment of protection from persecution by the country of his nationality? If 'protection' means some form of diplomatic or consular assistance that might be the case, but such an interpretation would be inconsistent with the meaning of 'protection' in the dominant element in the interpretation of article 1A(2) CSR51. To adopt a different meaning in article 1C would be to undermine its structural correspondence with article 1A(2). It would also run against the clear purpose of article 1C(1) in the overall CSR51 scheme, which is to identify the point at which status under article 1A(2) ceases.

This question is resolvable once it is understood that the acquisition of documents, or consular contact otherwise, has no decisive significance *per se*, but may be of considerable importance in showing that an individual has re-engaged with national protection from persecution. Contact with the consular or other authorities of the State whilst abroad has no special status as such, but may be seen in some contexts as evidence of re-availment of protection from persecution by the State of nationality. Another act which might evidence re-availment is return across the border of the State in question. Either action, depending upon the context, might indicate that a refugee has ceased to be such, because he or she has voluntarily re-availed himself or herself of the protection (from persecution) of the State of origin. In turn this would indicate the cessation of inability or unwillingness to rely upon national protection from persecution, which is a requirement of article 1A(2) CSR51. **7.10**

National practice has varied. In 1986 Grahl-Madsen observed that: **7.11**

> Some countries of refuge strictly apply two rules to passport acquisition by refugees. First, a person applying for refugee status must surrender his national passport. Second, a refugee who acquires a new passport or renews an old one loses refugee status. Switzerland, in particular, has stressed these rules. Certain other countries apply them less rigidly or not at all. For many years, Sweden required refugees to keep and renew their passports, so that Swedish residence permits could be stamped in them. The Swedish practice, which has since been abandoned, proved problematic, as it forced refugees to maintain contact with the consular agents of the regime from which they had fled. The Swiss practice corresponds more closely to the intentions of the drafters of the Convention on the Status of Refugees, and has since become the general practice. While it does not lend itself to obvious criticism, it does not address the intrinsic character of passports and their relation to protection in general. While the passport plays an important role in diplomatic and consular protection, it is only a prima facie proof of citizenship ... Just as the possession of a passport is not sufficient for the exercise of active protection, it is also not necessary. A state may protect a citizen whether he has no passport, never possessed one, or even if he possesses a passport issued by some other state or agency.[7]

[7] A Grahl-Madsen, 'Protection of Refugees by their Country of Origin' (1986) 11 *Yale Journal of International Law* 362, 370.

7.12 It is undoubtedly correct that documentation of identity and status, and particularly documentation conforming to a common standard and acceptable to States, is an important part of the CSR51 regime as it was of the interwar regimes. But the focus upon documentation as possible evidence of re-availment of protection from persecution risks promoting the erroneous conclusion that the refugee cannot or should not have documentation of a State of nationality at all. That conclusion greatly overstates the case. If the drafters of CSR51 had meant this, they could easily have said so—it does not take substantial drafting skill to see how this could for instance have been integrated, whether at article 28 CSR51 which provides for documentation of identity and status for CSR51 purposes or elsewhere. But it is sometimes implied from the need to provide documentation to refugees that they are prohibited from possession or use of any other documentation, and most specifically from possession or use of documents issued by a State of reference, and the risk of misunderstanding is increased by the perpetuation of earlier errors or the treatment of general, purposive statements as specific, literal ones. A number of examples could be pointed to. For instance, Robinson in his early *Commentary* stated that:

> In his capacity as 'refugee', the refugee is prohibited from obtaining documents certifying his identity, from the authorities either of his former homeland or the country of his former residence. On the other hand, almost all states require foreigners to possess such documents. To alleviate this difficulty the Contracting States undertake under the Convention to issue identity papers, documents certifying who the refugee is (identification cards for instance), to refugee residing in their respective territory who do not possess a valid travel document.[8]

The first sentence above read naturally posits the existence of an absolute prohibition upon obtaining documents which cannot sensibly be ascribed to CSR51. The third sentence suggests a limitation on the duty to issue travel documents to persons not possessing documents from a country of origin. The first sentence is straightforwardly incorrect. There is no prohibition in article 1A(2) CSR51 upon obtaining documents *per se*. If there were, then article 1C could be expected to contain a provision to the effect that CSR51 'shall cease to apply to any person … if he [or she] obtains documents certifying identity from the authorities of a former homeland or country of his former residence'. The third sentence is also incorrect. By article 28, States Parties to CSR51 'shall issue to refugees, lawfully staying in their territory, travel documents for the purpose of travel outside their territory unless compelling reasons of national security or public order otherwise require'. They are neither required nor permitted to withhold travel documents where a refugee remains in possession of, for example, a valid passport from his or her country of origin. The authorities in the country of refuge may refuse to issue a

[8] N Robinson, *Convention relating to the Status of Refugees, its History, Contents, and Interpretation* (Institute of Jewish Affairs, 1953) 26.

travel document only for entirely separate reasons relating to national security or public order. Nothing in the Schedule to CSR51 relating to travel documents creates a new, separate category of individuals who may be refused travel documents. Whilst article 28 CSR51 also provides that States 'shall in particular give sympathetic consideration to the issue of such a travel document to refugees in their territory who are unable to obtain a travel document from the country of their lawful residence', this specifically negates Robinson's proposition by showing recognition in the text of CSR51 that some refugees retaining or able to obtain travel documents from 'the country of their lawful residence' will also be granted travel documents under article 28 CSR51.

Robinson seems at this point to have been attempting a colloquial description of the general circumstances of the refugee. It is of course correct that some, perhaps very many, refugees do not have adequate documentation of identity or nationality from their State of nationality, and cannot obtain this (or reasonably be expected to do so) by reason of the hostility or unwillingness of the authorities, or the collapse of the state apparatus, or some other matter. However, his statement is far too broad to reflect the correct position under CSR51. **7.13**

It is important to understand that, though domestic practices have differed (see para 7.11 above) there is in CSR51 no general prohibition upon the acquisition of documents from the authorities of a country which is a reference country for article 1A(2) CSR51 purposes. Those authorities may be willing and capable of providing documents through consular authorities, even if they are unable or unwilling to provide protection within the territory of the State. Indeed, the central authorities may themselves also be outside the State's territory, if for instance this is subject to belligerent occupation and the legitimate government continues only in exile or if the authorities are unwilling or unable for any other reason to provide sufficient protection within the State's territory. **7.14**

Although Grahl-Madsen sometimes treated protection as consular protection rather than protection from persecution, he identified the need for attention to context in judging whether obtaining a passport constituted a request even for consular protection. Between the conjectural examples he cites, there is obviously scope for a wide range of differing circumstances: **7.15**

> Nevertheless, there remains some merit to the view that a passport represents a request, albeit tacit, to foreign governments that they treat the bearer as the government of the issuing state would like to see its citizens treated. If a passport is issued and recognized in this spirit, its issuance may very well be considered a measure of protection. On the other hand, if its purpose is merely to enable a person to comply with the formal requirements of the alien and immigration laws of a particular state, and this is clearly understood by all concerned, the issuance of the passport will have little to do with protection in a more profound sense. Instead, those involved will perceive it as merely a practical document issued for practical purposes.[9]

[9] Grahl-Madsen, 'Protection of Refugees by their Country of Origin' (n 7 above) 369–70.

7.16 As already seen, it is easy to identify situations in which the proposition that a refugee will never have or be able to employ identity documents of a home State, because any use constitutes re-availment, is falsified. For instance, where the legitimate government of a State has gone into exile due to occupation of the territory by another State or an armed group, and refugees fear persecution because of the hostile attitudes and actions of the occupying forces, it would be remarkable were the obtaining or renewal of a passport from the government in exile said to constitute re-availment.

7.17 On the other hand, there is at least one situation in which obtaining a national passport seems likely to demonstrate re-availment in a high proportion of cases. That situation is the obtaining of a new national passport where the refugee has held that status by reason of denationalisation (or effective denationalisation) by a State of nationality, coupled with continuing exclusion. As Pill LJ observed in *EB (Ethiopia) v SSHD* [2007] EWCA Civ 809, [2009] QB 1, at [44]: 'Mr Blake [representing the appellant] accepts that, if effective nationality were to be restored, the appellant would cease to be a refugee. Until that happens, she is entitled to refugee status'.

7.18 Once the spectre of a general prohibition on possession or use of documentation from a State of origin is dispelled, it becomes easier to understand article 1C(1) CSR51. It applies where there is a re-availment of national protection in the sense of internal protection from persecution, in which cessation of unwillingness or inability to return by reason of relevant fear may be identified from certain positive actions—such as obtaining a passport or other national document—in circumstances which reasonably indicate the cessation of unwillingness or inability to return by reason of well-founded fear for relevant reason.

7.19 Identified as a starting point, the interpretation of 'protection' in article 1A(2) CSR51 provides a strong indication of the meaning of the same term at article 1C(1) CSR51—not simply because the terminology is common, but because article 1C has an obvious and direct correspondence with article 1A(2), in that it sets out conditions in which cessation of status is appropriate because there has been a negation of the inability or unwillingness to return by reason of well-founded fear of persecution. Expressed at another level, article 1C defines conditions for the ending of the status resulting from satisfaction of the definition at article 1A(2) CSR51.

7.20 The meaning of 'protection' in article 1C(1) is therefore not substantially different from its meaning at article 1A(2) CSR51.

7.21 It must be accepted in this context that Grahl-Madsen in writing on article 1C reached no certainty as to the meaning of 'protection', identifying different measures 'of some kind or other taken by [a State] in order to safeguard or promote the integrity, rights, or interests of an individual'– but also specifying that even 'physical presence in the territory of the home country does not *per se* constitute re-availment of protection in the sense of Article 1C(1) ... or, in other words, the normalization of the relationship between State and individual—which matters'.[10] In effect this recognised the relative absence of strong guidance in decided cases and affirmed the importance of avoiding a fixed position, whilst leaving some matters open—a course which on the material available to him half a century ago was typically careful and conscientious.

7.22 Hathaway and Foster criticise article 1C(1) as deriving from 'a highly formalistic and outmoded understanding of the notion of "protection"'.[11] This criticism of over-extensiveness directed at article 1C by Hathaway and Foster is well founded but goes not to article 1C itself, but rather to the understanding of that provision encouraged by past commentary and jurisprudence neglecting the essential starting point—adequate interpretation of the key term, 'protection'. Hathaway and Foster[12] also criticise the breadth of a statement by Goodwin-Gill and McAdam that in the re-availment context 'Protection comprises all such actions by the refugee as indicate the establishment of normal relations with the authorities of the country of origin, such as registration at consulates or application for and renewal of passports or certificates of nationality'.[13] That observation becomes unexceptionable if 'normal relations' is understood as meaning a situation in which the refugee ceases to be unwilling or unable to avail herself of the protection from persecution of the country of origin. A less open meaning of re-availment is identifiably present in the statement of Goodwin-Gill and McAdam that 'For the purposes of re-availment of protection, the refugee must not only act voluntarily, but must also intend to and actually obtain protection' which precedes their statement that 'All the circumstances of the contact between the individual and the authorities of the country of origin must be taken into account'.[14] These observations stressing the need for voluntariness, intention, and the consideration of all relevant circumstances, are correct and valuable, bringing the respective positions of Hathaway and Foster, on the one hand, and Goodwin-Gill and McAdam, on the other, considerably closer to each other. They are also consistent with the interpretation of article 1A(2) CSR51 set out herein.

7.23 On the best interpretation, therefore, re-availment of the protection of his county of nationality means re-availment of internal protection from persecution for a Convention reason. The obtaining of a passport to return might indicate the

[10] A Grahl-Madsen, *The Status of Refugees in International Law*, vol I (AW Sijthoff, 1966) 381–85, §141, quoted passages at 381 and 384. Physical presence in the reference country would of course mean that the requirement of article 1A(2) CSR51, that a refugee be 'outside the country of his nationality' or if stateless 'outside the country of his former habitual residence' was no longer met, though departure from the territory would restore it.

[11] Hathaway and Foster (n 5 above) 465.

[12] Ibid.

[13] Goodwin-Gill and McAdam (n 4 above) 136.

[14] Ibid, 137.

intention to do this, but is far from necessarily doing so. Hathaway and Foster have rightly criticised the contrary assumption as 'highly formalistic and outmoded',[15] citing Grahl-Madsen's observation in this regard:

> A person may seldom have well-founded fear of being persecuted by the members of the foreign service of his home country; the pertinent fact therefore is that he fears persecution in the case of his return to his country of origin.[16]

Grahl-Madsen's statement in this instance strongly supports internal protection from persecution as the true interpretation of the term 'protection' in this context. Not surprisingly, Grahl-Madsen, Hathaway and Foster, and Goodwin-Gill and McAdam agree in rejecting the proposition that on a correct interpretation of article 1C(1) passport acquisition is automatically to be treated as re-availment.

7.24 The jurisprudence related to article 1C(1) CSR51 is somewhat limited. Across different jurisdictions the decisions frequently do show laudable care and fact-sensitivity by judicial decision-makers. Although efforts at judicial interpretation of the provision have been limited, judicial pragmatism or common sense seems often to have led to an equation of the question of whether there has been re-availment with that of whether an individual continues to be unable and unwilling to avail himself of the protection of a reference State. In effect such cases apply a correct interpretation, it is suggested even if the interpretive route to the approach adopted is not fully delineated. In *Chandrakumar v Canada (Minister of Employment and Immigration)* 1997 CanLII 16770 (FCTD), Pinard J set aside a decision of the Convention Refugee Determination Division, concluding that this was erroneous in treating the act of renewing a passport as re-availment *per se*, without exploration of the applicant's motivation. In *Maqdassy v Canada (Minister of Citizenship and Immigration)* [2002] FCJ No 238, 2002 FCT 182, upholding a finding of re-availment, Tremblay-Lamer J said that:

> 16. It was reasonable for the Board to infer that the applicant would not have returned to Iraq if she had a well-founded fear of persecution. In some cases, claimants have been found not to have re-availed themselves of state protection. For example, *in Shanmugarajah v (Minister of Employment and Immigration)*, [1992] FCJ No 583, the claimant, who had returned to his country of origin to take care of his ill mother, was found not to have re-availed himself of state protection. However, in the case at bar, there was no such pressing reason for the applicant to return to Iraq (See *Ali v Canada (Minister of Citizenship and Immigration)* [1996] FCJ No 558).

7.25 A case cited with some frequency in Canada is *Nsende v Canada (Minister of Citizenship and Immigration)* 2008 FC 531 [2009] 1 FCR 49 in which the applicant stated that he had sought the renewal of his Congolese passport with the intention of using it to travel to Thailand for business purposes. Lagacé DJ found that the Board's decision was unclear as to why it found the applicant's explanations

[15] Hathaway and Foster (n 5 above) 465.
[16] Grahl-Madsen, *The Status of Refugees in International Law* (n 10 above) 379, §140.

unsatisfactory. The Court refused to accept reliance upon an inference that the fact of seeking renewal of a national passport without more constituted proof of an intention on the part of the applicant to re-avail himself of the protection of his country of nationality.

More recently, in *Canada (Minister of Public Safety and Emergency Preparedness) v Bashir* 2015 FC 51, [2015] 4 FCR 336, Bédard J on an application by the Minister declined to set aside a judgment of the Immigration and Refugee Board that there had been no relevant re-availment of national protection by Pakistan. The Board had found that the respondent had renewed his Pakistani document in order to travel to a third country to meet his parents, being unaware that he could obtain a travel document from the Canadian authorities for this purpose, and had wrongly understood that he would need a valid national document for his anticipated application for permanent residence. Bédard J sought guidance in the UNHCR *Handbook*: 7.26

> [50] The applicant's argument appears to be based on the premise that since the Board had found that the respondent genuinely believed he was required to have a valid passport for the purposes of his permanent residency application, it should then have concluded that his act was not voluntary. In my view, such a finding would have been open to the Board in light of the evidence, but the finding that the respondent had acted voluntarily was also open to it in light of the fact that no authority had asked or required that the respondent obtain a Pakistani passport. That said, the fact that the respondent voluntarily requested renewals of his Pakistani passport does not necessarily entail that, by doing so, he had the intention of re-availing himself of the protection of Pakistan. The two criteria are different and the same factual matrix can have a different impact depending on the criterion being assessed.
>
> [51] I also consider that the Board's finding regarding the second requirement, namely that the respondent did not intend to re-avail himself of the protection of Pakistan when he applied to renew his passport, has an evidentiary basis and is reasonable.

A particularly extreme case on its facts, *Rezaei v Minister for Immigration and Multicultural Affairs* [2001] FCA 129, was decided by Allsop J in the Federal Court of Australia. As to the correct approach, he referred to Grahl-Madsen and to the test as being 'normalisation' of the relationship between individual and State: 7.27

> 51. There is much to be said for what Grahl-Madsen said in *The Status of Refugees in International Law* (1966) vol 1 at p 384, that for there to be a re-availment of the protection of the country of nationality there needs to be shown the voluntary and conscious choice of subjection to the government of the relevant country. In other words, there has to be shown the normalisation of the relationship between State and individual. In such an assessment a use of presumptions is perhaps, as I have said, questionable.

The applicants had been issued protection visas in Australia in April 1998. Allsop J describes the subsequent history: 7.28

> 5. On 15 and 21 July 1998, each of the applicants was issued with a new Iranian passport issued by the Iranian embassy in Canberra. On 1 and 2 December 1998, protection visa labels were placed in the applicants' new Iranian passports. On 9 December 1998, both

applicants left Australia for Iran where they have remained ever since. While in Iran they adopted a child by a lawful process involving the Iranian legal system. Towards the end of 2000, they applied to the Australian authorities to sponsor a child for migration and return to Australia.

7.29 The application was heard in September 2001, by which time the applicants had remained in Iran for almost three years. Allsop J observed (at [52]–[53]) that, though no point was raised in the case:

> 52. However, it should not be forgotten that the 'protection' which is to be re-availed of is not limited to the protection brought about by physical presence within the relevant country, once again as a citizen, but includes the re-availment of consular and diplomatic protection: Grahl-Madsen 'Protection of Refugees by their Country of Origin' (1986) vol 11(2) *Yale J International Law* 362, esp pp 364–370, and see generally Weis 'The Concept of the Refugee in International Law' (1960) *Journal du Droit International* 928; Grahl-Madsen *The Status of Refugees in International Law* (1966) Vol 1, pp 367–392; Goodwin-Gill *The Refugee in International Law* (Clarendon, 2nd ed, 1998) pp 80–84; Hathaway *The Law of Refugee Status* (Butterworths, 1991) ch 6; Zambelli *The Refugee Convention* (Carswell, 1999) pp 246–247; Cartier, Hullmann and Galiano (eds) *Who is a Refugee? A Comparative Case Law Study* (Kluwer, The Hague, 1997) pp 16, 220, 433–36, 560–61; Notes on the Cessation Clauses, Executive Committee of the High Commissioner's Programme, 8th meeting 30 May 1997.
>
> 53. There has been no extensive analysis of Article 1C(1) in Australian courts, but see *A v Minister for Immigration and Multicultural Affairs* [1999] FCA 227 at paras [38]–[39] per Katz J. It is unnecessary for me to embark on any such analysis of the jurisprudence on Article 1C(1) in various jurisdictions. This is so because the application does not identify as a ground of complaint the identification of a wrong legal standard by the delegate by the application of, or decision by reference to, the UNHCR Handbook; rather, the complaint is the failure to take into account the actions of the Department in stamping the passports with the protection visas. Further, there seems to me to be a clear evidential basis for coming to the conclusion that there was, by the time entry was made into Iran, a re-availment in the sense discussed by Grahl-Madsen, *supra*.

It is suggested that the decision goes beyond what was necessary in considering consular and diplomatic protection to be re-availment, and that the true re-availment was return to and remaining in Iran for a substantial period of time, inconsistently with the existence of unwillingness or inability to return for any relevant reason.

7.30 Finally, in *NM (Afghanistan) v Secretary of State for the Home Department* [2007] EWCA Civ 214, Latham LJ (with whom Ward LJ and Charles J concurred) rejected (at [12]) the proposition that obtaining a national passport indicated re-availment *per* se. The appellant in that case had not returned to the reference country and stated he had sought and obtained an Afghan passport in order to advance his application for a United Kingdom driving licence. This decision however recognised that the action could be taken into account in the overall assessment of whether article 1C CSR51 applied article 1A(2):

> 12. The Immigration Judge concluded that, in the light of this paragraph in Article 1C, the obtaining of the passport provided a discrete and complete answer to the appellant's claim for asylum. In doing so, he clearly followed the Tribunal decision in *MW (national passport: re-availment of protection) Pakistan* [2004] UKIAT 00136. Unfortunately, the Tribunal in that case did not have the benefit of the copious citing of authority, both judicial and academic, on the proper application of Article 1C which we have had. From this it is abundantly plain that Article 1C is, in itself, of no relevance when the decision-maker is determining whether or not a person is a 'refugee' within the meaning of Article 1A. Article 1C contains what are properly described as 'cessation clauses'. They set out the circumstances in which a person who has been recognised as a refugee loses that status. That follows from the words: 'This Convention shall cease to apply to any person falling under the terms of section A'.
>
> 13. It follows that Article 1C(1) strictly has no relevance to the present appeal. That does not, however, mean that the facts relating to the appellant's obtaining of the Afghan passport are irrelevant. They form part of the evidence available to the Tribunal to determine whether or not, in truth, the appellant does have a well-founded fear of persecution were he to be returned to Afghanistan. The Immigration Judge was therefore perfectly entitled to have regard to them. But in seeking to apply some sort of 'rule' derived from Article 1C(1) as he appears to have done, he erred in law.

This appears to be an area of CSR51 in which obscurity of interpretation in the UNHCR *Handbook* and some early commentary has in practice not prevented the jurisprudence from developing pragmatically, leading to results in the cases cited above which are entirely consistent with a reasonable interpretation of article 1C(1) CSR51. Overall, what examination of the interpretation of article 1C(1) seems to highlight is the need for focus upon whether a refugee has become willing or able to rely upon internal protection against relevantly motivated persecution. Even return to the territory does not necessarily indicate this, though article 1A(2) CSR51 is disapplied whilst the individual is in his or her own country. After extension over a considerable time, return would seem almost bound to support the inference that the unwillingness or inability to look for protection from persecution internally had ceased, barring exceptional circumstances such as existence in a cave or desert beyond the control of potential persecutors. Various actions outside the reference country may also support such an inference, but, as the sources above illustrate, attention to the facts of each particular case is vital. **7.31**

B2. Article 1C(2): Voluntary Re-Acquisition of Nationality

The provision reads: **7.32**

> 1C(2) Having lost his nationality, he has voluntarily re-acquired it.

'Nationality' here means nationality as defined in chapter one. The provision is virtually self-evident beyond this definition. 'Re-acquired' uses the past tense, and it seems obvious that the intention is that article 1C(2) CSR51 applies only when **7.33** an individual *has* the nationality in question—not when she has begun to contemplate re-acquisition or even when an application has been filed. The requirement of voluntariness may reflect, in part if not in whole, hesitation in the international law commentators as to whether nationality may be *imposed* upon an individual save by birth or descent, particularly when the individual is outside the territory of a State, and also as to the efficacy of retrospective measures in the field of nationality—both issues extensively considered but not resolved in the discussion of the Nazi denationalisations between the 1930s and 1945, and the *sequelae* thereto.[17]

B3. Article 1C(3): Acquisition of New Nationality, with Protection of that State

7.34 This provision reads:

> 1C(3) He has acquired a new nationality, and enjoys the protection of the country of his new nationality.

7.35 As above, 'nationality' here means nationality as defined in chapter one. 'Acquired' uses the past tense, and there appears a clear intention that article 1C(3) CSR51 apply only when an individual *has* the nationality in question, not at any earlier point. As with article 1C(2) CSR51 it is relevant to note (although the term 'acquired' might be thought to imply a need for voluntariness in any event) the hesitation of the main commentators upon international nationality law as to whether nationality may be *imposed* upon an individual save by the 'original means' of acquisition—that is, birth or descent—particularly when the individual is outside the territory of a State. Accordingly, it might well be arguable in appropriate circumstances that article 1C(3) is not engaged by a State, even one willing to afford protection from persecution, which purports to bestow its nationality upon the refugee by derivative means without a valid acceptance by the individual. In such a case the issue of recognition would become relevant. As to 'protection', this means internal protection from relevantly motivated persecution.

B4. Article 1C(4): Voluntary Re-Establishment in Reference Country

7.36 This provision reads:

> 1C(4) He has voluntarily re-established himself in the country which he left or outside which he remained owing to fear of persecution.

[17] See for instance F Mann, 'The Present Validity of Nazi Nationality Laws' (1973) 89 *Law Quarterly Review* 194; F Mann, '*Oppenheimer v Cattermole* Revisited' (1981) 97 *Law Quarterly Review* 194, 220–22; I Brownlie, 'The Relations of Nationality in Public International Law' in *British Yearbook of International Law 1963* (OUP, 1965) 285.

Here it is relevant to note departure from the usage elsewhere which specifies a country as being the country either of nationality or of habitual residence. The term 'the country' is much more general. It does not on its face require statehood, as the term 'country of his nationality' does, and is capable of use as a synonym of the term 'territory'. It might refer either to a country of nationality or a country of former habitual residence, so long as she remained outside that country earlier 'owing to fear of persecution'. 7.37

B5. Article 1C(5): Cessation of Circumstances of Recognition as a Refugee as Regards Country of Nationality

Article 1C(5) reads: 7.38

> 1C(5) He can no longer, because the circumstances in connexion with which he has been recognized as a refugee have ceased to exist, continue to refuse to avail himself of the protection of the country of his nationality.
>
> Provided that this paragraph shall not apply to a refugee falling under section A(1) of this article who is able to invoke compelling reasons arising out of previous persecution for refusing to avail himself of the protection of the country of nationality.

The 'country of his nationality' in each paragraph is a State of nationality as delineated in chapter one, and its 'protection' is, as in previous usages of the term, internal protection from relevant persecution. This conclusion is supported by the decision of the Court of Justice of the European Union in *Abdullah (Area of Freedom, Security and Justice)* [2010] EUECJ C-178/08 that: 7.39

> 76. Refugee status ceases to exist when, having regard to a change of circumstances of a significant and non-temporary nature in the third country concerned, the circumstances which justified the person's fear of persecution for [relevant reason], on the basis of which refugee status was granted, no longer exist, and that person has no other reason to fear being 'persecuted' within the meaning of Article 2c of the Directive.

B6. Article 1C(6): Cessation of Circumstances of Recognition as a Refugee as Regards Country of Former Habitual Residence of Stateless Person

The relevant provision reads: 7.40

> (6) Being a person who has no nationality he is, because of the circumstances in connexion with which he has been recognized as a refugee have ceased to exist, able to return to the country of his former habitual residence.

Provided that this paragraph shall not apply to a refugee falling under section A(1) of this article who is able to invoke compelling reasons arising out of previous persecution for refusing to return to the country of his former habitual residence.

7.41 Article 1C(6) CSR51 is the analogue as regards stateless persons, to article 1C(5). The 'country of his former habitual residence' in each paragraph is that country, and its 'protection' is, as in previous usages of the term, internal protection from relevant persecution.

C. Conclusion

7.42 Given the close correspondence between article 1C and article 1A(2) CSR51, it is understandable that the former is pervaded by similar terminology, which equally requires interpretation consistent with the background international law. Interpretation taking this into account gives a fuller understanding of the significance of each of the provisions within article 1C CSR51.

8

Exclusion

Article 1E of the Convention Relating to the Status of Refugees 1951 (CSR51) provides an exclusion clause of limited application, applicable where persons are not nationals but are recognised by the competent authorities of the country of residence as having rights and obligations assimilated to those which are attached to the nationality of that country.

Contents

A. Introduction

A1. Text of Article 1E of the Convention Relating to the Status of Refugees 1951

8.1 Article 1E of the Convention relating to the Status of Refugees 1951 (CSR51) provides that status under article 1A CSR51 does not arise in particular circumstances:

> 1E This Convention shall not apply to a person who is recognized by the competent authorities of the country in which he has taken residence as having the rights and obligations which are attached to the possession of the nationality of that country.

A2. Context

8.2 The question generally prompted by first consideration of article 1E CSR51 is what status there could be which is not nationality, as defined in chapter one, but attracts access to 'the rights and obligations which are attached to the possession of the nationality of that country'? By definition article 1E CSR51 applies when something other than nationality itself, but resembling it in specified respects, arises.

A3. Scope of Interpretation

8.3 No attempt is intended to conduct an over-exhaustive analysis of this very rarely applied provision. However, an attempt to identify its meaning is valuable, and is a natural exercise continuing the examination herein of interpretive considerations relating to CSR51 and the international law of nationality and statelessness.

B. Interpretation

8.4 Historically article 1E CSR51, introduced into what is now CSR51 by the United Nations General Assembly in December 1950,[1] results from a taking into account of the particular situation of those persons of German ethnic background who left or were expelled from Eastern Europe pursuant to forced population transfers under the Potsdam Protocol of 1945. Such persons were generally categorised as *Volksdeutche*, ethnic German refugees who found refuge in Germany after the final defeat of the Nazi regime. For reasons variously including the feeling that German ethnic refugees in Germany should not benefit equally with other persons denoted refugees and the willingness of the post-war German authorities to integrate these incomers, which reduced their apparent need for protection elsewhere, a view was held by many States that this group should be left outwith the protective regime being established by the creation and adoption of CSR51.

8.5 Grahl-Madsen notes that a reason for the particular form and content article 1E CSR51 was that the newly established Federal Republic of Germany had on 23 May 1949 adopted its *Grundgesetz* (Basic Law). Article 116(1) thereof provides that:

> Article 116
>
> [Definition of 'German'—Restoration of citizenship]
>
> Unless otherwise provided by a law, a German within the meaning of this Basic Law is a person who possesses German citizenship or who has been admitted to the territory of the German Reich within the boundaries of 31 December 1937 as a refugee or expellee of German ethnic origin or as the spouse or descendant of such person.

---

[1] Section D Annex to UN Doc A/RES/429(V) of 14 December 1950.

German domestic law contemporaneously provided generous rights and benefits to *Volksdeutsche*.[2] In 1955, German law provided for the bestowing of full citizenship upon ethnic German refugees and expellees, but until citizenship was bestowed, members of the group benefitted from a non-citizen regime providing rights and obligations arguably coterminous in important respects with those normally granted to citizens.[3]

The Constitution of the International Refugee Organisation of 15 December 1946 and earlier drafts of CSR51 specifically excluded the *Volksdeutsche* from refugee status.[4] Robinson stated somewhat imprecisely in reference to article 1E CSR51 that: **8.6**

> the Convention is not applicable to persons to whom the country of refuge grants the rights attached to possession of the nationality of this state, such as in the instance of Germans who fled or were expelled from Eastern countries and live in Germany.[5]

Article 1E CSR51 was therefore primarily motivated by the desire to carve out of the protection of CSR51 a particular group for whom other alleviating help was seen as available: a ready functional parallel, which has not lost its relevance over time as might have been envisioned, is article 1D excluding 'persons who are at present receiving from organs or agencies other than [UNHCR] protection or assistance'. However, as Marx has noted, the wording of the article is sufficiently broad that it is not restricted exclusively to Germans displaced from Eastern Europe after 1945,[6] and there had been discussion in the Ad Hoc Committee referring not only to the *Volksdeutsche* and to Arab refugees, but also to refugees of Kashmiri and Indian background in South Asia.[7] Grahl-Madsen used the term 'con-national' refugees, and it is suggested that such refugees are distinguished by having reached an exceptionally high degree of legal assimilation into the country of residence.[8] **8.7**

'[T]he country in which he has taken residence' as a form of words does not require that 'country' be a State rather than a territory—but the requirement that there be 'rights and obligations attached to the nationality of that country' seems to indicate clearly that only a State satisfies this requirement. The language concretely indicates that the existence of a nationality must be current. If a potential **8.8**

---

[2] A Grahl-Madsen, *The Status of Refugees in International Law*, vol I (AW Sijthoff, 1966) 267–69, §102.

[3] Ibid, §102(ii).

[4] United Nations, Constitution of the International Refugee Organization, 15 December 1946, UNTS, vol 18, 3, Annex I.

[5] N Robinson, *Convention relating to the Status of Refugees, its History, Contents, and Interpretation* (Institute of Jewish Affairs, 1953) 13.

[6] R Marx, 'Article 1E' in A Zimmerman (ed), *The 1951 Convention Relating to the Status of Refugees and its 1967 Protocol: A Commentary* (OUP, 2011) 575, §17.

[7] Ibid, 572, §5.

[8] Grahl-Madsen (n 2 above) 265–70, §102(ii).

or lapsed nationality (that is, status attached to an entity not constituting a State) were meant, then it might be expected that article 1E would refer not to 'the rights and obligations attached to the nationality of that country' but to, for instance, 'the rights and obligations *which would be* attached to the nationality of that country'.

8.9 The content of 'the rights and obligations of the nationality of that country' is not dictated by international law. Though right of entry and residence might be taken as central, the existence of any such right exerciseable by the individual (as opposed to a State expelling an alien to a country of nationality) was disputable prior to the development of modern international human rights law. It may be that this question under article 1E could, like the question of the definition of 'persecution' in article 1A(2) CSR51, today be advanced by reference to human rights law and non-discrimination, through agency of the Preambular reference to human rights and non-discrimination, but against this is the fact that modern international human rights law generally does not denote rights as attaching by reason of nationality or citizenship rather than presence on the territory or relevant control. In 1966 Grahl-Madsen suggested treating the rights given under German law to the *Volksdeutsche* as a useful reference, listing those rights as freedom of assembly, association, movement within the territory of the State, free choice of occupation, workplace and educational institution, freedom from extradition, and civil rights and obligations including eligibility for election or appointment to public office.[9] This offers a useful illustration, but little assistance in identifying a principled basis for article 1E CSR51.

8.10 It does appear that it was only the expansiveness of the particular regime afforded to the *Volksdeutsche* by the Federal Republic of Germany which brought such persons within article 1E CSR51. Other expellees of German background who resettled in Austria, under a different and less advantageous local regime, were held not to be covered by article 1E CSR51 and therefore to be capable of satisfying the article 1A(2) CSR51 definition.[10]

C. Conclusion

8.11 Article 1E CSR51 was prepared substantially in the light of the particular situation of the *Volksdeutsche* in the Federal Republic of Germany after 1949, but in principle is capable of engagement today so as to exclude from protection an individual

---

[9] Ibid, 270.

[10] J Vernant, *The Refugee in the Post-War World* (George Allen & Unwin, 1953) 98; and Grahl-Madsen (n 2 above) 267, §102(i).

meeting the particular rubric. In practice it is likely that the rights and obligations required prior to exclusion are so substantial that their application to non-nationals can be expected to be very rare. If any case can be found today it may be found in persons belonging to categories linked to States but not considered to be nationals: for example, persons who are *ressortissants* or protected persons and not nationals. Marx cites reference by Goodwin-Gill and McAdam to the possibility of members of independent Commonwealth nations classed as British protected persons and subjects under the British Nationality Act 1948, who possessed a right of entrance to the United Kingdom, and extensive rights on the territory, coming within the scope of article 1E CSR51 until 1962 when their unconditional right of entry to the United Kingdom was reduced.[11]

[11] Marx (n 6 above) 576, §22; G Goodwin-Gill and J McAdam, *The Refugee in International Law* (3rd edn, OUP, 2007) 161–62.

Select Bibliography

Note: an attempt has been made at a loose classification of works below, with any specified work placed in the most appropriate section, but categories are not exact and a degree of approximation has been necessary.

International Law: General Works and Treaty Law

Books

American Law Institute, *Restatement of the Law, Third: The Foreign Relations Law of the United States*, vol 1 (St Paul MN, American Law Institute Press, 1987).
Aust, A, *Modern Treaty Law and Practice* (3rd edn, Cambridge, CUP, 2013).
Corten, O and Klein, P (eds), *The Vienna Conventions on the Law of Treaties: A Commentary* (Oxford, OUP, 2011).
Crawford, J (ed), *Brownlie's Principles of Public International Law* (8th edn, Oxford, OUP, 2012).
Dörr, O and Schmalenbach, K (eds), *The Vienna Convention on the Law of Treaties: A Commentary* (Berlin, Springer, 2012).
Gardiner, R, *Treaty Interpretation* (2nd edn, Oxford, OUP, 2015).
Grotius, H, *The Rights of War and Peace* (original publication 1625, trans Barbeyrac, this edn edited R Tuck) (Indianapolis IN, Liberty Fund, 2005).
Jennings, R and Watts, A (eds), *Oppenheim's International Law*, 9th edn, vol 1 ('*Peace*') (Oxford, OUP, 1992).
Lauterpacht, H, *The Function of Law in the International Community* (Oxford, OUP, 1933).
Schwarzenberger, G, *A Manual of International Law* (5th edn, London, Stevens & Sons, 1967).
Vattel, E de, *The Law of Nations, Or, Principles of the Law of Nature, Applied to the Conduct and Affairs of Nations and Sovereigns, with Three Early Essays on the Origin and Nature of Natural Law and on Luxury* (translated 1797, trans anonymous, B Kapossy and R Whatmore (eds)) (Indianapolis IN, Liberty Fund, 2008).
Villiger, M, *Commentary on the 1969 Vienna Convention on the Law of Treaties* (Leiden, Martinus Nijhoff, 2009).
The Online *Max Planck Encyclopaedia of Public International Law*, in particular:
Bingham, T, 'Alabama Arbitration'.
Bogdandy, A von and Häußler, S, 'Nations'.
Charlesworth, H, 'Universal Declaration of Human Rights (1948)'.
Dörr, O, 'Nationality'.
Dugard, J, 'Diplomatic Protection'.
Frowein, J, 'Recognition' and 'Non-recognition'.
Göcke, K, 'Stateless Persons'.
Hagedorn, C, 'Passports'.

Hailbronner, K and Gogolin, J, 'Aliens'.
Kälin, W, 'Aliens, Expulsion, and Deportation'.
Kiss, A, 'Abuse of Rights'.
Klein, N, 'Eritrea–Ethiopia Claims Commission'.
Hofmann, R, 'Denaturalization and Forced Exile',
Ruffert, M, 'Recognition of Foreign Legislative and Administrative Acts'.
Schmalenbach, K, '*Ahmadou Sadio Diallo Case (Republic of Guinea v Democratic Republic of the Congo)*'.
Spiro, PJ, 'Multiple Nationality'.
Trevisanut, S, 'Nationality Cases before International Courts and Tribunals'.

Other Works

Buffard, I and Zemanek, K, 'The "Object and Purpose" of a Treaty: An Enigma?' (1998) 3 *Austrian Review of International and European Law* 311.

International Law: Nationality, Citizenship, Recognition, Statelessness

Books

Aleinikoff, TA and Chetail, V (eds), *Migration and International Legal Norms* (The Hague, TMC Asser Press, 2003).
Amerasinghe, CF, *Diplomatic Protection* (Oxford, OUP, 2008).
Bar-Yaacov, N, *Dual Nationality* (London, Stevens & Sons, 1961).
Boll, A, *Multiple Nationality and International Law* (Leiden, Martinus Nijhoff, 2006).
Cassese, A, *Self-Determination of Peoples: A Legal Reappraisal* (Cambridge, CUP, 1995).
Chen, T-C, *The International Law of Recognition, with Special Reference to Practice in Great Britain and the United States* (London, Stevens, 1951).
Chetail, V and Bauloz, C (eds), *Research Handbook on International Law and Migration* (Cheltenham, Edward Elgar, 2014).
Crawford, J, *The Creation of States in International Law* (2nd edn, Oxford, OUP, 2006).
—— (ed), *Brownlie's Principles of Public International Law* (8th edn, Oxford, OUP, 2012).
Donner, R, *The Regulation of Nationality in International Law* (2nd edn, Irvington-on-Hudson NY, Transnational, 1994).
Dugard, J, *Recognition and the United Nations* (Cambridge, Grotius Books, 1987).
Edwards, A and Waas, L van, *Nationality and Statelessness under International Law* (Cambridge, CUP, 2014).
Fransman, J, *British Nationality Law* (3rd edn, London, Bloomsbury, 2011).
Goodwin-Gill, G, *International Law and the Movement of Persons Between States* (Oxford, Clarendon Press, 1978).
Hannum, H, *The Right to Leave and Return in International Law and Practice* (Dordrecht, Martinus Nijhoff, 1987).
Henckaerts, J-M, *Mass Expulsion in Modern International Law and Practice* (The Hague, Martinus Nijhoff, 1995).
Hirsch Ballin, E, *Citizens' Rights and the Right to be a Citizen* (Leiden, Brill Nijhoff, 2014).
Jones, JM, *British Nationality Law and Practice* (Oxford, Clarendon, 1947).

Kelsen, H, *Principles of International Law* (2nd edn, New York, Holt, Rinehart and Winston, 1966).
Ko Swan Sik, *Nationality and International Law in Asian Perspective* (Leiden, Martinus Nijhoff, 1990).
Lauterpacht, H, *Recognition in International Law* (Cambridge, CUP, 1947) (reprinted in paperback with new 'Introduction' by J Crawford, Cambridge, CUP, 2013).
Manby, B, *Struggles for Citizenship in Africa* (London, Zed Books, 2009).
Panhuys, HF van, *The Role of Nationality in International Law* (Leiden, Sijthoff, 1959).
Plender, R, *International Migration Law* (2nd edn, Leiden, Martinus Nijhoff, 1988).
Sawyer, C and Blitz, B, *Statelessness in the European Union: Displaced, Undocumented, Unwanted* (Cambridge, CUP, 2011).
Tomuschat, C, *The Modern Law of Self-Determination* (Leiden, Martinus Nijhoff, 1993).
Tomuschat, C and Thouvenin, J-M (eds), *The Fundamental Rules of the International Legal Order: Jus Cogens and Obligations Erga Omnes* (Leiden, Martinus Nijhoff, 2006).
Waas, L van, *Nationality Matters: Statelessness under International Law* (Antwerp, Intersentia, 2008).
Weis, P, *Nationality and Statelessness in International Law* (London, Stevens, 1956).
—— *Nationality and Statelessness* (2nd edn, Alphen aan den Rijn, Sijthoff & Noordhoff, 1979).

Other Works

African Commission on Human and Peoples' Rights, *The Right to Nationality in Africa: Study Undertaken by the Special Rapporteur on the Rights of Refugees, Asylum Seekers and Internally Displaced Persons pursuant to Resolution 234 of April 2013 and approved by the Commission at its 55th Ordinary Session* (Banjul, ACHPR, 2014).
Aiena, C, *Stripping of Nationality as a Weapon of Political Suppression: The Cases of Bahrain, United Kingdom, United Arab Emirates and Kuwait* (Islamic Human Rights Commission, 2014).
Batchelor, C, 'Stateless Persons: Some Gaps in International Protection' (1995) 7(2) *International Journal of Refugee Law* 232.
—— 'UNHCR and Issues Related to Nationality' (1995) 14(3) *Refugee Survey Quarterly* 96.
—— 'Statelessness and the Problem of Resolving Nationality Status' (1998) 10(1) *International Journal of Refugee Law* 156.
Blackman, J, 'State Successions and Statelessness: The Emerging Right to an Effective Nationality Under International Law' (1998) 19 *Michigan Journal of International Law* 1141.
Brownlie, I, 'The Relations of Nationality in Public International Law' in *British Yearbook of International Law* 1963 (1964, Oxford, OUP).
Campbell, JR, 'The Enduring Nature of Stateless in The Horn of Africa: How Nation-States and Western Courts (Re)define Nationality' (2011) 23(4) *International Journal of Refugee Law* 656.
Dawidowicz, M, 'The Obligation of Non-Recognition of an Unlawful Situation' in J Crawford, A Pellet and S Olleson (eds), *The Law of International Responsibility* (Oxford, OUP, 2010).
Diplock, K, 'Passports and Protection in International Law' (1946) *Transactions of the Grotius Society* 42.

Dugard, J, 'South Africa's "Independent" Homelands: An Exercise in Denationalization' (1980) 10 *Denver Journal of International Law and Policy* 11.
—— 'The Denationalization of Black South Africans in Pursuance of Apartheid: A Question for the International Court of Justice?' (1984) 33 *Review of the International Commission of Jurists* 49.
Fischer Williams, J, 'Denationalization' (1927) 8 *British Yearbook of International Law* 45.
Fripp, E, 'Deprivation of Nationality and Public International Law—An Outline' (2014) 28(4) *Journal of Immigration, Asylum & Nationality Law* 367.
—— 'International Humanitarian Law and the Interpretation of "Persecution" in Article 1A(2) CSR51' (2014) 26(3) *International Journal of Refugee Law* 382.
Glynn, I, 'The Genesis and Development of Article 1 of the 1951 Refugee Convention' (2011) 25(1) *Journal of Refugee Studies* 134.
Groot, R de, *Survey on Rules on Loss of Nationality in International Treaties and Case Law* (Brussels, Centre for European Policy Studies, 2013).
Holborn, L, Review of *Nationality and Statelessness in International Law* by Paul Weis and *The Refugee and the World Community* by John George Stoessinger (1957) 51(2) *American Political Science Review* 528.
Jefferis, D, 'Institutionalizing Statelessness: The Revocation of Residency Rights of Palestinians in East Jerusalem Protecting Recognized Geneva Convention Refugees outside their States of Asylum' (2012) 24(2) *International Journal of Refugee Law* 202.
Lauterpacht, H, 'The International Protection of Human Rights' Hague Academy of International Law, *Recueil des cours*, vol 70 (Paris, Recueil Sirey, 1947) 1.
—— 'The Nationality of Denationalized Persons' in E Lauterpacht (ed), *International Law; Being the Collected Papers of Hersch Lauterpacht* (Cambridge, CUP, 1977) (first published in (1948) *Jewish Yearbook of International Law* 164).
Lawand, K, 'The Right to Return of Palestinians in International Law' (1996) 8(4) *International Journal of Refugee Law* 532.
Makarov, AN, 'Règles générales du droit de la nationalité' Hague Academy of International Law, *Recueil des cours*, vol 74 (Paris, Recueil Sirey, 1949) 269.
Mann, FA, '*R v Home Secretary ex p L (Case Comment)*' (1945) 61 *Law Quarterly Review* 126.
—— 'Review of *Festgabe Makarov*' in *British Yearbook of International Law* 1958 (Oxford, OUP, 1959) 425.
—— 'The Present Validity of Nazi Nationality Laws' (1973) 89 *Law Quarterly Review* 194.
—— '*Oppenheimer v Cattermole* Revisited' (1981) 97 *Law Quarterly Review* 194.
—— 'The Judicial Recognition of an Unrecognised State' (1987) 36 *International and Comparative Law Quarterly* 348.
Meindersma, C, 'Population Exchanges: International Law and State Practice—Part 1' (1997) 9(3) *International Journal of Refugee Law* 335.
—— 'Population Exchanges: International Law and State Practice—Part 2' (1997) 9(4) *International Journal of Refugee Law* 613.
Merrills, JG, 'One Nationality or Two? The Strange Case of *Oppenheimer v Cattermole*' (1974) 23 *International & Comparative Law Quarterly* 143.
—— '*Oppenheimer v Cattermole*—The Curtain Falls' (1975) 24 *International and Comparative Law Quarterly* 617.
Parry, C, 'The Duty to Recognise Foreign Nationality Laws' in C Bilfinger (ed), *Festgabe für Alexander N Makarov (Zeitschrift für Ausländisches Offentliches Recht und Völkerrecht)* (Stuttgart, W Kohlhammer, 1958).

Plender, R, 'The Right to a Nationality as Reflected in International Human Rights Law and the Sovereignty of States in Nationality Matters' (1995) 49 *Austrian Journal of Public International Law* 43.
Reut-Nicolussi, E, 'Displaced Persons and International Law' Hague Academy of International Law, *Recueil des cours*, vol 73 (Paris, Recueil Sirey, 1948) 1.
Ronen, Y, 'Status of Settlers Implanted by Illegal Territorial Regimes' in *British Yearbook of International Law* 2008 (2009, Oxford, OUP) 194.
Rosard, E, 'The Right to Return under International Law Following Mass Dislocation: The Bosnia Precedent' (1998) 19 *Michigan Journal of International Law* 1091.
Sanderson, M, 'Statelessness and Mass Expulsion in Sudan: A Reassessment of the International Law', 12 *Northwestern Journal of International Human Rights* 74 (2014).
Sibley, N, 'The Passport System' (1906) *Journal of the Society of Comparative Legislation* 26.
Zimmermann, A, 'State Succession and the Nationality of Natural Persons: Facts and Possible Codification' in P Eisemann and M Koskenniemi (eds), *Succession: Codification Tested against the Facts* (The Hague, Hague Academy of International Law/Martinus Nijhoff, 2000).

International Law: Human Rights

Books

Eide, A, Alfredsson, G et al (eds), *The Universal Declaration of Human Rights: A Commentary* (Oslo, Scandinavian University Press, 1992).
Joseph, S and Castan, M, *The International Covenant on Civil and Political Rights: Cases, Materials, and Commentary* (3rd edn, Oxford, OUP, 2013).
Kälin, W and Künzli, J, *The Law of Human Rights Protection* (Oxford, OUP, 2009).
Liu, G, *The Right to Leave and Return and Chinese Migration Law* (Leiden, Martinus Nijhoff, 2007).
Mole, N and Meredith, C, *Asylum and the European Convention on Human Rights* (5th edn, Strasbourg, Council of Europe, 2010).
Nowak, M, *UN Covenant on Civil and Political Rights: CCPR Commentary* (Kehl, K Engel, 1993).
Nowak, M et al, *The United Nations Convention against Torture: A Commentary* (Oxford, OUP, 2008).
Reid, K, *A Practitioner's Guide to the European Convention on Human Rights* (4th edn, London, Sweet & Maxwell, 2012).

Other Works

Adjami, M and Harrington, J, 'The Scope and Content of Article 15 of the Universal Declaration of Human Rights' (2008) 27(3) *Refugee Survey Quarterly* 93.
Baluarte, DC, 'Inter-American Justice Comes to the Dominican Republic: An Island Shakes as Human Rights and Sovereignty Clash' (2006) 13(2) *Human Rights Brief* 25–28, 38.
Goldston, J, 'Holes in the Rights Framework: Racial Discrimination, Citizenship, and the Rights of Noncitizens' (2006) 20(3) *Ethics & International Affairs* 321.

Kinninmont, J, 'Citizenship in the Gulf', in Ana Echagüe (ed.), *FRIDE Report: The Gulf States and the Arab Uprisings* (Brussels/Madrid, Fundación para las Relaciones Internacionales y el Diálogo Exterior, 2013).

Middle East Centre, London School of Economics, *Challenges to Citizenship in the Middle East and North Africa Region*, Collected Papers Volume 2 (London, LSE, 2014).

Saul, B, 'Cultural Nationalism, Self-Determination and Human Rights in Bhutan' (2000) 12(3) *International Journal of Refugee Law* 321.

Zayas, A-M de, 'International Law and Mass Population Transfers' (1975) 16 *Harvard International Law Journal* 207, 255–57.

International Law: Refugee Law

Books

Anker, D, *The Law of Asylum in the United States* (7th edn, Eagan MN, Thompson Reuters, 2014).

Feller, E, Türk V and Nicholson, F, *Refugee Protection in International Law* (Cambridge, CUP, 2003).

Goodwin-Gill, G and McAdam, J, *The Refugee in International Law* (3rd edn, Oxford, OUP, 2007).

Grahl-Madsen, A, *The Status of Refugees in International Law*, vol I (Leyden, AW Sijthoff, 1966); vol II (Leyden, AW Sijthoff, 1972).

Hathaway, J, *The Law of Refugee Status* (Toronto, Butterworths Canada, 1991).

—— *The Rights of Refugees under International Law* (Cambridge, CUP, 2005).

—— (ed), *Human Rights and Refugee Law* (Cheltenham, Elgar, 2013).

Hathaway, J and Foster, M, *The Law of Refugee Status* (2nd edn, Cambridge, CUP, 2014).

Robinson, N, *Convention relating to the Status of Refugees, its History, Contents, and Interpretation: A Commentary* (New York, Institute of Jewish Affairs, 1953).

Sinha, SP, *Asylum and International Law* (The Hague, Martinus Nijhoff, 1971).

Symes, M and Jorro, P, *Asylum Law and Practice* (2nd edn, Hayward's Heath, Bloomsbury Professional, 2010).

Vernant, J, *The Refugee in the Post-War World* (London, George Allen & Unwin, 1953).

Waldman, L, *The Definition of Convention Refugee* (Markham ON, Butterworths Canada, 2001).

Weis, P, *The Refugee Convention, 1951: The Travaux Préparatoires Analysed with a Commentary by the Late Dr Paul Weis* (Cambridge, CUP, 1995).

Zimmermann, A (ed), Dörschner, J and Machts, F (assistant eds), *The 1951 Convention Relating to the Status of Refugees and its 1967 Protocol: A Commentary* (Oxford, OUP, 2011).

Other Works

Baluarte, DC, 'Denationalization as Persecution—Using a Human Rights Approach to Refugee Law to Address the Stateless Legal Limbo in the United States' (Panel paper, Global Forum on Statelessness, The Hague, September 2014).

Chan, E and Schloenhardt, A, 'North Korean Refugees and International Refugee Law' (2007) 19(2) *International Journal of Refugee Law* 215.

Forbes, S, '"Imagine There's No Country": Statelessness as Persecution in Light of *Haile II*' (2013) 61 *Buffalo Law Review* 699.
Fortin, A, 'The Meaning of "Protection" in the Refugee Definition' (2000) 12(4) *International Journal of Refugee Law* 549.
Foster, M, 'Protection Elsewhere: The Legal Implications of Requiring Refugees to Seek Protection in Another State' (2007) 28 *Michigan Journal of International Law* 223.
Fripp, E, 'International Humanitarian Law and the Interpretation of "Persecution" in Article 1A(2) CSR51' (2014) 26(3) *International Journal of Refugee Law* 382.
Gillan, S, 'Refugee Convention—Whether Deprivation of Citizenship Amounts to Persecution' (2007) 21(4) *Journal of Immigration, Asylum & Nationality Law* 347.
Goodwin-Gill, G, 'The Search for the One, True Meaning …' in G Goodwin-Gill and H Lambert, *The Limits of Transnational Law: Refugee Law, Policy Harmonization and Judicial Dialogue in the European Union* (Cambridge, CUP, 2010).
Grahl-Madsen, A, 'Protection of Refugees by their Country of Origin' (1986) 11 *Yale Journal of International Law* 362.
Hathaway, JC, 'The Evolution of Refugee Status in International Law: 1920–1950' (1984) 33 *International & Comparative Law Quarterly* 348.
—— Fourth Colloquium on Challenges in International Refugee Law, 'The Michigan Guidelines on Protection Elsewhere' (2007) 28 *Michigan Journal of International Law* 208.
Lambert, H, 'Comparative Perspectives on Arbitrary Deprivation of Nationality and Refugee Status' (2015) 64 *International & Comparative Law Quarterly* 1.
Lee, Tang Lay, 'Refugees from Bhutan: Nationality, Statelessness and the Right to Return' (1998) 10(1) *International Journal of Refugee Law* 118.
Mathew, P, 'Lest We Forget: Australia's Policy on East Timorese Asylum Seekers' (1999) 11(1) *International Journal of Refugee Law* 7.
Piotrowicz, R, 'Refugee Status and Multiple Nationality in the Indonesian Archipelago: Is there a Timor Gap?' (1996) 8(3) *International Journal of Refugee Law* 319.
—— 'Facing Up To Refugees—International Apathy and German Self-Help' (1998) 10(3) *International Journal of Refugee Law* 410.
—— 'Lay Kon Tji and Minister for Immigration & Ethnic Affairs: The Function and Meaning of Effective Nationality in the Assessment of Applications for Asylum' (1999) 11(3) *International Journal of Refugee Law* 544.
Sen, S, 'Stateless Refugees and the Right to Return: The Bihari Refugees of South Asia—Part 1' (1999) 11(4) *International Journal of Refugee Law* 625.
—— 'Stateless Refugees and the Right to Return: The Bihari Refugees of South Asia—Part 2' (2000) 12(1) *International Journal of Refugee Law* 41.
Sidhom, M, 'Jong Kim Koe v Minister for Immigration and Multicultural Affairs: Federal Court Loses Sight of the Purpose of the Refugee Convention' (1998) 20(2) *Sydney Law Review* 315.
Steinbock, D, 'The Refugee Definition as Law: Issues of Interpretation' in F Nicholson and P Twomey (eds), *Refugee Rights and Realities: Evolving International Concepts and Regimes* (Cambridge, CUP, 1999).
Storey, H and Wallace, R, 'War and Peace in Refugee Law Jurisprudence' (2001) 95 *American Journal of International Law* 349.
Weis, P, 'Legal Aspects of the Convention of 25 July 1951 relating to the Status of Refugees' (1953) 30 *British Yearbook of International Law* (Oxford, OUP, 1954) 478.

—— 'The International Protection of Refugees' (1954) 48 *American Journal of International Law* 193.
—— *The Concept of Refugee in International Law* (1961) (UN Doc HCR/INF/49).
Wolman, A, 'North Korean Asylum Seekers and Dual Nationality' (2013) 24(4) *International Journal of Refugee Law* 793.
Ziegler, R, 'Protecting Recognized Geneva Convention Refugees Outside their States of Asylum' (2013) 25(2) *International Journal of Refugee Law* 235.

Other

Books

Agamben, G, *State of Exception*, trans Kevin Attell (Chicago, University of Chicago Press, 2005).
Arendt, H, *The Origins of Totalitarianism* (2nd edn, New York, Houghton Mifflin Harcourt, 1973).
Campbell, JR, *Nationalism, Law and Statelessness: Grand Illusions in the Horn of Africa* (Oxford, Routledge, 2013).
Cohen, G, *In War's Wake: Europe's Displaced Persons in the Postwar Order* (Oxford, OUP, 2012).
Gatrell, P, *Free World? The Campaign to Save the World's Refugees: 1956–1963* (Cambridge, CUP, 2011).
—— *The Making of the Modern Refugee* (Oxford, OUP, 2013).
Holborn, L, *The International Refugee Organization, a Specialized Agency of the United Nations: Its History and Work, 1946-1952* (Oxford, OUP, 1956).
—— *Refugees: A Problem of our Time: The Work of the United Nations High Commissioner for Refugees 1951–1972* (Metuchen NJ, Scarecrow, 1975).
Hope Simpson, J, *The Refugee Problem, Report of a Survey* (Oxford, OUP, 1939).
Lewis, J, *FA Mann, A Memoir* (Oxford, Hart Publishing, 2013).
Macdonogh, G, *After the Reich: From the Liberation of Vienna to the Berlin Airlift* (London, John Murray, 2007).
Marrus, MR, *The Unwanted: European Refugees from the First World War Through the Cold War* (Oxford, OUP, 1985) and second edition with new Foreword by AR Zolberg (2nd edn, Philadelphia PA, Temple UP, 2002).
Skran, C, *Refugees in Inter-War Europe: The Emergence of a Regime* (Oxford, OUP, 1995).
Snyder, T, *Black Earth: The Holocaust as History and Warning* (New York, Tim Duggan Books, 2015).

Other Works

Weber, M, 'The Profession and Vocation of Politics' in P Lassman and R Speirs (eds), *Political Writings* (trans R Speirs, first publication 1919, this publication Cambridge, CUP, 1994).

Index

www.ingramcontent.com/pod-product-compliance
Ingram Content Group UK Ltd.
Pitfield, Milton Keynes, MK11 3LW, UK
UKHW021911150926
475560UK00003B/310

9 781782 259213